THOMAS C. PATTERSON

ARCHAEOLOGY
The Evolution of Ancient Societies

ARCHAEOLOGY
The Evolution
of Ancient Societies

ARCHAEO

Prentice-Hall, Inc.
Englewood Cliffs, New Jersey 07632

Temple University

THOMAS C. PATTERSON

 **The Evolution of Ancient Societies**

Library of Congress Cataloging in Publication Data

PATTERSON, THOMAS CARL.
   Archaeology, the evolution of ancient societies.

   Includes bibliographies and index.
   1. Civilization, Ancient. 2. Archaeology. 3. Proto
history. I. Title.
CB311.P34   930   80-16506
ISBN 0-13-044040-X

Prentice-Hall Series in Anthropology
David M. Schneider, Editor

Editorial Supervision: Serena Hoffman
Designer: Jayne Conte
Manufacturing buyer: Edmund W. Leone
Cover Photograph: Charles E. Lee

© 1981 by Prentice-Hall, Inc., Englewood Cliffs, N.J. 07632

Printed in the United States of America
10 9 8 7 6 5 4 3 2 1

Prentice-Hall International, Inc., *London*
Prentice-Hall of Australia Pty. Limited, *Sydney*
Prentice-Hall of Canada, Ltd., *Toronto*
Prentice-Hall of India Private Limited, *New Delhi*
Prentice-Hall of Japan, Inc., *Tokyo*
Prentice-Hall of Southeast Asia Pte. Ltd., *Singapore*
Whitehall Books Limited, *Wellington, New Zealand*

For Karen Spalding and Helen Moses who helped me break out
of old ways of thinking into new intellectual grounds

For Joel Brodkin, Lynn Donovan, Leslie Freeman, and Ann Golob
who validated this process with support, questions, and criticism

Preface

PART ONE
STUDYING ANCIENT SOCIETIES

1

The Scope of Archaeology   3

THE BUSINESS OF ARCHAEOLOGY   4
Objects 6   Associations 9   Cultures 10

THE QUESTION OF TIME   11
Establishing a Relative Sequence 12
Absolute Dating 12

CONCLUSION   19

2

Studying Society and Social Change   21

**THE DEVELOPMENT
OF ARCHAEOLOGICAL RESEARCH**   21
Geology versus the Bible 22
Comparing Societies 23
Accounting for Social Change 24
Archaeology in the Early Twentieth Century 27

**CONTEMPORARY THEORIES
OF SOCIETY AND SOCIAL CHANGE**   29
Positivism 29   Historical Materialism 30

**CURRENT TRENDS
IN ARCHAEOLOGICAL THOUGHT**   32
Cultural Ecology 32   Cultural Evolutionism 33
Culture History 35

CONCLUSION   36

CONTENTS

PART TWO

BECOMING HUMAN

3

Human Origins: A Paleobiological Perspective   41

THE ECOLOGICAL THEATER AND THE EVOLUTIONARY PLAY   43

THE ORIGIN AND EVOLUTION OF THE PRIMATES   47

HOMINID ORIGINS AND EVOLUTION   53
Hominid Evolution During the Pliocene 54
The Evolution of the Genus Homo 59

4

The Emergence of Toolmakers   67

THE EARLIEST TOOLMAKERS   68

TOOLMAKING DURING THE MID-PLEISTOCENE   72

DAILY LIFE 500,000 YEARS AGO   74
Evidence from Terra Amata 74
Evidence from Olorgesailie 78
Evidence from Choukoutieu Cave 79
The Evolution of Early Human Society 81

5

The Transition to Modern Human Beings   85

DAILY LIFE AMONG THE NEANDERTHALS   86
The Périgord Region 86   The Inhabitants
of the Périgord 87   Food and Fuel 89
Tools 90   Death and Disease 92

DAILY LIFE ON THE UKRAINIAN STEPPE   93

THE STRUCTURE OF HUMAN SOCIETY   94
Larger Groups 95   Fragmentation of Groups 95
Division of Labor 96   Sharing 97

6

The Appearance
of Modern Human Beings   99

LIFE IN SOUTHWESTERN FRANCE   101
Tools 101   Population Size and Structure 102
Camps and Caves 104   Obtaining Food 105
Cooperation and Division of Labor 107

LIFE IN CZECHOSLOVAKIA   108

LIFE ON THE SOUTH AFRICAN COAST   110

DAILY LIFE IN THE LEVANT   111

THE STRUCTURE OF HUMAN SOCIETY   114

PART

THREE

FROM THE REMOTE PAST TO CLASSICAL ANTIQUITY

7

The Beginning of Agriculture
in the Ancient East   121

EARLY FOOD-PRODUCING
COMMUNITIES   122
The Zagros Mountains 124   The Levant 128
Antaolia 132

SOCIAL AND ECONOMIC CHANGE
IN THE ANCIENT EAST   136
The Significance of Agriculture 137   New Social
Relations 137   The Role of Ancestors 137
The Organization of Labor 138   Exchange 138

8

Ancient Peoples of Mesopotamia   **140**

**EARLY COMMUNITIES
ON THE MESOPOTAMIAN PLAIN**   **142**
Umm Dabaghiyah 142   Tell es-Sotto 143
Yarim Tepe I 143   Tell es-Sawwan and Choga
Mami 144   The Halafian Villages 145

**THE EVOLUTION OF URBAN SOCIETY
IN SOUTHERN MESOPOTAMIA**   **146**
The Ubaid Phase 146   Cities and Satellites 148
The Temple Corporation 150
Social Differentiation 152

**SOCIAL DEVELOPMENT IN ANCIENT
MESOPOTAMIA**   **154**
Production Units 155   Alliances 155
The Conical Clan 156

9

Ancient Peoples
of the Indo-Iranian Frontier   **159**

ANCIENT IRAN   **161**
The Susiana Plain 161   The Iranian Sistan 162

ANCIENT TURKMENIA   **165**
The Kelteminar Peoples 165
Early Farming Communities 165
Division of Labor and Specialization 168
Trade and Social Classes 170

THE INDUS VALLEY   **170**
Farming Communities 171   Mohenjo-daro 172
Harappa 174   Indus Valley Society 175

**EXTERNAL EXCHANGE AND SOCIAL
DEVELOPMENT**   **176**

10

Ancient Peoples of the Far East   **180**

NORTH CHINA   **182**
Pan-p'o-ts'un 182   The Lungshan
Settlements 183   The Shang Dynasty 184
The Chou Dynasty 187
The Rise of Feudalism 189

SOUTH CHINA AND SOUTHEAST ASIA 190
The Early Hoabinhian Peoples 190
Non Nok Tha and Ben Chiang 191
The Development of Trade 192

11

Ancient Peoples
of Egypt and Africa 195

ANCIENT EGYPT 197
The Fayum A Settlements 198
Farming Villages 199
The Gerzean Towns 199
The Unification of Egypt 200
The First Intermediate Period 203
The Middle Kingdom 204
The Hyksos Invasion 204
The New Kingdom 205

AFRICA SOUTH OF THE SAHARA 206
Early Communities 206   The Pastoralists 207
Trade, Crafts, and Wealth 207
Social Development in Sub-Saharan
Africa 208

12

Ancient Peoples
of Europe 213

EARLY FARMING COMMUNITIES 216
Farming Communities in Greece 216
Farming Communities in the Balkans 217
The Western Mediterranean 219
The Linear Pottery Cultures 219

EUROPEAN SOCIETY FROM
4000 TO 2000 BC 221
Agriculture 222   Metalworking and Other
Crafts 222   Trade 223
Tombs and Monuments 223

THE MEDITERRANEAN WORLD 226
Minoan Culture 227   Mycenaean Culture 228
The Structure of Mycenaean Society 229
Trade in the Aegean 229

PART FOUR

PEOPLES OF OCEANIA AND THE AMERICAS

13

Peoples Out of Asia   **237**

**EARLY PEOPLES OF AUSTRALIA
AND THE PACIFIC**   **237**
Lake Mungo and Kosipe 238   Other Early
Settlements 240   The Lapita Pottery
Cultures 241   The Settlement of Polynesia 242
Social Structure in Polynesia 243
New Zealand 244

THE FIRST AMERICANS   **244**
The Old Crow Basin 244   Migration to the South
and East 246   Cultural Diversity 248
Subsistence Activities 249   The Extinction
of Large Herbivores 251

14

Ancient Peoples
of North America   **255**

THE AMERICAN ARCTIC   **256**
Toolmaking in the Arctic 257   Early Whale
Hunters 258   The Maritime Archaic Tradition 258

THE EASTERN WOODLANDS   **260**
The Koster Site 260   Poverty Point 261
Trade in the Eastern Woodlands 262
Burial Practices 263   The Hopewellian
Settlements 265   Cahokia 265

THE AMERICAN SOUTHWEST   **267**
Early Inhabitants 267   The Hohokam
and the Hakataya 268   The Anasazi 269

15

Ancient Peoples of Mesoamerica 274

THE EARLY PEOPLES
OF MESOAMERICA 276
The Tehuacán Valley 276   Permanent Villages
and Social Stratification 278

THE OLMEC 279

THE DEVELOPMENT OF CITIES 282
Teotihuacán 282   The Effects of Import
Replacement 286

THE MAYA 288
Early Settlements in the Lowlands 289
The Buffer Zone Settlements 290

THE TOLTECS AND THE AZTECS 291

16

Ancient Peoples of South America 296

ANCIENT PEOPLES OF THE ANDES 298
The Ideal of Self-Sufficiency 298
The Development of Agriculture 298
Construction and Water Management 302
Communication Networks 303   The Chavin
Influence 306   The Huari Empire 307
The Incas 309

THE TROPICAL FOREST AND BEYOND 313
The Amazon Basin 313   Exchange Networks
and Fiestas 315   Hostility, Raiding,
and Migration 315

Epilog 318

Glossary 320

Index 327

As I write this preface, my mind wanders back to a conversation I had with a colleague several years ago.

"You're what? Writing a textbook on world archaeology? You must be crazy! There's so much evidence! No one can hope to read all the available information, much less control it. Tell me, why are you writing a book, anyway?"

"I'm curious. Besides, its a helluva challenge!"

And so it has turned out to be.

Like many archaeologists, I have conducted most of my research in one part of the world. The area—the central Andes—and its archaeology are familiar to me. The questions I asked about the social development of the ancient peoples who lived there were often the same as those that are asked about human history in other parts of the world. Unfortunately, the answers to these questions were often unique and applicable only to that area or a small part of it. As I continued to work in the same area, I gradually gained a deeper understanding and appreciation of the particular social and cultural forms that evolved there as the ancient inhabitants went about the business of solving the problems of daily life. Recognizing such forms, which emphasize the distinctive character of what happened in a particular area, provided me with a perspective from which seemingly unrelated facts about the ancient peoples of that area gained meaning. Such a perspective is absolutely essential, because it allows us to see relationships between various parts of a society in new ways. It can also be beneficial if we use it to organize our perceptions about the forms of other societies.

There is another perspective that is essential for understanding human society. It involves looking beneath the differences in social and cultural forms to discover the fundamental similarities in the structure and development of societies in different areas. This is the perspective I was interested in when I began writing the book. I became increasingly more curious about it as the writing progressed and my own ideas began to crystallize. Do

societies, in fact, develop along similar pathways in different areas? What is the nature of the similarities that underlie different societies? How can we account for the similarities—the repetitions—that we see in the archaeological records of different areas? How can we account for the differences? Why do similarities and differences occur? These are only a few of the questions that arose out of this viewpoint.

One of the problems I faced in writing this book was to organize it in such a way that both perspectives came into play. Ultimately, I chose to organize the contents geographically. This method has the advantage of giving the reader a taste of the archaeology of a given area. The major drawback is that a lot of current thinking in archaeology is focused on such topics as the origin of agricultural economies, the beginning of urban life, or the rise of stratified societies and the state, all of which happened in more than one part of the world, often quite independently. That is why there is repetition in the archaeological record.

Two major theoretical positions—positivism and historical materialism—dominate much of archaeological thought today. They are the products of a debate that has been taking place in the social sciences for more than a century. The two positions share a number of beliefs about the aims of scientific inquiry, the nature of evidence, the ways in which theories should be assessed, and the idea that there are standards for adequate explanation. They disagree, however, on what constitutes an adequate explanation, because each position involves certain assumptions that lead to different views about what societies are like and how they change. Generally, advocates of both positivism and historical materialism would agree on what the archaeologist has found and disagree on how this evidence fits into the broader picture.

I have chosen not to lay out in endless detail the theoretical positions adopted by various archaeologists on every question of current interest. To do so would confuse and obscure. Instead, I have written a book that reflects a personal view of what I see as the most probable and useful way of interpreting various pieces of evidence. I hope this view will provoke readers into forming their own opinions about how human societies developed.

I wrote the book for myself as much as for my friends and students, who questioned me about the evolution of human beings as both biological and social animals. I could not have written it without keeping in mind the questions they posed. Nor could I have written it without the help of my colleagues, both past and present. I am deeply indebted to them for the evidence they provided and for their theoretical insights and clarity of thought. I particularly wish to acknowledge the help and encouragement of Joel Brodkin, Lynn Donovan, Leslie Freeman, Ann Golob, Helen Moses, and Karen Spalding. I also want to thank Ed Stanford, Stan Wakefield, and Serena Hoffman of Prentice-Hall and the battery of anonymous reviewers who read the various drafts of the book. Without their help, the book would have been quite different.

THOMAS C. PATTERSON

Temple University

ARCHAEOLOGY

The Evolution
of Ancient Societies

STUDYING ANCIENT SOCIETIES

How did the earliest groups of tool-using apes develop into modern societies? Why have there been so many different kinds of societies in the past? And how does one kind of society change into another? These are the most important questions in the history of human society. Throughout most of human history, however, people did not write down their thoughts, concerns, or observations. Since we cannot rely on written records to tell us what happened during this period, we have to use archaeological evidence to find out what these early societies were like and how they changed.

PART
ONE

The Scope of Archaeology

Sir Leonard Woolley and his colleague MacIver had been excavating at an ancient Egyptian town in the Sudan for nearly two months. They had searched in vain for the town's cemetery, which would provide them with valuable information about how the townspeople treated their dead. One evening, after working all day, they walked to the top of hill near the town to watch the sun set over the Nile River. Suddenly they both noticed that the plain below them was dotted with small, dark circles. Woolley ran down the hill, and as he approached the plain the circles began to disappear. MacIver called out from above, directing him to each of the circles in turn. Woolley made a small pile of earth in the middle of each. The next morning they began excavating at those piles. At every one they found the entrance to a stone-lined tomb that had been made by the ancient residents of the town. The dark patches—visible from the hilltop for only a few moments a day, when the sun's rays struck them at just the right angle—were produced by little splinters of stone from the bedrock that the townspeople had dug up when they made the tombs and covered them over with the dirt and rock from the hole they had made.

Sir Leonard's experience might lead us to suspect that most archaeological sites are found by chance. However, nothing is further from the truth. Archaeologists are continually on the lookout for those minute deviations from the natural—those subtle clues used by detectives—that indicate that some sort of human activity has occurred in one locality and not in another. If Woolley and MacIver had not been curious about the location of the cemetery in the Sudan, they might never have recognized the significance of those dark patches of earth.

THE BUSINESS OF ARCHAEOLOGY

The business of archaeology is bringing the past back to life. Archaeologists want to know how people lived at different times and in different places. To find out, they might excavate a 2-million-year-old site in East Africa to find out what our remote ancestors looked like and how they lived; they might dig in a 2,000-year-old garbage dump in the Illinois River Valley to find out what the inhabitants of that area ate during a particular season of the year; or they might study the ruins of a Roman villa in England to learn about the structure of provincial society in the days of the Roman empire. The reason they study such a vast array of ancient peoples and societies is to understand and explain how human society has evolved through time. To do this, they must be able to account for the similarities and differences they observe in the archaeological record and the processes that brought them about.

Archaeologists, of course, are not the only people who try to understand and explain what happened in the past. Historians also try to do just that. Clearly, the goals of the archaeologist and the historian are similar. However, it is also clear that most archaeologists are not historians and most historians are not archaeologists. Since their goals are the same, what distinguishes them from each other? Many distinctions have been suggested, but the only one that stands up under close scrutiny is based on the kinds of evidence they use and the techniques they have developed for analyzing this information.

Historians deal almost exclusively with written records and reconstruct the past on the basis of what those records say. Written evidence often presents a distorted view of what happened in the past. For example, until recently in some parts of the world and even today in others, only a small segment of the population was literate, and our understanding of what a society was like is based on the views and biases of its literate class. Written records also contain factual errors introduced either accidentally or deliberately by their authors. As a result, historians have developed a number of techniques for checking the accuracy of their evidence.

In reconstructing the past, archaeologists rely primarily on evidence that was not left intentionally—such as food scraps in a garbage dump, a child and his toys buried in a stone-lined tomb, or the remains of a house that burned down. Since they are using these remains for purposes very different from those of the people who left them, archaeologists are not particularly concerned about the views of ancient peoples about themselves or others. They do have to worry about whether the evidence they have found accurately reflects what took place and, if not, what factors are distorting the archaeological record.

Archaeologists rely on two kinds of evidence, which we can call objects and associations, to reconstruct what ancient societies were like and how they

(a)

(b)
Archaeologists locate sites in various ways. (a) Remains, like the local chieftain's palace at San Juan de Pariache in Peru, are often exposed on the surface. (b) Remains, like this portion of an ancient platform mound at Ancón, Peru, are frequently exposed by construction or archaeological excavation.

Archaeological sites are places where people have carried out some activity in the past and traces of it have been preserved. Occasionally a series of activities were carried out in the same place at different times, and traces of them are stacked one on top of the other. In an excavation on the London waterfront, the wooden pilings (bottom) were part of a quay that was built around the middle of the second century AD. Toward the end of the fourth century, the Romans built a massive stone defense wall over the quay because of the increased danger and frequency of pirate raids. At different times in the twentieth century, construction workers laid water and sewer pipes (top) in the fill and ground covering the old remains. During the same period, a deep pit was dug into the ground. Brian Hobley, Recent rescue archaeology in London, **Archaeology,** 31, no. 3 (May 1978), 57. Courtesy of the Museum of London.

developed through time. They are found at places where people did something in the past—such as burying their dead, quarrying rock to make tools or buildings, or even growing grapes to make wine. Since ancient peoples, like their modern counterparts, were messy, they often modified the natural setting by leaving debris that provides us with clues about what they did. The range of human activities, traces of which are found at archaeological sites, is almost as infinite as the range of human behavior itself. The size of archaeological sites also varies. At one extreme are sites with surface areas of a few square yards that were formed when someone dropped a pot or made a stone tool. At the other extreme are ancient cities like Teotihuacán, Mexico, which covered more than nine square miles in AD 500 and witnessed the daily activities of nearly 200,000 people.

Objects

Objects are things that were manufactured, modified, or moved by people. Manufactured objects, or *artifacts* as they are usually called, can range in size and complexity from a pendant to a pyramid. They tell us a great deal about the artistic skills and technical achievements of ancient peoples. They reveal other things about the people as well, if we can determine how they were

(a)

(b)

After laying out a grid composed of standard-sized squares in order to locate objects relative to each other, archaeologists face two problems when they excavate a site. One is to determine the sequence of occupation layers; the other is to expose enough of each layer to discover how structures, features, and remains are distributed. The two problems necessitate different excavation strategies. (a) Deep trenches are excavated to expose a small portion of each occupation layer at the site; the archaeologists may actually excavate a number of trenches in the same site to ensure that they have a complete record of the occupations there. Kent V. Flannery, ed., **The early Mesoamerican village.** (New York: Academic Press, 1975), fig. 3-6, p. 70. (b) A large area is excavated and the location of contemporary structures and objects and their spatial relationships to each other are recorded. The archaeologists record this information in terms of the grid system that they have imposed on the site. Photograph courtesy of Christopher B. Donnan.

(a)   (b)

Shovels are usually the largest digging implements used by archaeologists. (a) More often, they excavate with trowels, ice picks, or paintbrushes. Kent V. Flannery, ed., **The early Mesoamerican village** (New York: Academic Press, 1975), fig. 2.2 p. 18. (b) The earth is screened to recover small objects as well as plant and animal remains. Stuart Struever, Flotation techniques for the recovery of small-scale archaeological remains. Reproduced by permission of the Society for American Archaeology from **American Antiquity,** 33, no. 3 (July 1968), 354.

used. For example, we can learn a great deal about the characteristics of ancient musical instruments by playing them, which tells us something about their music.

Modified objects can also tell us something about the behavior of the people who altered them. At an increasing number of sites archaeologists are finding chunks of siliceous rocks that look dramatically different from the way they look at places where they outcrop naturally. These chunks frequently have a pinkish color, are slightly glossy, and feel a little greasy. These characteristics can be duplicated experimentally by heating rocks for sustained periods. Besides altering the rock's appearance, heating changes its crystalline structure and makes it a more desirable material for the manufacture of chipped-stone tools than it would be in its natural, unmodified state.

Unmodified or natural objects that have been moved also provide valuable information about human life and activities in the past. Raw materials—metallic ores, for example—that have been moved great distances provide us with information about the existence of ancient exchange networks and focus our attention on questions about how the materials were obtained and transported. Plant and animal remains are particularly useful because they help answer a number of questions about the people who used them:

Did they have domesticated plants and animals? What were the ages and sexes of the animals they herded and hunted? At what times of the year were they able to use the plants and animals they exploited? How did they perceive and utilize the resources found in the environment in which they lived? Which of the plants and animals provided food and which furnished materials for making useful objects? What kinds of foods did they actually prefer? These facts provide both qualitative and quantitative information about the activities of ancient peoples that allows us to develop a rather detailed picture of their subsistence economy.

Associations

The other kind of archaeological evidence consists of *associations*—the spatial relationships of objects to each other and to features of their surroundings. Associations showing that objects or ideas were in use simultaneously are particularly important because they provide a context for viewing and interpreting the remains that even the most detailed study of the objects themselves would not yield. The famed Rosetta stone, a basalt slab discovered in Egypt in 1799, provides an excellent example. The face of the slab is composed of three panels, each containing a different kind of writing. The upper panel contains Egyptian hieroglyphics, which had been observed earlier but not understood. The middle register contains Demotic script, a previously unknown writing system that ultimately turned out to be a shorthand derived from the hieroglyphic system. The bottom panel contains an inscription written in ancient Greek—a language that was well understood when the Rosetta stone was discovered. Priests from Memphis wrote the Greek text in 196 BC to extol the deeds and virtues of their king, Ptolemy Epiphanes of Egypt. Ancient rulers apparently were like those of today: They wanted their press secretaries to tell people what they had said, whether or not it was important or even comprehensible to those who spoke or read another language. Using this premise, it was reasonable to assume that the upper two panels contained the same message as the lower one. This was proven twenty-three years later, when the texts of the upper panels were finally deciphered. Besides showing that there were at least three writing systems and two languages in use in Egypt toward the end of the third century BC, the Rosetta stone shows that there was enough contact between Egypt and Greece to warrant bilingual statements of messages.

The importance of associations for interpreting the past cannot be overemphasized. Like the Rosetta stone, associations of contemporaneity—such as the various objects found in a tomb, the contents of a house that burned down before its occupants could remove their belongings, the refuse thrown into a garbage dump for a short period, or the remains of an entire settlement covered suddenly with volcanic ash—allow archaeologists to group together those objects and associations which were characteristic of the daily lives and activities of an ancient people. Such an array of contemporary objects and associations from a single archaeological site is called an *assemblage*. Perhaps the most famous archaeological assemblage, and potentially one of the richest in terms of the information it can provide, comes from Pompeii, a Roman town at the foot of Mt. Vesuvius that was completely covered by ash when the volcano erupted in AD 79. As a result of the eruption a detailed record of the daily activities of the townspeople has been preserved: It includes such diverse pieces of information as the shape of the loaves of bread they ate, the location of various kinds of workshops, the location and layout of their vineyards and orchards, the tools they used to work their agricultural lands, and even the grafitti inscribed on bathhouse walls and directions to the "red light" district (which were inscribed on the streets). The archaeological remains from Pompeii and its companion settlement, Herculaneum, provide us with more information about the daily activities of the Romans than written records from that time.

Cultures

Archaeologists usually have to consider assemblages from a number of sites in an area in order to reconstruct what life was like there at some time in the past. What they usually find is that contemporary assemblages from that area contain the same kinds of objects and the same kinds of associations. For example, the houses may have been laid out in roughly the same way, and the same kinds of bottles, pans, and cutlery are found in their kitchens. The uniformity of these assemblages indicates that the people who produced them were in fairly close contact with each other. Archaeologists refer to similar assemblages from contemporary sites in the same area as a *culture*.

The kinds of objects and the patterns of associations that occur in an area at a particular time in the past—its culture—give it a particular form or feeling that distinguishes it from other areas. For example, the brick row houses of Philadelphia differ in layout from contemporary stucco houses in southern California or wooden Cape Cods in New England; the fact that these houses contain many of the same kinds of objects and associations indicates that their residents participate to a greater or lesser degree in the same socioeconomic network. The fact that these houses have different layouts and contain different arrays of objects and associations from those found among the Bushmen of the Kalahari Desert, Chinese peasants, or Moscow apartment dwellers indicates that there are a number of different cultures in the world today. It also shows that contemporary peoples living in different parts of the world participate in different networks of socioeconomic relationships.

The same was true in the past. Peoples who lived in different parts of the world at the same time had different cultures. They participated in different networks of social relationships, and they learned the appropriate ways of doing things and of viewing the world from their elders.

Like writers describing modern societies, archaeologists use cultural differences to distinguish one society from another. The culture of a people gives them their identity—a consistency of style, a character that distinguishes them from other groups. Culture is the product of human activity and exists only in connection with people and their activities. It is the sum of the products of their activities—their social experience, knowledge, ways of doing things, and so on—which is handed down as social information from one generation to the next. People internalize or learn their own culture at the same time that they are creating it. As a result, cultures develop through time as people do things in new ways and their views of the world change.

While culture gives form and meaning to people's actions, it does not tell us how or why they do things the way they do. Archaeology, like the rest of the social sciences, is based on the premise that human beings are more like each other than they are different from each other. Without this premise, it would be impossible to compare the organization and development of different societies, because their cultures make each of them unique. In order to make these comparisons it is necessary to strip away cultural overlays and examine the human relationships that underlie them and produce the particular cultural patterns we observe. By examining these social relationships, we can begin to compare the organization and development of ancient societies.

THE QUESTION OF TIME

Archaeologists usually have to consider assemblages from a number of different sites in the same area in order to determine what happened in that part of the world. Whether they are concerned with how human behavior changed through time in a particular region or how it varied from one region to another during the same period, they ultimately have to determine the chronological relationships of the various assemblages. They must establish which assemblages are the oldest, which are the most recent, and which are contemporary before they can make any meaningful statements about how societies developed in that area and how they were similar to or different from societies in other areas.

Archaeologists distinguish two kinds of time: relative and absolute. *Relative time,* or dating, means placing the various assemblages from an area in chronological order from the oldest to the most recent. Relative dating tells us the sequence in which various activities occurred; however, it does not tell us how old a particular assemblage is or how long it lasted. To answer these questions, archaeologists must rely on *absolute dates* expressed in terms of some unit of time such as years or centuries. These units are usually correlated with the Christian calendar. Thus, when archaeologists say that a particular assemblage is 5,000 years old, they are saying that it existed at about 3025 BC. Relative and absolute dates express different things, and they are obtained in different ways.

Archaeologists can establish a relative sequence using two methods: *stratig-raphy* and *seriation*. Usually both methods are used. What underlies both is the fact that objects and associations change through time. If this were not so, archaeologists could not distinguish a 2-million-year-old assemblage from one that was 200 years old.

There are two principles of stratigraphy. The first is the *law of superposition,* which states than an assemblage found at the bottom of an undisturbed deposit is older than those found on top of it. The superposition of assemblages can occur in various ways—a tomb is dug through the floor of an abandoned house; a pyramid is built on top of a layer of refuse; or a pile of garbage is dumped on top of another layer of garbage.

The second principle of stratigraphy has been called the *law of strata identified by their contents* by some archaeologists and the *law of faunal dissimilarity* by paleontologists. It says that the various assemblages found at an archaeological site can be distinguished by differences in the kinds of objects and associations they contain and in the proportions in which they occur. That is, if the contents of the two assemblages are different and the difference is not due to the fact that they reflect different activities, the assemblages are of different ages. If the assemblages contain the same materials in the same proportions, they are contemporary, since no differences can be discerned between them.

The most important thing about stratigraphy is that it allows archaeologists to keep things from different periods separate; however, they have to apply both laws simultaneously in order to establish a relative chronology. Superposition allows them to determine the sequence in which various assemblages occur; however, unless they notice contrasts in the contents of the various assemblages, they have to treat them as if they were contemporary, even if there is superpositional evidence showing that one assemblage is more recent than another. These contrasts can involve insignificant things—the ways in which people decorate their pottery or the grills they put on their cars—or things of fundamental importance, like the ways in which they satisfy basic human needs and how they organize themselves to do so.

Seriation involves arranging assemblages from the same region in a chronological sequence by some technique other than superposition. The premise underlying all seriation arguments, regardless of whether they involve particular kinds of objects or associations or entire assemblages reflecting the total array of human activity—is that change is a gradual process. As a result, those objects, associations, or assemblages which are most similar to each other in content will be closer together in the sequence and in age than those which are less similar to each other and, consequently, further apart in time.

Relative dating provides us with information about the succession of assemblages through time; however, it does not tell us how old they are or how long they lasted. To answer these questions, archaeologists rely on some kind of absolute dating technique. The absolute ages of assemblages and their durations in time can be determined in various ways. Perhaps the simplest of these is through direct historical information about the site. For example, there are historical statements referring to the volcanic eruption that covered Pompeii and Herculaneum in AD 79. Another relatively simple technique can be used when objects of known historical age appear in an assemblage; these objects allow archaeologists to bracket the age and duration of the assemblage. For example, we know that the Spaniards introduced blue glass beads to the Americas shortly after AD 1492; consequently, any archaeological assemblage in the New World that contains such beads cannot be earlier than that date, though it may be more recent. The blue glass beads provide the lower age limit of the assemblage. If the assemblage that immediately follows the one with blue glass beads contains objects that can be dated historically to AD 1550, then we also know the upper age of the assemblage with the beads. It cannot be more recent than AD 1550. In other words, the duration or time span represented is no more than 58 years; as a result, the assemblage dates to a period beginning no earlier than 1492 and ending no later than 1550.

Where there were ancient calendrical systems with recorded inscriptions—as in Egypt, China, Mesopotamia, and the Maya region of southern Mexico and Guatemala—it is possible to date some archaeological assemblages in terms of the calendar that was being used. There are two major problems with this method. First, archaeologists have to be able to correlate the indigenous calendrical systems with the Christian calendar. There are different correlations for a number of these calendars; for example, the two more plausible correlations of the Maya Long Count calendar with the Christian one differ by a little more than 256 years. The other difficulty is that the indigenous calendars are useful only for dating assemblages that are not older than the calendrical systems themselves.

Only a small portion of the known archaeological assemblages have been dated directly in terms of some calendrical system because of historical information about them or because they include objects of known age such as a pot with a Maya Long Count date inscribed on it. As a result, archaeologists usually rely on other techniques for absolute dating such as tree rings, radiocarbon, or potassium–argon dating. These techniques and others like them are called *chronometric dating methods*. They measure the rates of such natural phenomena as the formation of tree rings, the disintegration of radioactive carbon, or the formation of argon gas from radioactive potassium. Consequently, these techniques are independent of human activity.

Dendrochronology, or tree ring dating as it is more commonly known, is based on the fact that trees add concentric growth rings each year. This is especially true in areas where there are marked seasonal changes in the weather each year and the growth of the tree occurs during a few months of the year. When a tree is cut down or a core is taken from it, we can tell the age of the tree by counting the number of rings. The width of these rings can vary from year to year and reflect variations in the weather. The rings tend to be wider in years in which the climatic conditions favor growth and narrower in those in which conditions are less favorable. By comparing the ring sequences from different trees with overlapping ages and matching the pattern of wide and narrow rings, scientists can build a master chronology. This technique was first used in the American Southwest, where experts used ponderosa pine trees to construct a calendar that stretched back to 53 BC. Using the California bristlecone pine, they have developed a master chronology that now extends more than 8,000 years into the past.

Archaeologists have used tree ring dating effectively in the American Southwest and, to a lesser extent, in continental Europe, where a combination of Celtic and Roman beams provides a rough calendar that extends from about 700 BC to AD 339. For a tree ring–dated piece of wood to be useful to archaeologists, they must know its archaeological significance: Was it contemporary with the rest of the materials in the assemblage, or was it picked up and used at a later date?

Radiocarbon dating can be used to date assemblages up to about 60,000 years old. The method is based on the fact that a radioactive isotope of carbon—carbon 14—is produced by cosmic ray bombardment of nitrogen

Archaeologists use absolute chronologies established by matching ring patterns on trees cut at different times in the past. Jesse D. Jennings, **Prehistory of North America,** 2nd ed. (New York: McGraw-Hill, 1974), fig. 1-4, p. 15. Copyright © 1974 McGraw-Hill Book Company. Used by permission.

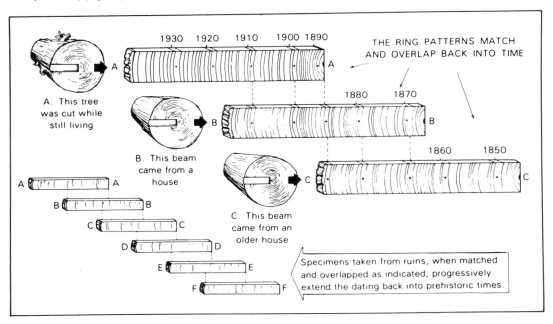

THE RING PATTERNS MATCH AND OVERLAP BACK INTO TIME

A. This tree was cut while still living

B. This beam came from a house

C. This beam came from an older house

Specimens taken from ruins, when matched and overlapped as indicated, progressively extend the dating back into prehistoric times.

atoms in the upper atmosphere and is eventually absorbed by every living thing on earth. Since living organisms are continually absorbing and eliminating carbon 14, they all contain roughly the same percentage that is found in the atmosphere and in other living organisms. When the organisms die, they no longer absorb carbon compounds from their environment, and their proportion of carbon 14 begins to diminish as the radioactive atoms disintegrate. After 5,730 years they have lost half of their carbon-14 atoms. Since the disintegration of radioactive atoms occurs at a known rate, called the half-life, scientists can determine the age of an organic material by measuring its radioactivity, that is, by counting the number of particles emitted by a known amount of material over a given period. By doing so, they can calculate how much radioactive carbon is still present in the material and, as a result, how old the material is.

Archaeologists can collect radiocarbon samples from any of a wide range of organic materials that occur in archaeological assemblages. These include charcoal from a fireplace, burned bone or shell, wood, or any other organic material that is clearly associated with the assemblage. Scientists in the laboratory convert the sample into an organic compound and place it in a chamber surrounded by devices that count radioactive decay. Dates obtained by this technique are expressed as probability statements. For example, a sample of organic material might yield an age of 1000 ± 200 radiocarbon years BP. This statement means a number of things. BP means "before the present," which is arbitrarily defined as AD 1950. The phrase "radiocarbon years" indicates that scientists are aware that a radiocarbon year might not have the same duration as a year defined in terms of the Christian calendar. The statement 1000 ± 200 indicates that there is a 67-percent chance that the actual age of the sample falls between 800 and 1,200 radiocarbon years and that there is a 95-percent probability that it falls between 600 and 1,400 radiocarbon years.

The radiocarbon dating method involves a number of assumptions, the most important of which is that the amount of carbon 14 produced in the upper atmosphere is relatively constant from one year to the next. At least three factors affect this assumption. First, the use of coal, oil, and other fossil fuels has tremendously increased the amount of ancient carbon in the atmosphere since the beginning of the industrial revolution in the later years of the eighteenth century; this has produced a decrease in the proportion of carbon 14 in the atmosphere and living organisms. Second, the hydrogen bomb explosions that have occurred since the 1950s have greatly increased the amount of carbon 14 and other radioactive debris in the atmosphere and elsewhere. Unfortunately, the "industrial effect" and the "atom bomb effect" do not cancel each other out. Third, there have been long-term variations in the intensity of the earth's magnetic field and changes in the amount of solar energy reaching the upper atmosphere. This means that there were times in the past when more carbon 14 was being produced in the atmosphere, as

Table 1-1: Calibration of Conventional Radiocarbon Dates (5568 Half-life) Using the Calibration Curve in Graph Found on p. 18

Radiocarbon Date bp	ad	Calendar Date† AD	BP	Radiocarbon Date bp	bc	Calendar Date† BC	BP
50	1900	—	—	2550	600	800	2750
100	1850	1895, 1820	55,130	2600	650	840	2790
150	1800	1685	265	2650	700	880	2830
200	1750	1650	300	2700	750	925	2875
250	1700	1625	325	2750	800	975	2925
300	1650	1580	370	2800	850	1030	2980
350	1600	1495	455	2850	900	1100	3050
400	1550	1470	480	2900	950	1175	3125
450	1500	1440	510	2950	1000	1250	3200
500	1450	1420	530	3000	1050	1320	3270
550	1400	1400	550	3050	1100	1385	3335
600	1350	1375	575	3100	1150	1440	3390
650	1300	1350	600	3150	1200	1495	3445
700	1250	1315	635	3200	1250	1550	3500
750	1200	1255	695	3250	1300	1595	3545
800	1150	1220	730	3300	1350	1650	3600
850	1100	1170	780	3350	1400	1710	3660
900	1050	1070	880	3400	1450	1770	3720
950	1000	1030	920	3450	1500	1835	3785
1000	950	990	960	3500	1550	1900	3850
1050	900	950	1000	3550	1600	1975	3925
1100	850	880	1070	3600	1650	2035	3985
1150	800	815	1135	3650	1700	2095	4045
1200	750	760	1190	3700	1750	2160	4110
1250	700	720	1230	3750	1800	2230	4180
1300	650	685	1265	3800	1850	2305	4255
1350	600	640	1310	3850	1900	2385	4335
1400	550	595	1355	3900	1950	2455	4405
1450	500	535	1415	3950	2000	2520	4470
1500	450	470	1480	4000	2050	2595	4545
1550	400	430	1520	4050	2100	2670	4620
1600	350	390	1560	4100	2150	2755	4705
1650	300	345	1605	4150	2200	2850	4800
1700	250	280	1670	4200	2250	2910	4860
1750	200	245	1705	4250	2300	2970	4920
1800	150	215	1735	4300	2350	3030	4980
1850	100	185	1765	4350	2400	3095	5045
1900	50ad	120AD	1830	4400	2450	3175	5125
1950	0ad	60AD	1890	4450	2500	3245	5195
2000	50bc	0AD	1950	4500	2550	3310	5260
2050	100	95	2045	4550	2600	3370	5320
2100	150	160	2110	4600	2650	3430	5380
2150*	200*	205*	2155*	4650	2700	3485	5435
2200*	250*	370*	2320*	4700	2750	3530	5480

16

Table 1.1: (continued)

Radiocarbon Date		Calendar Date[†]		Radiocarbon Date		Calendar Date[†]	
bp	ad	AD	BP	bp	bc	BC	BP
2250	300	400	2350	4750	2800	3580	5530
2300	350	425	2375	4800	2850	3635	5585
2350	400	450	2400	4850	2900	3685	5635
2400*	450*	490*	2440*	4900	2950	3730	5680
2450*	500*	600*	2550*	4950	3000	3785	5735
2500*	550*	755*	2705*	5000	3050	3835	5785
5050	3100	3885	5835	5800	3850	4630	6580
5100	3150	3935	5885	5850	3900	4680	6630
5150	3200	3990	5940	5900	3950	4760	6710
5200	3250	4040	5990	5950	4000	4845	6795
5250	3300	4095	6045	6000	4050	4920	6870
5300	3350	4160	6110	6050	4100	4975	6925
5350	3400	4250	6200	6100	4150	5030	6980
5400	3450	4325	6275	6150	4200	5085	7035
5450	3500	4375	6325	6200	4250	5130	7080
5500	3550	4410	6360	6250	4300	5170	7120
5550	3600	4450	6400	6300	4350	5215	7165
5600	3650	4485	6435	6350	4400	5255	7205
5650	3700	4520	6470	6400	4450	5300	7250
5700	3750	4555	6505	6450	4500	5350	7300
5750	3800	4590	6540	6500	4550	5415	7365

Source: R. M. Clark, "A Calibration Curve for Radiocarbon Dates." **Antiquity,** 49, no. 196 (December 1975), 264–65.

[†]Calendar dates are rounded to the nearest 5 years.
*See supplementary table 1.2 for calibration of dates in this region.

Table 1-2: Supplementary Table for Radiocarbon Dates

Radiocarbon Date		Calendar Date(s)				
bp	bc	BP		bp	bc	BP
2150	200	2155		2430	480	2510
2160	210	2165		2440	490	2530
2170	220	2175, 2270, 2285		2450	500	2550
2180	230	2190, 2250, 2305		2460	510	2565
2190	240	2230, 2315		2465	515	2575, 2620, 2655
2200	250	2320		2470	520	2585, 2605, 2665
2420	470	2480		2480	530	2680

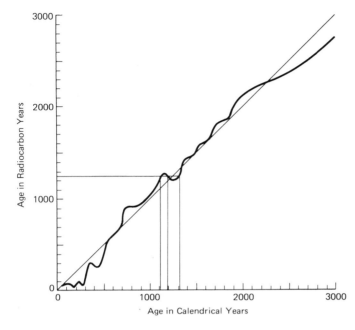

Radiocarbon dates are expressed in the form of probability statements — for instance. 1250 ± 100 radiocarbon years B.P. (before the present, which is arbitrarily defined as A.D. 1950). In this example, 1250 is the mean, and the ± 100 indicates that there is a 67 percent probability that the actual age of the sample falls between 1150 and 1350 radiocarbon years or 100 radiocarbon years on either side of the mean value. Thomas C. Patterson, **America's past: a new world archaeology** (Glenview: Scott Foresman & Co., 1973), p. 11, fig. 1-2.

well as times when less was being produced. Scientists discovered these variations by dating ancient wooden samples of known age and comparing the radiocarbon and tree ring ages of these samples. They have also worked out correction curves in which carbon 14 dates are calibrated with those obtained by dendrochronologists (see Tables 1.1 and 1.2).

Potassium–argon dating has been used to date rocks that range in age from about half a million to more than 4 billion years. It is based on the fact that a radioactive isotope of potassium disintegrates into the gas argon. By measuring the amount of argon that has accumulated in potassium-bearing minerals—such as many volcanic rocks and ashes—in a mass spectrometer, scientists can determine the age of the sample. The value of this technique is that it can be used to date materials well beyond the range of the radioactive carbon method. In fact, the older the sample, the more accurate the technique becomes. Its limitations are that it can be used only in areas where there once was volcanic activity and that the crystal structure of the rock sample cannot be porous (otherwise argon gas would have been added or lost through the holes in the crystals). Archaeologists and paleontologists have used the potassium–argon method to date samples associated with the first humans and their ancestors, who lived more than 2 million years ago.

In spite of the problems with these methods of absolute dating and others that are now being developed, archaeologists have to rely on them to determine the age and duration of most assemblages. Consequently, it is important to be aware of their limitations and not accept their results uncritically or use them carelessly. Scientists are refining these techniques so as to improve their accuracy. In addition, they are developing new ones—thermoluminescence, fission track dating, paleomagnetic dating—that will increase the range and variety of materials that can be used for absolute dating.

CONCLUSION

Archaeologists have to deal with only two kinds of evidence: objects of all kinds and the contexts in which these occur. In this sense there is very little to archaeology, for the range of evidence is limited to the traces of past human activities that have survived to the present. In another sense, however, there is a great deal to archaeology, particularly when it involves interpreting the meaning and significance of this evidence. Archaeologists can enhance our understanding of the past not just by focusing our attention on the objects and associations they find but, more important, by directing our attention to the broader patterns underlying these data and to questions of how and why the patterns and processes are similar and different from one region to another and from one period to the next. Through this kind of examination we can increase our understanding of the mechanisms that produce social change and development.

FURTHER READINGS

Childe, V. Gordon
1951 *Social evolution.* C. A. Watts, London.
1956 *Piecing together the past; the interpretation of archaeological data.* Praeger, New York.
1962 *A short introduction to archaeology.* Collier Books, New York.
Daniel, Glyn
1975 *One hundred and fifty years of archaeology.* Gerald Duckworth, London.
Deetz, James
1967 *Invitation to archaeology.* Doubleday, Garden City, N.Y.
Fagan, Brian M.
1978 *Archaeology; a brief introduction.* Little, Brown, Boston.
Flannery, Kent V.,
1977 *The early Mesoamerican village.* Academic Press, New York.
Heizer, Robert F., and John Graham
1967 *A guide to field methods in archaeology.* National Press Books, Palo Alto, Calif.
Hole, Frank, and Robert F. Heizer
1973 *An introduction to prehistoric archaeology.* Holt, Rinehart and Winston, New York.

Michael, Henry N., and Elizabeth K. Ralph, eds.
1971 *Dating techniques for the archaeologist.* M.I.T. Press, Cambridge, Mass.

Michels, J. W.
1973 *Dating methods in archaeology.* Seminar Press, New York.

Patterson, Thomas C.
1963 Contemporaneity and cross-dating in archaeological interpretation. *American Antiquity,* 28, no. 3, January, pp. 389–392.

Rowe, John H.
1959 Archaeological dating and cultural process. *Southwestern Journal of Anthropology,* 15, no. 4, Winter, pp. 317–324.
1961 Stratigraphy and seriation. *American Antiquity,* 26, no. 3, January, pp. 324–330.
1962 Stages and periods in archaeological interpretation. *Southwestern Journal of Anthropology,* 18, no. 1, Spring, pp. 40–54.
1962 Worsaae's law and the use of grave lots for archaeological dating. *American Antiquity,* 28, no. 2, pp. 129–137.

Wheeler, Mortimer
1956 *Archaeology from the earth.* Penguin Books, Baltimore.

Studying Society and Social Change

Archaeology did not develop in a vacuum. It is the product of intellectual currents that swirled through different generations in Europe over a span of four centuries. The ideas and activities associated with each of these currents have their own history. They were born in the Italian Renaissance of the fifteenth century, nurtured during the Age of Discovery, and brought together in the last half of the nineteenth century to form the field of archaeology as we know it today. These currents involve the development of new ideas about the world and the place of people in it, new perspectives on the age of the world and its inhabitants, the use of nonliterary evidence to piece together the past, and new ideas about the nature of human society and its development.

THE DEVELOPMENT OF ARCHAEOLOGICAL RESEARCH

The Italian humanists of the early fifteenth century recognized that their art, language, literature, and philosophy—their culture—were different from those of ancient Rome and that those differences were worthy of study. They soon began to make systematic studies of ancient ruins; they combined this archaeological evidence with literary and epigraphical evidence to reconstruct the Roman past. Through the fifteenth and sixteenth centuries these antiquarians slowly extended their investigations eastward to Greece, Egypt, and the great empires of the Ancient East—Persia and Assyria. As humanistic philosophy, with its special perspective on cultural differences, was embraced in northern Europe, antiquarians began to study the ruins and relics of England, France, and Germany.

2

By the beginning of the seventeenth century, social philosophers were coming to grips with explorers' reports of societies in the Americas that were dramatically different from those that were familiar to the peoples of Europe. At the same time, they were beginning to deal with the implications of the great astronomical and mathematical discoveries of Copernicus, Galileo, Newton, and others. The impact of the exploration and scientific advances of the day shattered existing world views by depriving humanity of its sense of uniqueness and importance. The old world views—a mixture of biblical revelation, interpretations of medieval mythology and classical writers, and the humanist notion of the superiority of the classical world over that of the present—no longer provided satisfactory explanations. For the new rationalists, with their emphasis on direct observation, experimentation, and inductive reasoning, natural laws governed the movement of everything in the universe—including human society.

Geology versus the Bible

One thing the rationalists and their contemporaries agreed on was the age of the earth. No one thought the world was very old. The date of the creation had become firmly fixed in the Protestant countries of northern Europe during the Reformation because of the unquestionable authority of the Bible as a historical source. Scholars studied the Old Testament to determine as precisely as possible the time of the creation. Following more than a century of scholarship on the biblical time scale, Archbishop James Ussher fixed the time of this event at nine in the morning of October 23, 4004 BC. Biblical time scales were frequently printed in the margins of the Bible and acquired almost as much authority as the text itself.

In 1593 biblical scholars began to examine other kinds of evidence in their quest to establish a chronology for the Old Testament. At first they confined their inquiries to the historical information found in ancient Persian, Babylonian, and Egyptian sources. A few of them pointed out that there were inconsistencies in the time scale provided by the Scriptures and that there were discrepancies between such chronologies and those derived from ancient Near Eastern sources. In the middle of the seventeenth century, they began to consider chronological evidence provided by traditions recorded in the Americas and China to resolve these contradictions. Finally, in the last quarter of the century, they began to look at evidence provided by the earth itself. These assessments of the age of the earth combined the biblical accounts of the creation and flood with recent advances in physics, astronomy, and geology. By themselves, they did not shed any new light on the age of the earth; however, they did stimulate a number of naturalists to publish their own views about the origin of the earth and the changes that had occurred since then. By the middle of the eighteenth century, the naturalists were relying entirely on geological and other kinds of scientific information to reconstruct the earth's history.

Geologists made great strides during the last half of the eighteenth century. In 1756 they showed that the geological formations of the earth's crust were stratified, one on top of another, and that these strata followed one another in a definite order. In 1796 they showed that different geological strata contained different kinds of fossil plants and animals and that each stratum contained its own particular assemblage. In other words, the earth's crust contained a long succession of former worlds, each with its own varieties of plants and animals. The most important discovery of the period, however, occurred in 1785, when James Hutton formulated the principle of *uniformitarianism*. This principle states that the geological processes altering the face of the earth today are the same as those that modified it in the past. Scientists grasped the significance of this principle almost immediately. Since these processes operate very slowly today, the succession of past worlds must also have formed slowly over a long time. In other words, the earth was much older than the Bible indicated.

Almost immediately, scientists began to ask whether some ancient peoples might have lived simultaneously with extinct animals. Circumstantial evidence accumulated. In 1859, for the first time, it was shown that human beings had, in fact, lived at the same time as certain kinds of extinct animals—first at Brixham Cave in England and then at Abbeville, France. More recently, new methods of absolute dating have shown that the age of the world must be measured in *billions* rather than millions of years, and as our understanding of the fossil record has increased, the age of our earliest human ancestors has slowly but steadily been pushed further back in time.

Comparing Societies

While the biblical scholars and naturalists were trying to establish the age of the earth, the social philosophers and theorists were searching for laws that would explain the functioning and development of human society. Seventeenth-century rationalists were preoccupied with two questions: the natural state of human society and the intellectual development of people as members of human society. As a result, they wrote numerous tracts on natural law, natural politics, natural religion, and natural economic laws. They based their writings largely on philosophical arguments about the natural, or primitive, state of human society. However, only a few actually bothered to use historical information or data provided by the voyage and travel literature, facts that they selected very carefully to bolster their arguments.

The other concern of the seventeenth-century social theorists was the intellectual development of human society. At first this concern was limited largely to comparing the intellectual achievements of the ancient Greeks and Romans with those of modern Europeans. The humanists and their successors with their deep reverence for the classical world, argued that human society had deteriorated with the passage of time and that the peoples of today were clearly inferior to those of classical antiquity. The rationalists countered such claims. Bolstering their argument with the great geographic and scientific discoveries of the day, they claimed that the peoples of modern Europe were intellectually superior to those of the classical world. This debate, called the quarrel between the ancients and the moderns, was waged largely during the first half of the seventeenth century and was clearly won by the modern rationalists.

For the next fifty years Europeans saw themselves as more advanced than the peoples of the classical world. However, as the volume of the travel literature grew, the newly discovered peoples of the Americas, Africa, and the South Seas presented the social theorists of the eighteenth century with a very distressing problem. How could so many different kinds of societies develop in a world that was governed by laws that operated in the same way everywhere? They attempted to solve this problem in a variety of ways. Some saw the differences in the manners and customs of different peoples as the products of learning. Others saw them as the products of various driving forces—climate, government, religion, or economics—that shaped society and gave direction to its movement. However, the view that ultimately won out in the late eighteenth century was that these primitive non-European societies were representatives of earlier stages in the development of civilization—particularly European civilization—than the peoples of the classical world. This idea is called the *comparative method.*

Accounting for Social Change

The social theorists of the nineteenth century continued to concern themselves with the laws that gave order to human society; however, their quest for these laws differed somewhat from that of their predecessors. They saw the rules governing social change as the key to understanding how order was maintained in human society. For the positivist philosophers—Auguste Comte, John Stuart Mill, Herbert Spencer—it was essential to understand the laws of social change so that the existing social order could be maintained. For the historical materialists—Karl Marx and Friedrich Engels—it was essential to understand the laws of social change in order to direct the movement of society toward higher stages of social development.

As we shall see later, the positivists and the historical materialists had very different ideas about what human societies are like. In fact, it has been said that much of the content of the social sciences today is the product of an ongoing debate between the positivists and the historical materialists. Modern archaeologists have been influenced by both theoretical positions.

By the seventeenth century antiquarians were beginning to make systematic surveys of ancient peoples mentioned in the writings of classical authors. At first they preferred the evidence provided by these writers and in inscriptions over archaeological evidence. This was particularly true for the ancient Greeks and Romans because of the relative abundance of literary evidence and inscriptions describing them. It was much less true in the northern countries—England, France, and Germany—where there was very little

(a)

(b)

(c)

By the end of the sixteenth century, drawings of American Indians were influencing how Europeans perceived their ancestors. The artist, John White, visited Virginia in about 1585 and drew (a) an American Indian while there. He returned to England and drew (b) "A Native Briton" and (c) "A Pict." Thomas D. Kendrick, **British antiquity** (London: Methuen, 1950), pls. 12, 13. Reproduced by permission of the Trustees of the British Museum.

literary evidence and virtually no inscriptions. As a result, the antiquarians of the northern countries had to rely to a much greater extent on archaeological evidence to piece together the past. By the end of the century the northern antiquarians saw archaeological evidence as superior to that found in the writings of classical authors. They brought direct observation into historical inquiry and ultimately pointed out the need for new kinds of historical writing by questioning the completeness of classical sources. For them, the accounts of classical authors and the writings of contemporary philosophers and social theorists on the development of human society no longer sufficed.

However, when the northern antiquarians used archaeological evidence to piece together the past they systematically attributed the relics and ruins they described to peoples mentioned by classical writers. They usually saw these peoples—the Britons, the Gauls, or the Franks—as the earliest inhabitants of their countries. Because the antiquarians accepted the biblical time scale, none of those peoples were thought to be of great antiquity. When they wrote about the history of humanity in the seventeenth century, they did it in terms of four empires—those of Greece, Rome, Assyria, and Persia—that were both earlier than and contemporary with Christianity. Later, in the eighteenth century, they wrote about the history of humanity in terms of ancient, medieval, and modern peoples. They assumed that in the ancient Near East and the classical world there were relatively short periods between the creation of the world and the earliest peoples mentioned in written sources. In northern Europe, where there was little or no Roman influence and Christianity penetrated relatively late, the period between the creation of the world and the first historically documented peoples was much longer. For the northern antiquarians, this prehistoric period was shrouded in darkness and fog; they had no way of imposing order on the relics they found.

A number of things helped to change this situation between 1775 and 1816. First, a few rationalist philosophers, particularly those in Scotland, became interested in the early stages of human society; some of them stressed the importance of economic factors in these developments. Second, in 1773 an English antiquarian, Governor Pownall, was describing archaeological evidence from New Grange in two very distinct ways. At the same time that he was writing in terms of peoples with fixed historical names, he was also discussing human development in terms of a succession of economic stages in which the first human beings—hunters and gatherers—were gradually succeeded by settled land workers, or farmers. Third, the northern antiquarians became even more closely allied with the naturalists because of the lack of literary evidence concerning what had happened in those countries in the past. This made them much more aware of the advances that were taking place in geology during the last quarter of the eighteenth century. Fourth, in 1816 the Danish antiquarian Christian Jurgensen Thomsen used the idea of a succession of three technological stages, known as the *Three Ages*. A stage in which stone tools were used, succeeded by ones in which bronze and then iron tools were made, were the basis for organizing archaeological collections at the National Museum in Copenhagen. For the first time, antiquarians were able to recognize order in the prehistoric past of northern Europe.

Excavations in the Danish bogs and Swiss lake dwellings during the 1840s provided stratigraphic proof of the succession of Thomsen's Three Ages. The Three-Age idea became widely accepted in western Europe during the 1850s. However, in the 1860s the excavations at Brixham Cave and in the Somme gravels at Abbeville, which provided conclusive evidence of the great antiquity of humanity, created a new problem. Archaeologists recognized that the stone tools used by the human contemporaries of extinct animals were different from the ones found in the Danish bogs. By 1865 they had divided the Stone Age into earlier and later parts: Chipped-stone tools were characteristic of the Paleolithic, or Old Stone Age, and polished-stone tools were used by the peoples of the Neolithic, or New Stone Age. This set the pattern for an activity that was very popular among archaeologists for the next fifty years—dividing and subdividing the Three Ages into an ever-increasing number of stages on the basis of technological or stylistic differences in their artifacts.

Many archaeologists of the day saw these successions of technological ages as analogous to the succession of geological strata. In fact, for many scientists of the late nineteenth century archaeology was the link between geology and history. However, they wrote about the early differences in terms of people who migrated into an area from the outside and brought with them new ways of doing things, or they saw them in terms of the spread of tools, techniques, or ideas from one area to another. By so doing, they were able to deal, at least superficially, with the fact that similar cultures need not have flourished simultaneously in different parts of the world.

Archaeology in the Early Twentieth Century

This concern with cultural differences marked the beginning of a new orientation in archaeology. Archaeologists no longer saw the development of ancient societies as analogous to the succession of different types of fossils in the earth's crust. Instead, they were beginning to adopt anthropological and historical perspectives that emphasized that ancient societies were groups of human beings who learned particular ways of doing things as they grew up. Archaeologists increasingly stressed the fact these ideas and behaviors were learned. It was culture—learned ideas and behavior—that distinguished one group of people from another. V. Gordon Childe popularized this orientation in the late 1920s when he published *The Dawn of European Civilization* and *The Danube in Prehistory*.

At about the same time that they began to study groups of artifacts and associations—cultures—as distribution patterns in time and space, archaeologists began to examine and explain these patterns in terms of the prehistoric landscapes in which they occurred. In the 1920s and 1930s Cyril Fox and other archaeologists began to plot the distribution of archaeological materials from different periods on a series of ecological maps that reflected the environmental changes that had occurred in Europe during the past 10,000 years. They observed that there was a close correlation between the geographic distributions of the environmental resources of a particular period and archaeological materials from the same period. This correlation implied that there was a close relationship between an archaeological culture and its natural habitat. The nature of this relationship was clarified by the early 1950s, when archaeologists began to emphasize that the economic base of a society represented an adjustment between the needs of its members and the physical and biological conditions in which they lived. In other words, culture—particularly its technological and economic aspects—was the way in which a group of people adapted to its environment.

As archaeologists increasingly turned their attention to analyzing the relationships between ancient societies and their environments, they gradually renewed their interest in explaining the changes and developments that had occurred in different parts of the world. Through the 1940s they relied largely on explanations of social change and development that stressed *diffusion,* or the spread of innovations from one place to another. This orientation, which combined the ideas that the cultural differences were due to different environmental adaptations and that social change was a product of diffusion, forced archaeologists to focus on the particular events and processes that occurred in each area and effectively prevented them from looking at the underlying similarities in the structure and development of different societies.

In the 1950s archaeologists once again began to look behind the differences to examine similarities in the historical development of various societies. Their explanations increasingly emphasized the relationship between the organization of work, technology, and resources provided by the natural environment and how this organization affects other aspects of the society. Some explanations also implied that societies with similar environmental situations—for example, the so-called hydraulic societies in the Near East, Egypt, Peru, and elsewhere—developed in the same manner. However, once again social theory provided a number of different ways of looking at human society and its development.

By the 1960s archaeologists who were concerned with the development of human societies relied on theoretical formulations that were developed largely, if not entirely, outside of the field itself. Their reconstructions of ancient societies and how they changed or developed through time were based on the premises of positivism and historical materialism. In the section that follows we will consider these theoretical positions in more detail and examine how they have influenced and been incorporated into archaeological thought.

CONTEMPORARY THEORIES OF SOCIETY AND SOCIAL CHANGE

As mentioned earlier, two philosophical positions—*positivism* and *historical materialism*—dominate thinking in archaeology and the other social sciences today. Each involves certain assumptions that lead to different views about what societies are like and how they change. There tends to be some mixing of the tenets of these philosophical positions, since social scientists arrive at their views of society and social change in response to the questions being asked in particular intellectual climates. As a result, few archaeologists would subscribe completely to a single position, and none would completely disregard what they consider valuable in each. In other words, most archaeologists are eclectic in the sense that they pick and choose from the various position, emphasizing some tenets while ignoring others. However, some seem to pick and choose more than others.

Positivism

The positivists assume that they can study only observable social or historical facts, which are analogous to the facts studied by natural or physical scientists. These facts are derived from the activities of the individual, who is the basic unit of society. The facts are linked to each other by sets of constant and unchanging relationships that reflect universally applicable laws. In other words, what is true about the behavior of one person—either alone or in a group—is true about the behavior of all other individuals, regardless of when or where they lived.

A truly positivist social science is both behaviorist and reductionist. It is *behaviorist* because it avoids reference to the internal mental states of people, their beliefs and values, and their reasons and motives for acting. It is *reductionist* because the scientific study of society is a quest to discover the general laws that govern human behavior and reduce them in number so that each law explains the greatest possible variety of social and historical facts.

Positivists view society as composed of a number of individuals who interact with each other in particular ways. The behavior of these individuals is learned. Consequently, when positivists examine the structure of a society they are concerned with the various kinds of groups these individuals form and the kinds of relationships, or institutions, that arise from their activities in those groups. For them, a society is analogous to a biological organism or a cybernetic system. It is composed of a number of interrelated parts—groups, institutions, or systems—that interact in such a way that the social organism or system is maintained in some state of stable or dynamic equilibrium so that it can continue to function or operate.

Since the positivists view stability and order as the normal conditions of human society, they are forced to rely on other models to view and explain social change. In fact, they view social change from several different perspectives. For some, it is a product of some force that impinges on the social system from the outside. For others, it is a product of some internal contradiction that is generated in the society when one institution or activity becomes more important than others and disrupts the normal functioning of the system. For a third group, it is a product of the normal growth of various social institutions.

| Historical Materialism | The historical materialists see societies as groups of individuals who interact with one another to satisfy the material needs of life—food, shelter, and clothing—and to ensure the continuity or reproduction of the group from one generation to the next. Consequently, the behavior of individuals can be understood only in terms of their membership in a group and their participation in its activities. People satisfy the basic needs of production and reproduction through work. This involves making tools and devising techniques so that the objects of nature can be used. In order to carry out these activities, they enter into definite relationships with each other that are called the *relations of production*. These relations include the patterns of specialization and cooperation involved in the process of production, the exchange of labor resulting from the division of labor, and the ways in which the socially valuable goods produced are distributed throughout the society. The relations of production also express different forms of property ownership. In societies in which the means of production are owned communally, everyone has equal access to the goods produced, and relations of cooperation and mutual assistance are established. In societies in which the means of production are owned by individuals or by some segment of the society, relations based on domination and subjugation develop because some individuals have greater access to the socially valuable goods produced by others.

The productive forces of a society—the natural objects its members use, the tools with which they exploit those resources, and the labor power of the people who use those tools—express the relationship of the society to its environment, and the level of their development indicates the extent of its control over nature. However, the relations of production are the basis, the economic foundation, of all other social relations, ideas, and views that form the political and ideological superstructure of a society. In other words, the historical materialists see society as consisting of three interacting and interdependent levels: an economic base, a political level consisting of institutions and norms that regulate the functioning of the society, and an ideological level with corresponding forms of social consciousness. The historical materialists also recognize that not everything in a society—its art and language, for example—can be reduced to the economic base or be considered mere reflections of it.

According to the historical materialists, the ideological level of a society consists of the ideas people have about the world, their attitudes, and their customary behavior in particular situations. These ideas are not only subjective scientific statements that describe reality, but also social statements full of imaginary elements that express the memories, hopes, and aspirations of people. Ideologies help people adapt to the reality of the world in which they live by providing explanations of their relations with this world as they perceive it. In societies with social classes, the different classes may have different ideological tendencies that reflect their position in the productive process.

The political level of a society consists of those institutions and norms which help its members regulate the functioning of the group. The existence of the political level is based on the social division of labor. In every society there is a need for people to organize and administer different activities in the productive process. In simple societies, where the division of labor is minimal, the individual who organizes and supervises one work activity may be supervised by a different person when another activity is being carried out. In class societies, these administrative functions are carried out by the state. The principal function of the state, however, is to ensure the continued political domination of the class that owns the means of production. In modern capitalist societies this is done by controlling institutions like the police, the courts, the schools, or the media. In other words, the state legitimizes and perpetuates the existing social order.

Historical materialists believe that every society has an underlying structure that can be abstracted from social reality by studying the relations that develop between people as they satisfy the basic needs of production and reproduction through their labor. This underlying structure is an abstraction composed of one or more *modes of production* that express the relationships between the forces of production and the relations of production. There are relatively few modes of production, and the same one can provide the dominant underlying structure in a number of different societies existing at various times and places. In other words, the particular combination of modes of production and the relative position or importance of each vary from one society to another.

Each mode of production has its own laws that govern its functioning and development. Consequently, the concepts that are essential for understanding the functioning and development of one mode of production have little or no value for understanding another. For example, information about kinship or the relationship between lord and serf is essential for understanding the primitive and feudal modes of production; however, it does not explain the structure and development of the capitalist mode of production, which is based on the existence of social classes.

Modes of production succeed each other in a definite progression, since the seeds for each new mode are found in the contradictions that developed in the preceding one. Each new generation must initially accept the existing productive forces and relations of production before modifying them to satisfy their needs in a more adequate fashion. In other words, there is continuity in the development of the productive forces of a society. However, beyond a certain point in the development of society the relations of production act as a brake that limits the further development of the productive forces. When this happens, the relations of production have to change to correspond with the new level of development of the productive forces. At first this change may affect only that small sector of the economy which controls the new productive forces. However, as these new forces become more important, the old relations of production can be adapted to some extent, but the degree to which this can happen is limited. As the contradiction between the old and new forces in the society becomes more apparent, the old relations of production are replaced by the new ones, which reflect the conscious activities of those classes which hope to create ideological, political, and economic conditions favorable to the further development of the new forces of production. As this happens, the aspirations of the rising classes come into conflict with the institutions and regulations of the state, which function to maintain the interests of the class that already controls the means of production. This conflict, or contradiction, is ultimately resolved only when the rising class overthrows the established one and remolds the institutions and ideology of the society to fit its own vision of what that society should be like.

CURRENT TRENDS IN ARCHAEOLOGICAL THOUGHT

Archaeologists have used elements of both positivism and historical materialism to construct their descriptive or explanatory models. In fact, one or the other of these philosophical positions underlies virtually all the theoretical models produced or used by archaeologists today. Some of these theories adhere rather closely to the tenets of positivism, while others incorporate premises—often in the form of assumptions—from both perspectives. The theories described in the following paragraphs are not mutually exclusive, and the same individual might well subscribe to two or more of these positions.

Cultural
Ecology

Concern with the relationship between societies and their natural environments flourished during the 1930s. This growing interest took place against the background of the Great Depression, a period during which anthropologists and other social scientists became increasingly aware of the importance of economic factors in shaping social relationships. The term *cultural ecology* was coined by Julian H. Steward, who was concerned with the economic and sociopolitical organization of the Great Basin Shoshone and how these peoples adapted to the environment in which they lived.

For Steward, cultural ecology dealt with the social organization of work or how people made use of those elements of their environment which they perceived as resources. The organization of this work reflects not only the tools and techniques people employ, but also the resources they exploit by these means. This cultural core—tools, techniques, the organization of production, and knowledge of the environment—reflects the way people impinge on their environment and the way their environment impinges on them. Historically, the activities and institutions involved in the cultural core constitute a major dynamic factor in the development of any society.

It appears that Steward and other cultural ecologists see the determinative effect of the environment as greatest in societies with relatively simple technologies and with food-collecting rather than food-producing economies. In more complex societies, in which subsistence activities have been solved by some form of food production, elements of the sociopolitical superstructure, rather than the environment, may be more important determinants of further social development than the economic base. In other words, the rules governing the development of more complex societies—that is, those that produce their own food—are different from the rules regulating the development of groups that harvest rather than grow their food.

Cultural ecologists are not environmental determinists. They see the relationship between a society and its environment as an important factor, but not the only one, producing social change. The environment offers a range of possibilities to the peoples residing in it. Groups with different histories—forms of labor organization, tools, techniques, and perceptions of what constitute resources—might well adapt to similar environmental conditions in quite different ways.

Recently some archaeologists have begun to incorporate the ideas and terminology of general systems theory into their ecological models. They see human society as an integral part, a subsystem, of a larger system that also includes the physical landscape and the biological environment. They are concerned with examining how certain combinations of cultural traits—such as subsistence strategies—function in this larger system to produce an adaptation of the social system to the other parts of the larger system. They are interested in those factors or mechanisms which promote stability and change in the larger system. These are often referred to as "homeostatic" and "negative feedback" mechanisms.

**Cultural
Evolutionism**

V. Gordon Childe, Leslie White, and Julian Steward reopened the study of *cultural evolution* during the late 1940s. They were interested in how human society had developed from our earliest tool-using ancestors to the present. Most cultural evolutionists share a general view of what a society is like; they see it as composed of a series of levels—a techno-economic base with sociopolitical and ideological superstructures. These levels are interrelated, but their respective roles in the process of social development are different.

For Childe and White, the economic base—the way a people impinged on the world around it—was the driving force that determined, to a large extent, the nature of the sociopolitical and ideological levels. The technological and economic aspects of a society change more readily and rapidly than either the sociopolitical or ideological levels; when the contradiction between the economy and the rest of the society became large enough, changes occurred in the social institutions and ideology of the group. For Steward, changes in the cultural core—which may consist of institutions and regulations from the economic, sociopolitical, and ideological levels of Childe or White—played the most important role in determining the direction of social development.

More recently, archaeologists have begun to examine the role of other factors that might be driving forces that underlie or determine the direction of social development. Some have focused on single factors like the managerial requirements of irrigation systems, warfare, population growth, or trade between peoples living in resource-deficient areas. Others—such as Robert Adams and Kent Flannery—have argued that cultural evolution is a product of the interaction of a number of factors or variables, including those that their opponents view as primary driving forces.

For most archaeologists, cultural evolution occurs when the members of a society adapt to some aspect of their natural and social environment in such a way that they can optimize some aspect of their behavior. By and large, this process is unidirectional, because human society becomes more complex as people gain greater and greater control over the forces of nature. In other words, most cultural evolutionists accept the idea of progress, which reflects the ability of a people to generate new ideas, new skills, and new kinds of tools as well as its capacity to adopt concepts, techniques, and tools developed by others, to make these more efficient, and to find new applications for them.

Most cultural evolutionists see society as developing through a series of organizational levels, or stages, which are usually defined in terms of some combination of population size, subsistence strategy, complexity of social organization, and type of political organization. There are a number of schemes of this sort, for example, from egalitarian, or nonstratified, to stratified or from band to tribe to chiefdom to state. In the latter scheme, bands—the earliest developmental stage—consist of a small number of related families in which leadership is situational and whose hunting and gathering subsistence economy is based on a division of labor along the lines of sex and age. Tribes, the next developmental stage, range in size from 500 to several thousand individuals who belong to groups of families related by descent from a common ancestor or by membership in some corporate, property-holding group such as a clan. Tribes are common among simple agriculturists, often have weak political leadership, and are frequently held together by elaborate ceremonies and rituals. Chiefdoms, the third developmental level in this scheme, are characterized by relatively larger populations than tribes, distinctions between "noble" and "commoner" social units in terms of property ownership, some form of intensified food production, and a division of labor that includes at least part-time craft specialization. The most advanced developmental stage, the state, is characterized by a highly centralized government with a full-time bureaucracy, social stratification, an economic structure controlled by a hereditary elite whose members also dominate the state apparatus, full-time craft specialization, and large populations that occasionally number in the millions.

If there is an area of disagreement among cultural evolutionists today, it concerns the universality of the shaping effect of the economic base in determining the form and content of the sociopolitical and ideological superstructures in different environmental situations. For Childe, White, and others, this effect is universal, regardless of the environment. For Steward and adherents to his position, the shaping effect of the economy has to be determined for each particular society.

Culture
History

Culture historians like Alfred Kidder, Max Uhle, and George Reisner had a major impact on the field of archaeology in the United States during the first half of the twentieth century. In fact, culture history was undoubtedly the predominant approach in American archaeology during this period. The reason for this was the close relationship between archaeology and anthropology, a field that was heavily influenced by the historical empiricism of Franz Boas and his students. The culture historians generally shared the empiricist philosophy of the anthropologists and historians of the period. This position held that the task of the historian was to study events in order to show what happened in the past; that these events resulted from the activities of individuals; and that once the events had been ordered and analyzed, it would be possible to arrive at more general statements about human behavior.

The culture historians view culture as a set of rules that are shared and learned by the members of a group and determine the patterns of their behavior. These rules can be discerned by observing how people usually do something or how they interact with each other in given situations; for example, how they decorate pottery, how they dispose of the dead, or why they live where they do. A culture historian would ask such questions and be able to answer once enough information was available about a particular group of people.

Since culture—these shared rules that pattern behavior—varies from one group to another, one of the most important tasks of culture historians is to determine the distribution of different cultures in time and space. They do this by collecting evidence from different archaeological sites, comparing this information, and combining similar assemblages from different sites into larger, more inclusive units. Once this has been accomplished, it is possible to describe what the culture was like at a given time and how it changed.

Culture historians explain change in two ways. Some cultural or social changes are products of internal factors, like the invention and gradual adoption of some new object or way of doing something. Other cultural or social changes are products of factors that originate outside the members of the group but ultimately impinge on their behavior—for example, they borrow and gradually adopt some item from another group; they are invaded or conquered by another group; or the environment in which they live changes in some way.

CONCLUSION

Any discussion of the development of human society must take place within a theoretical context in which certain questions, certain kinds of information, and certain models of explanation have significance. The positivists and historical materialists share a general conception of science as an objective rational inquiry whose aim is to develop true explanations of the world around us. Both believe that scientific theories can be judged by reference to empirical evidence. Both believe that there are things that exist independently of our views about them. Both believe that there are standards that apply to methods of explanation, use of evidence, and application of scientific theories. However, they differ on what those standards are. The positivists attempt to explain events by showing that there is some regularity in nature; their laws express relationships in nature. The historical materialists find these explanations inadequate because they do not tell us how or why a particular event occurred. For an explanation to be adequate, they believe, it must show not only why something happened, but also what changes have occurred in order to bring about this new state of affairs; this involves describing both the structures that were present initially and the mechanisms that were operating to bring about change.

FURTHER READINGS

Binford, Lewis R.
1972 *An archaeological perspective.* Seminar Press, New York and London.

Bock, Kenneth E.
1956 The acceptance of histories; toward a perspective for social science. *University of California Publications in Sociology and Social Institutions,* vol. 3, no. 1. University of California Press, Berkeley and Los Angeles.

Childe, V. Gordon
1946 *What happened in history.* Penguin Books, Harmondsworth, England.
1963 *Social evolution.* Meridian Books, Cleveland.

Daniel, Glyn
1963 *The idea of prehistory.* World, Cleveland and New York.
1975 *One hundred and fifty years of archaeology.* Gerald Duckworth, London.

Eiseley, Loren C.
1961 *Darwin's century; evolution and the men who discovered it.* Doubleday, Garden City, N.Y.

Flannery, Kent V.
1967 Culture history v. cultural process: a debate in American archaeology. *Scientific American,* 217, no. 2, pp. 119–122.
1972 The cultural evolution of civilizations. *Annual Review of Ecology and Systematics,* 3, pp. 399–426.

Haber, Francis C.
1959 *The age of the world; Moses to Darwin.* Johns Hopkins Press, Baltimore.

Heizer, Robert F.
1962 *Man's discovery of his past; literary landmarks in archaeology.* Prentice-Hall, Englewood Cliffs, N.J.

Hobsbawm, Eric J.
1972 Karl Marx's contribution to historiography. *Ideology in social science; readings in critical social theory,* ed. by Robin Blackburn, pp. 265–283. Pantheon Books, New York.

Klejn, Leo S.
1977 A panorama of theoretical archaeology. *Current Anthropology,* 18, no. 1, March, pp. 1–42.

Legros, Dominique
1977 Chance, necessity, and mode of production; a Marxist critique of cultural evolutionism. *American Anthropologist,* 79, no. 1, March, pp. 26–41.

McMurtry, John
1978 *The structure of Marx's world-view.* Princeton University Press, Princeton.

Momigliano, Arnaldo D.
1966 Ancient history and the antiquarian. *Studies in historiography,* pp. 1–39. Harper & Row, New York.

Morgan, Charles G.
1973 Archaeology and explanation. *World Archaeology,* 4, no. 3, February, pp. 259–276.

Murphy, Robert F.
1970 Basin ethnography and ecological theory. In *Languages and cultures of western North America,* ed. E. H. Swanson, pp. 152–171. Idaho State University Press, Pocatello.

Rowe, John H.
1959 Archaeological dating and cultural process. *Southwestern Journal of Anthropology,* 15, no. 4, pp. 317–324.
1964 Ethnography and ethnology in the sixteenth century. *The Kroeber Anthropological Society Papers,* no. 30, pp. 1–20. Berkeley.
1965 The Renaissance foundations of anthropology. *American Anthropologist,* 67, no. 1, February, pp. 1–20.

Steward, Julian H.
1955 *Theory of culture change; the methodology of multilinear evolution.* University of Illinois Press, Urbana.

Watson, Patty Jo, Steven A. LeBlanc, and Charles L. Redman
1971 *Explanation in archaeology; an explicitly scientific approach.* Columbia University Press, New York.

White, Leslie A.
1949 *The science of culture.* Farrar, Straus & Giroux, New York.

BECOMING HUMAN

In the preceding chapters we saw what archaeological evidence is and how archaeologists use it to understand what has happened in the past. In this part of the book we will look more closely at how we became human. Becoming human was a slow process; the initial steps were hesitant ones. However, it gained momentum as time passed, and today the nature of humanity is changing more rapidly than ever before. We will view this process in two ways. First we will look at it as a paleobiologist would; that is, we will watch a lineage of apes become less and less like their relatives with the passage of time. Then we will view it as an archaeologist would, and watch the same lineage expand its needs and develop novel ways of satisfying them.

PART

TWO

Human Origins: A Paleobiological Perspective

3

People are animals. They share a remarkable number of anatomical and behavioral features with other kinds of animals. They have bilateral symmetry; an internal skeleton including vertebrae that protect the spinal nerve and a skull that encloses the brain and protects the sense organs of the head; a complex circulation system in which oxygenated blood is pumped throughout the body by a chambered heart; powerful muscles along the sides of the body that are used for locomotion; well-developed sense organs; and bisexual reproduction. All of these features are also characteristic of fish, amphibians, reptiles, and birds.

More specifically, people are *mammals* because they share features that are characteristic of this particular group of animals. They have body hair; their body temperature is constant; they give birth to live infants; and they suckle their infants. There are many different kinds, or orders, of mammals, each of which has its own particular characteristics. For example, dogs, cats, and other members of the carnivores are flesh eaters and have teeth that are specialized for biting, tearing, and shredding flesh; rats, beavers, and other rodents have teeth that are well suited for gnawing hard materials like wood or nuts.

People belong to an order called the *primates,* which also includes apes, monkeys, and prosimians. The primates have very large brains and skulls, small snouts and relatively flat faces, eyes that have rotated toward the front of the skull, a small bony structure around the nose, nails instead of claws, and paired breasts located high on the chest. Classifying human beings as primates is a way of saying that their closest relatives in the animal kingdom are the other animals of this order. This means that the different kinds of primates living today evolved from a common ancestor that lived in the distant past—65 to 70 million years ago, according to the fossil record—

The relationships between the living families of the Order Primates and the geological epochs when those families first appeared in the fossil record.

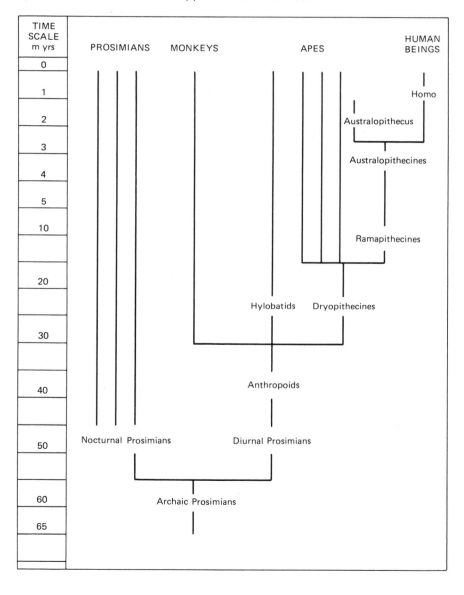

and that the order diversified through time. Some lineages became extinct while others survived and changed through time.

How did these processes of change, diversification, and extinction take place? How did human beings evolve from their primate ancestors? And what changes have taken place in the human lineage?

THE ECOLOGICAL THEATER AND THE EVOLUTIONARY PLAY

The title of this section comes from a book by G. Evelyn Hutchinson.[1] It is an elegant statement of some fundamental aspects of the history of life. The evolution of life has taken place in a wide variety of environmental situations that are themselves continually changing. The evolutionary process, then, is like a long play being performed on a stage of global proportions. The theater is essential for the performance; without it, the play could not take place. In other words, evolution can be understood only in terms of what is happening in the environment. Ecology and evolution are interdependent; they are two different ways of looking at the same story. Ecology focuses on the relationships and interactions among the performers on stage at a particular moment in time; evolution is concerned with how the plot developed to allow those particular characters to be there at that moment.

When biologists use the term *ecology* they are referring to the relationships between organisms and their environments. Any environment is a complex situation produced by the interaction of a number of physical and social factors. For example, one part of the environment is defined by the intersection of such physical factors as temperature, topography, soil conditions, and the availability of water. These and other variables interact to produce a situation in which some kinds of plants and animals can live and others cannot. The other part of the environment is a social one; it is produced by the interrelationships and interactions among the organisms that reside there and what happens between them and their physically defined surroundings.

We can distinguish various levels in the interactions between organisms and their natural and social environments. They can be arranged along a continuum. At one extreme, we can focus on what happens between an individual and its natural and social environment. At the other, we can focus on the interrelationships between the different kinds of plants and animals that live in a particular habitat—a tidal pool along a rocky coast or a tropical rain forest—and on the interactions between them and the physical conditions in the area they occupy. Obviously, there are intervening positions along this continuum, each of which represents a slightly different way of viewing the ecological theater and what is happening on the stage.

---

[1]G. Evelyn Hutchinson, 1965, *The ecological theater and the evolutionary play,* Yale University Press, New Haven and London.

For biologists, the word *evolution* means change through time or descent with modification. That is, today's plants and animals are the modified descendants of different organisms that lived in the past. These changes may be morphological ones that affect the appearance of the organisms or behavioral ones that influence how they interact with their contemporaries.

The word *evolution* is usually associated with Charles Darwin, who made the first serious attempt to describe or interpret biological change through time as a product of a number of conflicting forces or a balance among them. Today evolutionary biology incorporates many ideas that were vague in Darwin's day, and the modern synthesis, as the current theory is called, is a much more powerful way of explaining biological change through time than were Darwin's original formulations.

Evolution can also be defined as changes in the genetic composition of a population. This is different from the way Darwin defined it. Such a definition is useful because it focuses on the ideas of population, heredity, and variation. It also asks the questions, Where does variation come from? How is it transmitted from one generation to the next? What causes it to change through time?

We all know that the individual is the basic unit of life. It is the individual who is born, is nurtured, and grows to maturity. Individuals always live in groups, and their actions can be understood fully only in terms of how they interact with the members of their group. Biologists deal with two levels of groups: populations and species. Briefly, a *population* is composed of a number of individuals who live in the same region at a particular time and mate successfully with each other. For example, the people of Pitcairn Island form a population; they mate and produce offspring. The people of New York form another population. A *species* is a more inclusive group; it consists of a number of similar but isolated populations whose members are capable of mating and producing viable offspring. For example, someone from Pitcairn Island could mate with someone from New York and they could have a child, even though they come from different populations.

We are all aware that like produces like. Dogs mate and have puppies; cats mate and produce kittens. Tall people mate, and their children tend to be tall; shorter individuals who mate tend to have children who are relatively short, like their parents. That is, individuals tend to resemble their parents physically—or phenotypically, as biologists say—but they are not identical to them. The important question is, How does this inheritance take place? The answer was provided by Gregor Mendel, who raised garden peas and bred them over a number of successive generations. He noted the relationships between seven visible characteristics, such as seed form and color, of each plant and the patterns of inheritance between them and each of their offspring. Mendel concluded that hereditary features were transmitted by a large number of independent particles that we now call *genes*. These are contributed in equal numbers by each of the individual's parents. Furthermore, the genes that affect the appearance of one trait are inherited independently from those that determine the appearance of other features.

All of the genes of the individuals of a particular population constitute what is called a *gene pool.* The genes of individuals whose parents belong to this population are derived from this gene pool. In other words, the gene pool is a reservoir of hereditary material that is passed from one generation to the next. Many individuals or only a few may contribute to and share the gene pool. It may be distributed over a wide area or a small one. It may be stable through time or change from one generation to the next.

No two individuals in a population have exactly the same combination of genes, including identical siblings—who are born with identical genetic systems but are subjected to different environmental situations so that different genes mutate. This genetic variation contributes to the fact that the people of a population are physically different from each other.

There are three reasons for the amount of genetic variation in a population: recombination, gene flow, and mutation. *Recombination* is what happens when two individuals mate and their offspring receive half of their genes from each parent. The mathematics of this process are impressive when we consider that any two individuals probably differ by 30,000 genes. The continual reshuffling of genes through recombination is a major source of the genetic variation that exists in a population. *Gene flow* is the second source of genetic variation; it occurs when there is some exchange of genetic material between populations. In other words, a person from one population mates with one from another population, thereby introducing new genes into one of the populations. *Mutation,* the third source of variation, is the ultimate source of every new gene. In the long run it is probably not as important as recombination or gene flow.

If recombination, gene flow, and mutation operated without checks, the genetic diversity of populations would far exceed anything that exists naturally. The continued increase in the genetic diversity of a population is limited by natural selection and sampling accidents. These forces restrict the potential for unlimited variation and channel it into certain pathways or directions.

Natural selection is by far the more important and effective of the two forces that limit variation. It is based on four fundamental facts of life. First, survival is limited; the number of eggs and sperm produced greatly exceeds the number of individuals born, which in turn exceeds the number that survive to the reproductive stage and can contribute genetic material to the next generation by producing viable offspring. Second, there is hereditary variation among the individuals of a population owing to genetic differences. Third, there is differential survival; some individuals have a greater chance of becoming adults and reproducing than others because they possess genes that are advantageous in the environment where they live. And fourth, these advantageous genes have a greater chance of being inherited because more individuals with such genes are likely to reach adulthood and contribute genetic material to the next generation.

Natural selection permits any advantageous gene or combination of genes to accumulate in a population at the expense of those that are less favorable or deleterious. This may be a long process requiring many generations. Differential survival and reproduction are the testing ground for natural selection, where genes with survival value are either fixed in or eliminated from the gene pool. Natural selection modifies the gene pool so as to increase the congruity, or harmony, between the population and its environment.

Any hereditary characteristic that increases this congruity or promotes an individual's success in surviving and contributing genes to the next generation is called an *adaptation*. Adaptations enable the individual to obtain food, avoid predators, survive to the reproductive stage, and produce offspring. They take many different forms and may involve morphological, physiological, or behavioral features. They make it possible for the members of a population to function more efficiently in their environment. Natural selection is the driving force that produces adaptations, which it does by using the opportunities provided by the population's gene pool.

There is an important relationship among the genetic variability of a population, its adaptation at a given time, and its potential for change in an environment in flux. Populations with low variability—in which most of the members are similar to each other, and atypical individuals are few—are usually very well adapted to their environments; however, they usually are not very successful in adapting to even slight changes in these conditions because of the homogeneity of their members. Populations with a great deal of variability and wide ranges of variation—in which there are relatively few typical individuals and a lot of unusual ones—may be less well adapted for life in a particular set of environmental conditions, but they have a greater chance of adapting to new conditions and occupying previously unoccupied environments. This means that populations with low variability and limited ranges of variation are disadvantaged in a continually changing world, since they have fewer available options for change. The most successful groups with regard to survival are those with wide ranges of variation and the ability to adapt productively and effectively to many different environmental settings.

Most populations live in environments that offer them a much greater range of habitats than they are willing to occupy and many more resources than they are willing or able to exploit effectively. Another way of viewing evolution, therefore, is to see it as a series of changes in the kinds of interactions that occur between a population and its environment. From this perspective, a major feature of evolution is the entrance of a population into a new environmental niche; this move may be real or figurative. Often the population really does not go anywhere; the new environment comes to it through climatic change or the appearance of new plants and animals. If the population can utilize these new resources, its members have "moved" in an evolutionary sense. The fossil record shows numerous instances in which, once a group of animals has entered a new environmental zone, its descendants often become highly diversified. This process is called *adaptive radiation*. The new populations become increasingly specialized by focusing their activities on certain parts of the new environment and using them more efficiently than their predecessors did.

THE ORIGIN AND EVOLUTION OF THE PRIMATES

The first primates appeared more than 65 million years ago in the tropical forests that covered North America and Europe. They evolved from a group of shrewlike insectivores that lived on the ground and had well-developed senses of touch and smell. The first primates moved into the lower canopy and shrub layer of the tropical forests—an environmental zone that seems to have been unoccupied earlier. After entering this new environment these early primates, or *archaic prosimians,* diversified rapidly.

During the Eocene, which extended from 58 million to 34 million years ago, at least one group of early primates began to rely on eyesight, rather than touch or smell, as they hunted insects amid the vines and slender branches in the lower layers and marginal growth of the tropical forests. They had evolved a number of adaptations that facilitated these activities. Their eyes had rotated forward on the skull, producing stereoscopic vision with good depth perception. Bony sockets surrounded the eyes and protected them from injury. The cerebral cortex had become larger, and there had been a reduction in the relative size of the snout, which suggests that the sense of smell was less important than it had been earlier. The middle ears were larger and had been reorganized to provide improved balance—a highly advantageous adaptation for animals that move on slender supports and leap from one place to another. The hands and feet had opposable thumbs and big toes and digits with nails instead of claws. These adaptations allowed such animals to achieve better control over their movements as they stalked insects among the narrow branches and vines overlooking the forest floor. They grasped these supports with their feet and used their hands to catch and hold their prey.

This group of prosimians was the first to share a number of anatomical and behavioral features with modern prosimians; hence, they have been called the first primates of modern aspect. This group diversified rapidly during the Middle Eocene. Perhaps the most important dichotomy that occurred during this period involved the time of day when different kinds of primates were active. Some prosimian groups continued to be active at night, while others moved into a daytime activity niche. This move selected for improved vision among the daytime, or diurnal, primates, and they developed brains with relatively larger visual centers than those of their nocturnal relatives. The

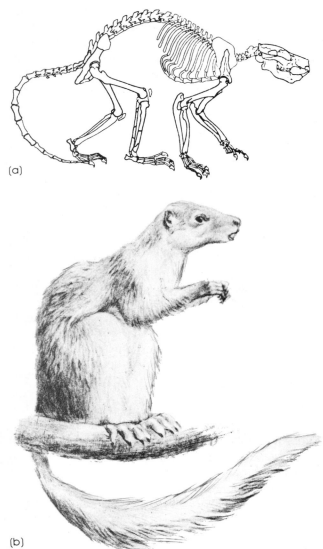

(a)

(b)

The **Plesiadapidae,** an extinct family of archaic prosimians, lived in North America and Europe during the Paleocene Epoch (65 to 59 million years ago), when the climates of these areas were milder than they are today. The two land masses had separated recently because of continental drift, and the kinds of plants and animals found on them became progressively more different as time passed. The fact the **Plesiadapidae** occurred in both places indicates that the separation took place shortly after the first primates appeared in the fossil record. The **Plesiadapidae** shared many features with their insectivore ancestors: They lacked the encircling bony rims that protected their eyes, and the facial portions of their skulls were enormous compared with their brain cases. Their skeletons indicate that they probably moved like squirrels. (a) A skeletal reconstruction of **Plesiadapis.** Elwyn L. Simons. **Primate evolution; an introduction to man's place in nature** (New York: Macmillan, 1972), fig. 39, p. 111. Reprinted with permission of Macmillan Publishing Co. Inc. Copyright © 1972 by Elwyn L. Simons. (b) A reconstruction of **Plesiadapis** based on skeletal remains from France and Colorado. Richard E. Leakey and Roger Lewin, **Origins** (New York: E. P. Dutton, 1977), p. 39. Robert Harding Picture Library.

ancestors of monkeys, apes, and humans are to be found among the diurnal primates of the Eocene.

Fossil jaws and teeth found in the Pondaung Hills of central Burma appear to be transitional between those of the prosimians and those of more advanced primates. These specimens—*Amphipithecus* and *Pondaungia*—show a number of similarities in shape to the jaws and teeth of monkeys and

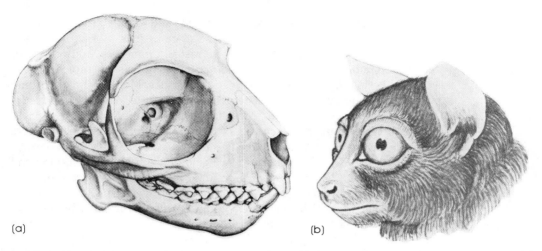

(a)

(b)

Necrolemur antiquus lived in Europe toward the middle of the Eocene Epoch (58 to 34 million years ago). It is the best known of the early primates with modern anatomical features such as enlarged eyes rotated forward on the skull and protected by bony rims, and relatively large brain cases in proportion to the facial part of the skull. (a) Reconstruction of the skull of **Necrolemur.** Elwyn L. Simons, **Primate evolution; an introduction to man's place in nature** (New York: Macmillan, 1972), fig. 64, p. 164. (b) Reconstruction of the facial appearance of **Necrolemur.** Elwyn L. Simons, **Primate evolution; and introduction to man's place in nature** (New York: Macmillan, 1972), fig. 65, p. 165. Both figures reprinted with permission of Macmillan Co., Inc; Copyright © 1972 by Elwyn L. Simmons.

apes. This suggests that they may be the common ancestor of the fossil and modern anthropoids, or at least something close to that ancestor. The deposits they come from are more than 40 million years old and date to the later part of the Eocene.

The earliest monkeys and hominoids—a taxonomic group that includes both the great apes and human beings—appeared about 30 million years ago. Their ancestors had moved into Africa during the Eocene or earlier, and their remains have been found in the Fayum Depression of northern Egypt. At that time the Fayum was crossed by a series of slow, vegetation-clogged streams that flowed into brackish estuaries and lagoons; trees lined the banks of these streams and gradually merged with grasslands farther from the water courses. Since most of the anthropoids incorporated in the Oligocene deposits at the Fayum were immature, it appears that these young animals fell out of the trees and drowned in the streams below.

The earliest monkeys of the Old World—*Parapithecus* and *Apidium*—were leaf eaters resembling the colobus monkeys of Africa and Asia today. They were highly arboreal quadrupeds whose cheek teeth were specialized for chewing leaves. Judging by the paucity of their remains in deposits more than 12 million years old, they seem to have been a small, almost insignificant element of the African fauna. At that time, during the Late Miocene, they spread into various kinds of forest, woodland, and grassland environments that were developing in Eurasia and sub-Saharan Africa. Some of the leaf-eating monkeys had gradually become terrestrial omnivores, and once they had moved into the new environmental zone, they diversified rapidly. These ground-dwelling monkeys are called cercopithecines. Monkeys have become much more abundant in the fossil record since the Late Miocene, which suggests that they have competed successfully with a number of other species.

The first *hominoids* (ancestors of both apes and human beings) were fruit eaters who exploited the outer edges of the tree canopy. They were small quadrupeds capable of hanging and swinging beneath branches. By the end of the Oligocene, 25 million years ago, they had already diverged into two lineages. One group, the *hylobatids,* became increasingly specialized end-of-the-branch feeders, while the other group, the *dryopithecines,* became increasingly terrestrial during the Miocene, possibly as a result of competition with some of the omnivorous and frugivorous cercopithecine monkeys that were evolving at that time and moving into new environmental zones. Both of these hominoid lineages survive today. Gibbons and siamangs, the modern hylobatids, are found in the rain forests of Southeast Asia. The great apes—modern descendants of the forest-dwelling dryopithecines—live in the forests of Africa and Southeast Asia.

The dryopithecines evolved in Africa and spread into Eurasia during the Miocene, which has been called the "age of the apes" because of their variety and abundance in the fossil deposits of that epoch. Once the dryopithecines had moved into the forests of Eurasia, they developed a variety of feeding strategies, judging from differences in the shapes of their teeth. One African species, perhaps the ancestor of the modern gorilla, lived on heavily forested mountain slopes and ate a variety of plant foods. Another African species, like the modern chimpanzee, lived in a slightly more open area; its teeth suggest that it relied on fruits and other kinds of plant foods. Some of the northern dryopithecines may have lived in oak and chestnut forests; as a result, their diets would have differed significantly from those of their relatives in the tropics.

A group of hominoids, the *ramapithecines,* appeared in the fossil records of Africa, eastern Europe, and Asia by the Middle Miocene. The species in this group probably evolved from isolated populations of forest-dwelling dryopithecines that lived in areas where mixed environments composed of forests, woodlands, and savannas gradually appeared in response to changes in the world's climate. These species—*Ramapithecus, Sivapithecus,* and *Gigantopithecus*—all have jaws and cheek teeth that are proportionately larger than those of their dryopithecine ancestors and contemporaries. This suggests that the feeding strategies of the two groups were different. The ramapithecines presumably made use of the wide range of roots, tubers, seeds, and grains found along the edges of the forests and in the more open

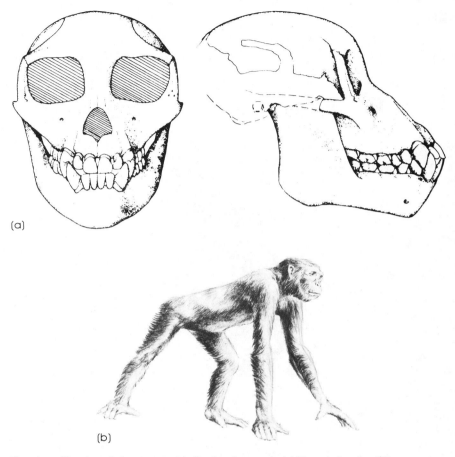

(a)

(b)

The dryopithecines first appeared in the fossil record of Africa during the Oligocene Epoch (34 to 25 million years ago). The family spread into Eurasia and diversified during the Miocene Epoch (25 to 8 million years ago). (a) Reconstruction of the skull of **Dryopithecus africanus,** a middle Miocene fossil from East Africa with apelike jaws and dentition. S. I. Rosen, **Introduction to the primates; living and fossil** (Englewood Cliffs, N.J.: Prentice-Hall, 1974), fig. 10-2, p. 166. (b) Reconstruction of the appearance of **Dryopithecus africanus.** Richard E. Leakey and Roger Lewin, **Origins** (New York: E. P. Dutton, 1977), p. 57. Robert Harding Picture Library.

areas of their environment. This was potentially a much greater range of food resources than was available to their forest-dwelling dryopithecine contemporaries. All three ramapithecine species lived in the same area of Pakistan during the Middle Miocene, which suggests that each had a slightly different feeding behavior. *Ramapithecus,* for example, has been found at Fort Ternan in East Africa in association with long antelope bones that seem to have been

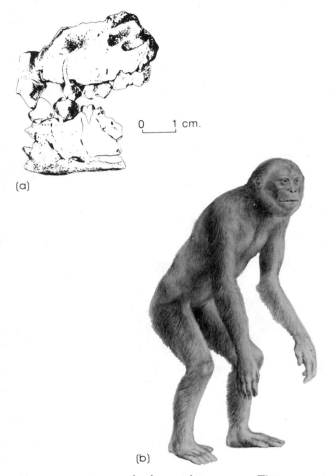

0   1 cm.

(a)

(b)

The ramapithecines appeared in the fossil record during the middle Miocene and are often found in the same deposits as the dryopithecines. The ramapithecines have jaws and cheek teeth that are proportionately larger than those of the dryopithecines apes, which suggests that they had different feeding strategies. (a) The left maxilla articulated with the left mandible of **Ramapithecus wickeri,** a ramapithecine from Fort Ternan, East Africa. C. P. Andrews, **Ramapithecus wickeri** from Fort Ternan, Kenya, **Nature,** 231 (1971), 192–194. (b) Reconstruction of **Ramapithecus wickeri,** Richard E. Leakey and Roger Lewin, **Orgins** (New York: E. P. Dutton, 1977), p. 67. Robert Harding Picture Library.

cracked open for marrow. This suggests that meat may have played some role in the diet of *Ramapithecus* and possibly in that of the other ramapithecines as well.

When the ramapithecines moved into this new environmental zone, other aspects of their behavior and morphology may also have been affected. For example, they have teeth that are much more like those of modern humans than those of their dryopithecine contemporaries. There was a great deal of wear between adjacent teeth, which suggests that the tooth row was crowded. There was no gap between the canine and first molar of *Ramapithecus,* which suggests that it chewed with a rotary or sideways motion like modern people rather than with the up and down motion characteristic of the contemporary apes. The chewing surfaces of the front cheek teeth are much more worn than those of the rear ones. This delayed sequence of

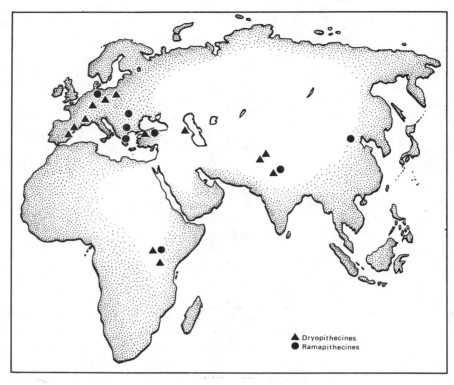

Distribution of dryopithecine and ramapithecine hominoids.

dental eruption indicates that the ramapithecines may have matured more slowly than the apes and that the period of infant and juvenile learning was prolonged.

HOMINID ORIGINS AND EVOLUTION

Hominids (human beings and their more immediate ancestors in the fossil record) evolved during the Pliocene; however, we do not yet know which of the hominoid species was the ancestor of the hominids. Australopithecines are the earliest well-known hominid fossils of the Pliocene. A 5-million-year-old australopithecine jaw fragment was found in Lothagam in Kenya.

After about 4 million years ago, hominid fossil remains become relatively abundant. Since then, the hominids have evolved a number of behavioral and morphological characteristics that distinguish them from the hominoids: They have smaller front teeth; they have an upright posture and

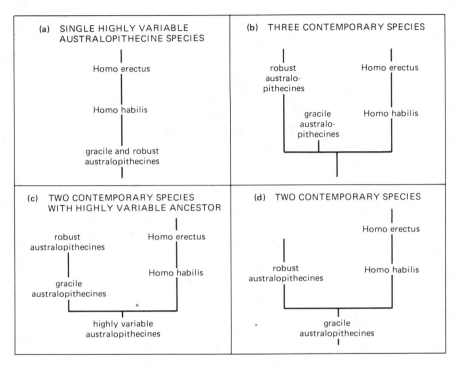

Human phylogeny. Several alternatives have been proposed in recent years. (The author favors c.)

walk bipedally; they have enlarged and reorganized brains; they have opposable thumbs and the motor skills to make tools; they have less body hair than their nonhuman contemporaries and, presumably, than their ancestors; and they use spoken language as an effective mode of communication. This complex of traits, which appeared at different times in the fossil record and evolved at different rates, reflects a progressive adjustment to conditions that were emerging in a continually changing terrestrial environment. To maintain themselves in this environment, the hominids not only had to adapt to the conditions that existed at any given moment, but they also had to be flexible enough—both genetically and behaviorally—to respond to the changes that were taking place.

Hominid Evolution During the Pliocene

While paleoanthropologists generally agree on the overall features of human evolution, they hold divergent views about the specific features of human evolution during the Pliocene—a period that extended from 6 million to about 2 million years ago. The reason for these discrepancies is that different

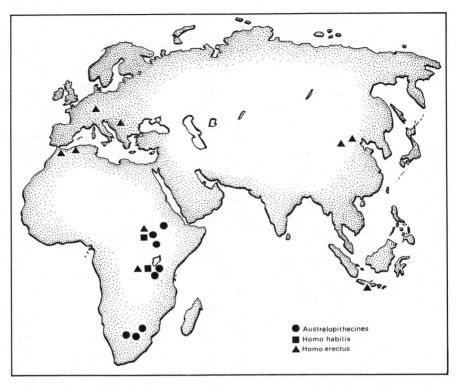

Distribution of sites where australopithecines, **Homo habilis,** and **Homo erectus** have been found.

paleoanthropologists interpret fossil evidence differently. They hold different views about the meaning of variations in the size and shape of particular anatomical structures in different specimens; they emphasize the importance of some specimens and deemphasize that of others for interpreting the human fossil record; and they have different ideas about the relationships among the various fossil remains and how these should be classified.

Essentially, there are three positions. The first is that there were two parallel lineages of hominids—*Homo* and *Australopithecus*—that diverged from each other about 2.5 to 3.0 million years ago and coexisted until about 1.2 million years ago, when the latter became extinct. The second is that there were three parallel hominid lineages that diverged from their common ancestor about 5 million years ago; these were *Homo,* a small australopithecine, and a large australopithecine—all of which coexisted until about a million years ago, when the latter two became extinct. The third position is that there was never more than one hominid lineage at any time in the past. In the remainder of this section we will follow those paleoanthropologists who expound the first position because it seems to offer the best explanation of the evidence that is now available.

The earliest well-known hominid remains belong to a small australopithecine, *Australopithecus afarensis,* which lived in the open woodlands and grasslands of Africa during the Pliocene. Remains of this species have been found at Laetotil in northern Tanzania and at several locations around Hadar in southeastern Ethiopia. The Laetotil fossils, as well as two sets of footprints found with them, are between 3.6 and 3.8 million years old. The Hadar fossils, representing at least thirty-five individuals, are somewhat younger; they range in age from 2.6 to 3.3 million years.

Australopithecus afarensis, like modern human beings, was fully bipedal although its brain was less than one-third the size of the human brain today. The members of this species showed marked sexual dimorphism; that is, the males were considerably larger than the females. They were between three and four feet in height and weighed between 40 and 60 pounds. Judging from the shape of their pelvis and feet, they probably ran more easily than they walked; their toes pointed in, and their torsos probably swayed from side to side when they moved rapidly. Their jaws were set under their faces, which improved the efficiency with which they chewed, ground, and sliced food by facilitating the rotary and lateral movement of the lower jaw. Their cheek teeth had flat crowns and thick enamel, which suggests that they were basically vegetarians who ate the fruits, tough seeds, tubers, shoots, and stems pro-

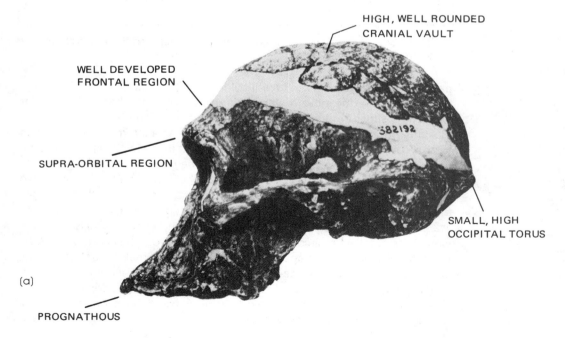

HIGH, WELL ROUNDED CRANIAL VAULT

WELL DEVELOPED FRONTAL REGION

SUPRA-ORBITAL REGION

382192

SMALL, HIGH OCCIPITAL TORUS

(a)

PROGNATHOUS

vided by their open woodland and savanna environment. Their molars show differential wear, which indicates a delayed sequence of tooth eruption that was undoubtedly associated with a prolonged period of maturation. Finally, they probably sweated a lot to dissipate heat and drank small amounts of water fairly frequently during the daytime to prevent dehydration under the tropical sun.

This species split into two distinct lineages about 2.5 to 3.0 million years ago. One of these was *Homo,* the direct ancestor of modern human beings and the other was *Australopithecus,* a hominid lineage that retained many of the primitive characteristics of *A. afarensis* and became extinct about a million years ago. What this means, in biological terms, is that the members of one lineage could mate successfully with their contemporaries in that lineage but not with individuals from the other. In other words, the members of the two lineages were reproductively isolated.

A question of considerable interest is, How did this reproductive isolation develop? The process is called *speciation.* What probably happened is that different populations of *A. afarensis* gradually began to make use of the food resources found in slightly different environments in the same area. At first there may have been some gene exchange between them. However, as each population became better adapted to the conditions that prevailed in its environment, the amount of gene exchange between them decreased, either because of the unavailability of living spaces for hybrids or as a result of less frequent interactions between the two populations. Eventually the reproductive isolation was complete in the sense that the members of the two species could not mate successfully.

The australopithecine lineage is composed of two species: an earlier, gracile form known as *Australopithecus africanus* and a

(b)

The small, or gracile, australopithecines first appeared in the fossil record about 2.5 million years ago. (a) Side view of the skull of **Australopithecus africanus.** S. I. Rosen, **Introduction to the primates; living and fossil** (Englewood Cliffs, N.J.: Prentice-Hall, 1974), fig. 11-4, p. 182.
(b) Reconstruction of the appearance of **Australopithecus africanus.** Richard E. Leakey and Roger Lewin, **Origins** (New York: E. P. Dutton, 1977), p. 95. Robert Harding Picture Library.

later, more robust form known as *Australopithecus robustus* or *Australopithecus boisei.* They are essentially smaller and larger versions of the same creature. The differences in the size of their brains, cheek teeth, and musculature associated with chewing and grinding food were directly related to differences in their body size. The species in this lineage share a number of features that were not found in *A. afarensis;* these include an increase in the relative size of the cheek teeth and increased robustus and buttressing of the lower jaw and the musculature associated with chewing. This suggests that the members of this lineage developed an increasingly specialized feeding strategy involving a diet—presumably fruits, nuts, seeds, stems, and shoots—that required heavy mastication.

Australopithecus africanus, the earlier member of this lineage, is best known from a series of South African sites that probably date from between 2.0 and 2.5 million years ago. In addition, they have also been found in the Omo Basin of southern Ethiopia. With the exception of the changes in their facial structure due to their increasingly specialized chewing apparatus, the members of this species probably were not very different in appearance from their immediate ancestors. They weighed between 40 and 60 pounds and were three to four feet tall.

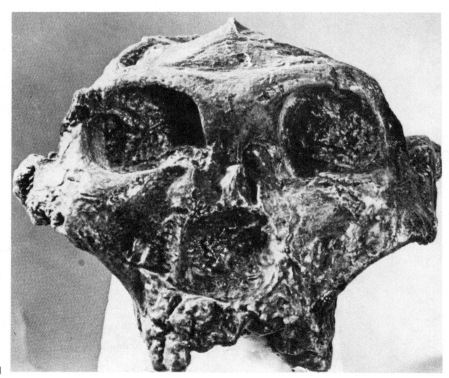

(a)

Australopithecus robustus, the later member of the lineage, is known from sites in both South and East Africa. These individuals weighed 70 to 100 pounds and were four to five feet tall. The later ones had enormous cheek teeth and jaws, compared with those of human beings today. The muscles that supported this structure and provided the power for chewing were attached well up on the top of the skull; the result is that a number of the robust australopithecines have a sagittal crest on the top of the skull.

The Evolution of the Genus Homo

The australopithecines became extinct about a million years ago. It is clear that these tropical hominids were preyed on by large cats, packs of wild dogs, and perhaps even members of the other hominid lineage. However, predation was probably not the reason why they ultimately became extinct. It is one way in which population size is regulated, but predator and prey do not compete with each other for food. It is more likely that competition was the major factor involved in the extinction of the australopithecines. Their competitors may well have been terrestrial cercopithecine monkeys—like baboons—who were able to use the plant food resources of the tropical savannas of eastern and southern Africa more efficiently than did the australopithecines.

The other hominid lineage, whose earliest representative was *Homo habilis,* evolved into modern human beings. The early members of this lineage gradually created a new, distinctly human ecological niche. Their brains had volumes of 635 to 780 cubic centimeters—roughly 25 to 50 percent larger than those of their australopithecine contemporaries. Their teeth—rela-

(b)

The robust australopithecines appeared later than the smaller forms. (a) The skull of **Australopithecus robustus** from Swartkrans, South Africa, showing the sagital crest, where powerful muscles associated with chewing were attached. S. I. Rosen, **Introduction to the primates; living and fossil** (Englewood Cliffs, N.J.: Prentice-Hall, 1974), fig. 11-8, p. 186. Courtesy of S. I. Rosen. (b) Reconstruction of the appearance of **Australopithecus robustus.** Richard E. Leakey and Roger Lewin, **Origins** (New York: E. P. Dutton, 1977), p. 110. Robert Harding Picture Library.

tively small molars and broader incisors—suggest that their food required less mastication than that of the australopithecines, and imply that their feeding strategy was becoming increasingly different from that of the other lineage. The presence of chipped-stone tools at 2-million-year-old archaeological sites in Tanzania and Kenya indicates that they had the motor skills to make and use tools on a regular basis. The existence of these sites indicates that these early peoples brought food and other materials back to their camps, and implies that they may have shared these goods with other members of their group. The presence of an indentation on the interior surface of a skull corresponds to Broca's area of the brain—a center that controls the production of words and word sequences—and suggests that our ancestors were already using spoken language to communicate information.

So far, *Homo habilis* has been found only in the tropical grasslands of East and South Africa in deposits that date from about 1.7 to 2.1 million years ago; however, it will not be surprising if they are eventually found in other tropical areas of the Old World as well.

The next structural stage in human evolution is best represented by a series of specimens from Java and China that are now called *Homo erectus*. Similar fossils have also been found in Africa, Europe, and the Near East. They range in age from about 1.9 million years to about 300,000 to 400,000 years. The oldest *Homo erectus* specimens come from the Djetis Beds in Java and, not surprisingly, resemble contemporary *Homo habilis* specimens from Olduvai Gorge and Lake Turkana in East Africa. The later specimens from the Djetis Beds, which are probably about a million years old, resemble *Homo erectus* remains found in Eurasia and Africa.

The differences between *Homo habilis* and *Homo erectus* indicate that two interrelated sets of changes were taking place. The jaws and teeth of humans were becoming smaller while their brains were becoming larger. The cranial capacities of the early *Homo erectus* specimens average about 800 cubic centimeters, whereas those of some of the later specimens range from 850 to more than 1400 cubic centimeters and average over 1000 cubic centimeters. The human brain expanded differentially during this period. The parietal and temporal lobes—which are associated with motor skills and adaptive behavior—grew more rapidly than the rest of the brain. As a result, the shape of the skull changed. It became higher and more rounded, while the frontal region became less flattened.

The remains of *Homo erectus* in Europe and China show that human beings were beginning to live in temperate areas outside of the tropics. Stone tools in Vallonet Cave in southeastern France indicate that the movement into the temperate regions began about a million years ago. One of the ways people survived in these temperate regions was by living in caves and building

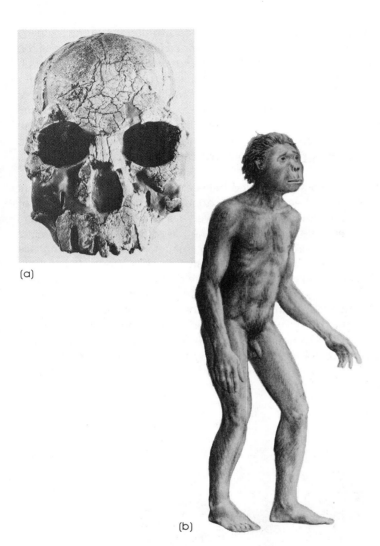

(a)

(b)

Homo habilis was the earliest representative of the genus **Homo**. (a) Front view of a skull from the Lake Turkana region of Kenya. Richard E. Leakey and Roger Lewin. **Origins** (New York: E. P. Dutton, 1977), p. 87. (b) Reconstruction of the appearance of **Homo habilis**. (Richard E. Leakey and Roger Lewin, **Origins** (New York: E. P. Dutton, 1977), p. 107. Both figures courtesy of Robert Harding Picture Library.

fires to provide both heat and light. Cooking may also have originated during this period. This belief is based on the fact that the cheek teeth of *Homo erectus* were becoming progressively smaller with the passage of time. As a result, the jaws and muscles associated with chewing were also becoming smaller. Since cooked food puts less strain on the jaw and chewing muscles, the regular cooking of food may actually have facilitated changes in the shape of the head.

The major structural changes that have occurred in the human lineage during the past 300,000 years have been confined largely to the shape of the head. The cranial capacities of the archaic *Homo sapiens,* who lived 300,000 years ago, averaged about 1200 cubic centimeters. Those of modern *Homo sapiens* average about 1450 to 1500 cubic centimeters. The older forms looked a little like some of the late *Homo erectus* specimens. This is not surprising, since there is an evolutionary continuity between ourselves and the *Homo erectus* populations that lived before us. In general, our faces have become flatter, our brow ridges less pronounced, and the backs of our skulls more rounded.

The archaic *Homo sapiens* lived between 70,000 and 300,000 years ago. Their remains have been found in Indonesia, Europe, and Africa. All of these remains are quite fragmentary; however, it is clear that the major difference between the earlier and later specimens was in the size of their brains. Cranial capacities increased by 250 cubic centimeters or more during this period. The archaic *Homo sapiens,* taking both the earlier and the later forms, were remarkably similar in appearance in spite of the differences in their cranial capacities. This suggests that populations living in different parts of the Old World were subjected to the same selection pressures during this period.

The later archaic *Homo sapiens* gave rise to a highly varied series of populations known as Neanderthals. The Neanderthals are usually divided into two groups. One consists of a relatively homogeneous series of fossils

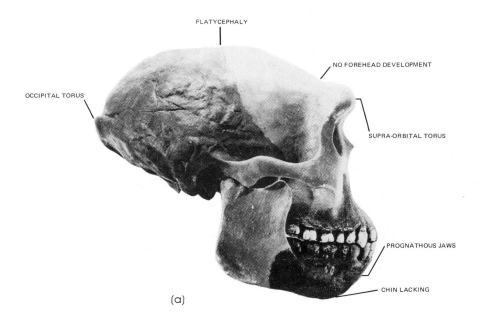

PLATYCEPHALY

NO FOREHEAD DEVELOPMENT

OCCIPITAL TORUS

SUPRA-ORBITAL TORUS

PROGNATHOUS JAWS

CHIN LACKING

(a)

from the sheltered, well-watered valleys of Western Europe; these individuals lived between 70,000 and 45,000 years ago. The members of this group are called classic Neanderthals. The other group lived outside of Western Europe during this period; its members were much more varied in appearance than their contemporaries. Specimens that are more than 60,000 years old tend to share more morphological features with the classic Neanderthals than those that are more recent.

The classic Neanderthals provide us with the popular stereotype of the cave man: a short, brutish-looking fellow with a sloping forehead and a receding chin who stood at the entrance of his lair dressed in a bear skin with a wooden club resting on one shoulder. They lived in regions just outside of the borders of the frozen ground and tundra vegetation that covered much of northern and western Europe during the early part of the last glaciation. The individuals of this population had large cranial capacities—larger than those of modern humans—but their heads were shaped differently. Their skulls bulged along the sides and backs, and their foreheads sloped. They had prominent cheekbones, large brow ridges, and receding chins. They were short, with thick, barrel-like chests and short, stubby extremities. Many of their physical characteristics are also found among modern populations that live in cold environments; these features are usually interpreted as adaptations to life under cold conditions. The early part of the last glacial cycle was, of course, the first time human beings lived continuously in exceptionally cold areas.

The remarkable uniformity of the classic Neanderthals suggests that they were a product of rather intense selection pressures that operated uniformly on the peoples of western Europe during the early part of the

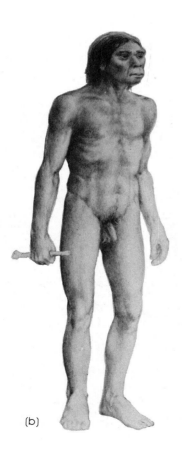

(b)

Homo erectus was the first hominid to live outside of the tropics. (a) Side view of the skull of **Homo erectus.** S. I. Rosen, **Introduction to the primates; living and fossil** (Englewood Cliffs, N.J.: Prentice-Hall, 1974), fig. 12-8, p. 212. Courtesy of the American Museum of Natural History.
(b) Reconstruction of the appearance of **Homo erectus.** Richard E. Leakey and Roger Lewin, **Origins** (New York: E. P. Dutton, 1977), p. 123. Robert Harding Picture Library.

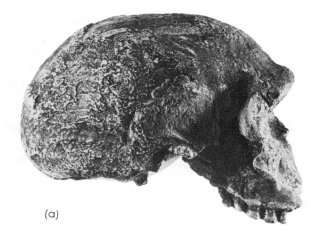
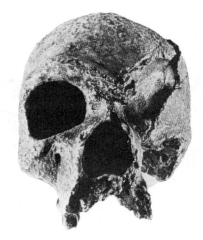

(a)

(b)

Archaic **Homo sapiens** appeared about 300,000 years ago. (a) Side view of the skull from Steinheim that is between 150,000 and 200,000 years old. S. I. Rosen, **Introduction to the primates; living and fossil** (Englewood Cliffs, N.J.: Prentice-Hall, 1974), fig. 13-2, p. 220. Courtesy of S. I. Rosen.
(b) Reconstruction of the appearance of a classic Neanderthal. Richard E. Leakey and Roger Lewin, **Origins** (New York: E. P. Dutton, 1977), p. 130. Robert Harding Picture Library.

last glaciation. Contemporaries living in warmer environments lacked many of the features that were so characteristic of the classic Neanderthals, suggesting that they were subjected to different selection pressures. Another way of looking at the situation is that the classic Neanderthals were a fringe population living under the extreme environmental conditions that prevailed along the periphery of the area inhabited by human beings, and that the inhabitants of the warmer, more central areas were subject to different or less intense selection pressures and, as a result, were more varied in appearance.

Fully modern human beings appeared in the fossil record about 40,000 years ago at Niah Cave in Borneo and at various localities in the Near East. The first fully modern human skeletons in western Europe are about 25,000 years old—15,000 years more recent than the latest classic Neanderthals. Between 30,000 and 40,000 years ago human beings moved across the narrow water barriers that separated Australia and North America from the Eurasian landmass. With these movements, they occupied the last major uninhabited portions of the world.

As people moved into new lands during the Pleistocene, they were also moving into new ecological niches that presented them with new selection pressures and new challenges. New anatomical and physiological adaptations emerged in response to settlement in such varied habitats as arid deserts, tundra, or high mountains. Genetic and behavioral differences developed as people adapted to the conditions that prevailed where they lived. These differences are the products of evolutionary forces that began to operate millions of years ago and continue to operate today.

FURTHER READINGS

Birdsell, Joseph B.
1975 *Human evolution; an introduction to the new physical anthropology.* Rand McNally, Chicago.

Boughey, Arthur S.
1968 *Ecology of populations.* Macmillan, New York.

Cartmill, Matt
1975 *Primate origins.* Burgess, Minneapolis.

Grant, Verne
1963 *The origin of adaptations.* Columbia University Press, New York and London.

Hamilton, Terrell H.
1967 *Process and pattern in evolution.* Macmillan, New York.

Holloway, Ralph L.
1974 The casts of fossil hominid brains. *Scientific American*, 231, no. 1, July, pp. 106–115.

Howell, F. Clark, and the Editors of Time–Life Books
1970 *Early man.* Life Nature Library, Time–Life Books, New York.

Johanson, D. C., and T. D. White
1979 A systematic assessment of early African hominids. *Science*, 203, no. 4378, January 26, pp. 321–330.

Jolly, Alison
1972 *The evolution of primate behavior.* Macmillan, New York.

Kolata, Gina Bari
1977 Human evolution; hominoids of the Miocene. *Science,* 197, no. 4300, July 15, pp. 244–245, 294.

Kennedy, Kenneth A. R.
1975 *Neanderthal man.* Burgess, Minneapolis.

Leakey, Richard E., and Roger Lewin
1977 *Origins.* E. P. Dutton, New York.

Martin, R. D.
1975 Ascent of the primates. *Natural History,* 84, no. 3, March, pp. 52–61.

Mettler, Lawrence E., and Thomas G. Gregg
1969 *Population genetics and evolution.* Prentice-Hall, Englewood Cliffs, N.J.

Pilbeam, David
1972 *The ascent of man; an introduction to human evolution.* Macmillan, New York.

Pilbeam, David, and Stephen Jay Gould
1974 Size and scaling in human evolution. *Science,* 186, no. 4167, December 6, pp. 892–901.

Poirier, Frank E.
1974 *In search of ourselves; an introduction to physical anthropology.* Burgess, Minneapolis.

Romer, Alfred Sherwood
1959 *The vertebrate story,* 4th ed. University of Chicago Press, Chicago and London.

Simons, Elwyn L.
1972 *Primate evolution; an introduction to man's place in nature.* Macmillan, New York.

Walker, Alan, and Richard E. Leakey
1978 The hominids of East Turkana. *Scientific American,* 239, no. 2, August, pp. 54–66.

The Emergence of Toolmakers

Human beings are strange primates. The modern ones are anatomically unique. They walk upright on their hind legs; they have long, narrow feet that are very well suited to striding; they have curved spines with large heads balanced on top of them; their faces are short, and their teeth are arranged in parabola-shaped arcs; and they have large, opposable thumbs that give them both power and precision in grasping and manipulating objects. In the last chapter we saw that these anatomical characteristics evolved at different rates and appeared in the fossil record at different times.

Modern human beings are also peculiar in ecological terms. They have a wider geographic range than any other primate species; in fact, they have a greater range than most other animal species. Until about a million years ago human beings were tropical animals residing in the grassland areas of the Old World. Then they began to move slowly into the temperate regions of Eurasia and, finally, into the colder regions to the north. More recently, they were able to cross water barriers and move into the New World, on the one hand, and Australia and New Guinea, on the other.

Like other primates, human beings live in groups, and their behavior can be understood only in terms of their membership in one of these social units. However, human societies are very different from those of other primate species. They are much more variable in both size and organization. Human groups have ranged in size from a few individuals to many millions of people. They have organized themselves in various ways to satisfy the basic needs of life, and they have erected a wide variety of sociopolitical and ideological structures on these economic foundations. Much of what is unique about human social behavior depends on the use of language as the primary means of communicating information about the world. For instance, only human beings stand around talking to each other in order to convey what they are thinking or what they want another person to know. These and other aspects of human behavior have evolved through time as responses to new situations. Human behavior is not static. It is continually changing, sometimes slowly and barely perceptibly, at other times with amazing rapidity.

Human beings are also distinctive from the archaeologist's viewpoint. Three things distinguish them from other kinds of animals: they make tools; they are incredibly messy, so that their garbage and other debris accumulate at places where they did something in the past; and they share food and other goods that they have carried to a home base or camp. Other animals occasionally use tools. For example, sea otters will place rocks on their chests and smash clamshells on them in order to get meat, and chimpanzees will lick a stick and put it down a termites' nest in order to harvest the insects. However, these activities and use of objects are qualitatively different from toolmaking. Modern apes even build nests; however, so little happens around their campsites that virtually nothing is preserved for more than a day or so; consequently, little, if anything, about their daily activities would be preserved in the archaeological record. Chimpanzees will tolerate another animal's feeding on the same large chunk of meat; however, they do not share vegetable foods, which constitute the bulk of their diet. This is a far cry from the exchanges of food that take place between human adults and between adults and children when the hunter and collector return to camp bearing meat and vegetable foods, which they pool in order to feed themselves and other members of the group.

THE EARLIEST TOOLMAKERS

The earliest manufactured tools discovered to date come from the Koobi Fora area east of Lake Turkana in northern Kenya. The deposits containing these chipped-stone tools are about 1.8 million years old. The most distinctive tools in the Koobi Fora assemblage are choppers with working edges formed by flakes struck off in two directions from one end or along the side of a *cobble,* or a large pebble. The rest of the assemblage consists of flakes, battered cobbles, and broken chips. Preliminary excavations carried out in 1970 show that these tools came from a campsite where people lived for some time. Broken bones were also scattered over the floor of the camp, and not far away were the remains of a hippopotamus that had apparently been butchered. It is not clear whether the inhabitants of the camp killed the hippopotamus and then butchered it or whether they were scavengers. We know very little about the people who made and used the tools at Koobi Fora. Presumably, they belonged to the species *Homo habilis;* however, even this can be debated, since two different kinds of hominids lived in East Africa during this period.

The best information about the activities of the earliest toolmakers comes from Olduvai Gorge, a valley in the Serengeti Plains of northern Tanzania. This Y-shaped canyon is more than thirteen miles long and about 150 to 250 feet deep. Archaeological sites have been found at a number of locations in the gorge, and many of these sites were intensively studied during the 1960s. The older sites occur in the deposits that form Beds I and II. These geological formations range in age from about 1.8 to 1.0 million years. This means that the oldest archaeological assemblages at Olduvai Gorge are about the same age as those at Koobi Fora.

The stone tool assemblages from the Olduvai Gorge sites contain a wider variety of tool types than the ones from Koobi Fora. The earliest assemblages are called Oldowan and include a variety of cobble choppers, polyhedrons with three or more working edges, disc-shaped cobbles with jagged working edges, several kinds of light- and heavy-duty scrapers, awls, burins, and flakes. Oldowan assemblages are found throughout the deposits of Beds I and II, and the kinds of tools that occur in them change gradually with the passages of time. For instance, the latest Oldowan assemblages contain a kind of tool, called a proto-biface, that is bifacially flaked along both lateral edges and comes to a point.

Stone tools from Koobi Fora, east of Lake Turkana in northern Kenya. (A–D) Cobble choppers. (E) Flake struck from a cobble chopper to resharpen its edge. Mary Leakey, Early artifacts from the Koobi Fora area, **Nature,** 226 (1970), 228–230, fig. 1.

One of the sites from the lower part of Bed II is a chert factory. It is about 1.6 million years old. The inhabitants of the gorge went to this locality to quarry *chert,* a stone that was suitable for the kinds of tools they wanted to manufacture. The quarry contains a wide variety of broken nodules of chert discarded at various stages in the process of manufacture, as well as whole and broken flakes, a few tools, and lots of chipping debris. When these materials were compared with the chert flakes found at a contemporary campsite in another part of the gorge, it was clear that the ancient residents of this camp preferred chert flakes of a certain size. They selected these flakes at the quarry and then carried them back to their campsite, where they were used for various tasks. This suggests that the early inhabitants of the gorge were capable of planning a relatively complex sequence of activities around the use of stone tools.

The campsites at Olduvai Gorge were located close to water, either on the shores of lakes or along the edges of streams, judging from the presence of crocodile and fish remains, the bones of aquatic birds, and casts of reeds. One of the camps was almost completely excavated. Its oblong central area contained large numbers of stone artifacts and broken bones. It was surrounded by a relatively barren area with little debris. Outside of this barren zone debris became more plentiful, and the materials were more complete than in the central area. This suggests that the central living area may have been enclosed by a windbreak made of bushes, which corresponded with the barren zone. The objects found outside of the windbreak were presumably thrown there by the inhabitants of the camp.

Similar circular areas with concentrations of artifacts and broken bones were found at other campsites in the gorge. In fact, one campsite had two such areas, indicating that there were two windbreaks instead of one; this suggests that more people resided there. Another campsite had a semicircular pile of rocks about sixteen feet across that probably formed the base of a windbreak. Each of these simple structures enclosed an area of about 200 square feet.

The size of the windbreaks allows us to make some rough estimates about the number of people who may have used these flimsy structures as shelter. Anthropologists examining the relationship between house size and number of residents have compiled information from a number of societies and found that a figure of 20 square feet per person for the first six residents and 100 square feet for each additional resident is fairly typical. This suggests that each windbreak at Olduvai Gorge sheltered about seven individuals. Evidence of a different kind from the Hadar area of Ethiopia corroborates the idea that groups of this size existed several million years ago. Sediments between 2.6 and 3.3 million years old have yielded the remains of an *Australopithecus afarensis* group composed of two children and three to five adults, all of whom were killed at the same time by a flash flood.

Broken bones from a wide variety of animal species, including australopithecines, have been found scattered over the surfaces of the campsites at Olduvai Gorge. These animals ranged from frogs and small rodents to elephants. Small and medium-sized animals like antelopes and pigs are the more common forms at the campsites; large animals like elephants, giraffes, and

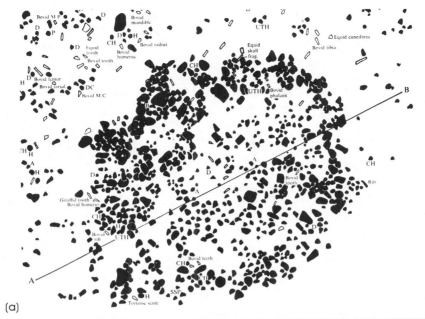

(a)

(b)

Campsite on the DK living floor at Olduvai Gorge. (a) Plan of the stone circle and the remains surrounding it, including artifacts (shown in black) and fossil bones (shown in outline). M. D. Leakey, **Olduvai Gorge** (Cambridge and New York: Cambridge University Press, 1971), vol. 3, fig. 7. (b) A rough shelter made by the Okombambi of Southwest Africa with a semicircular ring of stones supporting the bases of the branches. M. D. Leakey, **Olduvai Gorge** (Cambridge and New York: Cambridge University Press, 1971), vol. 3, pl. 3.

buffaloes occur but are not very common. It is clear that the inhabitants of the gorge consumed meat from fauna of all sizes, but that small and medium-sized animals provided the bulk of the meat. Furthermore, there is some indication that the ancient inhabitants of the gorge ate different kinds of animals during the wet and dry seasons.

Some of the antelopes found at one campsite had depressed skull fractures, which suggests that they were killed at close range. Large animals like elephants were discovered at several localities along the edges of ancient watering places. This suggests that the animals were either driven into the muddy flats along the margins of lakes or streams or became mired there accidentally. In either case the animals were butchered, and pieces of meat were carried back to the campsites. It is obvious that the early peoples of Olduvai Gorge acquired some meat by hunting; they may also have acquired some meat, presumably from large animals, by scavenging. Since they brought meat back to their camps, it is clear that they shared their food.

TOOLMAKING DURING THE MID-PLEISTOCENE

Stone tools and their associations are our main source of information about human behavior from roughly 1.5 million to 500,000 years ago. Unfortunately, the sites dating from this time have not provided as much information as we would like about this critical period of human history. There are several reasons for this situation. Not many sites from this period are known, and many of those that are known were located along the edges of ancient streams or lakes. Few of these sites have been studied adequately, and preservation conditions at the ones that have been examined are poorer than those prevailing at earlier sites like Olduvai Gorge. Finally, some of the localities where stone tools have been found are not archaeological sites at all but, rather, ancient river gravels containing materials that were carried from other sites and redeposited. As a result, we probably know less about this stage of human history than about what happened before and after it.

The earliest standardized toolmaking tradition emerged between 1.5 and 1.0 million years ago and is called the *Acheulean tradition*. Assemblages belonging to the Acheulean tradition have high proportions of bifacially chipped stone tools, the best known and most distinctive of which are hand axes. These are made on large flakes or cobbles. Flakes have been removed from two directions along a major portion of their circumference to produce a flat, sharp working edge. This chipping often extends far back from the edges of the tool and frequently covers all of the two opposed surfaces. Usually, one end of the hand ax is pointed and the other rounded. These tools probably evolved from the "proto-bifaces" found in some of the later Oldowan assemblages. Another distinctive tool in Acheulean assemblages is the cleaver, which is like a hand ax except that it has a straight edge or end instead of coming to a point. The flakes formed by making these tools were frequently made into other kinds of tools, such as scrapers or knives. The hand axes may have been used as mattocks, while the cleavers may have been used for chopping, scraping meat from bones, or cutting through ligaments and bones. The flakes that were the by-products of the manufacture of the larger implements were also used, presumably to cut meat, remove it from hides or bone, or shape wooden sticks.

The Acheulean tradition changed over time. Toward the end of the mid-Pleistocene, perhaps 300,000 years ago, the makers of stone tools began to use a variety of prepared-core techniques; that is, they chipped the surface of a suitable rock or cobble in such a way that the shape and size of the flakes to be removed from it were predetermined. These prepared-core techniques, of which the best known is called the *Levallois,* or tortoise core technique, were widespread in Europe, North Africa, and the Near East. Assemblages with prepared cores have also been found at various localities in sub-Saharan Africa.

Other kinds of stone-working technologies besides the Acheulean were also used during the mid-Pleistocene. Assemblages containing Oldowan-like implements have been found from South Africa to western Morocco and southern Europe. For example, the assemblage from Vallonnet Cave in southern France, which is about a million years old and is the earliest evidence of human occupation in Europe, is composed of a few cobble choppers with flakes removed from one direction along part of their edges, along with retouched flakes and the broken bones of extinct animals such as the woolly rhinoceros. The assemblages from Vértesszöllös in Hungary, which is 500,000–600,000 years old, yielded a number of choppers and chopping tools made from both flakes and cobbles and a wide variety of tools made on flakes.

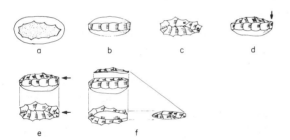

The Levallois or prepared-core technique. (a) The sides of a cobble are trimmed by direct percussion flaking. (b) The top of the cobble is trimmed. (c) A striking platform is prepared at one end of the core through a combination of percussion flaking and grinding. (d) The prepared flake, with its predetermined form, is removed from top of the core by a blow directed at the striking platform. (e) Top and side views of the prepared core and the flake struck from it. Thomas C. Patterson, **America's past: A new world archaeology** (Glenview, Ill.: Scott, Foresman, 1973), fig. 2-6, p. 29. Copyright © 1973 by Scott, Foresman and Company. Reprinted by permission.

There are numerous non-Acheulean assemblages from eastern and southern Asia that date to the mid-Pleistocene. These have been found from northwest India to northern China and southward through the Malay Peninsula to Java. These assemblages are composed of choppers with cutting edges flaked from one direction, chopping tools with edges worked from two directions, and a variety of flake tools. These implements were made from cobbles and flakes. The toolmakers obtained some of the flakes by using the bipolar technique, which involves placing the core on a stone anvil and removing flakes from it.

The distribution of stone tool assemblages during the mid-Pleistocene indicates that some human beings successfully colonized new environments about a million years ago. They moved out of the tropical areas of Africa and Eurasia into the temperate zones of southern Europe and the Far East. Through this move they expanded their range. Judging from the paucity of archaeological remains in these areas dating to this period, the colonization process must have been a slow one, and the population density must have been exceptionally low for many thousands of years.

Some of the plants and animals found by the colonists in these new lands were probably familiar, while others, perhaps even a majority, may have been unknown. At first, the colonists had to rely on familiar food resources like those that existed in the "staging areas" from which they came. Gradually, as they became acquainted with the seasonal and permanent food resources of their new environment, they began to use new food items. In this way they became better adapted to the conditions that prevailed in these new lands. These adaptations involved not only information about the local flora and fauna but also new tools and techniques—for example, the use of fire.

DAILY LIFE 500,000 YEARS AGO

A number of sites dating from between about 300,000 and 500,000 years ago have yielded significant amounts of information about the daily lives of our distant ancestors. The archaeological remains at these localities were left by humans belonging to the species *Homo erectus*.

Evidence from Terra Amata

Perhaps the richest of these sites is Terra Amata, located in Nice on the French Riviera in deposits that are roughly half a million years old. When the site was occupied, the Mediterranean stood about 85 feet higher than it does today and the climate was somewhat cooler and more humid than it is now. The people at Terra Amata lived on a sandy beach strewn with cobbles and on a sand dune behind it that overlooked a small cove. The camp was sheltered from the winds that blew almost continuously from the north and west. Saltwater plants grew along the edge of the cove, and a small freshwater stream that flowed by the campsite was covered with waterlilies during the spring. Pine and oak trees grew on the coastal plain and foothills behind the dune. Farther up the hills fir and Norway pine were abundant. Small herds of elephants, oxen, and rhinoceroses browsed on the trees and bushes of the coastal lowlands. Red deer also browsed in the lowlands and on the tree-covered slopes beyond. Wild boars and ibex were found in the forested areas at higher elevations.

The people lived in oval huts that ranged from 26 to 49 feet in length and from 13 to 20 feet in width. The walls of the huts were formed by wooden stakes about three inches in diameter that were driven into the sand and held in place by rocks and boulders piled against them. Inside each hut were several posts about a foot in diameter that probably supported a ridge pole, which in turn supported the stakes and branches that formed the sides of the structures.

Twenty-one of these flimsy structures have been found. Four were on a sandbar; six were on the beach; and eleven were built on the sand dune. The houses probably collapsed shortly after they were abandoned and were then covered with a thin layer of windblown sand. The fact that the eleven living floors on the sand dune are superimposed almost exactly on top of one another suggests that the site was occupied for eleven consecutive years, presumably by the same group of people.

Reconstruction of one of the oval huts found at Terra Amata on the French Riviera. Henry de Lumley, A Paleolithic camp at Nice, **Scientific American,** 218, no. 5 (1969), 43. Copyright © 1969 by Scientific American, Inc. All rights reserved.

There was a hearth in the center of each hut. This was a shallow pit or pebble-paved area about a foot or two in diameter. Frequently, a small stone wall was built on the northwestern perimeter of the fireplace, presumably to protect the fires from the northwesterly winds that prevailed in the area. This suggests that the huts were drafty and that their sides were nothing more than branches stuck into the ground.

The people carried out various activities in their huts. In one, a tool-maker sat in the corner on an animal skin amid the chips and other debris produced by making stone tools. In another corner there was a spherical wooden bowl with a rough bottom; it was filled with something that had dried into a nondescript whitish substance. Not far away from the bowl were some lumps of red ocher worn to a point; these pencils made of a natural red pigment may well have been used by the inhabitants to color themselves, perhaps for some ritual purpose. They may have sat on flat limestone slabs, which also made convenient surfaces for chopping meat and breaking animal bones. Meat was probably cooked over open fires in the hearths, and at night the inhabitants of the huts probably wrapped themselves in animal skins and slept, huddled together, on the debris-free ground around the fire.

If we use the same value for the relationship between house size and number of residents that we employed in determining group size at Olduvai Gorge, we find that human social groups had become significantly larger. The population of Terra Amata may have ranged from about nine to fifteen or more individuals. Judging from the variation in the size of the huts, the number of people residing at the site probably differed somewhat from one year to the next. These differences may reflect the amount of food that was available around the camp during that year or what happened to the group during the preceding season, when food items may have been in short supply.

A footprint was found outside one of the huts. It was 9½ inches long. There is a rough correlation between the height of an individual and the length of his or her foot. Using this correlation, the person who left the imprint found at Terra Amata was about five feet tall. Using another very rough correlation between height and body weight, we estimate that the person probably weighed between 90 and 100 pounds.

Another person defecated outside one of the huts. Scientists analyzed the contents of the fossilized human feces and found the pollen of plants that flower in the late spring and early summer. This suggests that the group came to Terra Amata around late April, rebuilt the huts, and stayed there until June. The fact that one of the stone tools found at the site was made from rock that outcrops about thirty miles away suggests that the group moved from one place to another during the year. Since the quarry for this rock is located in a coastal area near Cannes, the inhabitants of Terra Amata may have spent a good part of the year in places like Nice. We cannot determine how far they roamed beyond this area. Perhaps they resided in caves during the winter months.

The people of Terra Amata ate turtles, birds, and a variety of mammals. Although they hunted small animals like rabbits and rodents, they seem to have preferred larger animals. Judging from the relative abundance of the remains of the various animals, they were especially fond of red deer. This species was followed in popularity by elephants, wild boars, ibex, rhinoceroses and oxen. In general, the hunters avoided healthy adult animals as prey; instead, they selected the very young, the very old, and sick or injured animals because they were easier to kill. They also ate mussels, oysters, and limpets gathered along the shore of the cove; the presence of fish bones in the refuse around the camp indicates that they occasionally consumed fish.

Evidence from Torralba

An open site in north–central Spain that is roughly the same age as Terra Amata provides us with additional information about the hunting activities of our mid-Pleistocene ancestors. The site is called Torralba. When it was used, the climate of the area was probably about 5° to 10° F cooler than it is today. Torralba lies in a small, steep-sided valley. Pine trees grew on the plateau above the cliffs forming the edge of the valley. A river flowed slowly across the valley floor through ponds and marshes choked with reeds and sedges. Areas covered with low grasses bordered these seasonal swamps. Hunters standing on the cliffs and ledges must have watched animals graze in these natural pastures. Game was probably always more abundant in the grasslands than on the pine-covered plateau above. This must have been particularly true during the seasons when elephants, horses, wild cattle, and other large herbivores moved through the valley.

Judging from the virtual absence of small-animal and bird remains at the site, the hunters of Torralba apparently were interested principally in animals that were large enough to be seen as they moved through the grassy areas of the valley. Elephants were the largest animals they killed, and perhaps the most desired. They also hunted other large animals, such as horses, red deer, rhinoceroses, and oxen. On some of the occupation floors at Torralba, the remains of horses were almost as plentiful as those of elephants.

Animals occasionally wandered away from the herds that were grazing on the grassy floor of the valley. These lone animals were watched carefully. Some of them strayed too close to the edge of the swamp and became stuck in the muddy ground. The hunters saw these accidents from the cliffs and ledges overlooking the valley. They left these perches and moved quickly toward the mired animals. By the time the hunters arrived, the animals were already exhausted by the struggle to free themselves, and after the mud rose above their knees they were virtually helpless. Perhaps the hunters waited a while, watching the helpless animals thrash about and then become still. Finally they killed them efficiently and quickly with wooden spears and stones.

At other times the hunters set a series of grass fires on the valley floor. Herds of animals rushed madly in front of the flames that were sweeping along the valley. Some of them fled toward the swamp and got stuck as they tried to cross the water to the solid ground on the other side. The hunters gradually congregated on the banks amid the still-smoldering grass and waited for the animals to tire before killing them.

Fires were built near the dead animals, presumably to keep insects away and smoke the meat that was being removed from the carcasses. They skinned the animals with small, sharp flakes, which were discarded when they became dull. On one valley floor the hunters cut off the legs of an elephant and laid them end to end so that they formed a bridge that stretched from the dead animals to

The linear arrangement of tusks and leg bones at Torralba, Spain, suggests that ancient hunters placed them this way. F. Clark Howell and the Editors of Time–Life Books, **Early man** (New York: Time–Life Books, 1972), 97.

solid ground. Individuals presumably carried heavy slabs of meat across this crude causeway in order to avoid sinking into the muddy bottom of the swamp. They butchered the various kinds of animals in different ways. For example, they frequently removed whole limbs from small animals such as horses or red deer; consequently, the skeletal remains of these species are generally incomplete and are scattered over the site. Large animals like elephants were usually butchered on the spot, and slabs of meat were carried away; as a result, the skeletons of large species are usually disarticulated but fairly complete.

Evidence from Olorgesailie

Our ancestors seem to have responded quickly and efficiently to animals that might have competed with them for food resources. At Olorgesailie, a 450,000-year-old site in Kenya, a group of hunters may have massacred a troop of giant baboons. The remains of at least fifty subadult and adult animals, as well as thirteen juveniles, were found scattered over a living floor in association with more than 500 hand axes and cleavers that were blunted by use. Presumably, the hunters came upon the baboon troop while the animals were dozing in the afternoon sun. They dislodged the terrified animals from the trees and killed them before the troop could organize its defenses.

It is clear that the mid-Pleistocene hunters did far more than scavenge dead animals or wait for one to have an accident that would reduce its mobility. They knew a great deal about the behavior of their prey and their competitors because they had spent long hours watching these animals. The hunters were aware of seasonal variations in the behavior of their prey, and there is evidence from Olduvai Gorge indicating that at least some groups may have hunted different kinds of animals from one season to the next. Finally, it is obvious that a great deal of planning and cooperation was involved in the communal hunting activities of these groups.

Evidence from Choukoutien Cave

Our early ancestors ate vegetable foods in addition to meat. The inhabitants of Choukoutien Cave—a half-million-year-old site located near Peking—ate hackberries collected during the late summer and early fall. The inhabitants of Terra Amata may well have carried plant foods back to their campsite in wooden containers or animal skins to share with other members of the population. Unfortunately, we do not know how important plant foods were in the diets of these early populations. It is possible that they were more important to groups in some kinds of environment than to groups in other circumstances. Today, for example, peoples living in warm or tropical areas tend to eat much more plant food than animal protein, while groups living in cold or arctic environments consume much more meat and fish than vegetable food. If this was true during the mid-Pleistocene, then we would expect that groups living in tropical environments like Olorgesailie ate lots of fruits and vegetables and that groups living in areas with cold winters, such as Choukoutien Cave, consumed larger quantities of fish and game.

It is clear that the inhabitants of Choukoutien Cave were skilled hunters. They particularly liked the small deer and giant beavers that lived in the pine and beech forests that covered much of the landscape around the cave; they also hunted horses, bison, gazelles, and other animal species found in open country. Altogether, the skeletal remains of nearly ninety species of animals were found at the site. What makes this site important, however, is that human beings were among the species consumed by the occupants of the cave. The remains of about forty individuals were found scattered through the deep deposits of the cave. All of the skulls were pried open, and many of the long bones had been cracked and broken; presumably, the occupants were seeking brains and marrow. Both men and women were consumed, and more than 40 percent of the individuals were children who had died before the age of 14. The deposits of the cave were formed over a period of about 50,000 years, which means that one individual was consumed every 1,250 years. This suggests that cannibalism was not a particularly frequent practice and that human flesh was not a major source of animal protein.

Some writers have used the evidence from Choukoutien Cave to support the argument that humans are innately aggressive. The inhabitants of the

(a)

Choukoutien Locality I, outside Peking, China. (a) A general view of the cave with the excavation grid painted on the rock face of the cave. (b) The floor of the cave. Courtesy of the American Museum of Natural History.

(b)

cave killed these individuals for their meat. Presumably, the deceased belonged to a different social group, one that competed with the cave residents for scarce food resources. However, there is no factual basis for assuming that the dead belonged to another social unit. Nor is there any real evidence supporting the idea that they were killed for their meat. It is just as likely that they were eaten after they had died of natural causes and that they were consumed either out of respect and affection or because of a desire not to waste protein foods.

THE EVOLUTION OF EARLY HUMAN SOCIETY

This chapter has presented portraits of what life was like at two different times in the distant past. One of the questions these descriptions raise is, How and why did the uniquely human features of our society evolve in the first place? In the next few pages we will look at the process of becoming human from a slightly different perspective, one that incorporates the findings of neuroanatomists, developmental psychologists, and students of primate social behavior.

No human being leads a solitary life. This is another way of saying that humans are social animals who live in groups and that their behavior can be understood only in terms of the way they interact with other individuals in their social milieu. The fact that all diurnal primates are social animals suggests that this is an ancient characteristic of the order and implies that the earliest human beings—the ramapithecines or their immediate ancestors—also lived in social groups.

Early human groups were small. Evidence from the Afar Valley and Olduvai Gorge suggests that a typical human group living 2 million years ago had six or seven members and that the majority of these were adults. As time passed, human social groups became larger. By 500,000 years ago, human groups seem to have ranged in size from about nine to fifteen individuals; again, most members of the group were adults. The gradual increase in group size is probably related as much to the individual's need to share experience with others as to the requirements of defense or obtaining food.

Experience is shared with others through communication. There are various kinds of communication, of which the most important are empathy and speech. Empathic communication is earlier and more basic than speech. It involves sharing an emotion that is being experienced by another individual. Empathic communication is nonverbal, like much of the communication that takes place between a small infant and its mother. However, speech increases the capacity for empathic communication. It allows individuals to share experiences or information about what happened at different times and places. If empathy allows us to share information about what is happening here and now, then speech allows us to share what happened there and then.

Fortunately, we know a great deal about the neurological control of speech. One of the major areas involved in the production of speech is a bulge on the left frontal lobe of the brain called Broca's area. It controls the production of words and word sequences. Individuals with damaged Broca's areas speak slowly and have a great deal of difficulty articulating words. A recent study of a *Homo habilis* skull from the Lake Turkana area of East Africa showed the existence of an indentation on the interior surface that would correspond with Broca's area. This suggests that our ancestors were already talking with each other nearly 2 million years ago. Their speech may have been very rudimentary by today's standards; nevertheless, they were communicating verbally.

The left side of the brain is dominant for language in most human beings. The left hemisphere is dominant in other ways as well. For example, it controls the activity of the right hand. Today about six out of seven people are right-handed. Handedness is another distinctly human feature, since all nonhuman primates are ambidextrous. Since both speech and handedness are associated with hemispherical dominance in the brain, it is not surprising that the earliest evidence of handedness comes from three caves in South Africa that range in age from 2 to 3 million years. The human inhabitants of the caves killed a number of baboons by clubbing them on the head with the long bones of zebras. Roughly fourteen out of every fifteen baboons were killed by blows delivered by individuals who were right-handed.

Different individuals played different social roles in these early groups. In fact, each individual played a series of different roles during his or her lifetime. These depended on age and, perhaps to a lesser extent, sex. In both human and nonhuman primate groups, the first role learned, regardless of sex, is that of the infant. Infants are the centers of attention for other members of the group. They are small, helpless individuals to be nurtured, cuddled, played with, and protected from danger. Within an amazingly short time after birth, infants begin spending longer and longer periods away from their mothers in the company of other individuals who are not yet adults. The relationships they establish in these multi-age play groups are probably more important to their normal social development than are their associations with adults. In the context of these peer groups, juveniles learn through trial and success the skills required to get their needs met. They learn cooperation and compromise and begin to develop ideas of fairness and justice; in other words, they teach each other appropriate social behavior. The members of these juvenile peer groups are intensely curious about the world; consequently, they are usually the first to discover new things about it and, because of their curiosity about the world, frequently warn the larger group of potential danger. By adulthood, individuals have learned their sex roles.

Among many nonhuman primate groups, and presumably among our earliest ancestors as well, females provided maternal care for infants while adult males maintained order within the group and protected its members from dangers posed by the outside world. It is clear that males and females of different ages behaved differently in these early human societies. The allocation of various tasks to individuals on the basis of their age or sex was probably most apparent in those activities—like exploration, child care, or protection—which do not involve the procurement of food or other items. Two million years ago individuals were carrying meat and other items, such as raw materials for making stone tools, back to their home base and sharing these goods with other members of their groups. Sharing involves a relationship between the individual who collected or produced the object and the individual who consumed or used it. This relationship is a social one consisting of rights to appropriate and obligations to reciprocate. What is less clear is who was sharing what with whom.

Does sharing reflect a situation in which each individual collected the total range of foods—seeds, fruits, and game—as well as other goods and then shared some of these items with the other members of the group? Or does it reflect some rudimentary division of labor based on sex and age differences in which adult males, adult females, and children provided different items to the group as a whole? Food sharing, whatever its nature, involves a degree of cooperation that does not exist in nonhuman primate societies today and presumably did not exist in the past. It is a distinctly human attribute that appeared when individuals found it useful or necessary to split the task of getting food into two or more distinct activities that could be performed separately, either at different times or in different places. It involves not only a higher degree of cooperation between individuals, but also new levels of trust and confidence in the motivations of others. Sharing provides the basis for increased specialization of production; it allows people to commit time to activities that are productive but do not in themselves allow the group to survive and reproduce itself.

FURTHER READINGS

Birdsell, Joseph B.
1975 *Human evolution; an introduction to the new physical anthropology.* Rand McNally, Chicago.

Bordes, François
1968 *The Old Stone Age.* McGraw-Hill, New York and Toronto.

Butzer, Karl W.,
1971 *Environment and archaeology; an ecological approach to prehistory.* Aldine-Atherton, Chicago.

Clark, J. Desmond
1970 *The prehistory of Africa.* Praeger, New York.

Clark, J. Desmond, and F. Clark Howell, eds.
1966 Recent studies in paleoanthropology. *American Anthropologist Special Publication,* 68, no. 2, pt. 2.

DeLumley, Henry
1969 A Paleolithic camp at Nice. *Scientific American,* 218, no. 5, May, pp. 42–50.

Gould, Richard A.
1971 The Old Stone Age. In *Man, culture, and society,* ed. Harry L. Shapiro, pp. 47–94. Oxford University Press, London, Oxford, and New York.

Howell, F. Clark, and the Editors of Time–Life Books
1970 *Early man.* Life Nature Library, Time–Life Books, New York.

Isaac, Glynn L.
1969 Studies of early cultures in Africa. *World Archaeology,* 1, no. 1, June, pp. 1–28.
1971 The diet of early man; aspects of archaeological evidence from Lower and Middle Pleistocene sites in Africa. *World Archaeology,* 2, no. 3, February, pp. 278–299.
1978 The food-sharing behavior of protohuman hominids. *Scientific American,* 238, no. 4, April, pp. 90–108.

Jolly, Alison
1972 *The evolution of primate behavior.* Macmillan, New York.

Kolata, Gina Bari
1975 Human evolution; life-styles and lineages of early hominids. *Science,* 187, no. 4180, March 14, pp. 940–942.

Lancaster, Jane B.
1975 *Primate behavior and the emergence of human culture.* Holt, Rinehart and Winston, New York.

Leakey, Mary D.
1971 *Olduvai Gorge,* vol. 3, *Excavations in Beds I and II, 1960–1963.* Cambridge University Press, Cambridge, England.

Lee, Richard B., and Irven DeVore, eds.
1968 *Man the hunter.* Aldine-Atherton, Chicago.

Lewis, Michael, and Leonard A. Rosenblum. eds.
1975 *Friendship and peer relations.* Wiley, New York.

Montagu, Ashley, ed.
1973 *Man and aggression.* Oxford University Press, London, Oxford, and New York.

Pearce, Jane, and Saul Newton
1963 *The conditions of human growth.* Citadel Press, Secaucus.

Pfeiffer, John E.
1972 *The emergence of man.* Harper & Row, New York.

Sahlins, Marshall
1972 *Stone Age economics.* Aldine-Atherton, Chicago.

Siskind, Janet
1978 Kinship and mode of production. *American Anthropologist,* 80, no. 4, December, pp. 860–872.

Speth, John D., and Dave D. Davis
1976 Seasonal variability in early hominid predation. *Science,* 192, no. 4238, April 30, pp. 441–445.

Tunnell, Gary G.
1973 *Culture and biology; becoming human.* Burgess, Minneapolis.

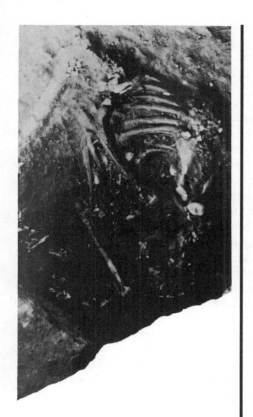

The Transition to Modern Human Beings

The transition from ancient to fully modern human beings occurred between 300,000 and 40,000 years ago. We know relatively little about what happened during the early stages of this transformation, the period that lasted from 300,000 to about 70,000 years ago. There are only a few human fossils from this time, and these are fragmentary and incomplete. The archaeological sites that have been studied so far have, on the whole, provided less information about human activities than earlier or later sites. By comparison, we know a great deal about the later phases of the transition, those that lasted from 70,000 to 40,000 years ago, when classic Neanderthals roamed Western Europe and their collaterals lived elsewhere in the Old World.

Given what we know about the appearance of ancient and fully modern human beings, we can be quite certain that the major anatomical changes that occurred during the early stages of the transition were confined largely to the shape of the head. These changes reflect the expansion of the parietal and temporal lobes of the brain. They were adaptive responses to a social milieu in which increased memory, capacity for speech, and facility at integrating and associating sensory information were advantageous.

Human behavior changed slowly during the transition, at least by today's standards; however, it was changing many times more rapidly than it had at any previous time. The early archaic *Homo sapiens* continued to do many things the same way their mid-Pleistocene ancestors did them. For example, they continued to use Acheulean tools that were only slightly different in shape from those used by their remote ancestors half a million years

5

earlier; however, they made tools in a new way, called the *Levallois technique,* that made more efficient use of raw materials than earlier stoneworking methods did.

When we compare what daily life was like at the beginning of this period and at its close, it is clear that people were living differently by the end of the period and that their behavior had changed during those 250,000 years. By comparison, these changes were much more extensive than those that had occurred during a similar time span a million or so years earlier. For example, there was relatively little difference between the earliest tools found in East Africa and those found in deposits that are a half-million years more recent.

The reason human behavior changed so slowly during this period was that human groups were small; they probably numbered between ten and fifteen individuals. As a result, the multi-age juvenile play groups must have been even smaller. This was important because new behavior and perceptions of the world usually originate among individuals who have not yet learned the culturally accepted ways of doing things or viewing what is around them. These individuals were, and still are, concentrated among the younger rather than the older members of the group. In other words, the juvenile peer group provides the social context for learning and creativity. When this group is composed of only a few individuals, innovative behavior is less likely to be validated by other members. Consequently, many innovative ideas were stillborn, while others perished without a trace for lack of an audience that was responsive and supportive. The outcome of this situation was that old patterns of behavior and ways of looking at the world were perpetuated.

DAILY LIFE AMONG THE NEANDERTHALS

The classic Neanderthals and their immediate ancestors lived in the well-watered valleys of western Europe from about 120,000 to 40,000 years ago. They lived in caves in the limestone cliffs that form the edges of these valleys. Archaeologists have found remains of their activities in a number of caves, particularly ones located in the Périgord region of southwestern France.

The Périgord
Region

The Périgord region is located about 300 miles southwest of Paris near the village of Les Eyzies. The Dordogne River and its tributary, the Vézère, have gouged deep wide valleys out of a limestone massif. The valleys and the smaller canyons leading away from them are bounded by limestone cliffs that are several hundred feet high. Along the foot of the cliffs are rock shelters with enormous overhanging roofs and caves that extend far back into the cliffs.

Between 120,000 and 70,000 years ago the climate of the Périgord was warmer and moister than it is now. The winters were mild; the January temperatures averaged about 50° F, which is about 7° F warmer than the present average. This meant not only that it snowed less frequently, but also that the snow that did fall stayed on the ground for a shorter time. Grassy meadows and woodlands composed of oak, pine, and elm covered the low-lying areas during the interglacial period. Groves of pine trees interspersed with various kinds of alpine vegetation overlooked the valleys. Game abounded in the region. Elephants, oxen, horses, rhinoceroses, hippopotamuses, boars, and deer were plentiful.

The climate of the Périgord deteriorated rapidly shortly before the onset of the last major glacial cycle. It became both drier and colder. Temperatures were 20° F lower in July and more than 40° F lower in January than they are now. This meant that the summers averaged in the low 50s while the average winter temperatures were less than 10° F. The mixed forests that had covered the region were replaced by tundra and steppe at low elevations and by cold-adapted alpine plant formations at higher elevations. There were scattered stands of pine, and dwarf birch and alders were probably found along the river banks. The fauna of the Périgord consisted of both tundra and alpine species. Gigantic herds of reindeer must have grazed in the area, as well as musk oxen, mammoths, giant elks, and horses. Cave bears and ibex lived in the limestone uplands.

The Inhabitants of the Périgord

The inhabitants of the Périgord region occupied more than thirty caves during the first part of the last glacial cycle. This works out to about one cave every thousand years. However, radiocarbon measurements indicate that some of the caves were probably occupied simultaneously. This suggests that the population of the region increased in the period between 70,000 and 40,000 years ago.

The cave sites ranged in length from about 45 to 75 feet and were about 30 feet wide. Stakes 2 to 3 inches in diameter were driven into the ground around the entrances of the caves or in front of the large, open rock shelters. These stakes probably supported a wooden framework covered with animal hides and branches that served as a windbreak and kept out the cold during the winter months. These wooden frameworks were undoubtedly convenient for other things as well—a place to hang up game for butchering or suspend pieces of meat so they could dry in the sun.

If we use the same value for the relationship between house size and number of residents we used earlier—20 square feet per person for the first six inhabitants and 100 square feet for each additional one—we find that human groups were larger than before. In the Périgord region they would have ranged in size from about 18 to 27 individuals. At LaQuina, the largest site dating from this period, the population would have been about 36 individuals by this criterion. Other estimates of population size, using different criteria, do not disagree dramatically with these figures. Using the quantity of animal remains, archaeologists estimate that less than 40 people camped at the open site of Saltgitter-Lebenstadt for a few weeks during the summers about 55,000 years ago.

A study of thirty-nine Neanderthal burials provides us with some information about the population structure of these groups. Almost 40 percent of the individuals died in infancy or childhood, and another 10 percent died before their twentieth year. Adults who died between the ages of 21 and 30 constitute 15 percent of the sample, and those who died between 31 and 40 constitute 25 percent. Less than 10 percent of the population lived beyond age 40, and individuals who reached age 50 were very rare. Another way of saying this is that more than half of the individuals who were born died before they reached adulthood. Most women died before their thirtieth year; this was undoubtedly due to complications of childbirth in some cases. Men frequently lived beyond the age of 30. The effect of this differential mortality was that there were more men than women in these Neanderthal groups; the sex ratio was probably about twelve men to ten women.

Let us assume, for the moment, that this sample is representative of populations living during the early part of the last glaciation. In a group of thirty individuals there would have been about five women of childbearing age. If all of them were pregnant at the same time, then about five infants would be born each year; of these, three would survive, given the 40 percent infant mortality rate. This is an unrealistically high birth rate, however, since lactating women do not usually become pregnant. If a woman became pregnant every third year instead of every year, then five children would be born over the three-year period and three of them would survive. In other words, the juvenile peer groups would have been composed of about six individuals who would have been born within six years of each other.

The increased size of these juvenile peer groups is undoubtedly part of the reason human behavior began to change more rapidly. Larger juvenile peer groups meant that more individuals were available to validate new ideas and behavior and transmit these to other members of the group. The other factor that contributed to human behavior's changing more rapidly was that there may have been more than one group inhabiting the same general area. Given the size of a region like the Périgord, these groups must have interacted with each other on a face-to-face basis at least occasionally during the year. Even minimal contacts between groups would have facilitated communication and the spread of new ideas and behavior from the members of one social unit to those of another. This process—however infrequent, brief, and low-key the contacts may have been—created larger audiences, which meant that original ideas and behavior had a better chance of being validated. It also provided a larger group of people who could adopt innovations and introduce them into other social units.

Judging from the ages of the animals found in the refuse deposits of the sites in the Périgord region, some of the caves and rock shelters were inhabited more or less continuously throughout the year. The inhabitants of the caves clearly spent more time in their rocky homes during some seasons than others. Occasionally they left the caves altogether to camp along streams or in the mountains for short periods when game or plant foods were particularly plentiful.

This suggests that the human groups living in the Périgord region during this period were somewhat more sedentary than their ancestors. What permitted the inhabitants of the region to live in the same caves throughout the year? It may have been the fact that all of their food resources could be acquired within an hour or two's journey from the camp. One effect of residing in the same place throughout the year may have been that women had children more frequently. The reason for this was that the physical stress associated with child care—particularly carrying the infant from one place to another—was significantly reduced among these sedentary populations. This could happen without any dramatic change in the subsistence economy of the group.

Food and Fuel

The inhabitants of the Périgord region were particularly fond of reindeer; however, they hunted and consumed a wide variety of other large herbivorous mammals as well. Mammoths, woolly rhinoceroses, red deer, horses, oxen, boars, ibex, and roe and fallow deer are only a few of the other large species found in their camp dumps. Smaller mammals like hares and foxes were trapped and probably provided a substitute for the meat from large animals or furnished some raw material needed by the group. At Saltgitter-Lebenstadt, the summer camp in northern Germany, the people also hunted swans, ducks, and even a vulture, and fished for perch and pike in the stream that passed by their campsite. Undoubtedly the inhabitants of Europe also ate plant foods during this period, but the archaeological record is not clear about the kinds of fruits, seeds, and vegetables they consumed.

How much meat did a group consume? If we assume that each member ate about three pounds of meat a day, then a group of thirty would need about 2,700 pounds of meat each month. This meant they had to kill about twenty-two reindeer, which weigh roughly 250 pounds each and provide about 125 pounds of usable food. If they were hunting larger animals, such as mammoths or red deer, they needed fewer of them.

Hunting must have been particularly difficult during the winter months, when cold, icy winds swept across the snow-covered tundra of the Périgord valleys. The temperatures hovered around 0° F or below as the skin-clad hunters moved slowly toward the herds grazing on lichens and other plants that had poked their way through the thin layer of snow covering the frozen ground. Suddenly spears were thrown; the animals bolted and ran away from the hunters. A few minutes later the animals had disappeared. The snow was red and the ground covered with dead and dying animals. The hunters quickly dispatched the ones that were still alive. Efficiently they began cutting the carcasses into pieces that could be carried back to their rocky lairs.

Some of this meat was stored for later use. In one cave on the Isle of Jersey off the west coast of France, the inhabitants dug a large pit next to the wall on one side and put large chunks of meat in it—three rhinoceros skulls and pieces of at least five mammoths. They took chunks of meat out of this locker when they were ready to cook them over the fire that warmed and lit the cave.

Finding fuel was another problem for the inhabitants of the Périgord region. It must have been especially hard to find during the periods of glacial advance, when there were virtually no trees in the area, or during the winter, when it was difficult to walk through the snow. When wood was scarce, these people undoubtedly used grasses and shrubs as fuel. They burned animal bones, and they may even have used animal fat and dried animal droppings to light and warm their caves.

Tools

The people of the Périgord used *Mousterian* tools. These were made on stone flakes removed from carefully prepared cores shaped like tortoises. The tool-maker carefully chipped around the edge of a flint nodule, keeping in mind the shape of the final flake to be struck from the core. This is called the Levallois technique, and tools made in this fashion have been found from the Atlantic Ocean to the area north of the Black Sea and from England to North Africa. Mousterian assemblages contain many different kinds of tools: awls for piercing hides and wood, scrapers for removing meat, spear points for killing game, denticulates for sawing and shredding, and various kinds of knives for cutting.

The inhabitants of the Périgord region, and those of the Near East as well, used different tool kits to perform different tasks. For example, one tool kit contained two kinds of borers, a beak-shaped engraver, and some other tools that probably were used to make objects from wood and bone—spear shafts, handles, or pegs—and cordage from animal hides. Another kit contained several kinds of spear points and a wide variety of scrapers; these tools were probably used in killing and butchering animals. A third kit contained knives and sharp flakes that may have been used for cutting and preparing meat. Another contained denticulates and scrapers that presumably were used for shredding, sawing, and smoothing wood and other plant materials. A fifth kit contained spear points and various kinds of scrapers, including one that looked like a push plane. These tools were probably used for killing and butchering but may have been employed in more specialized activities as well.

The people of the Périgord region carried out various activities in their caves. On one side of the cave a person sat making pegs and cordage to support animal skins across the front of the lair; not far away another cut large

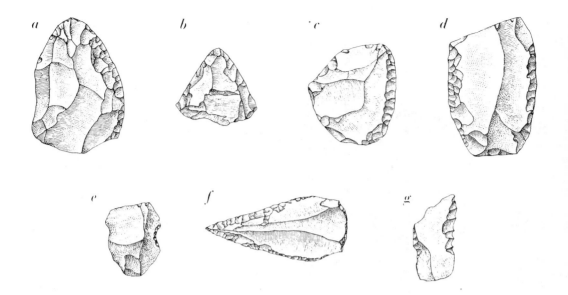

A Mousterian tool kit. (a–d). Side scrapers. (e) Notched tool. (f) Point. (g) Denticulate. Richard G. Klein, Ice-age hunters of the Ukraine. **Scientific American,** 230, no. 6 (1974), 72. Copyright © 1974 by Scientific American, Inc. All rights reserved.

chunks of meat into smaller pieces for roasting, while a third shredded vegetable materials with denticulates. Outside the cave an animal was butchered, and the stone tools used in this activity were discarded as they became dull.

The tools used to process foods—denticulates, scrapers, and knives—were frequently made of flint obtained in the immediate vicinity. The hunting tools—spear points and certain types of scrapers—were often made from raw materials found a mile or more from the base camp. This suggests that the inhabitants of the Périgord region used whatever raw materials were at hand when they made stone tools. What they may have carried with them were hammer stones and other implements used to make stone tools. They probably valued these much the way that today's artisans value their tools. Primary tools were probably much more important to the flintknappers than the implements they fashioned with them.

The toolmakers seem to have used the Levallois technique most frequently to manufacture tools for hunting. The hunting implements—spear points, knives, and several kinds of scrapers—were much more uniform or standardized in appearance than the denticulates and other tools associated with domestic or maintenance activities. The hunting tools were made on flakes of a predetermined size and shape, while those used for other purposes were often made on flakes of various sizes and shapes.

Death and Disease

Death was ever-present among these people. Many died in infancy and childhood, and most were dead by their fortieth year. In a group of thirty, two or three individuals died each year. In some instances we can determine what caused them to die. For example, a middle-aged individual from Monte Circeo, near Rome, was struck in the temporal region of the head and died as a result. An individual from Shanidar Cave in Iraq was stabbed and died with a stone spear point embedded in his thorax. Another individual from Shanidar died accidentally when the roof of the cave collapsed on him. He had already survived having his right arm amputated below the elbow and was recovering from head injuries inflicted by a sharp object.

A Neanderthal burial at Shanidar Cave, Iraq. Carol Ember and Melvin Ember, **Anthropology,** 2nd ed. (Englewood Cliffs, N.J.: Prentice-Hall 1977), p. 108.

Neglect was undoubtedly a major cause of death among early human groups, given the high infant and childhood mortality rates. This neglect probably took various forms—situational, unconscious, and conscious. For example, given the life expectancy of women, it is quite likely that the youngest children were not raised to adulthood by their biological mothers; this implies that they were cared for by other members of the group—other women, men and even older children. In such situations the orphaned infant or young child may be less adequately nourished or cared for than his or her more fortunate peers and, consequently, may be more susceptible to certain diseases. The mothering individual—the biological mother or someone else—might permit the infant or young child to wander away or get hurt while she was engaged in some other activity. Finally, child neglect and abuse are conscious activities in any society; there is no reason to assume that such behavior is of recent origin.

Disease was the other major cause of death among ancient populations. The people in these groups were susceptible to diseases such as trichinosis that are acquired by eating raw animal foods. They were also susceptible to zoonoses, infections of other animals that are transmitted by biting insects; among these were anthrax and botulism. Internal parasites such as hookworms or amoebas that are found in fecal matter were probably present as well. Tetanus, which is present in dirt, must have taken a heavy toll. Infectious diseases like mumps, measles, or smallpox were not important because the germs could not perpetuate themselves owing to the small size of the group.

The first deliberate burials occurred during the early part of the last glacial cycle. The inhabitants of Le Moustier, a site in the Périgord region, buried an 18-year-old with considerable care and tenderness. He was placed on his side, his legs bent and his head resting on his right arm as if he were going to sleep. Meat and stone tools were placed in the grave with him. A group living around La Ferrassie, another site in southern France, buried two adults and four children on the floor of the cave; they aligned the bodies in an east–west direction. The battered skull from Monte Circeo was placed on the floor of the cave and surrounded by a circle of rocks. Child burials were often quite elaborate. For example, a child from the site of Teshik-Tash in southern Russia was surrounded by half a dozen goat frontlets whose horns had been pushed into the ground. A young child was placed on a bed of wildflowers in Shanidar Cave before being covered with earth.

DAILY LIFE ON THE UKRAINIAN STEPPE

Molodova lies in the Dneister River valley about 200 miles northwest of Odessa on the Black Sea. People first lived at the site more than 45,000 years ago, when periglacial steppe covered the permanently frozen ground of the southwestern Ukraine. The winters were long and cold, but little snow fell; temperatures averaged around 0° F during the winter months. The summers were short, but warm enough for a variety of hardy grasses to grow and mature. These provided food for more than a dozen species of large and small herbivores. In the north, the hunters preferred reindeer and wild horse. To the south, they hunted steppe bison. Woolly rhinoceroses, aurochs, musk oxen, saiga antelope, red deer, and moose were among the herbivores that they hunted infrequently. The only carnivores they killed in any quantity were fox and wolf.

The ancient Ukrainians apparently resided in the river valleys during the long winter months when the rivers were frozen over and fierce winds swept across the steppe grasslands. Their houses were wooden frameworks covered with animal skins; the latter were held in place by mammoth bones, which the inhabitants seem to have collected especially for this purpose. The bone anchors were placed around the perimeter of the house as well as on top of it. Chemical tests on the mammoth bones from one site indicated that the animals had lived and died thousands of years apart. Skulls, tusks, shoulder blades, pelvises, and certain long bones were particularly suitable as weights.

One of the houses was an oval, about 33 feet long and 25 feet wide. Fifteen hearths lit and warmed the inside of this large, tentlike structure. Perhaps thirteen to fifteen individuals lived in such a hut during the winter months. They went outside for food and fuel as infrequently as possible. They apparently dressed in fox and wolf hides and lived on a diet that was rich in animal protein and fat.

During the summers they moved out of the river valleys onto the grass-covered steppes, where game was plentiful. Archaeologists have not yet found the remains of their summer camps, possibly because they were so transitory that little was left behind. This suggests that the inhabitants of eastern Europe, particularly the steppe areas, were much more nomadic than their contemporaries in southwestern France. The reason for this may be that the ancient Ukrainians were more dependent on migratory species as primary sources of food; as a result, they had to move seasonally with the herds of reindeer, horse, and bison. Their food procurement activities, like the locations of their camps, were closely linked to the seasonal cycles of these animals.

THE STRUCTURE OF HUMAN SOCIETY

Our ancestors of 50,000 years ago lived in a social milieu that was fundamentally different from anything we are familiar with today. There were no social classes, and there was no state to promote the welfare of individuals or pre-

Shelter found at Moldova I. (a) Reconstruction of the shelter. (b) Plan of the shelter. Each square in the grid is one meter on a side. Richard G. Klein, Ice-age hunters of the Ukraine, **Scientific American,** 230, no. 6 (1974), 67. Copyright © 1974 by Scientific American, Inc. All rights reserved.

(a)

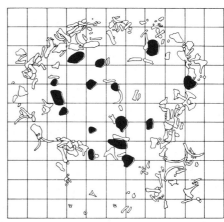

(b)

vent them from satisfying their needs. People lived in small groups. For days, perhaps even months, they saw only people they knew. The appearance of a stranger in their midst must have been a notable event, one that was both exciting and perhaps slightly frightening. People were totally dependent on each other for survival in a way that is very difficult for us to understand.

Larger Groups

Human groups had expanded in size. They may have contained as many as thirty or forty members at those times of the year when food was particularly plentiful. These larger social groupings had adaptive significance in the sense that they promoted the survival and well-being of their members over extended periods. In a larger group individuals had more opportunities to have their needs satisfied and more opportunities to expand their capacities by recognizing and meeting the needs of others. There were also significantly more opportunities for new kinds of behavior and ways of viewing the world to be validated and adopted by other members of the social unit. Spoken language facilitated all of this by allowing the members of a group to share information about the world they lived in.

Larger group size meant that the members of a social unit had to acquire more food in order to maintain a particular standard of living. In a sense every human group sets an upper limit on its size by defining what elements of the natural environment constitute resources and by developing the means—tools, techniques, and knowledge—to exploit those resources. When food resources are inadequate to sustain a group at a particular standard of living, the members have only a limited number of ways of dealing with the situation. These include redefining what elements of the environment constitute food so that more foodstuffs are available; or the group can also reduce the number of individuals relying on the food resources of a given area through some method of population control, such as splitting the group into two or more segments and having some segments move out of the area. It can increase the productivity of its labor through some technological or organizational innovation. It appears that all of these happened toward the end of the last interglacial period.

Fragmentation of Groups

The increased number and extent of archaeological sites dating from the transitional period suggests that human groups fragmented, moved into new territories or created them, and grew in size, repeating the process several times. This meant that the individuals organized themselves in such a way that group size was flexible. The group was able to split into two or more segments fairly easily. The process of division might have been a seasonal one that reflected the cyclical availability of food resources. It might have been a temporary one that occurred for short periods, perhaps when food was scarce or the members of the group were feeling antagonistic toward each other. Or it might have been a permanent division that occurred when one segment moved into a new territory while the rest of the group remained behind in the old one.

When a group fragmented, each functional segment seems to have contained about ten to fifteen members, judging from the size of the tent at Molodova as well as the size of caves in archaeological sites in southwestern France. Given the age structure and sex ratio of Neanderthal populations (derived from the burials), more than half of the individuals in one of these social units would have been adults and there would have been more males than females. For example, a group of thirteen might consist of a male over 30, three men and three women of reproductive age, and six infants and children. It is clear that the primary functions of these minimal social units were the acquisition of food, the production of goods, and the consumption of both of these kinds of objects.

Division of Labor

During the transition from ancient to modern human beings, the primary division of labor in human society may well have been based on age differences. We can distinguish three groups, each of which played a different economic role at any given moment. The adults, both men and women, composed the group that must have been largely responsible for the acquisition of food and the production of other goods. A second group was composed of infants and children—individuals who were too young to be engaged more than marginally in the productive process. The third group was composed of individuals who were too old to be effective food producers or who had some kind of illness or ailment that prevented them from being fully engaged in the productive process.

How did this tendency toward fragmentation, together with the age structure of early human society, affect the organization of work? Some of the subsistence activities, such as collecting wild plants, could have been carried out by a number of individuals working independently. Other subsistence activities, such as the hunting of large herbivores, were complex tasks that required the cooperation of a number of individuals. An important question is, How were these cooperative work groups organized? In a social setting where group size and membership were not completely stable because of sporadic or periodic fragmentation, it is likely that these work teams existed for short periods, just long enough to complete a particular task. It is also likely that their membership was not tightly or rigidly fixed. Given the age structure and size of these groups, it is likely that many of the same individuals participated in the same cooperative work teams again and again. In other words, the membership of the work teams was probably semipermanent, and members could easily be added or subtracted.

Sharing
It is clear that these hunters and gatherers shared the products of their labor with infants and children, on the one hand, and with old or ailing individuals, on the other. For example, they cared for a 50-year-old man from La Chapelle-aux-Saints who had relatively few teeth and a severe case of spinal arthritis for a period of at least several years. On at least two different occasions they cared for the man from Shanidar Cave whose arm had been amputated—once while he recovered from surgery and again while he was recuperating from a severe head injury. By sharing with and caring for the infants and children, the adults in the group were ensuring the continued existence of the group itself over a period that encompassed more than one generation.

The relationship between older and younger generations may well have been enmeshed in the division of labor between men and women. Many archaeologists assume that there was a sexual division of labor in early human societies. If they are correct, then the men in these social units pursued one set of productive activities, while the women carried out another. Furthermore, each sex had access to a portion of the goods produced by the other. This allowed the members of the group to undertake some risky productive activities such as long-range hunting, whose outcome was uncertain; they knew they would still have access to the more certain production—say, plant foods—of the other sex. The relationship between the sexes, in short, was one of sharing, which involves both rights and obligations.

It is not economics that provides the motivation for men and women to share with each other and with the members of other generations in their social unit. The driving force is an ideological one that can be couched in terms of relationships with the supernatural or ties of kinship between different members of the group. These social relations—sets of rules that define from whom an individual can claim labor and goods and to whom he or she must give them—may reflect the existence of kinship systems during the transitional period. The presence of burials among the Neanderthal populations of western Europe and their contemporaries elsewhere in the Old World around 50,000 years ago suggests that people may already have begun to define their social relationships in terms of kinship and descent. What is also clear, however, is that kinship systems—which occasionally coincide with our notions of biological or genealogical relations—were not essential for the maintenance and functioning of human societies at this stage of their development.

FURTHER READINGS

Binford, Lewis R., and Sally R. Binford
1966 A preliminary analysis of functional variability in the Mousterian of Levallois facies. *American Anthropologist Special Publication,* 68, no. 2, pt. 2, pp. 238–295.

Bordes, François
1968 *The Old Stone Age.* McGraw-Hill, New York and Toronto.

Cockburn, T. Aidan
1971 Infectious diseases in ancient populations. *Current Anthropology,* 12, no. 1, pp. 45–62.

Engels, Frederick
1972 *The origin of the family, private property and the state,* ed. with introduction by Eleanor Burke Leacock. International Publishers, New York.

Hindess, Barry, and Paul Q. Hirst
1975 *Pre-capitalist modes of production.* Routledge & Kegan Paul, London and Boston.

Kennedy, Kenneth A. R.
1975 *Neanderthal man.* Burgess, Minneapolis.

Klein, Richard
1973 *Ice-age hunters of the Ukraine.* University of Chicago Press, Chicago.

Konner, Melvin
1975 Relations among infants and juveniles in comparative perspective. In *Friendship and peer relations,* ed. Michael Lewis and Leonard A. Rosenblum, pp. 99–130. Wiley, New York

Lee, Richard B.
1972 Population growth and the beginnings of sedentary life among the !Kung Bushmen. In *Population growth; anthropological implications,* ed. Brian Spooner, pp. 329–342. M.I.T. Press, Cambridge, Mass.

Mellars, P. A.
1973 The character of the middle–upper palaeolithic transition in southwest France. In *The explanation of culture change; models in prehistory,* ed. Colin Renfrew, pp. 255–276. Gerald Duckworth, London.

Pearce, Jane, and Saul Newton
1963 *The conditions of human growth.* Citadel Press, Secaucus, N.J.

Pfeiffer, John E.
1972 *The emergence of man,* 2nd ed. Harper & Row, New York.

Terray, Emmanuel
1972 Historical materialism and segmentary lineage-based societies. In *Marxism and "primitive" societies; two studies by Emmanual Terray,* pp. 93–186. Monthly Review Press, New York and London.

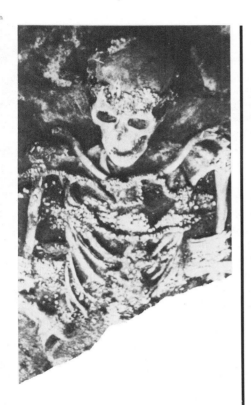

The Appearance of Modern Human Beings

Modern human beings—people who resembled the people of the world today—appeared about 40,000 years ago. They were undoubtedly as varied in their appearance as we are. The people who lived in one part of the world looked different from those who lived in other regions. Physical traits such as height, weight, skin color, and hair texture, varied as much then as they do today. This variation was always present and was always changing as human groups adapted first to one set of environment conditions and then to another.

Some groups developed technologies that allowed them to move into new lands where no humans had ever set foot before. One set of adaptations permitted people to live in polar areas like Siberia and the Arctic. These adaptations were cultural ones—warm clothing and shelter—that ultimately permitted them to use the Siberian north as a staging area for moving into the Americas, which they did around 35,000 years ago. At about the same time other groups crossed the sixty miles of open water that separated Australia and New Guinea from Indonesia, which was then part of the Asian mainland.

Many more sites are known from this period than from all of the preceding periods of human history. This implies that the total population of the world had increased significantly. Population growth was probably continuous, particularly after groups began to move into previously uninhabited areas. It is unlikely, however, that the growth rate was uniform from one region to another, given differences in availability of resources and in the economic orientations of the inhabitants of different places.

The productive forces of these early societies were not well developed. Their resource base was small; their tools were simple; and the labor available to wield these implements was minimal. The productivity of human labor was also low. Yet people were able to produce more than just what was necessary to meet their needs and ensure the continuation of the group into the future. They were able to carry out work activities above and beyond the labor that was necessary to sustain the group. The ability to perform this surplus labor, regardless of the amount, was absolutely essential for the further development of the society's productive forces. The effects of surplus labor were most noticeable when technological innovations were adopted and the productivity of labor, and in some instances the size of the group as well, increased. Without the time to try new ways of doing things, there would have been no innovations or they would have occurred much less frequently. The time to experiment was provided by the surplus labor of the group.

Progress occurred once people began to harness the forces of nature with increasingly sophisticated technological and scientific innovations. The reason for this is that the effects of technological and scientific innovations are cumulative. The most important precondition for the occurrence of innovations among the members of a group is that they have a history of adopting innovations. In other words, most technological and scientific innovations are based on prior achievements. Material progress reflects more than the capacity of a people to generate new ideas, new skills, and new kinds of tools; it also reflects the ability to adopt concepts, techniques, and implements developed by others, make them more efficient, and find new applications for them.

By itself, the number of individuals in a group is a neutral factor in the process leading to improvement of productive forces. If concentrations of individuals occur within a group and the processes of imitation, collaboration, and validation are encouraged, then there is a greater certainty that innovative ideas and behavior will appear. This is particularly true when these interactions take place in a social milieu that anticipates that change will take place and actively encourages it. Frequently the members of a group limit their expectation of change to certain aspects of their culture. For example, in our own society we expect car styles or women's dress fashions to change each year, but not many of us anticipate rapid changes in other areas, such as language or taboos against incest.

Progress—changes in the productive forces of a society—did occur during the last stages of the Pleistocene. It was accompanied by changes in the social relations of the members of these groups. In the following pages we will examine how people lived in various parts of the Old World during this period and consider the kinds of changes that occurred in their behavior.

LIFE IN SOUTHWESTERN FRANCE

The inhabitants of the Périgord region of southwestern France lived through a series of severe climatic changes between 35,000 and 10,000 years ago. At the beginning of this period the climate of the area was much like that of today. The well-watered valleys were covered with grassy meadows and woodlands composed of oak, elm, and pine trees. After about 30,000 years ago it became colder and drier. The winters were longer; the woodlands became smaller and almost disappeared from the area altogether; the lush grasses of the meadows were replaced by hardy bunch grasses that could grow in soils that were frozen most of the year, and by lichens that fastened themselves to rocks. The height of this cold, dry period occurred about 19,000 to 20,000 years ago. Around 17,000 years ago the climate became more humid, and stands of evergreens began to reappear in the river valleys. Later, when the climate became warmer, deciduous trees like oak and elm reappeared in the area.

Tools

The toolmakers of the area used a new technique for making stone implements called the *punch blade technique*. The stoneworkers prepared a roughly cylindrical core about four to six inches in length. Then they placed a bone or antler punch on the top edge of the core and struck it with a hammer. A long, narrow blade was removed from the side of the core. The toolmakers continued to remove blades from the core in this fashion until the core became too small to work efficiently. A small core weighing about two or three pounds would yield enough blades to make about 75 feet of cutting edge; this is roughly ten times as much cutting edge as could be obtained with earlier stoneworking techniques.

Stone tools were then made with these blades. The finished ones come in a much wider variety of shapes and forms than anything that had been used in the region before. Many of the tools had no antecedents in the earlier stone tool kits of the Périgord. The toolmakers of this period were highly original. They devised entirely new kinds of tools to use for particular purposes. This process occurred not just once or twice but repeatedly throughout the time from 35,000 to 10,000 years ago. The result was a series of stone tool assemblages, each with its own characteristic set of tools and tool shapes. The earliest of these are the so-called *Châtelperronian* assemblages, which date from between about 37,000 and 30,000 years ago. They were followed by *Aurignacian* (30,000 to 24,000 years ago), *Upper Perigordian* (24,000 to 20,000 years ago), *Solutrean* (20,000 to 17,000 years ago), and *Magdalenian* (17,000 to 12,000 years ago) assemblages.

Population Size and Structure

Roughly five times as many caves and rock shelters in the Périgord region were occupied during this 25,000-year period as had been occupied during the preceding 35,000 years. This suggests that the population of the region had increased substantially. The number of sites with Châtelperronian assemblages was roughly equivalent to the number of sites containing Mousterian assemblages. There was a significant three- to fourfold increase in the number of sites with Aurignacian assemblages. The number of sites stabilized and remained relatively constant during the time that the Upper Perigordian and Solutrean assemblages were being manufactured. But there was a twofold increase in the number of sites during the time that the Magdalenian assemblages were manufactured. This suggests that population growth in the area was not continuous. It increased dramatically on two different occasions—once during the time of the Aurignacian and again during the Magdalenian.

Furthermore, the occupation layers from this period are consistently larger than earlier ones in the region. Three of the rock shelters that were occupied during the time of the Aurignacian assemblages were more than 150 feet long and 30 feet wide. These caves would have had populations of about 50 individuals, assuming 20 square feet for each of the first six inhabitants and 100 square feet for each additional one. One of the caves that were occupied during the time from the Upper Perigordian to the Magdalenian—a site called Laugerie Haute—is nearly 500 feet long and 100 feet wide. It encloses an area of 50,000 square feet and could house about 500 persons, assuming that the same relationship between floor space and number of residents and assuming that the whole cave was a residential area. This estimate would be too high if part of the site was not residential. If we use another, more conservative means of estimating the population size of archaeological sites—the logarithm of the population equals half the logarithm of the surface area in square meters—then Laugerie Haute still had a population of about 70 persons. Another site, La Magdeleine, extends from the back of the rock shelter to the river and covers about 45,000 square feet—a little more than an acre; it may have had a population of about 65, using the second method of estimating population num-

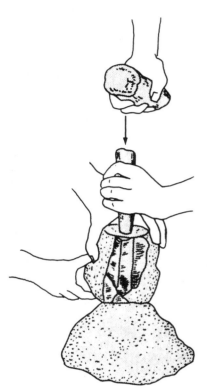

Many of the stone tools used in western Europe between 37,000 and 10,000 years ago were made on blades removed from cylindrical cores. A punch — made of bone, antler, or horn — was placed on the edge of the core and then struck with a hammer stone. The punch blade technique allowed stoneworkers to make much more efficient use of raw materials than earlier stoneworking techniques did. Brian M. Fagan, **In the beginning** (Boston: Little, Brown, 1972), p. 195.

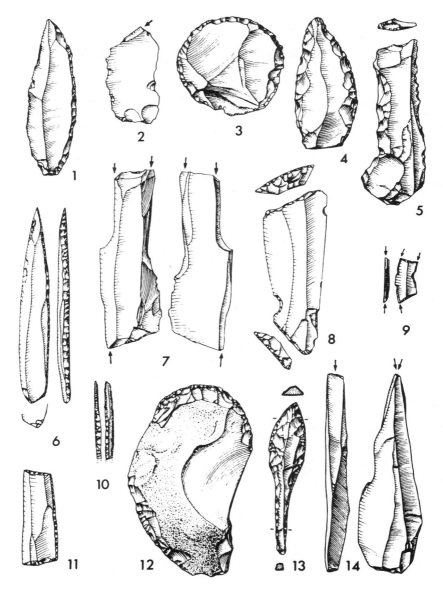

Stone tools from the Périgord region of southwestern France. (1) Chatelperron knife.
(2) Burin. (3) Scraper on a flake. (4) Mousterian point. (5) Denticulated blade. (6) Gravette
point. (7) Multiple burin. (8) Truncated blade. (9) Noailles burin. (10) Backed blade. (11)
Truncated blade fragment. (12) Flake scraper. (13) Font-Robert point. (14) Dihedral burin.
François Bordes, **The Old Stone Age** (New York: McGraw-Hill, 1968), fig. 54, p. 151.
Copyright © 1968 by McGraw-Hill Book Company. Used by permission.

bers. About twenty miles down the Dordogne River from La Magdeleine is another series of rock shelters that probably housed between 50 and 70 persons. A large, open site with an extensive Magdalenian occupation is located at Solvieux; it covers an area of more than 90,000 square feet and may have had a population of about 130 persons.

It is clear that human groups were larger than they had been earlier. At the beginning of the period, they ranged in size from about 50 to 100 individuals. By the end of the period, some settlements may have housed as many as 130 individuals. It is also clear that some of the occupation layers at different sites were contemporary with each other. This meant that the population of the Périgord region was even larger than the estimates for any given site suggest. It is conceivable that the region was inhabited by 500 to 1,000 persons during much of the period.

A study of seventy-six burials from Eurasia provides us with some insight into the population structure of groups living not only in southwestern France but also elsewhere on the Eurasian landmass. Roughly 40 percent of the individuals died in infancy or childhood; another 15 percent died before they reached adult stature. Another 20 percent died before they reached the age of 30. Fifteen percent died between the ages of 31 and 40, and 10 percent lived beyond the age of 40. Only about three individuals out of a hundred lived beyond the age of 50. This age structure was not dramatically different from those of earlier and later populations in Eurasia.

Camps and Caves

Judging from the ages of the animal remains found in refuse deposits at the larger sites in the Périgord region, many of these sites were occupied continuously throughout the year. Some of the smaller sites may have been camps that were inhabited for brief intervals—a week or less—by work parties of six to eight individuals that left the main campsite. Other sites, intermediate in size between the main settlements and the temporary hunting and collecting camps, were probably occupied by households of a dozen or more individuals on a more or less permanent basis.

Some groups went to considerable lengths to improve the appearance of the caves and rock shelters in which they lived. They dug out ancient deposits from the floors of several caves to produce a roomier, more regular living area. Sometimes they carried cobbles from nearby streams and carefully paved parts of the floor. Finally, they built stone walls along the edges of the living areas in some of the caves, presumably to support wooden or bone frameworks that were covered with animal skins. Tentlike structures were built in a number of the caves, particularly around the entrances. These presumably kept out the wind and cold. In the cave of Arcy-sur-Cure, located outside of the Périgord about 100 miles southeast of Paris, the residents put up a tent inside the cave and used mammoth tusks as stakes to support the

A middle-aged woman buried at Sungir near Moscow. USSR. The tomb is about 25,000 years old. More than 3,500 mammoth ivory and bone beads were sewn to a pullover shirt made of animal hide or fur; these beads took more than 1,000 hours to carve and were sewn in place at the time that she was buried. In addition to the shirt, she wore trousers with mocassins, a cape, and a cap with drilled fox teeth and beads sewn to it. On each of her arms she wore 25 ivory bracelets interspersed with beaded bracelets. An enormous amount of labor was invested in preparing the dead woman's clothing. Chester S. Chard, **Man in prehistory,** 2nd ed. (New York: McGraw-Hill, 1974), p. 170, fig. 13-1.

skin covering. At the Magdalenian sites living floors located outside the caves and rock shelters undoubtedly were also covered by large tents; one living floor at Pincevent, a site 35 miles southeast of Paris, had three separate sleeping areas, each with its own hearth to provide light and warmth during the summer and early fall evenings when the camp was occupied.

Obtaining Food

The inhabitants of the Périgord region hunted reindeer almost to the exclusion of all other terrestrial herbivores. Virtually all of the bones recovered from some garbage dumps are reindeer bones. Remains of other species do occur, but they are exceptionally rare in this region. Outside of the Périgord, other species were exploited. To the south, the inhabitants of the Pyrenees relied extensively on mammoth; to the north, the group at Solutré consumed enormous numbers of wild horses.

If we assume that each member of a group ate about three pounds of meat a day, then a group of 100 individuals needed about 300 pounds of meat each day; assuming that half of a 250-pound reindeer is usable, then they needed to kill 2.4 animals a day, or 72 per month. A group of 130 individuals would consume about 100 animals a month, or more than 1,200 each year. In the past, the hunters of the Périgord may have culled only adult individuals from the reindeer herds. During this period, they seem to have killed young individuals as well as more mature ones.

The inhabitants of the Périgord had more effective hunting weapons than their ancestors had. These were spear throwers—sticks about two feet long with a handle at one end and a hook at the other to hold the butt end of the spear. The spear thrower is an extension of the hunter's arm that gives the weapon both greater range and more striking power. The hunter holds the spear thrower by the handle and places a spear in it with the butt end firmly lodged against the hook. To launch the spear he swings his arm forward and releases the spear at the top of the arc created by his arm and the spear thrower. With the spear thrower, the hunter could heave spears over 400 feet and kill at ranges of about 100 feet. This meant that he no longer had to get as close to his prey as his ancestors did.

Although it has not been proved, many archaeologists believe that the inhabitants of the Périgord region had bows and arrows. The evidence for this is slim. The oldest known bows come from Denmark and are about 8,000 years old; some stone-tipped wooden arrow shafts have been found in 10,000-year-old reindeer hunter camps in northern Germany. And some small stones with representations of feathered projectiles scratched on them

Men using spear throwers. These simple rods with a hook at one end allowed hunters to hurl spears with much greater velocity. This not only increased the killing power of the spear but also enabled people to remain farther from their prey.

have been found in 20,000-year-old archaeological deposits at La Colombière in France.

Perhaps the most effective means of acquiring animals involved repeated cooperation by several work groups. Teams of hunters collaborated with each other to stampede herds of animals over cliffs or into pitfalls. They did this with considerable skill. At Predmost in Czechoslovakia hunters drove more than 1,000 mammoths into pits dug especially for that purpose. Beneath the cliffs at Solutré are the skeletons of more than 100,000 horses killed by the inhabitants of that area about 20,000 years ago. Of course, not all of the horses were killed at the same time. The accumulation of skeletons represents animal drives that were carried out sporadically over a period of perhaps 1,000 years.

The inhabitants of the Périgord region dramatically expanded their food supply about 20,000 years ago, when they developed fishing equipment and techniques for catching fish in large numbers. Fishing became a particularly important activity by the time of the Magdalenian, when many of the large settlements were located in close proximity to river banks. The great majority of the fish bones identified to date belong to salmon, which spawned in the Dordogne and Vézère Rivers and their tributaries during the fall. Remains of other species, such as trout, pike, and chub, also occur but are much less plentiful.

It is not difficult to imagine what fall was like along one of these rivers. The waters churn with millions of salmon making their way upriver to the spawning grounds where they were born. Fishermen stand on the edges of pools and shallow rapids, harpoon in hand, waiting for the right moment or the right fish. Nearby, two or three people are catching fish with nets made of thongs and weighted with cylindrical stones. Not far away, thousands of fish are trapped in a fish weir built in the middle of the stream. As the fish trap fills with fish, people wade into the enclosure and spear them with leisters—long poles with three-pronged ends. The fish are strung by ropes pushed through their gills; the fisherman hauls his catch with him until the load becomes too heavy. Then he wades to solid land and gives it to another person, who guts the fish and prepares them for drying or smoking over an open fire.

Cooperation and Division of Labor

It is clear that some of the tasks involved in acquiring food—such as large-scale animal drives or intensive fishing along the rivers when the salmon were running—required the cooperation of large numbers of people. This work consisted of a series of overlapping tasks that required the collaboration of a number of work teams working sequentially and independently to achieve a particular goal. The animal drives or intensive fishing did not take a lot of time—perhaps no more than a few weeks. However, in all likelihood they were performed every year. This implies that the people involved could organize themselves in such a way that they could muster enough individuals to do the work that needed to be done. Furthermore, when work projects are carried out on this scale by large numbers of people, it is impossible to determine who owns the final product because it belongs to everyone in general and no one in particular. This means that the people of the Périgord must have had a set of rules governing the redistribution of these communally produced commodities to all the members of the group. It also means that they had the ability to cooperate on projects that were not directly related to survival.

There was probably some division of labor of the large-scale subsistence activities. During the fall months, for example, reindeer herds were migrating to winter pastures at about the same time that salmon were moving up the rivers to spawn. This meant that two of the major sources of meat protein were available at the same time. Thus, there were conflicting demands for the time and labor of the group. The conflict could be solved in several different ways. Some work teams could hunt while others were engaged full time in fishing. The work teams could also fish one day and hunt the next; however, this is not a particularly efficient way of allocating time and energy. Undoubtedly there was some variation in the ways in which different groups solved this problem.

The increased productivity that characterized this period facilitated the development or performance of other activities that were not directly involved with the acquisition of food. For example, one toolmaker fashioned elaborate stone spear points that were too large and thin ever to be used for work; one of their functions must have been to display his workmanship. At the same time, the inhabitants of the area were beginning to make personal ornaments—necklaces of perforated animal teeth and carved shells that had been brought from places more than 100 miles distant. They carved beads and pendants out of bone, antler, and ivory, and both men and women must have worn them with pride. They also carved small figurines out of soft stone and painted slabs of rock with a wide variety of animals and figures; some of these were used to decorate their homes, while others were painted on walls and ceilings far back in the caves. The latter could be seen only with the aid of lamp—a stone bowl filled with animal fat and a burning wick. In one of these caverns, more than 200 feet from the opening of the cave, archaeologists found the footprints of half a dozen 15-year-olds who had packed the earth down as they walked around in a circle under the animals painted on the walls. This may well be the remains of the earliest known ritual—perhaps a rite of passage from the world of the child to that of the adult.

LIFE IN CZECHOSLOVAKIA

Dolni Vestonice was a small settlement located next to a stream that flowed swiftly out of the Pollau Mountains of central Czechoslovakia into the marshy bottom lands of the Thaya Valley. People lived there about 25,000 years ago.

The settlement was built on a peninsula that jutted out into the marsh, so its houses were surrounded on three sides by swamp. The area was not glaciated then; the edge of the ice sheet was several hundred miles to the north. It was intensely cold, however. The winters were long and the summers short and cool. Pine and willow trees grew in the sheltered valleys, while tundra grasses, mosses, and lichens covered the open plains during the short summers. Mammoths, reindeer, bison, wolves, and hares—all cold-adapted animals—abounded in the area.

The settlement consisted of four huts built inside a compound. A fifth hut overlooked the others from the hillside next to the stream. Piles of mammoth bones stood near the huts; more bones were strewn along the banks of the stream and in it. Tusks and other large bones formed parts of the wall and were laid against the skin tents to keep them from blowing away. The huts were oval; the largest was 45 feet by 27 feet and had five hearths to light and heat the inside.

The fifth hut, somewhat more recent than the others, was a circular, semisubterranean structure about 18 feet in diameter. It was located about 250 feet uphill from the rest of the settlement. There was a clay oven in the center of the hut; several thousand pieces of clay—some shapeless and others representing parts of animals—were scattered on the floor. This hut does not seem to have been lived in; instead, it appears to have been the center of some specialized activity that involved the manufacture of small clay figurines.

About 25 percent of the animal remains at Dolni Vestonice are from mammoth; hare and fox account for another 25 percent, and reindeer and wolf compose about 10 percent. Other animals were present, but they were much less common. Young mammoth probably provided the bulk of the animal protein; the inhabitants of the settlement probably ate water nuts, arctic berries, hazelnuts, and wild grasses collected from the marshy area around the camp.

The annual cycle of the people of Dolni Vestonice was probably closely tied to the movement of the mammoths. During the summer months, the mammoths dispersed over the grasslands, where each adult mammoth consumed 400 to 600 pounds of grass a day. In the winter, the mammoths moved into sheltered wooded areas, where they browsed on twigs and branches that had relatively little nutritional value. They drew upon the fat they had stored during the summer months and became progressively leaner as the winter progressed.

The human group dispersed and followed the mammoths onto the grasslands during the summer months. As fall approached and the animals began to move into the sheltered valleys, they returned to the camp at Dolni Vestonice. Plant foods were gathered from the nearby marsh, and like their neighbors at Predmost, 50 miles to the north, the inhabitants of Dolni Vestonice began to kill mammoths in preparation for the long winter ahead.

The settlement at Dolni Vestonice and its way of life, which focused on the seasonal movement of the mammoths, provide some clues to the social and economic organization of the central European groups of 25,000 years ago. The fact that the four huts of the winter camp were surrounded by a wall suggests that their residents formed a group. This social unit was divided into four living groups, each occupying a separate hut and consisting of about fifteen individuals. Both the living groups and the larger group they formed had their own social and economic realities. For certain activities—say, hunting mammoth during the summer months, when the animals were dispersed —the basic economic unit may have been the living group, which followed the animals across the grasslands of central Europe. As fall approached, the groups came together once again with old acquaintances—individuals they had known since childhood. Now, with the animals coming together and the size of the herds increasing daily, the basic economic unit, or work team, shifted from the members of a single living group to the members of the larger unit. Work teams that had produced food independently during the summer months now cooperated with each other to accumulate food for the whole group for the approaching winter.

Another question that is relevant to discerning the social organization of the residents of Dolni Vestonice has to do with the isolated hut on the hill overlooking the main camp. What was it? During the excavation of the hut archaeologists found a small ivory tablet engraved with a female human head. The left side of the woman's face was deformed in such a way that the side of her face appeared to be paralyzed. Earlier excavations at the camp had produced another representation of a woman's head, this one sculpted in three dimensions. The left side of her face also appeared to be paralyzed. Archaeologists also recovered an isolated burial at the camp. A small woman had been buried beneath two mammoth shoulderblades. Her head and chest had been sprinkled with red ocher, and she held the remains of a fox in her hand. A stone spear point had been placed next to her head. What is most striking about this small, delicate woman, however, is that the entire left side of her face was deformed. When she was alive her face had the same slack appearance as that of the woman in the two carvings. In all likelihood she was the model for the carvings. Someone made an accurate three-dimensinal representation of her while she was alive. A few generations later she was represented again, this time in two dimensions in a carving with a masklike quality. Evidently her memory was associated with the activities performed in the hut on the hillside. This structure may have served as the locus for ceremonial activities related to the manufacture of small figurines.

LIFE ON THE SOUTH AFRICAN COAST

Nelson Bay cave overlooks the Indian Ocean about 300 miles east of Capetown. The cave is carved into a 200-foot-high sandstone cliff. It faces the south.

It is about 100 feet wide and 100 to 150 feet deep. A small spring rises at the back of the cave, so there is always a supply of fresh water.

The first inhabitants of the cave lived there about 18,000 years ago. At that time the ocean was more than 50 miles away, and the inhabitants rarely went there to get food. Instead, they used what could be found in the immediate vicinity of the cave. They hunted antelopes, ostrich, baboons, giant buffalo, bush pigs, and wart hogs. They also collected seeds and berries from the plants that grew in the grasslands in front of the cave.

The inhabitants of the cave added a number of features to make it more comfortable. They built small stone windbreaks around their fireplaces and a large semicircular windbreak between the hearths and the mouth of the cave. Saplings were stuck into the top of this stone wall, and animal skins were stretched between them to keep out the cold. This would have been particularly comfortable on winter nights, when frost or even a light sprinkling of snow covered the ground.

The life style of these people changed dramatically about 16,000 years ago as the glacial ice melted and the seas began to rise. The 50-mile-long plain that stretched from the cave to the Indian Ocean was gradually inundated. By 10,000 BC waves were breaking just a few miles from the mouth of the cave. The animals that formerly grazed in front of the cave had gradually moved as their pasture disappeared. The inhabitants were no longer able to stay in the cave on a year-round basis.

During the summers, they dispersed and moved inland to collect plant foods and hunt the animals grazing in the park savanna of the African coast. In the winter months, they returned to the cave to harvest the resources of the sea. They collected limpets and pried abalone from the rocks in the tidal zone. Another work team walked a few miles along the coast to a rocky prominence that had become a breeding ground for seals. They must have walked into the rookery and killed the seals with clubs. Other work teams or individuals sat on beaches and rocky points to fish. They baited their lines with pieces of mussels taken from the rocks; the bait was placed over a bone or wooden gorge that snapped open once the fish had taken the bait and chewed on it a little.

The people of Nelson Bay moved regularly from one environment to another, from a settled life on the coast during the winter months to a transient, migratory existence in the interior during the summer. Their diet changed from seafood to a combination of meat and vegetables as they moved from their ocean-front cave to the interior.

DAILY LIFE IN THE LEVANT

About 18,000 years ago a new way of life began to emerge among the inhabitants of the coastal plain of Palestine and the hills beyond. At that time marshes covered much of the plain. Hippopotamuses and wart hogs were the largest residents of these swampy places, and the birds there must have been varied and plentiful. Human beings lived on sand dunes and in oak forests located on high ground overlooking the marshy areas. Their settlements were still small—no more than 2,000 square feet—but much more numerous than they had been earlier.

Deer, gazelles, and wild cattle grazed on the grass-covered hills overlooking the coastal plain. Small streams rose in these hills and flowed into the Mediterranean during the rainy season, which lasted from January to March. The eastern slopes of these hills overlooked the Jordan Valley, which was covered with stands of grass interspersed with oak and pine trees and lower shrubs that were well adapted to the long, dry summers of the area.

Animal bones from the refuse deposits at the human campsites indicate that the people of the area were exploiting a much greater range of animal resources than their ancestors had. Large animals—gazelles, goats, and deer—still provided the bulk of the meat; however, small animals like rodents, tortoises, snails, and birds were also consumed. The skins, teeth, shells, and feathers of these animals may well have been used for other purposes—decorating clothes or making jewelry.

The animal remains from a few camps contrast markedly with the general pattern of using a wide selection of the available resources. At these camps, the inhabitants seem to have concentrated on certain animals almost to the exclusion of other species. For example, at Wadi Madamagh, a camp near Petra, goat bones compose 80 percent of the faunal remains. Gazelle bones compose three-quarters of the faunal assemblage from Nahal Oren, a camp near Mt. Carmel outside of Haifa. The inhabitants of these camps may have been specialized hunters. However, the vegetation of the areas immediately surrounding the camps would not have supported very large numbers of these animals. In fact, these animals would have been in competition with other species, such as deer, for plant foods. One estimate is that about 200 deer could live in the area around one of the camps. With a herd of this size, there would have been an annual surplus of roughly thirty-five animals, which would have yielded about 1,600 pounds of meat. At three pounds a day per person, this was enough meat to sustain a group of twenty individuals for twenty-seven days. Given the fact that both goats and gazelles were competing with other animal species for food resources, the number of these animals found around a camp would have been somewhat smaller than 200. This means that they would have supported a group of specialized hunters for an even shorter period.

It appears that the residents of these and other sites on the hills overlooking the eastern Mediterranean rounded up as many goats or gazelles as they could catch, particularly females and young, and began herding them. This assured the human population a reliable supply of meat throughout the year. It also meant, however, that they could stay in one place only as long as pasture was available. When the animals had depleted the wild grasses, the

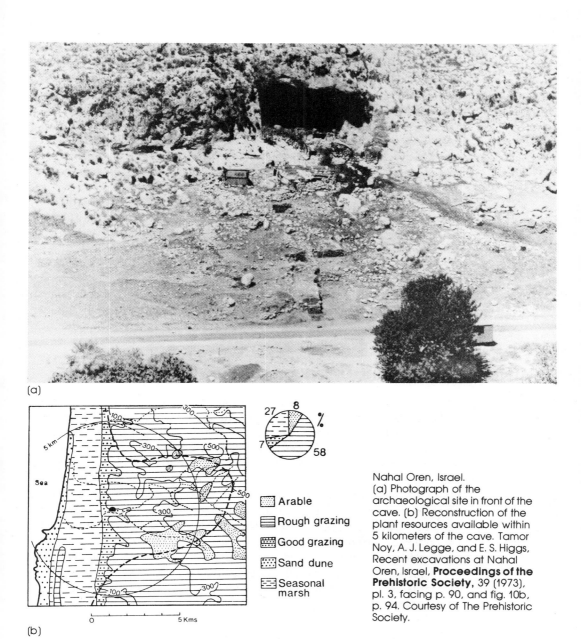

(a)

(b)

Nahal Oren, Israel.
(a) Photograph of the archaeological site in front of the cave. (b) Reconstruction of the plant resources available within 5 kilometers of the cave. Tamor Noy, A. J. Legge, and E. S. Higgs, Recent excavations at Nahal Oren, Israel, **Proceedings of the Prehistoric Society,** 39 (1973), pl. 3, facing p. 90, and fig. 10b, p. 94. Courtesy of The Prehistoric Society.

27 — 8
7 — 58 %

☒ Arable
☰ Rough grazing
▦ Good grazing
⬚ Sand dune
⊟ Seasonal marsh

group had to move to a locality where fresh pasture was available. One of the areas they moved into, probably during the late spring, was the Jordan Valley, a broad grassland with scattered stands of trees.

At Ain Gev, a small site on the shores of Lake Tiberias in the Jordan Valley, archaeologists found a number of round houses that date from this period. Inside one of them were grinding slabs, a mortar, and small stone blades with silica sheen on them. This sheen was produced when grass was cut with the chipped-stone implements. This indicates that the inhabitants of the camp were using the wild grasses that grew in the area. Two grasses that must have been particularly abundant there in late April, after the rains had stopped, are wild wheat and barley. With very primitive stone tools a small group of three or four individuals can harvest enough wild grain in an hour to feed themselves for several weeks.

What these groups may have done was to keep their small herds away from stands of wild cereals that they could use. This would ensure them a supply of grain, while their animals could graze on plants that lacked economic importance. As wheat and barley became less plentiful in the valley and the animals began to deplete their pasture, the herders may have moved up into the limestone hills to the west, where the cereals were just beginning to ripen and fresh pasture was available for the animals. This combination provides the environmental base for the later development of agrarian economies—a transformation that we will consider in more detail in the next section.

THE STRUCTURE OF HUMAN SOCIETY

The cooperative nature of the major food procurement activities described earlier in this chapter suggests that there was a network of stable social relationships that existed before the work activity was carried out and specified how the goods produced would be distributed among the members of the work team and the members of the larger social unit. In modern hunting and gathering societies these relationships are usually enmeshed in kinship networks. Today there is often a person who coordinates and supervises the labor of work teams, or production units. The individual occupying this socially useful position does not have to have a different status from those of the other members of the larger social unit. He or she might occupy this supervisory position only for the duration of a particular work activity; when the task is completed, such services are no longer needed. When a different work activity is being performed, the same individual might well be a laborer instead of an organizer or supervisor.

In some areas, like southwestern France, human groups had abundant food resources and the means to exploit the economically important elements of their environments efficiently. Consequently, the populations of these groups were often large—perhaps as high as 200 in some instances—and their members often lived together in the same settlements for much, if not all, of the year. These groups probably had a number of independent work teams, or production units, that were simultaneously engaged in the same food procurement activity and produced food for different groups of consumers in the larger society. The organization and supervision of these autonomous production units may have been identical to that of smaller groups. It seems likely that the fragmenting process that took place in early hunting and gathering societies probably occurred along the lines between competing production units.

The productivity of human labor increased significantly toward the end of the Pleistocene. By 20,000 years ago individuals or groups in various societies were carrying out activities that were not directly related to the acquisition of food. As mentioned earlier, a toolmaker in France fashioned elaborate spear points that were too large and thin to be used for hunting. People in the Périgord were making necklaces from seashells brought from places more than 100 miles away. These groups, as well as ones in northern Spain, painted slabs of rock and cave walls with elaborate scenes. Throughout Europe people carved small human figurines out of bone and soft stone, and a group in Czechoslovakia made fired-clay figurines of animals and people.

At certain times of the year there were probably technical divisions of labor in these societies. Such divisions occurred when their members were confronted with the problem of exploiting several seasonal resources that became available at the same time. One way of resolving the conflicts created by this kind of situation may have been to establish a set of priorities and to schedule food procurement activities in terms of those priorities. For example, the members of a given production unit might harvest wild fruits and trap small animals 50 percent of the time, hunt large game and collect wild grains another 25 percent of the time, and fish and gather aquatic resources for the remainder. These activities may well have involved a division of labor by age and sex. Another way of resolving the crisis created by the simultaneous availability of different economic resources is to have one production unit engage in one food procurement activity while another work team carries out a different set of activities.

When technical divisions of labor exist it is absolutely essential that *exchange* take place if the society as a whole is to survive and reproduce. Without exchange, or the circulation of goods, a society could not survive, since no individual or production unit is totally self-sufficient. In other words, the members of a production unit share the products of their labor with the members of their consumption unit, and the members of different consumption units share the products of their labor with each other. At first this kind of exchange may have occurred only within a given society. However, as the various production and consumption units began to establish wider and wider networks of relationships with other groups both within the society and outside of it, the archaeological record begins to change. Exotic materials that are not available locally and goods that were not produced locally begin to appear with increasing frequency. These items were often luxury goods—like the seashells used for jewelry—rather than products that were directly related to the society's subsistence needs. One effect of these exchanges was to create alliances between different units—not only units within the same society but also between those in different societies.

If a society were organized in such a way that it had several independent production units that were simultaneously engaged in the same food procurement activity, these work teams probably produced different amounts of food and other goods in any given year. There are several reasons why this variation would occur; the more obvious of these are demographic ones that reflect small group size and continual change. For example, there is a close link between productivity and the age and sex composition of a given production unit. The age and sex composition of one production unit might not be particularly well suited for producing everything the members of that group needed; as a result, the members of this unit might not be able to acquire enough food to meet their needs. Another production unit with a large number of individuals in the age and sex categories that hunted or harvested wild plant foods might well be able to acquire more of these items than it needed. While the first one did not produce enough, the second one was able to produce a surplus.

Evidence from the 23,000-year-old site at Sungir, near Moscow, indicates that some units were able to produce or accumulate more than others and that access to these goods was often ascribed—a result of membership in one of these highly productive units—rather than achieved. For example, the tunic of a middle-aged woman was decorated with more than 3,500 beads of mammoth ivory and bone that took more than 1,000 hours to carve; these were sewn on her fur shirt at the time that she was buried and represent an enormous investment of labor by others in activities that were not directly related to the survival needs of the group.

It is clear that some societies dating to late Pleistocene times could produce significant surpluses of both labor and goods, and these surpluses seem to have been generated within the group rather than being acquired through exchange with other peoples. These societies were able to generate surpluses because their productivity had increased to the point at which they could produce more, if they so desired, than just the items that were essential for the maintenance and reproduction of the group. Some of this surplus labor, at least at Sungir, seems to have been used to express differences in status, wealth, or access to labor.

FURTHER READINGS

Barnett, Homer G.
1953 *Innovation; the basis of cultural change.* McGraw-Hill, New York.

Fairservis, Walter A., Jr.
1975 *The threshold of civilization; an experiment in prehistory.* Scribner's, New York.

Flannery, Kent
1969 Origins and ecological effects of early domestication in Iran and the Near East. In *The domestication and exploitation of plants and animals,* ed. Peter J. Ucko and G. W. Dimbleby, pp. 73–100. Gerald Duckworth, London.

Hindess, Barry, and Paul Q. Hirst
1975 *Pre-capitalist modes of production.* Routledge & Kegan Paul, London and Boston.

Mellaart, James
1975 *The Neolithic of the Near East.* Thames & Hudson, London.

Mellars, P. A.
1973 The character of the middle–upper palaeolithic transition in southwest France. In *The explanation of culture change; models in prehistory,* ed. Colin Renfrew, pp. 255–276. Gerald Duckworth, London.

Pfeiffer, John E.
1972 *The emergence of man,* 2nd ed. Harper & Row, New York.

Prideaux, Tom, and the Editors of Time–Life Books
1973 *Cro-Magnon man.* Time–Life Books, New York.

Ucko, Peter J., and Andrée Rosenfeld
1967 *Palaeolithic art.* McGraw-Hill, New York and Toronto.

Viti-Finzi, C., and E. S. Higgs
1970 Prehistoric economy in the Mount Carmel area of Palestine. Site catchment analysis. *Proceedings of the Prehistoric Society,* 36, pp. 1–37. Cambridge.

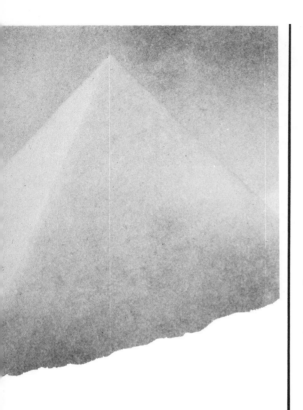

THREE

FROM THE REMOTE PAST TO CLASSICAL ANTIQUITY

For most of human history groups of people foraged and hunted for the food and other goods they needed to sustain themselves and ensure the survival of their children. But about 10,000 years ago a new economic pattern began to emerge, a pattern based on the use of domesticated plants and animals. At first it occurred only in a few widely scattered parts of the world: the Near East, China and northern Indochina, Mesoamerica, and tropical South America. As time passed, peoples living elsewhere in the world gradually adopted new modes of food production and incorporated them into their own economies.

The transformation of human society from bands of hunters and gatherers to peoples dependent on agriculture for their livelihood—a transformation known as the Neolithic revolution—was a gradual process that occurred slowly over thousands of years. It was an uneven process that occurred earlier in some areas than in others and more rapidly in one place than in another. Nevertheless, its impact has been enormous, regardless of where, when, or even how fast it happened.

The Neolithic Revolution was based on new patterns of work and the new kinds of social relations that arose out of them.

What distinguishes the farmer from the hunter is the nature of work and its implications. For the farmer, work consists of a number of tasks—such as clearing fields, planting, weeding, and harvesting—that have to be carried out sequentially over an extended period. This means that the membership of a production unit must be stable enough so that these tasks can be performed every year. In addition, the payoff from agriculture—the consumption of plant and animal foods—is delayed for many months after the first work tasks have been completed. The economic orientation of the farmer lacks some of the immediacy and opportunism of that of the hunter. Finally, the activities of the farmer have to be carried out at particular times of the year, and this may well interfere with the acquisition of other food resources that might also be available at those times.

Food production, with its need for networks of stable social relations, ultimately permitted high population densities, the formation of permanent settlements, and the development of societies with marked class distinctions. At first these social relations reflected ties between equals and were probably expressed in terms of the various systems of kinship and descent that characterized early food-producing societies. However, as people began to form larger, more complex societies, the social ties were no longer simply a matter of relations between equals. Instead, they gradually took the form of relationships between classes of people, some of which had greater access to the society's wealth than others.

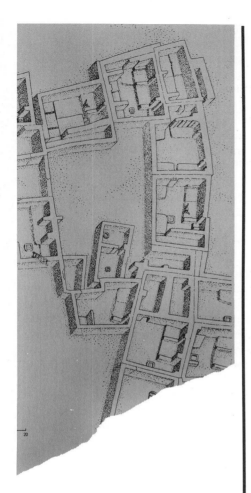

The Beginning of Agriculture in the Ancient East

The ancient East is part of the great desert that stretches almost uninterrupted from the Atlantic Sahara to the Gobi of Mongolia and from there to the gates of Peking. For our purposes it extends from the Nile River Valley northward along the Mediterranean coast of the Levant to the Anatolian Plateau of southern Turkey, and eastward across the rolling plains of Mesopotamia to the Iranian Plateau and from there to the Indus River Valley. Mountain ranges and barren tracts of stone and sand divide this vast area into a series of smaller deserts, each of which has its own ecological peculiarities. The ancient East is thus an ecological mosaic with rich alluvial river valleys, swamps, tree-covered foothills, and fertile mountain valleys, as well as seemingly endless stretches of desert.

Between 9,000 and 11,000 years ago, groups living in the foothills and mountainous areas surrounding the great alluvial plain of Mesopotamia domesticated sheep and goats. Later, they domesticated wild cereal grasses—emmer and einkorn wheat and barley. Still later, they added other plants and animals to their repertory of domesticated foodstuffs. Over the years archaeologists have developed and discarded a number of explanations for the origins of agricultural production in this region and elsewhere. One of the early explanations was the "garbage heap" hypothesis: As people brought wild plants back to their camps, seeds were scattered on the disturbed soils; plants eventually grew, and the people were able to harvest these plants in the immediate vicinity of their homes. A second explanation, the "oasis" theory, was quite popular

7

during the first half of this century: Temperate environmental zones shifted northward at the close of the last ice age and the Near Eastern environments became drier; as a result, human beings—as well as various economically important plants and animals—became concentrated in areas with permanent water supplies and the interactions between them intensified, with domestication being one of the outcomes. A third explanation, the "nuclear area" hypothesis, came into prominence in the 1950s: Environmental changes in nuclear areas such as the hilly flanks of the Near East were minimal at the end of the last ice age and had nothing to do with the origins of food production, which developed gradually in these ecologically diverse areas as people began to understand and manipulate the plants and animals around them.

Today two kinds of demographic explanations have come to the forefront. One is a "population pressure" model: Human population increased because of ample food supply that was becoming available at the end of the Pleistocene; this allowed for increased sedentism, which led to population growth and an increased demand for food that was ultimately met by agricultural production. The other is a "demographic shift" explanation: People moved out of the areas that were optimal for the wild progenitors of domestic plants and animals and into marginal lands; there they introduced plants and animals from the nuclear area that could flourish only under the controlled conditions of agricultural production.

In this chapter we will examine two related problems in the light of current views about the origins of agriculture: (1) How did early food-producing communities develop in the Near East? (2) What were they like?

EARLY FOOD-PRODUCING COMMUNITIES

The peoples of the ancient East had developed a variety of life styles by 10,000 years ago. Some groups continued to move from one place to another throughout the year, hunting a variety of animals and harvesting wild plant foods as these became available. Other groups had developed new ways of making a living. They lived in large, nearly permanent settlements with 50 to 100 or more residents; they hunted game animals in the valleys, fished in lakes, harvested wild cereal grasses in the nearby foothills, and exchanged bitumen, salt, sulfur, or fresh water for more exotic materials like turquoise, obsidian, or cowrie shells. These changes involved not only new kinds of relationships between people and their environments but also new patterns of social relations between members of the same group and between different social units.

By 10,000 years ago the ancient peoples of the Near East had already developed new perceptions of what parts of their environments constituted economically important resources; some of these elements were used for food while others were used for tools, jewelry, or goods to be exchanged with distant peoples. They intensified the acquisition or production of these goods by spending more time to exploit them or exploiting them more efficiently with new kinds of tools, techniques, or forms of labor organization. And they entered into new kinds of relations with the wild animals and plants they used for food. They restricted the movement of herd animals like goats and gazelles; they captured and tamed young animals; they modified the age and sex structure of herds; and eventually they controlled breeding within the herd. They brought wild grains and then other plants out of their natural habitats, planted them near their settlements, harvested them once they had ripened, and saved some of the seeds to plant the following year. By controlling animal breeding and planting seeds in places where the plants did not grow naturally, these groups were subjecting the wild species to new selection pressures that ultimately modified their appearance and genetic composition and slowly made them economically more desirable. Agriculture probably began among those groups which increased production to meet demands for greater per capita food consumption; it originated in those contexts in which the demand for more food outstripped the regenerative capacity of the local environment and domesticated plants and animals eventually became more important than the indigenous wild species.

Early food-producing settlements in the Near East.

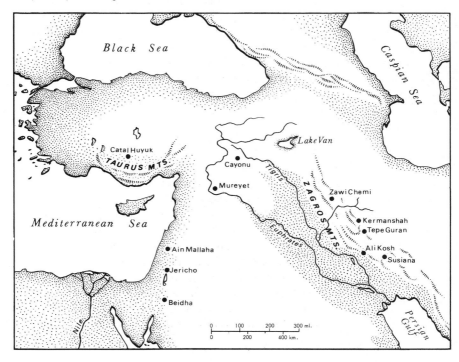

The kinds of social relations that were developing in this area facilitated some of the economic changes that were taking place. These relations reflected new patterns of cooperation and competition and new forms of property ownership that were unknown to the most ancient peoples in the area. As particular localized resources—a herd or a certain field—gained importance, people began to live more or less permanently in close proximity to the animals or pieces of land they claimed as their own. Resources that had once been shared with the members of other social units were now defended by members of the controlling community. Judging from burial practices that developed early, this sense of community—of belonging to the same social unit—was expressed in terms of descent from a common ancestor. As a result, each social unit included both living and dead members. The dead were particularly important because they were the connecting links between the living and the common ancestor; they defined an individual's place in the group and his or her share of its wealth. The construction of year-round settlements in close proximity to the property owned by the group and to the cemeteries where the dead were buried enhanced other tendencies that were already present among these early peoples: the desire to accumulate objects; the need to construct immobile facilities like storage pits, canals, or dams; the need to increase production even further; and the tendency for the group to become larger as labor becomes more valuable. Finally, judging from the continual increase in both the quantity and the variety of exotic materials found at archaeological sites, these peoples were entering into alliances or exchange relationships with groups living at ever-greater distances.

The transformation of hunting and gathering societies into societies with effective food-producing economies occurred in different ways and at different rates in various parts of the ancient East. Since there were various pathways leading to the development or adoption of effective food production, let us trace how this transformation took place in three different areas of the Near East.

The Zagros Mountains	The Zagros Mountains mark the western edge of the Iranian Plateau and separate it from the Mesopotamian lowlands of modern Iraq. The Zagros consist of a series of parallel mountain ranges rising between 2,000 and 5,000 feet above sea level. These ranges are separated by intermontane valleys formed by both permanent and seasonal rivers wending their way to the great plain of Mesopotamia. The summers are hot and dry in the Zagros; it rains during the cool winter months, and the parched earth turns green with vegetation. Wild wheat and barley occur naturally in the region and ripen in late spring after the rains have stopped. Oak and pistachio trees grow on the slopes overlooking the intermontane valleys.

Zawi Chemi   Between 9000 and 8000 BC small groups of hunters and gatherers moved seasonally through the valleys of the Zagros, following migratory game and stopping at different places when local plant foods such as wild cereal grasses, lentils, acorns, and pistachios ripened. Zawi Chemi, located in the oak–pistachio woodlands of northernmost Iraq, was one of these seasonal camps. People camped here on and off during the summer months for nearly 1,000 years. The first inhabitants hunted a variety of wild animals; the bones recovered at the site indicate that they were particularly fond of goat, sheep, and red deer.

By 8000 BC the people of Zawi Chemi were no longer engaged exclusively in hunting and wild-plant collecting. The high proportion of bones from young male sheep in the refuse deposits suggest that herding was becoming an economically important activity along the edge of the Zagros Mountains. The sheep in these deposits are anatomically similar to wild forms rather than to the later domesticated forms found in the area. This suggests that the people had captured wild sheep and were keeping herds composed mainly of females and young juveniles; presumably, a few males were kept for breeding purposes.

The group moved its herd from one place to another as pasturage became available. At Zawi Chemi, the people probably lived in small, circular, temporary huts. The presence of storage pits, mortars, grinding slabs, and basket impressions in contemporary deposits in a nearby cave indicates that they also collected and processed wild plant foods.

Ali Kosh   Ali Kosh on the Khuzistan Plain in east–central Iran provides us with more information about the daily lives of these nomadic herders and their descendants. The site is located in the winter grasslands outside the oak and pistachio woodlands on the flanks of the Zagros. When the settlement was first occupied, about 7900 BC, winter rains filled a natural depression on the plain, and at that time it may have been a semipermanent swamp bordered by rushes and sedges.

During the earliest occupation of Ali Kosh—the *Bus Mordeh Phase*— the inhabitants built small, rectangular houses of unfired clay bricks. The rooms were no more than six by eight feet. They had wide doorways and floors of stamped mud or clay. The roofs were made of mats woven from rushes or sedges collected at the nearby swamp. These huts were scattered over an area of about an acre, and the population of the settlement was probably between 50 and 100.

In the spring the residents of Ali Kosh collected wild plant foods such as wild alfalfa, milk vetch, and the fruit of wild capers, which were native to northern Khuzistan. In addition, they planted emmer wheat and two-row hulled barley, two annual grasses that are not native to the region. These economically important plants were probably grown in the mud flats around the swamp. Goat herding was a major subsistence activity. Most of the goats that were consumed were young; only one-third of the flock reached the age of 3, and most of these individuals were females chosen for breeding. The goats were almost identical to the wild forms found in the mountains to the west. Sheep were also herded, but they were only one-tenth as numerous as goats. Hunting and fishing constituted the other major subsistence activities that were at least as important as herding. The people of Ali Kosh hunted gazelles in tremendous numbers and also consumed wild oxen, onagers, and pigs. Seasonal waterfowl, which visited the swampy area between November and March, also formed an important part of the diet, as did fish, freshwater mussels, and turtles.

The absence of summer products in their refuse suggests that the residents of Ali Kosh left their homes at this time of the year and took their herds to summer pastures in the high mountain valleys to the east. They undoubtedly encountered other groups in the mountains during the summer months, and it is clear that they exchanged both information and commodities with those peoples. For example, a small portion of their stone tools were made of obsidian from the Lake Van region of Turkey, which is located more than 500 miles to the north. They also wore beads made of cowrie shells from the Persian Gulf, some 200 miles to the south.

As time passed, the inhabitants of Ali Kosh relied less on wild legumes and more on cultivated winter cereal grasses, which they grew in the mud flats around the marsh. This suggests that they probably increased the amount of land under cultivation, thereby reducing the abundance of wild plants in the vicinity of the settlement. They continued to consume goats, which by now were clearly domesticated, and the number of sheep in their herds was gradually increasing. They hunted gazelles, onagers, and wild cattle with increased vigor. Their village was still the only one in the area, and its population was not noticeably larger than it had been earlier. They still pastured their herds in the high mountain grasslands during the summers, and continued to meet peoples from other communities who were also pasturing their animals in the mountains. Their goats came into contact with those from other herds; they mated with them in the late summer, and new genetic traits, such as medially flattened horn cores, gradually became established in the Ali Kosh herds. The people also acquired things from distant places while they were residing in these summer herding camps: seashells from the Persian Gulf, obsidian from eastern Turkey, copper from central Iran, and turquoise from the area around the Afghanistan border.

The people of Ali Kosh still grew only emmer wheat and two-row barley during the *Mohammad Jaffar Phase,* which lasted from 6000 to 5600 BC. However, they had changed the appearance of the area around their village. A lot of the natural ground cover had been removed as the area under cultivation and the amount of grazing land increased. Changes in the kinds of weeds found in the refuse indicate that the farmers had to weed their fields carefully and that some of the fields stood fallow in any given year. As the amount of farm land increased, the herders had to go farther afield to find pasture for their animals. Judging from the animal bones in the refuse, herding was much more important economically than it had been earlier. As the herds became larger, the amount of pasture available to gazelles and other herbivores diminished. The residents of Ali Kosh still hunted these ungulates, perhaps more intensively than before, which suggests that they kept sheep and goats for their wool, hair, and milk rather than their meat.

Their village now covered nearly three acres and may have had as many as 150 to 270 residents. Furthermore, there may have been two other settlements nearby that were roughly the same size as Ali Kosh. The people of these villages were very much like those of Ali Kosh. They farmed, herded, and hunted wild animals and birds during the winter and early spring. As the hot, dry summer approached, they left their homes on the plain and traveled with their herds to pastures high in the mountains, where they would stay until the fall.

Tepe Guran   Their contemporaries 100 miles or more to the north in Luristan and around Kermanshah were beginning to organize their lives differently. They lived in the same place throughout the year. The earliest year-round village in Luristan appeared about 6200 BC at Tepe Guran. The inhabitants lived in mud-walled huts and exploited the wide range of resources found on the valley floor and in the neighboring hills. They grew barley, collected pistachios, herded sheep and goats, and hunted a variety of wild animals, especially small species like hedgehogs that had been relatively unimportant before. It is quite likely that the reason they were able to live in the same place all year was that the resources they needed in different seasons were found in close proximity to each other; as a result, the villagers never had to travel more than an hour or so in any direction to get what they needed.

Villages of the Deh Luran Plain   Between 5500 and 5000 BC an important change occurred on the Deh Luran Plain, where the old village of Ali Kosh was located. The people began to use simple water management systems that ultimately increased agricultural production. By this time they had moved their villages from the edge of the seasonally flooded marsh to places near the streams that flowed out of the mountains to the north. The streams provided water during the winter rainy season, and with very little effort this water could be diverted through ditches to nearby fields. Although farming probably continued to depend mainly on rainfall during this period, any water control system, however simple, provided insurance against crop failures or poor harvests in years when the rains were late or inadequate. The farmers used hoes of polished stone attached to wooden handles with asphalt to break up the alluvial soils around the streams. They planted new, more productive varieties of wheat and barley as well as the older forms. They also raised lentils, vetch, and flax or linseed and left behind the remains of almonds that may have either been grown or collected from wild trees on the hills overlooking the plain.

The villagers also raised domestic goats and sheep. The latter were becoming the most common domesticated animals in the region, possibly because they have a panting mechanism that allows them to survive better than other animals in the hot, dry climates of the Khuzistan steppe. Domestic cattle, smaller than the wild forms, also appeared for the first time. They were used for food at first and later as beasts of burden.

At least six villages on the margins of the Deh Luran Plain date to this period. Each was as large and populous as the earlier villages in the area. The total population of the area probably ranged between 600 and 1,500. Seventy miles to the southeast on the rolling plain of Susiana, more than thirty villages were occupied on a year-round basis at this time. Each of the villages on the Deh Luran Plain, as well as those at Susiana, was probably surrounded by intensively cultivated fields. As time passed, however, these fields became increasingly saline as the irrigation waters brought various salts to the surface. The villagers began to grow greater amounts of barley, which had a higher tolerance for alkaline soils than wheat. The new farming methods led to the destruction of extensive areas of natural vegetation, and ultimately to a decline in the number of wild ungulates found in the region.

There is no evidence that the villages on the Deh Luran Plain were linked to each other either economically or politically at that time. Although it is clear that their residents exchanged ideas and information with each other, there is no way of demonstrating that one village was more important or more prestigious than another. In terms of production, the village may well have been the largest production unit, owning both the agricultural fields and the herds. The household, composed of a relatively small number of individuals, was probably the consumption unit for most commodities. There is some evidence for a technical division of labor in the sense that some economically important activities—for example, farming and herding—had to be performed during the same season. It is also clear that some members of the community spent part of their time weaving wool and flax or making pottery during the summer months.

The Levant

Between 10,000 and 8000 BC small groups of people moved seasonally through the ecological zones of the Levant in which wild cereal grasses grew. They harvested wild wheat and barley as these grains ripened in April and May. Later in the year they collected acorns and pistachios from the woodlands on the hills overlooking the Mediterranean plain and the rocky country around the Jordan Valley. The high proportion of goat bones at sites like Beidha, near Petra, suggest that some groups herded these animals. The same sites also yield the remains of wild animals such as fallow deer, gazelles, and wild pigs, suggesting that game was used to supplement the meat provided by the herds. The nature of hunting undoubtedly varied from one area to another, depending on the kinds of wild animals present. At sites located near permanent water supplies, the inhabitants fished and hunted migratory waterfowl during the winter months.

Ain Mallaha Ain Mallaha, a settlement near the Jordan River that dates to this period, covered an area of more than 20,000 square feet. Its residents lived in fifty or so semisubterranean circular huts. The diameters of the huts ranged from about 8 to 27 feet, and their floor areas ranged from 50 to more than 500 square feet. Perhaps as many as 200 individuals lived in this camp. They buried their dead outside the houses. Some of the burials were

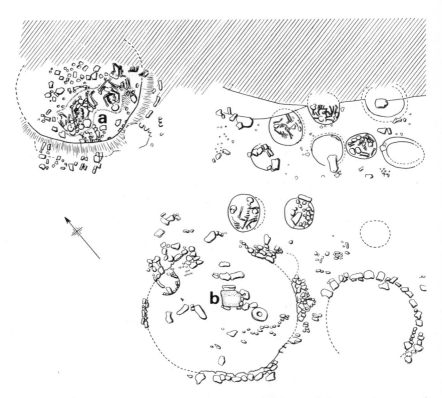

A portion of the village at Ain Mallaha with circular houses and storage pits, some of which were reused for burials. James Mellaart, **Earliest civilizations of the Near East** (London: Thames and Hudson Ltd., 1965), fig. 5, p. 23.

primary in the sense that the individual was interred at the time that he or she died. Others were secondary; the individual had presumably died elsewhere and his or her remains had been brought back to the base camp. Jewelry was common in the burials at Ain Mallaha; there were frontlets, bonnets, and necklaces made of dentalium shells from the Mediterranean, and necklaces made from gazelle bones.

Mureybet   Mureybet is a somewhat more recent settlement on the east bank of the Euphrates River in the steppe country south of Aleppo. It was first occupied about 8600 BC, during the *Natufian Phase*. Around 8000 BC the inhabitants of Mureybet lived in about 200 round huts. They hunted a variety of steppe-dwelling herbivores such as gazelles and aurochs. They also relied extensively on shellfish and aquatic birds from the river. Wild einkorn wheat and barley have been found in the refuse deposits, along with vetch and lentils. The legumes and weeds were probably part of the natural vegetation of the area. However, wild einkorn wheat and barley would have been found naturally only in the higher lands more than 100 miles to the north. This suggests that the inhabitants of Mureybet brought the wild cereal grasses from their natural habitat in the high country and planted them in a manmade environment near their camp. The process of planting, weeding, and caring for the young plants, as well as protecting them from birds and other animal pests, requires continual attention. Thus, the villagers must have decided that it was advantageous to stay near their fields and settlement for a major portion of each year.

By 7500 BC the village of Mureybet covered more than seven acres and its residents lived in rectangular houses with walls made of limestone slabs. One house had nearly 200 square feet of floor space, and another was divided into four rooms, each about five feet square. The residents placed the horn cores from cattle in the walls of one structure. They placed detached human skulls in the corners of three rooms and covered them with debris and red clay. They reburied several individuals, who had presumably died elsewhere, under the floors of several other buildings.

Jericho   About the same time, a small village in the Jericho oasis near the modern city of Jerusalem was becoming larger. The inhabitants lived in round or oval houses with diameters of 15 feet or more; the houses were made of molded mud bricks and sunk into the ground. They were spread out over an area of ten acres and completely engulfed the earlier settlement at the oasis. Later the inhabitants built a stone wall around the village, which may have housed as many as 650 people by that time.

There were no domesticated animals at Jericho during this period. The villagers either hunted or herded gazelles, their main source of meat; they also hunted wild cattle, pigs, and goats. By 7500 BC or shortly afterward they were growing two-row hulled barley and emmer wheat. The inhabitants of Jericho had brought these plants out of their natural habitats in the oak–pistachio woodlands of the upland areas and had planted them in the well-watered lowlands around the oasis. In addition, they were collecting lentils and figs, which probably grew naturally around the settlement.

Cayönü A different pattern of development occurs at Cayönü, a settlement on the banks of a stream south of the Taurus Mountains that was occupied from 7500 to 6800 BC. The first inhabitants had domesticated dogs. They hunted a variety of wild animals—sheep, goats, pigs, cattle, and red deer—and grew wild forms of emmer and einkorn wheat. Wild barley, which was native to the area, was economically unimportant. They also gathered pistachios, almonds, vetch, and flax from the nearby area. The later residents of Cayönü relied extensively on domesticated animals—sheep, goats, and probably pigs; however, they continued to hunt wild cattle and red deer in considerable numbers. They grew domesticated forms of emmer and einkorn wheat, lentils, and chick peas, and gathered nuts and berries from the surrounding hills. Within a few hundred years the economic orientation of the villagers had shifted from hunting and gathering to food production supplemented by significant amounts of wild game and plant foods.

Cayönü is located about 15 miles from a source of native copper and malachite ores. The inhabitants of the settlement were obviously attracted by the shining red copper ore and the bright green malachite ores, which could be shaped into objects. The earliest known cold-hammered copper objects—pins and drilled beads—occur there.

Beidha In about 7000 BC the inhabitants of Beidha, a site in the rocky desert of southern Jordan, lived in clusters of round houses. Each cluster contained a few houses and some storerooms, enclosed by a stone wall. Open work spaces separated the clusters. The village burned down in about 6600 BC; when it was rebuilt, a group of large rectangular houses dominated the center of the settlement. Later the residents built rectangular rooms that were grouped together and opened off long corridors. Heavy buttresses in the walls of these corridor houses suggest that some of them may have supported second stories. The lower rooms off the corridors may have been workshops in which the residents made bone tools, polished-stone implements, and drilled beads.

Archaeologists have found a number of headless burials at various sites dating from the seventh millenium BC. Sometimes the head was buried near the rest of the body, but more often it was buried separately or kept in a room. The inhabitants of Beidha, Jericho, and other sites in the Levant restored the facial features of these skulls with plaster and paint. The elaborately restored skulls are frequently assumed to indicate some form of ancestor worship. At Jericho, archaeologists have found fragments of a number of life-sized plaster figures that may have been substitutes for real skulls.

The Economy of the Levant   The subsistence economy of the peoples of the Levant was based on a combination of herding, hunting, agriculture, and wild-plant collecting. Domesticated goats were the most common herd animals, though sheep were also known at some settlements. The people hunted a variety of game animals—gazelles, aurochs, wild pigs, and deer—which continued to provide a significant portion of the meat they consumed. Interestingly, they no longer hunted birds or fished, as their ancestors had. The cereal grasses—wheat and barley—were the plants they grew most often. These were grown at virtually every settlement in the Levant during this period. The inhabitants of the Levant also collected a variety of wild plants—acorns, almonds, pistachios, chick peas, and lentils—from the woodlands and fields around their settlements. These wild plant foods provided them with important vegetable fat and protein supplements.

Anatolia

The Anatolian Plateau of Turkey lies between two mountain ranges: the Pontic Mountains to the north and the Taurus to the south. Grassy steppe and fertile basins cover this gently rolling plain. Archaeologists have found a number of ancient settlements on the plateau; they are particularly abundant in the southern half.

Catal Hüyük is perhaps the most important of the early sites. It is located on the Konya Plain of southern Anatolia. The plain lies about 3,000 feet above sea level and is a region of interior drainage, like the Great Basin of the Western United States, where streams flowing out of the mountains empty into saline lakes or disappear. The Konya Plain was probably covered with lakes about 10,000 years ago. As these began to dry up at the end of the Pleistocene, fertile land appeared and a variety of plants and animals invaded the newly exposed lands from the surrounding areas. A large marsh filled the sink in the center of the basin, and the Carsamba River flowed out of the mountains toward the swampy area in the middle of the plain. A wide variety of animals—deer, aurochs, gazelles, leopards, ibex, sheep, goats, and pigs—lived in the complicated life zones of the Taurus Mountains and the Konya Plain. Birds and tortoises were plentiful around the swamp, and the lakes and rivers teemed with fish and freshwater clams.

Catal Hüyük straddled one of the branches of the Carsamba River that flowed out of the mountains to the south and ultimately disappeared on the arid steppe lands of the Konya Plain. The ancient site covered more than 32 acres, of which about one acre was excavated during the early 1960s. Radiocarbon measurements from various early levels indicate that it was occupied between 6500 and 5600 BC. The excavations revealed more than a dozen building stages during this period, as well as the existence of still earlier cultural deposits that have yet to be excavated. The most thoroughly studied levels date from about 6000 BC.

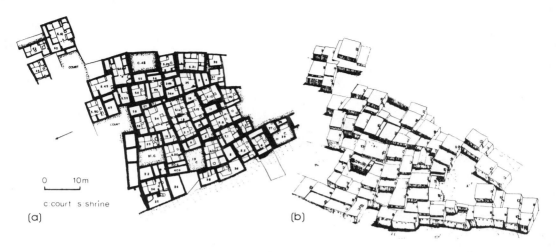

Catal Hüyük. (a) Plan of the southeast quarter of the settlement. (b) Reconstruction of the southeast quarter. James Mellaart, **The Neolithic of the Near East** (New York: Scribner's, 1975), fig. 46, p. 101. Copyright © 1975 by Thames and Hudson, Ltd. Used by permission of Charles Scribner's Sons.

The residents of Catal Hüyük built their houses on a gentle slope overlooking the river and the plain that stretched in the distance. Their houses were rectangular, about 15 by 20 feet, and consisted of a single room with a raised platform extending around three walls. The platform on the south wall was a kitchen area with a hearth, an oven, and a place to store fuel. There was a hole in the flat roof above the kitchen area that allowed smoke to leave the room and through which people entered, crawling down a ladder to the floor. A small window high on the downhill wall admitted light to the room. Many of the white plastered walls were painted with murals that depicted scenes from the daily life of the settlement. The people built their houses next to each other and shared small courtyards where they disposed of garbage and sewage.

Each household probably consisted of three to eight individuals. The total population of the town, assuming that all 32 acres were occupied at the same time, varied from 2,000 to almost 10,000 persons, with a figure of about 4,000 to 5,000 most likely. More than 400 burials were recovered in the excavations, and these reveal a great deal about the people who lived at Catal Hüyük. Infant and child mortality were high. Nearly 40 percent of the infants died before reaching maturity. Women lived to be about 30, while men had a life expectancy of about 34 years. The typical woman who survived to the age of 30 had four children. Some of the individuals who lived at Catal Hüyük had at least one parent who had been born elsewhere, as determined from hereditary features of teeth and skeletons. Many of the

133

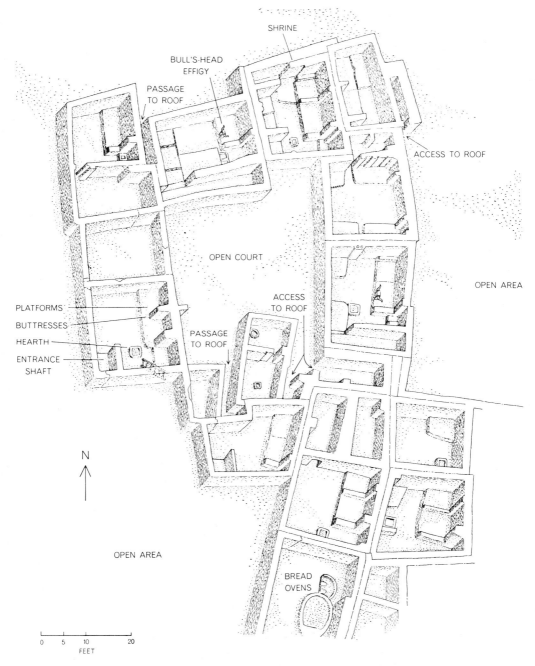

PASSAGE TO ROOF

BULL'S-HEAD EFFIGY

SHRINE

ACCESS TO ROOF

OPEN COURT

OPEN AREA

PLATFORMS

BUTTRESSES

HEARTH

ENTRANCE SHAFT

ACCESS TO ROOF

PASSAGE TO ROOF

N

OPEN AREA

BREAD OVENS

0   5   10   20
        FEET

Çatal Hüyük. The arrangement of households, shrines, and courtyards in the community.
James Mellaart. A Neolithic city in Turkey, **Scientific American,** 210, no. 4 (1964), 95.
Copyright © 1964 by Scientific American, Inc. All rights reserved.

people suffered from malaria, which undoubtedly affected their life expectancy. Others suffered broken bones from falling, and still others were injured in fights. At least one individual was gored by a bull and died as a result.

The inhabitants grew einkorn and emmer wheat in the wet ground around the swamp a little way downriver from the settlement. The need to use wet ground for farming forced them to live close to the swamp, in spite of the fact that there were many malaria-carrying mosquitoes there. Five or six miles from the town, the ground was higher and drier, offering a much more satisfactory place to live, but the moisture in the soil was not dependable enough for growing crops. To live in a drier and healthier place, the people would have had to have walked more than five miles to the swamp. This would have taken far too much time, so they chose to live closer to their fields, where they could also drive off unwanted predators like birds and hunt deer and other ungulates, which provided meat and other important raw materials. Their wheat fields undoubtedly attracted wild game and, as a result, actually enhanced the importance of hunting in their economy. Besides hunting and farming, the people of Catal Hüyük harvested wild legumes from the area around the settlement and collected nuts and wild fruits from the hills to the south. They had small herds of domesticated cattle that provided roughly 90 percent of the meat they consumed, as well as transport for raw materials like wood and obsidian that were brought from the hills.

Nearly one-quarter of the structures excavated at Catal Hüyük have been identified as shrines. These vary in size but tend to be larger and more elaborately decorated than other buildings in the settlement. They often have highly elaborate wall paintings, plaster reliefs of animals or rows of cattle horns set into the walls, and statues or human skulls arranged on the platforms next to the walls. In addition, women and children were often buried under the floors or under the benches around the walls. The individuals interred in the shrines tend to have more goods buried with them, including items like Red Sea cowrie shells or Syrian flint daggers that came from places hundreds of miles away.

People were also buried in the houses, under the floors and under the sleeping platforms around the walls. When an individual died, his or her body apparently was exposed to the elements until the flesh had disappeared. The skeleton was then wrapped in cloth or animal skins and placed in the house, where it usually joined other burials. Most of the burials lacked grave goods, except for a few containers of food and occasional tools or weapons.

The murals on the shrine walls are particularly important because they provide information about the organization of some of the economic activities conducted at the settlement. A mural in one shrine depicts a hunting scene with fifteen men attacking a stag. Another mural in the same shrine shows a group of thirty individuals, mostly men, standing around a great bull; one of the individuals in the scene is more elaborately dressed and seems to be standing back and overseeing the activities of the others. These wall paintings suggest that hunting was carried out by groups of fifteen to thirty men, depending on the quarry. The men in these hunting parties may well have belonged to the same production units, which were centered in the shrines. For certain activities the members of two or more shrines may have banded together. It is also likely that the men depicted in these hunting scenes resided in different households and belonged to different consumption units.

SOCIAL AND ECONOMIC CHANGE IN THE ANCIENT EAST

By 5000 BC many people in the Near East sustained themselves through agricultural production and lived in small villages with about 100 residents. These farming communities developed along different pathways in different areas. The groups living in the Zagros Mountains had already domesticated animals by 8900 BC; later they domesticated wheat and barley, which occurred naturally in small stands throughout the area; eventually they adopted plants that had been brought under domestication elsewhere. Agricultural production slowly gained importance among the inhabitants of this ecologically diverse area. At first domesticated animals were far more important than plants. This fact was reflected in the settlement patterns of these peoples. They lived in small, transient settlements that reflected the seasonal movement of animals from one pasture to another; year-round settlements, presumably with division of labor between farmers and herders, did not become common until the sixth millenium BC.

The inhabitants of the Levant lived in substantial permanent or semipermanent settlements with several hundred residents well before they brought plants and animals under domestication or adopted any that had been domesticated elsewhere. They built villages with substantial architecture in localities with considerable ecological diversity—that is, along the boundaries between different environmental zones; since they could exploit the resources of these different areas, they enhanced the range of wild plant and animal foods available to them in the immediate vicinity of their homes. Although domesticated plants were known as early as 7000 BC, agricultural production based on domesticated animals as well as plants did not become economically important in this area until the sixth millenium BC.

The people of the Anatolian Plateau domesticated indigenous plants and animals during the eighth millenium BC. Initially they depended more on wild species than on domesticated ones; however, the shift from wild species to domesticated ones occurred more rapidly here than elsewhere in the Near East. This change was reflected in the relatively early—seventh millenium BC—appearance of permanent settlements in the area.

The Significance of Agriculture

Agriculture began among those peoples who had to deal with demands for greater per capita production. Four factors contributed to the initial success and further development of agricultural production in the Near East. First, new relations of production emerged among the inhabitants of the area. Second, these peoples developed new kinds of tools and techniques to exploit economically important resources in a more efficient manner. Third, the practices of stockbreeding and planting ultimately led to changes in the frequency with which certain genes appeared—genes that produced traits that were viewed as either desirable or economically important. Fourth, as herding and agriculture became increasingly important activities and took place over wider areas, those areas were modified as large numbers of unimportant wild species were gradually replaced by a smaller number of domesticated ones; while the productivity of these areas increased, their ecological diversity and stability were reduced.

New Social Relations

Let us consider the new kinds of social relations that developed at this time in more detail. It is clear that the late Pleistocene societies of the Near East had all the necessary prerequisites for developing efficient food-producing economies. These small, highly mobile groups had relatively stable memberships —a fact that undoubtedly was related to their attachments to particular herds of animals and perhaps to particular stands of wild cereal grasses and plants. This stability of membership—reflected in concepts of ownership or access to property, such as a particular herd or localized resource area —meant that labor could be organized on a more or less permanent basis and that the members of the group could carry out a series of tasks that had to be performed sequentially over an extended period. This kind of labor organization was absolutely essential for any sort of reliance on agricultural production, with its clearly defined sequence of tasks and delayed payoffs.

The Role of Ancestors

The elaborate burial practices that developed in the Near East, especially in the Levant and Anatolia, suggest that these ancient peoples had an ideology in which the dead played important roles. This ideology emphasized descent, stressed the continued involvement of the departed ancestors in the daily affairs of the group, and reflected the maintenance of ownership of localized resources over a number of generations. The dead defined the individual's place in the group and, consequently, his or her share of its wealth; these relationships undoubtedly were expressed in terms of kinship, with the kinds of rights and obligations that kin ties involve. Moreover, the dead were brought back to permanent or semipermanent settlements, where they were interred as secondary burials under house floors and their skulls were kept as mementos in the corners of rooms. The presence of deceased ancestors was a symbolic expression of ownership, not only of the settlements themselves but also of the localized resource areas found in close proximity to them. Differences in the quality and quantity of grave goods from one burial to another reflected differences in the status or wealth of the various production or consumption units that made up the larger society.

The Organization of Labor

Labor was organized in various ways in these early communities. Certain craft activities, such as pottery making and weaving, apparently were carried out by the members of each residential unit, presumably on a seasonal and part-time basis; the goods produced in their workshops were used by the members of that residential unit or perhaps by a small number of closely related residential units. Other craft activities—jewelry making, for example—were also carried out in household workshops; however, there were fewer such workshops, which suggests that the goods produced in them had wider circulation in the community as a whole. The work associated with other productive activities—herding, hunting, farming, or fishing—seems to have been carried out by production units that included individuals from more than one household. It is also clear that there were technical divisions of labor in these early social units, judging from the fact that their members were simultaneously carrying out a series of different economically important activities. The various work teams, or production units, engaged in these activities shared the products of their labor with each other. At first this exchange occurred within the group; it may have been nothing more than the reciprocal exchange of one product for an equivalent amount of something else. As time passed, however, various communities began to establish wider networks of relationships with other groups, and the volume of exchange began to increase. This is reflected in the archaeological record by the appearance of exotic materials from distant places, by the presence of new genetic traits in the goat herds of Ali Kosh, and later by the evidence of genetic admixture to the population of Catal Hüyük.

Exchange

Exchange may have been one of the methods used by the members of these communities to level out differences in the amounts produced by different production units. Units that produced surpluses—more than their members needed for a particular period—may have given feasts for the rest of the community at which they shared their surplus production with less fortunate relatives. They gained prestige in return for their generosity. In other words, exchange was a means for creating alliances, not only between different production units in the same community but also between different communities.

FURTHER READINGS

Bender, Barbara
1978 Gatherer–hunter to farmer: a social perspective. *World Archaeology,* 10, no. 2, October, pp. 204–222.

Fairservis, Walter A., Jr.
1975 *The threshold of civilization; an experiment in prehistory.* Scribner's, New York.

Flannery, Kent V.
1969 Origins and ecological effects of early domestication in Iran and the Near East. In *The domestication and exploitation of plants and animals,* ed. Peter J. Ucko and G. W. Dimbleby, pp. 73–100. Gerald Duckworth, London.
1972 The origins of the village as a settlement type in Mesoamerica and the Near East; a comparative study. In *Man, settlement and urbanism,* ed. Peter J. Ucko, Ruth Tringham, and G. W. Dimbleby, pp. 23–54. Gerald Duckworth, London.

Hole, Frank
1968 Evidence of social organization from western Iran, 8000–4000 BC. In *New perspectives in archaeology,* ed. Sally R. Binford and Lewis R. Binford, pp. 245–266. Aldine-Atherton, Chicago.

Hole, Frank, Kent V. Flannery, and James A. Neely
1969 Prehistory and human ecology of the Deh Luran Plain. *Memoirs of the Museum of Anthropology, University of Michigan,* no. 1.

Mellaart, James
1975 *The Neolithic of the Near East.* Scribner's, New York.

Redman, Charles L.
1978 *The rise of civilization; from early farmer to urban society in the ancient Near East.* W. H. Freeman, San Francisco.

Wright, Gary A.
1971 Origins of food production in southwestern Asia; a survey of ideas. *Current Anthropology,* 12, nos. 4–5, pp. 447–578.

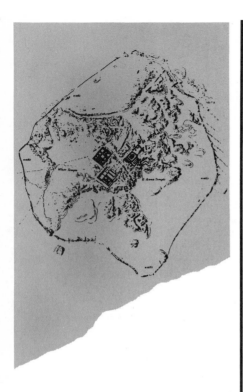

Ancient Peoples of Mesopotamia

Mesopotamian civilization developed in Iraq and the adjacent parts of Iran, Turkey, and Syria during the fourth millenium BC and flourished into the first millenium AD. The phrase *Mesopotamian civilization* expresses the unity of what happened there, the particular form of civilization that emerged and transformed itself, without playing down the fact that within the area different peoples solved the problems of daily life in different ways. They had to import plants and animals that had been domesticated elsewhere to make life livable in a country continually threatened by drought, floods, and the ever-present danger of the desert spreading onto arable land. They had to find more and richer land for their crops. They had to protect themselves from the torrential floods that occurred each year along the rivers. And they had to build elaborate systems of canals, dams, and reservoirs to control and store the water that was so necessary for their survival.

The plains of Mesopotamia are composed of a number of different landscapes. There are stretches of fertile land along the Tigris and Euphrates rivers and their tributaries where irrigation agriculture is possible. There are narrow valleys along the edges of the plain and in the foothills beyond where there is enough rain each year to grow cereal grains and fruit trees. There are areas between the two rivers where crops can be grown, but the productivity of these lands varies enormously because of differences in soil quality and rainfall. There are areas between the cultivated fields and the barren stretches of stone and sand where herds of sheep and goats can graze. And finally there is the desert itself, a sea of continually shifting sand that flows relentlessly into the fields and pastures of the peoples who dwell on the plain.

8

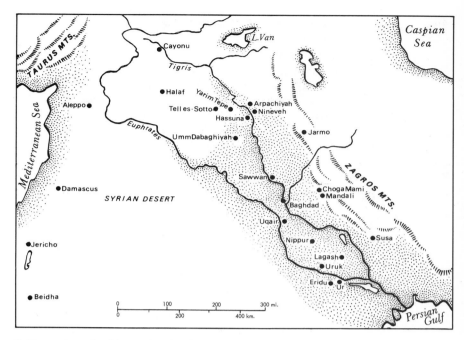

Settlements on the Mesopotamian Plain.

Each of these landscapes supported a particular combination of food resources. These resources became available at different times of the year, required different amounts and kinds of labor, needed different kinds of capital investments (such as specialized tools or elaborate irrigation systems), and varied enormously in productivity. These landscapes rarely existed in isolation. As a result, most of the ancient peoples that lived on the Mesopotamian plain utilized the resources found in a cluster of adjacent landscapes.

These economic facts helped create the various ways of life that emerged in different parts of ancient Mesopotamia. To use the resources found in the various constellations of landscapes, the ancient peoples developed different combinations of tools, techniques, and labor power. For example, the productive forces required to work an area composed mainly of small garden plots where spring and summer vegetables were grown were different from those needed to work large fields of wheat or barley or to herd animals that had to move from one pasture to another.

The tools the people used and the experience and skills they had were not the only factors involved in satisfying the necessities of life. In order to produce what they needed, the ancient peoples of Mesopotamia entered into socially defined relationships of production, which, in turn, conditioned their political structures and ideologies.

Thousands of clay tablets recovered from a number of settlements in ancient Mesopotamia provide insights into the nature of those relationships.

These tablets are concerned with economic matters. They record the day-to-day workings of bureaucracies that organized agricultural and commodity production; administered long-distance trade for raw materials that were not available locally; rented fields and gardens; collected taxes; provided rations and wages to work forces composed of men, women, and children; and managed the distribution of food and other goods among the members of powerful temple or palace communities.

The lords of these temple or palace communities, be they gods or kings, were central figures in the economic units that owned much of the arable land, controlled production and exchange, and shaped the daily lives of people through labor drafts and rationing. In the south, these organizations exerted political control over small regions that, in later times, consisted of a city surrounded by towns, farming hamlets, manorial estates, agricultural lands, and pastures. The center of these political entities was the main temple of the city, which provided certain services to the people it served and received cooperation and loyalty in return. In the north, palace organizations exerted political control over dispersed farming communities. The king was the center of these political entities, which combined the idea of royalty with that of a national religion.

In this chapter we will examine two related problems: (1) How did the temple and palace organizations develop in ancient Mesopotamia? (2) How did they function?

EARLY COMMUNITIES ON THE MESOPOTAMIAN PLAIN

Rich winter pasture covers the rolling plain of Mesopotamia, and herds of gazelles, onagers, and other herbivores grazed over much of the area for thousands of years. The plain was undoubtedly inhabited by wandering bands of hunters and gatherers, and perhaps herders, long before the first permanent settlements were established there. However, there is little archaeological evidence from the period before 6000 BC, for two reasons. One reason is that archaeologists have only recently begun to explore the ancient land surfaces of northern Mesopotamia. The other reason is that each year the land surfaces of southern Mesopotamia are covered by new layers of alluvium deposited by the flooding Tigris and Euphrates rivers; as a result, ancient archaeological sites are likely to be covered by many feet of soil that has accumulated over the years.

Umm
Dabaghiyah

One of the earliest settlements in northern Mesopotamia was Umm Dabaghiyah, which was occupied briefly around 6000 BC or not long afterward. The village covered about two acres in a steppe environment at the very edge of the area where rainfall agriculture was possible. The buildings were made of packed mud. Two of the buildings contained regular rows of small, cell-like rooms that were entered through the roof. These were probably communal storehouses that enclosed three sides of a central courtyard. The houses consisted of a series of small rooms connected by low doorways through which the inhabitants crawled when they wanted to go from one room to the next. Hooded fireplaces and plastered cupboards lined the south walls of the kitchen—living areas. Grinding stones were set in the plastered floors nearby. In some of the houses toeholds had been cut into the plastered and painted walls, which suggests that they had trapdoors opening onto flat roofs. The houses also had doorways that opened into narrow alleys leading toward the central courtyard.

The agricultural lands around Umm Dabaghiyah are only marginally productive today; however, traces of einkorn and emmer wheat, barley, peas, and lentils in the refuse deposits around the settlement suggest that at least some of the 100 or so residents of the village engaged in farming on a part-time basis. The villagers also had a variety of domesticated animals—cattle, goats, sheep, pigs, and dogs; however, gazelles and wild onagers provided most of the meat they consumed. In fact, onager hunting may have been the villagers' major occupation. A wall painting in a building near the central courtyard depicts five running onagers surrounded by hooked figures that have been interpreted as wooden stakes supporting a net; behind the onagers are hunters brandishing weapons and stampeding the animals into the enclosure. It may well be that Umm Dabaghiyah was a trading outpost whose residents were involved primarily in exporting onager skins and other animal products to other communities.

Tell es-Sotto

Tell es-Sotto lies seventy miles north of Umm Dabaghiyah. The site is important because of the cultural stratigraphy that occurs there. The first inhabitants used pottery and other tools that were essentially identical to those found at Umm Dabaghiyah. The later occupants of the settlement used a kind of pottery known as *Hassuna,* which has been found at more than forty other archaeological sites in northern Mesopotamia that date between about 5500 and 5000 BC.

Yarim Tepe I

Yarim Tepe I, located at the foot of the Sinjar Hills near Tell es-Sotto, is perhaps the most revealing of the Hassuna Phase settlements in northern Mesopotamia. The earliest inhabitants of Yarim Tepe I lived in small multi-room dwellings separated from each other by open spaces that permitted easy circulation through the settlement. As time passed, they enlarged the original houses by adding rooms to them, presumably to incorporate more people into the households. This construction gradually blocked the streets and alleys of the village, and movement from one place to another became progressively more difficult. After a generation or two the villagers redesigned their settlement with more open space in order to cope better with the problems of congestion created by their ancestors.

The residents of Yarim Tepe I grew cereals and legumes in the marginal farmlands near the Sinjar Hills and kept small herds of cattle, sheep, goats, and pigs. However, they obtained most of their meat from the wild cattle, boars, and gazelles that grazed beyond the limits of the settlement.

There was a great deal of industrial specialization at Yarim Tepe I. Some individuals were involved in a sophisticated metallurgy that involved smelting both copper and lead. Others made pottery in two-staged pottery kilns. Both of these activities were carried out in clearly defined areas of the settlement. In addition, communal storehouses identical to those found at Umm Dabaghiyah were used; this suggests that these structures were in widespread use during the second half of the sixth millenium BC. The inhabitants of Yarim Tepe I also used stamp seals, which, in later times, were used to identify the manufacturer or owner of portable objects.

Tell es-Sawwan and Choga Mami	Contemporary with Yarim Tepe I and other settlements where Hassuna pottery was used are towns and villages with *Samara Phase* assemblages. These settlements, dating from between about 5500 and 5000 BC, are located to the southeast, upstream from Baghdad along the alluvial plain of the Tigris River and near Mandali at the foot of the Zagros Mountains. The Samarran towns and villages are found well south of the area where rainfall agriculture is possible. Evidence from Tell es-Sawwan on the Tigris River and Choga Mami on the Mandali Plain indicates that the inhabitants of these settlements used irrigation canals to water their agricultural fields. In the Mandali area, the Samarran towns and villages are located along natural contours that parallel the nearby hills and cross natural water channels at right angles. Excavations at Choga Mami have revealed an irrigation canal following one of these contours. Small feeder channels lead from the downhill side of the large canal into arable land. The residents of the Samarran settlements were among the first people in the Near East to use irrigation systems to farm the rich alluvial soil of areas with insufficient rainfall.

At both Tell es-Sawwan and Choga Mami the people grew emmer and bread wheat as well as several varieties of barley and linseed. At Choga Mami they also grew lentils and peas and collected wild pistachios from the nearby hills. The people of Sawwan fished and gathered freshwater mussels from the river and hunted gazelles, onagers, and wild cattle. At Choga Mami fishing was not important. The inhabitants hunted deer in the hills and raised domesticated sheep, goats, and cattle. Given the abundance of cattle bones on alluvial sites by the fifth millenium BC, it is conceivable that inhabitants were already using animals to pull some kind of plow to break up the soil for planting; however, the earliest actual evidence for the use of plows dates to the latter part of the fourth millenium BC.

Tell es-Sawwan and Choga Mami were large settlements, each covering an area of ten to twelve acres. Tell es-Sawwan was built on a bluff overlooking the Tigris River; the other three sides of the settlement were surrounded by a massive wall and ditch. A tower guarded the only entrance excavated so far at Choga Mami. The inhabitants of both settlements used mold-made, dried-mud bricks to construct their buildings. The T-shaped buildings of Sawwan and the rectangular ones at Choga Mami consist of a number of small rooms separated from each other by thin interior walls. Some of the rooms were connected to form households; each household had a doorway leading to the outside. At Choga Mami, and perhaps at Tel es-Sawwan as well, a number of structures were built on top of earlier houses and incorporated the older walls as foundations. The strict adherence to the outlines of old buildings may reflect property boundaries. There is also a massive wall surrounding a number of houses at Choga Mami; it may well have enclosed some larger social unit composed of a number of distinct households.

There was a cemetery underneath one of the earliest structures at Tell es-Sawwan. More than 100 individuals, mostly infants, had been buried below the floors of the rooms in this building. The building itself contained no household goods. An alabaster statuette of a woman stood in a niche in one of the rooms, suggesting that the structure may have served as a shrine. The burials were covered with red ochre in many cases, and were wrapped in mats. They wore necklaces and bracelets made of shells and stones brought from distant places; female figurines made of alabaster and a variety of alabaster bowls and jars accompanied many of the burials. These ground-stone objects, which number in the hundreds, provide evidence of specialized craftmanship and suggest that some of the productive forces of the community were diverted to the production of what seem to be luxury goods.

The Halafian Villages

Halaf Phase settlements, which date from between about 5300 and 4400 BC, were widespread in northern Mesopotamia and beyond. Initially, the villages where high-quality Halaf pottery was used were found along the well-watered foothills of the Taurus Mountains between the upper portions of the Tigris and Euphrates Rivers. However, by about 5000 BC Halaf pottery had a much more extensive geographic distribution; it was traded as far west as the Mediterranean and northward into the Lake Van region of eastern Anatolia, where extensive obsidian deposits occur.

Arpachiyah, a small village on the Tigris River upstream from Nineveh, and Yarim Tepe II near the Sinjar Hills are the best-known Halafian settlements. The architecture of the two settlements was distinctive. There were circular buildings with stone foundations; the earlier ones had diameters ranging up to 21 feet, while the later ones were even larger—up to 35 feet in diameter, with rectangular anterooms more than 50 feet long. The circular portions of these structures were domed, while flat or gabled roofs covered the anterooms. The structures stood near the centers of the two settlements and were approached by stone-paved streets. The absence of habitation refuse around them and the fact that a large number of female figurines were found in one of the buildings at Arpachiyah have led to speculations that they served some sort of ritual purpose. Smaller, beehive-shaped dwellings made of sun-dried mud surrounded the larger public structures in both settlements. The latest buildings at Arpachiyah were rectangular rather than circular; one of them was a large hall surrounded by storerooms and workshops where potters and stoneworkers plied their craft.

The inhabitants of the Halafian villages apparently grew wheat, barley, and flax in the rain-fed fields around their settlements. The presence of flax suggests they may also have been producing linen cloth, perhaps for export. They kept small herds of goats and sheep in the pastures beyond their fields; the residents of a few villages also kept domesticated cattle.

Several lines of evidence suggest that the inhabitants of the Halafian villages produced luxury goods and may have controlled overland trade between the Mesopotamian plain and eastern Anatolia, where copper, lead, and obsidian deposits were found. Part of this evidence is that pottery kilns, workshops stacked with pottery, and a stone carver's workshop stood at the center of Arpachiyah, which suggests that the settlement may have been a center for the production of fine pottery and stone bowls—a factory and trading town rather than a farming community. A second line of evidence is the presence of Halafian settlements in eastern Anatolia, an area that provided much of the obsidian found in Mesopotamia and its environs after about 7000 BC. Further evidence is the fact that the residents of the Halafian villages were among the first people in Mesopotamia to use metal objects made of copper and lead—two resources that do not occur on the Mesopotamian plain.

THE EVOLUTION OF URBAN SOCIETY IN SOUTHERN MESOPOTAMIA

Seven thousand years ago the earliest known inhabitants of southern Mesopotamia lived in small villages on the flood plain of the Euphrates River. Marshes covered much of the area, stretching eastward toward the grasslands of Khuzistan at the foot of the Zagros Mountains and southward toward the head of the Persian Gulf. At the beginning of historical times, a series of lakes and tidal lagoons extended inland from the shores of the Persian Gulf to the area around the ancient settlements. Today, the remains of these villages are found in the desert along old, silted-up channels of the Euphrates, well away from the modern course of the river.

The 'Ubaid
Phase

The earliest of these *'Ubaid Phase* communities, as they are called, had a very limited geographic distribution; all were located between the ancient settlements known as Warka and Eridu. The site of Eridu has provided archaeologists with a long sequence of 'Ubaid building stages. Fourteen of the nineteen building levels under the corner of a ziggurat (temple platform) that dates from the latter part of the third millenium BC contained 'Ubaid pottery.

The earliest dwellings at Eridu consisted of reed huts and mud brick houses. One of the huts was divided into a number of rooms, two of which had low platforms used for cooking. The reed huts in the lower levels were often built next to mud brick walls, and at least one of them was actually an annex to a mud brick building.

The most important discovery at Eridu was the first of a series of shrines built one on top of another in the same place over a period of nearly 3,000 years. The earliest shrine was a small building about 12 feet on a side, with a projecting bay opposite the narrow doorway. An altar stood in the middle of the room; offerings were burned on it, and their ashes fell to the floor at its base. In later times these offerings included fish and birds caught in the nearby marshes. As time passed, larger, more elaborate shrines were built that preserved the basic pattern of the first one: an altar set in the middle of a small room. The seventh shrine built at Eridu was a spacious temple almost 50 feet long. It had a central nave with small rooms projecting from it; the altar was located at the narrow end of the building. The structure itself was built on a raised platform that overlooked the settlement and the marshes beyond.

By about 4800 BC 'Ubaid pottery was being used and perhaps manufactured as far north as Nippur and east of Baghdad in the Mandali oasis. Late 'Ubaid pottery, dating from between about 4400 and 4000 BC was widespread. It has been found in Saudi Arabia opposite the island of Bahrein, where it appears as an intrusive element in the debris left by the non-pottery-using peoples of the Arabian Peninsula. It also occurred in northern Syria, where timber was plentiful; in northern Iraq; and in southern Iran, where copper deposits are found. The expansion of the 'Ubaid peoples into these regions may be the first attempt by the inhabitants of southern Mesopotamia to gain direct access to raw materials—such as pearls, timber, stone, and metal ores—that were absent in their homeland.

Little is known about the subsistence activities of the first 'Ubaid peoples. However, charred seeds from the 'Ubaid levels of Ur and the location of that settlement relative to the position of the Euphrates River at the time indicate that they practiced irrigation agriculture. They undoubtedly grew emmer wheat, barley, and linseed. Animal bones from Eridu and the smaller settlement at Ras al 'Amiya indicate that they fished in the marshes, hunted wild onagers, and raised domesticated cattle, sheep, and goats. However, goats and sheep were not plentiful in southern Mesopotamia; this contrasted markedly with the situation that prevailed on the plains of Khuzistan, a few hundred miles away, where rainfall agriculture was possible and goats and sheep were plentiful.

The 'Ubaid peoples were ingenious artisans who made excellent use of local materials. At first their pottery was handmade. Later, as their influence spread into the north, they began to mass produce pottery. This involved using molds and decreasing the amount of painted decoration that appeared on each vessel. A number of changes accompanied the shift to mass production. On the Susiana Plain large, centralized workshops replaced smaller ones. Furthermore, pottery production was concentrated in a few of the 'Ubaid settlements in the area instead of being common to all of them, as it had been earlier. These changes must have been accompanied by changes in the ways in which locally produced commodities were distributed among the inhabitants of the area as a whole.

The largest of the 'Ubaid settlements, Tell 'Uqair, covered more than 27 acres and may have had as many as 3,000 or 4,000 residents by 4000 BC. There were several other settlements in southern Mesopotamia that were nearly as large as Tell 'Uqair. However, the majority of the 'Ubaid settlements were smaller—an acre or two in area, with populations of about 100. The smaller settlements were generally located in close proximity to the larger towns. These clusters of settlements were separated by expanses of swamp or desert. Such geographically imposed separation set limits on the size of political units and effectively prevented political unification of the country as a whole.

Cities and Satellites

By 4000 BC social and economic differences were already developing between the large town in a cluster and the villages and hamlets that surrounded it. For example, the range of stamp seals found in the towns is greater than that of the seals found in the surrounding settlements. These seals have designs impressed on them and were used to prevent unauthorized people from opening containers such as a pottery storage vessel or a basket. Clay would be placed over a knot and stamped with a seal representing the group or village that had produced the commodity. The presence of a large variety of discarded stamp seals in the towns indicates that the townspeople were receiving shipments of commodities produced in the satellite communities and suggests that they were acting as middlemen—shipping what they received from one community to the residents of another.

A number of towns in southern Mesopotamia grew considerably during the fourth millenium BC as their inhabitants began to produce a greater variety of goods and export them to villagers living in the surrounding areas. Uruk, for example, covered about 25 acres in 4000 BC. Nine centuries later the town covered nearly 200 acres and may have had 10,000 residents. Uruk grew explosively during the next 200 years. The town covered more than 1,000 acres and was surrounded by a high wall that was more than 6 miles long. Its population swelled to more than 20,000. It appears that more than two-thirds of the people living in the region around Uruk lived in the city itself.

At first Uruk had only one sanctuary. As time passed and the settlement grew in importance, a second sanctuary appeared in the new part of the city.

A contour plan of the walled city of Uruk. M. E. L. Mallowan, **Early Mesopotamia and Iran** (London: Thames and Hudson Ltd., 1965), fig. 1, p. 14.

About 3200 BC, the inhabitants built an enormous terrace that connected the two temples. A century later, the older of the shrines was abandoned and the newer one enlarged. The people erected a platform and built the sanctuary on top of it. The new sanctuary included a temple similar to those at Eridu and a large number of administrative and storage rooms.

Special buildings or rooms associated with the town sanctuary have been found at other cities in the area. Such buildings were not found at the smaller settlements—the villages and hamlets surrounding the urban centers. At Susa, a city located about 150 miles northeast of Uruk, buildings with specialized functions—scribal and storage areas—were built on top of the sanctuary platform and in the area surrounding it. Archaeologists recovered a large number of stamp seals and discarded seal impressions in this part of the settlement. This suggests that the users of these buildings were opening a variety of containers received from other places and that they were sealing and shipping these containers as well. After about 3300 BC the users of these buildings around the central platforms at Susa and other cities in southern Mesopotamia prepared cuneiform tablets to record economic transactions. They invented a writing system in response to the needs created by the centralized administration of economic activities.

The Temple Corporation

By historic times the individuals using these buildings belonged to the *temple corporation*. They looked after the worldly affairs of the main god of the temple. They organized and managed agricultural production on the lands outside the city that were owned by the deity, and rented other temple lands to sharecroppers. They organized and supported craft guilds—weavers, brewers, smiths—that produced commodities for foreign exchange to acquire materials that were not available locally. They supported the merchants who managed the traffic in textiles and other manufactured goods and acted as intermediaries between the temple and the mining and smelting centers to the north. They performed certain cultic services for the community as a whole, for which they received tribute. And they assumed certain social responsibilities, insuring the welfare of the underprivileged by providing food or granting loans.

In theory, the entire city belonged to the main god of the temple. In practice, however, the temple corporation owned only a portion of the land in the city and beyond; individuals or noble families held the rest as private property. By virtue of its wealth the temple corporation had the means to overcome the progressive salinization of its irrigated farmlands and mount the labor force required to clean out the silt deposited in large canals or repair dams and dikes that had weakened with the passage of time. As a result of their ability to carry out such work, the temple corporations of many cities increased in size and importance well into the middle of the second millenium BC by buying up the lands of the less fortunate members of the community.

The temple corporation—the officials and administrators of the sanctuary, craftsmen, and other personnel—accounted for only a small portion of the city's population. The vast majority of the townspeople were farmers, cattle breeders, boatmen, fishermen, merchants, scribes, artisans, laborers, or slaves. Some of the families were wealthy and owned estates covering hundreds of acres. Some of the artisans sold their goods in the market or bartered them for other commodities.

The temple itself was the largest and most impressive building in the city. Outside the sacred area around the temple were the residential quarters—narrow, unpaved streets winding their way through a jumble of large and small houses. These occasionally opened onto streets lined with

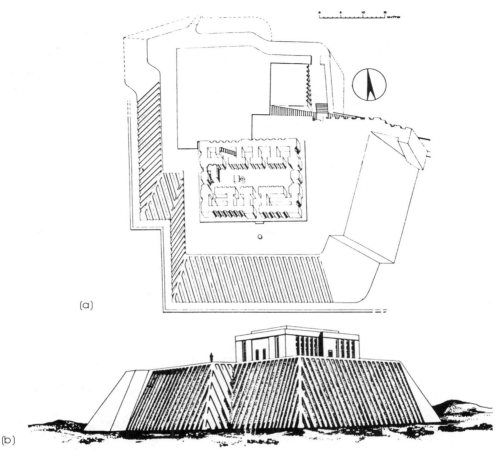

(a)

(b)

The White Temple at Uruk during the later part of the fourth millenium BC.
(a) Reconstruction of the structure showing the sanctuary on the temple tower.
(b) Reconstruction of the White Temple from ground level. M. E. L. Mallowan, **Early Mesopotamia and Iran** (London: Thames and Hudson Ltd., 1965), figs. 28, 29, p. 39.

awning-covered booths or small plazas next to gates in the city wall. Most of the houses were small, mud brick buildings with several rooms grouped around a courtyard. Family burial grounds were often located beneath the houses.

The economic base of Mesopotamian society was agriculture, which was carried out in the rural area around the city. Farming was conducted at several different levels: on the extensive lands owned and administered by the temple corporation, on private lands held by individuals or noble families, and on small plots worked by the urban poor or nomadic shepherds. Deeds of sale and other records from the archives at Lagash indicate that land was frequently held by kin groups and that many of the individual "owners" were, in fact, representatives of kin-based groups. This suggests that food production was organized to a large extent around groups of individuals related to each other by descent from a common ancestor. Although industrial production on a large scale was carried out primarily in the workshops of the temple corporation, it appears that the craftsmen working in these shops frequently belonged to the same kin group. Consequently, it is clear that kin groups played important roles in both agricultural and craft production in southern Mesopotamia during the third millenium BC, and presumably earlier as well.

Production and exchange were controlled to a large extent by an urban institution—the temple corporation. The amount of goods and services that passed through the temple corporation was apparently quite large in relation to the total amount of these goods and services that was available. It is also clear that much of the wealth of the outlying villages and hamlets—their agricultural and craft production— was drawn off to support the temple personnel in the city.

Social Differentiation

Social stratification was much more apparent in the cities than in the surrounding villages and hamlets. The existence of social classes, defined in terms of access to economic resources, is confirmed not only by written records but also by archaeological evidence from cemeteries. One of the clearest indicators of wealth in southern Mesopotamia was the presence of copper or more precious metals in tombs. Wealth tended to be concentrated in the urban centers. For example, 20 of the more than 1,300 burials excavated at the city of Ur contained a wide range of metal objects—gold and silver ornaments, copper and gold vessels, gold and silver daggers, and large numbers of bronze tools and utensils. More than 400 other tombs had a few copper or bronze tools or objects such as mirrors, bowls, or razors. The rest of the tombs lacked grave goods or yielded only pottery or stone vessels. At a contemporary nearby village only 18 of the 94 burials contained metal objects, and only 4 of these contained more than one such object.

Social differentiation apparently increased in the cities between 2900 and 2400 BC. At first most of the tombs in urban cemeteries lacked metal objects. A small number of tombs contained a few copper objects like daggers or toilet articles. A smaller number contained a significant quantity of copper objects, including stands that held stone vessels; the value of the copper in these stands was enough to buy a fair-sized piece of farmland at the going prices of those days. As time passed, copper and other precious metals became more plentiful in southern Mesopotamia, and metal objects were placed in more tombs in the urban centers. There was an almost continuous gradation from the tombs that contained a lot of metal objects to those that contained none.

At the top of the social hierarchy were the noble families headed by important men. They owned large estates that were worked by free clients or slaves. At Lagash the individual who assumed political leadership and religious responsibility for the successful management of the temple corporation probably came from a noble family with its own estates separate from those of the city god. Commoners who owned land as members of kin groups formed a second stratum of Mesopotamian society; they probably composed more than half the population of Lagash. Clients, supported by the temple corporation or by the noble families, formed a third segment of the population. At the bottom of the social hierarchy were slaves, who occupied a variety of legally distinct positions. Slaves performed tasks in those sectors of the economy which were involved with industrial, or commodity, production. For example, the Bau community at Lagash had 250 to 300 slaves out of a total work force of 1,200 individuals; most of these were women who, with their children, were employed in a weaving workshop. This suggests that roughly one-quarter of the labor resources above the subsistence level were devoted to the production of thread and cloth and that slaves played the major role in the production of these items, which were used for exchange not only in the local economy but also in the long-distance trade through which essential raw materials like timber and metals were obtained.

During an emergency the city put itself in the hands of a *lugal,* or "big man," who assumed certain cult responsibilities and control over the temple

The cities of Sumer and Akkad.

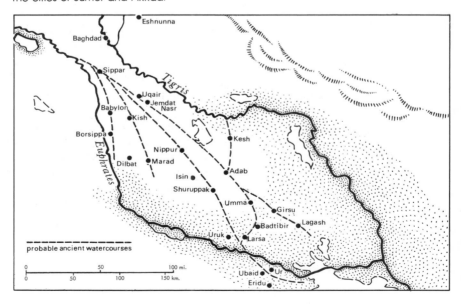

and city. When the emergency was over, his authority reverted to the temple corporation and to an assembly composed of noblemen and commoners. In other words, both the authority of the *lugal* and his term of office were temporary. However, after about 2500 BC, as the cities grew larger and more numerous, the threat of danger was never really absent. Fields, irrigation canals, and safe transport were all areas of potential dispute between neighboring cities. For example, the cities of Lagash and Umma fought a destructive war with each other over a few pieces of arable land; this war lasted more than five generations. Under these conditions the office of *lugal* seems to have become a permanent one in a number of cities. The term *lugal* gradually came to mean paramount political leadership and later was used as the royal title.

The king acted on behalf of the assembly and the city god. His rule was sanctioned by the city god, who could withdraw his approval at any time. Consequently, the formation of dynasties had no basis in the Mesopotamian theory of kingship during the third millenium BC. However, dynasties did exist during this period in several cities; their existence was interpreted as a favor bestowed by the gods.

SOCIAL DEVELOPMENT IN ANCIENT MESOPOTAMIA

By 3500 BC or perhaps earlier, societies in ancient Mesopotamia were dominated by large palace or temple corporations that owned most of the arable land, controlled production and exchange, and organized the daily lives of people through complicated systems of record keeping and rationing. A question of considerable theoretical importance is, How did this social form develop out of the small, permanently occupied agricultural communities that existed on the Mesopotamian Plain and in the areas around it two millenia earlier? This transformation was an important one that included the development of new productive forces and new relations of production. It reflected changes in the relations among people as they developed new ways to extract, transform, distribute, and use the energy provided by nature. It also reflected the establishment of property—a relationship between a person and a thing that recognizes and legitimizes the inequality between that person and other individuals in the society. In other words, this transformation saw the beginnings of social stratification—a situation in which the various groups in a society have differential access to its wealth and surplus production—and the state—institutions of social control that ensure not only that the supervisory and administrative necessities of the society are performed but also that they are carried out by the elite and that the interests of this group are maintained and protected from those of the rest of the society. Using what we know about ancient Mesopotamian society, let us speculate about the mechanisms underlying this transformation.

Production Units	The early farming communities in Mesopotamia were composed of a number of production units. Given the importance of the dead in this area and its environs, membership in these production units was probably defined in terms of descent from a founding ancestor, who, in turn, was the descendant of some higher unity, or supernatural being, who stood above the community as a whole and controlled the distribution of wealth and prosperity. These production units included both living and dead members. The latter were particularly important because they defined who belonged to the group and who had access to its surplus production; the dead also defined the relationship between the living members of the unit and the higher unity—a city god in later times—who stood above the human members of the community and was the sole proprietor of the resources they used.

The various production units in a community undoubtedly produced different amounts of food and other goods in any given year. The most obvious reasons for this are demographic ones resulting from size and chance. A unit with too few farmers or herders might not produce enough food to meet the needs of its members, while one with a lot of farmers or herders might produce a surplus. In a community with an ideology emphasizing the role of a supernatural being as the sole owner and distributor of wealth, differences in production had to be explained in terms of supernatural intervention. Units that produced surpluses must have founding ancestors that were more influential with the god than those of production units that could not produce enough to satisfy the needs of their members.

Alliances	Another important feature of the relations of production in these communities was the alliances created by exchanges between different production units. Groups that produced surpluses gained prestige by sharing the products of their labor with less productive units. The members of these less productive units wanted to enter into alliances with their more fortunate kin in order to ensure their survival and continued existence. They could establish such alliances in various ways. The less fortunate units might give the more prosperous ones gifts in return for food or for having their influential ancestors intercede with the god. Or the less fortunate units might give laborers to the more prestigious groups in return for favorable consideration.

These alliances had a number of important effects on the community. First, they made each production unit in the society dependent on other groups for its survival. Second, they tended to level out differences in the amounts of food produced by the various production units in the community. Third, assuming that the alliances were matrimonial ones, as the genetic admixture data from Catal Hüyük suggest, they played an important role in determining the distribution of wealth and labor in the community as a whole by affecting the rate at which any given production unit could accumulate surplus. Prestigious production units—those that produced surpluses—were more desirable alliance partners; consequently, they received laborers and perhaps goods from other production units. As a result, they had growing labor forces and could produce a little more than they had produced before.

Initially the differences in productivity of the various production units in a community probably were not great. A group that was relatively prestigious and eagerly sought after as an alliance partner at a particular time might at a later time suffer a reversal in its fortunes and find itself seeking closer ties with formerly dependent production units whose fortunes had risen. This give-and-take pattern continued as long as all the production units in the community saw themselves as equally descended from the supernatural being through different ancestors. However, once a production unit succeeded in convincing other groups in the community that its wealth and prosperity were due to the fact that its founding ancestor had better connections or closer ties with the supernatural being, it could insert itself as the mediator between the god and the rest of the community. When this happened, the structure of the community changed dramatically as new patterns of social relations developed.

The Conical Clan

No longer was the community composed of more or less equal groups— production units defined in terms of descent from founding ancestors who were ultimately related to the supernatural being. What was important was the degree of relationship: which founding ancestor was most closely connected with the supernatural being. In the new structure the founding ancestor of the production unit that inserted itself in the position of mediator was viewed as more closely related to the god than the ancestors of other groups in the community. This social form is called a *conical clan*; all relations of social rank are defined in terms of genealogical proximity or distance from the higher unity that stands above the larger community.

Once a particular production unit succeeded in occupying this position—in setting itself apart from the rest of the community—its members were able to control a greater portion of the labor of the community as a whole by requiring tribute and labor payments in return for performing the activities necessary to ensure the continued well-being of the community. Only that production unit could perform these essential activities because of its monopoly of access to the imaginary source of surplus production—the higher being. As a result, the highest-ranking production unit had increasing control over the labor force and the objects of wealth that circulated in the exchange network that linked the various groups together.

At first the differences between the highest-ranking production unit and the rest of the production units in the society may not have been great. The members of the most prestigious group probably still labored in the fields and shops, with only a little help from the laborers they had acquired—debt "slaves" from production units that were unable to meet their obligations, or captives from outside the community. As time passed, social hierarchies became more developed; bureaucractic functions emerged and multiplied among the elite group; and an ever-increasing portion of the surplus production was drained off to support administrative activities and the continually increasing standard of living of the elite. This shift was accompanied by a separation of the powerful elite group from the lower-ranking groups in the society and by the gradual creation of a class of exploiters and an exploited class consisting of captives, debt slaves, and the members of low-ranking production units. The separation of the wealthy—the royalty and the nobility— from the commoners involved severing the kinship relations that had once existed between these units while maintaining through various ideological means, such as the maintenance and performance of old rituals, the fiction that the commoners were still socially dependent on the wealthy. This shift also witnessed the development of various institutions and rules of social control—the state—which ensured that necessary work would get done and that the interests of the elite would be protected and maintained.

As long as surplus production continued to increase under the existing forces of production, social stratification increased as the technical and social divisions of labor became more developed. Artisans came to places where the elite controlled production or exchange. They became full-time craft specialists supported by the surplus production of the rest of the community; they gave their labor to the supernatural being and to the elite as its earthly representatives. However, when surplus production stopped growing at its former rate because of conflicts between neighboring communities over arable land, the demand of city dwellers for food and other goods continued unabated. This ultimately led to a lower standard of living for the population as a whole and to increased social stratification. Land became a negotiable item that could be bought and sold. The wealthy—the temple corporation and the noble families—began to accumulate land, while the commoners became increasingly dependent on the rich for their security and livelihood as they were slowly separated from their land and the products of their labor.

FURTHER READINGS

Adams, Robert McCormick
1965 *Land behind Baghdad; a history of settlement on the Diyala Plains.* University of Chicago Press, Chicago and London.
1966 *The evolution of urban society; early Mesopotamia and prehispanic Mexico.* Aldine-Atherton, Chicago.
1972 Patterns of urbanization in early southern Mesopotamia. In *Man, settlement, and urbanism,* ed. Peter J. Ucko, Ruth Tringham, and G. W. Dimbleby, pp. 735–750. Gerald Duckworth, London.

Adams, Robert McCormick, and Hans J. Nissen
1972 *The Uruk countryside; the natural setting of urban societies.* University of Chicago Press, Chicago and London.

Diakonoff, Igor M.
1969 *Ancient Mesopotamia, socio-economic history; a collection of essays by Soviet scholars.* Nauka Publishing House, Moscow.

Friedman, Jonathan
1975 Tribes, states, and transformations. In *Marxist analyses and social anthropology,* ed. Maurice Bloch, pp. 161–202. Malaby Press, London.

Johnson, Gregory A.
1972 A test of the utility of central place theory in archaeology. In *Man, settlement, and urbanism,* ed. Peter J. Ucko, Ruth Tringham, and G. W. Dimbleby, pp. 769–786. Gerald Duckworth, London.

Kramer, Samuel Noah
1963 *The Sumerians; their history, culture, and character.* University of Chicago Press, Chicago and London.

Mallowan, Max E. L.
1965 *Early Mesopotamia and Iran.* McGraw-Hill, New York.

Nissen, Hans J.
1972 The city wall of Uruk. In *Man, settlement, and urbanism,* ed. Peter J. Ucko, Ruth Tringham, and G. W. Dimbleby, pp. 793–796. Gerald Duckworth, London.

Oates, David
1972 The development of Assyrian towns and cities. In *Man, settlement, and urbanism,* ed. Peter J. Ucko, Ruth Tringham, and G. W. Dimbleby, pp. 799–804. Gerald Duckworth, London.

Oates, David, and Joan Oates
1976 *The rise of civilization.* E. P. Dutton, New York.

Oppenheim, A. Leo
1964 *Ancient Mesopotamia; portrait of a dead civilization.* University of Chicago Press, Chicago and London.
1967 *Letters from Mesopotamia; official, business, and private letters on clay tablets from two millenia.* University of Chicago Press, Chicago and London.

Postgate, J. N.
1972 The role of the temple in the Mesopotamian secular community. In *Man, settlement, and urbanism,* ed. Peter J. Ucko, Ruth Tringham, and G. W. Dimbleby, pp. 811–826. Gerald Duckworth, London.

Redman, Charles L.
1978 *The rise of civilization; from early farmers to urban society in the ancient Near East.* W. H. Freeman, San Francisco.

Wright, Henry T.
1969 The administration of rural production in an early Mesopotamian town. *University of Michigan Museum of Anthropology, Anthropological Papers,* no. 39.

Wright, Henry T., and Gregory A. Johnson
1975 Population, exchange, and early state formation in southwestern Iran. *American Anthropologist,* 77, no. 2, pp. 267–289.

Young, T. Cuyler, Jr.
1972 Population densities and early Mesopotamia urbanism. In *Man, settlement, and urbanism,* ed. Peter J. Ucko, Ruth Tringham, and G. W. Dimbleby, pp. 837–842. Gerald Duckworth, London.

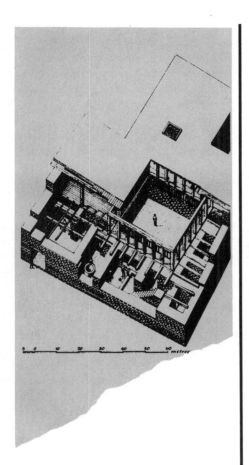

Ancient Peoples of the Indo-Iranian Frontier

East of Mesopotamia lies the Iranian Plateau, a vast desert that stretches one-third of the way across Asia, separating the Tigris and Euphrates Rivers from the Indus Valley and the lands beyond. The plateau resembles an enormous raised block surrounded on three sides by broad ranges of mountains. The northern rim of the Plateau is less well defined between the Caspian Sea and the Hindu Kush Mountains, where it dips and merges with the vast plains and deserts of central Asia.

The summers are hot on the Iranian Plateau; temperatures often exceed 100° F. The winters are mild, and rain falls in the mountains. Rain-fed rivers flow from the mountains onto the plateau during the winter months before disappearing into sinks and marshes. This moisture supports a variety of plant formations through the foothills and along the river channels, areas that were favored by the plateau's early settlers. Caves were used as butchering stations more than 40,000 years ago, and by the fourth millenium BC there were strings of farming communities through the southern mountains and along the northern edge of the plateau.

Caravan routes crossed the plateau in historic times; these were undoubtedly ancient roads that connected the peoples of the Iranian Plateau with those of Mesopotamia. The northern route passed along the Elburz Mountains to Meshed and brought the peoples of both Iran and Mesopotamia into contact with the inhabitants of the steppes and deserts of central Asia. This route then passed through Afganistan and crossed the Hindu Kush Mountains at the Khyber Pass, where it followed the Indus River southward through the high valleys of Pakistan. The southern route led from southern Mesopotamia through Khuzistan along the Fars and opened into the hills of Baluchistan, which overlook the Indus Valley.

Small streams rising in the Hindu Kush and Himalaya Mountains flow southward through deep valleys and come together on the semiarid plains of Punjab to form the Indus River. The Indus then meanders southward across the vast alluvial fan of the Sind before emptying into the Arabian Sea. The land becomes drier as one moves southward through the desert landscape of the Sind and westward into the hills of Baluchistan.

The Indus River carries enormous amounts of silt—twice as much as the Nile and nearly ten times as much as the Colorado. As a result, natural levees build up along the course of the river in the southern Punjab and the Sind. When the rains are exceptionally heavy in the mountains, the river often overflows these levees and floods thousands of square miles of the surrounding countryside. These alluvial soils are rich, and luxuriant forests grow naturally on them. These gallery forests become less dense away from the river banks and their composition changes as they gradually merge into savannas and then into the desert itself.

Ancient societies were located on the Iranian Plateau and in Turkmenia and the Indus Valley. How did these ancient societies develop? And what kinds of relationships existed between the peoples of these regions and those of Mesopotamia?

Ancient settlements on the Indo-Iranian frontier.

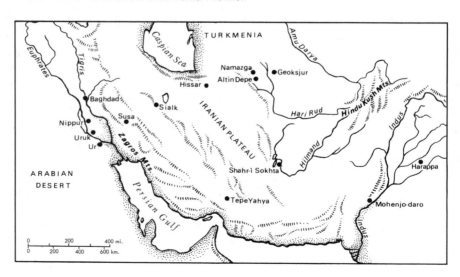

ANCIENT IRAN

The earliest inhabitants of the Iranian Plateau lived in caves along its northern rim near the Caspian Sea. The first residents of the caves lived there more than 40,000 years ago and used Mousterian tools to butcher animals. About 12,000 years ago people inhabited a number of caves at the southeast corner of the Caspian Sea. At first they relied heavily on gazelles for protein, supplemented by sheep, goats, horses, pigs, and even seals from the Caspian. These caves were abandoned and then reoccupied about 7500 BC. Their inhabitants herded sheep and goats and harvested wild cereals like barley and emmer wheat that were native to the area. Their contemporaries to the south at Tepe Asiab in Luristan collected freshwater shellfish, their major source of protein during the winter months.

The Susiana Plain

The Susiana Plain lies a few hundred miles east of southern Mesopotamia on the western slopes of the Zagros Mountains. It is a large plain covering more than 1,000 square miles, and it is watered by several streams that rise in the Zagros. People first lived on the plain about 8,000 years ago. Their lives were probably not much different from those of their contemporaries to the north at Ali Kosh or Tepe Guran. During the fourth millenium BC, a complex society resembling those of southern Mesopotamia began to develop on the plain. By 3500 BC, more than 20,000 people lived in the 50 settlements that dotted the area. The largest of these later became the city of Susa, the capital of Elam, a state that dominated much of Iran during the second millenium BC. In 3500 BC it covered thirty acres and was surrounded by three towns and 46 villages. In other words, there was a hierarchy of small, medium, and large settlements on the plain. This resembled the kind of settlement structure that existed around Uruk and other cities in southern Mesopotamia at the same time. A few centuries later, around 3300 BC, a fourth level of settlement appeared on the Susiana Plain. While Susa itself grew to cover more than 60 acres, a difference developed between large villages and small ones. The large ones covered about six acres, while the small ones covered an average of about two acres. Three hundred years later Susa grew rapidly, and by 2500 BC it covered more than 175 acres and probably had a population of around 10,000.

Settlement hierarchies like the ones that developed around Susa and Uruk develop under conditions in which villages, towns, and cities are incorporated into a market network. After 3500 BC, for example, pottery workshops became concentrated in the three largest communities on the Susiana Plain. This implies that potters in these communities were providing pottery for the rest of the inhabitants of the region. It is also interesting to note that they made bowls in three sizes; the medium-sized one held about two-thirds of a quart, which is roughly the amount of grain needed to make the amount of bread consumed daily by an adult in the region today. This suggests the existence of rationing—that the workers on the Susiana Plain during the fourth millenium BC were issued standard portions. In other words, production, distribution, and consumption were being mediated by an administrative elite.

| The Iranian Sistan | The situation that prevailed on the Susiana Plain after 3500 BC was not very different from the situation in southern Mesopotamia. However, it was different from what was happening to the east and north. There were only two levels of settlement in Iranian Sistan, which is located 800 miles east of Susa. The largest settlement in the region, Shahr-i Sokhta, covered more than 200 acres at the beginning of the third millenium BC. It was surrounded by small villages, none of which covered more than four acres. A similar settlement pattern—the large center surrounded by small villages—may have occurred around Tepe Yahya, 500 miles southeast of Susa in a valley near the Arabian Sea, and at Tepe Sialk, more than 200 miles northeast of Susa in a valley overlooking the central desert.

Tepe Yahya and Tepe Sialk were very closely related to Susa after 3500 BC. Writing appeared in Susa at about that time. The tablets found there were written in proto-Elamite—a different language from Sumerian, which was used in the settlements of southern Mesopotamia. Tablets with proto-Elamite inscriptions have also been found at Tepe Yahya and Tepe Sialk. This suggests that the inhabitants of these centers spoke proto-Elamite as well, and that they were closely related to the people of Susa. Although tablets have not been found at Shahr-i Sokhta, it is clear that its residents also had economic dealings with the people of Susa.

Tepe Yahya was first occupied more than 6,500 years ago by people who grew domesticated cereals and herded cattle, sheep, and goats. Camel bones were also present; however, it is not clear whether these animals were domesticated. The inhabitants also used a soft green stone, known as steatite, that could be obtained in the area. A steatite figurine was found in the earliest occupation level. By 3500 BC the village had grown. One building was an administrative center. It contained pottery bowls in standardized sizes like those found at Susa; near them were two dozen jar stoppers marked with seal impressions, and ninety tablets, six of which bore proto-Elamite inscriptions recording the receipt or shipment of goods. The presence of blank tablets in the room suggests that the writing was done there. The goods referred to in these tablets may well have been steatite bowls. By 3000 BC the residents of the settlement were engaged primarily in the manufacture of steatite bowls. One workshop contained more than 1,200 fragments of vessels in various stages of manufacture. Some of them were undecorated, while others had design motifs that appeared on steatite bowls found in sites in both Mesopotamia and the Indus Valley.

It probably took a worker at Tepe Yahya a day to hollow out a couple of steatite bowls and carve standardized design motifs on their exteriors. The workers used bronze-like chisels, awls, and pins to do this. At first these tools were made from copper ores that contained a lot of arsenic. Copper ores with arsenic impurities do not outcrop around Tepe Yahya; consequently, the inhabitants must have imported either the ore or ingots made from it from another locality on the Iranian Plateau. Later, by 3000 BC, they were getting the ore, ingots made from it, or the tools themselves from another place. A bronze dagger found in a level dating from this period was 3 percent tin. Copper ores with tin impurities do not occur around Tepe Yahya.

The activities at Tepe Yahya give us some insight into what happened elsewhere on the Iranian Plateau. There does not seem to have been an elite district in the settlement with larger or more luxurious quarters. This suggests that the people who benefited most directly from the production of steatite bowls lived elsewhere—perhaps at Susa or a large settlement like Shahr-i Sokhta. What did the residents of Tepe Yahya receive as they became increasingly involved in the production of steatite bowls? It may well have been perishable objects such as cereals, textiles, and protein foods that they had once produced themselves; as they spent more time making steatite bowls and exporting them, they spent progressively less time producing the staples they needed. These commodities—grain, textiles, and dried fish—were among the surplus products of the Mesopotamian city–states. The people of the communities in areas where three- or four-level settlement hierarchies occurred probably profited from the production that took place at Tepe Yahya.

Shahr-i Sokhta probably had 10,000 inhabitants during the first half of the third millenium BC. None of the thirty villages around it seem to have had populations of more than 100–150. The residents of the area farmed the delta of the Hilmand River, which flows out of the mountains to the east. They probably had herds as well. However, their most important economic activity was the manufacture and export of lapis lazuli, a blue crystal that was highly valued throughout the ancient East. They mined the mineral, which is often embedded in limestone, high in the Hindu Kush Mountains and brought chunks of it by camel caravan to large workshops in Shahr-i Sokhta itself. In one of the workshops archaeologists found lapis lazuli embedded in chunks of limestone just as it had come from the mines; they also found lapis lazuli objects in various stages of manufacture. This suggests that most of the work was done by craftsmen in the workshops.

The residents of one part of Shahr-i Sokhta lived in large multiroomed dwellings, while those of other parts of the city and the surrounding villages had smaller houses. This suggests that there were social classes in the area

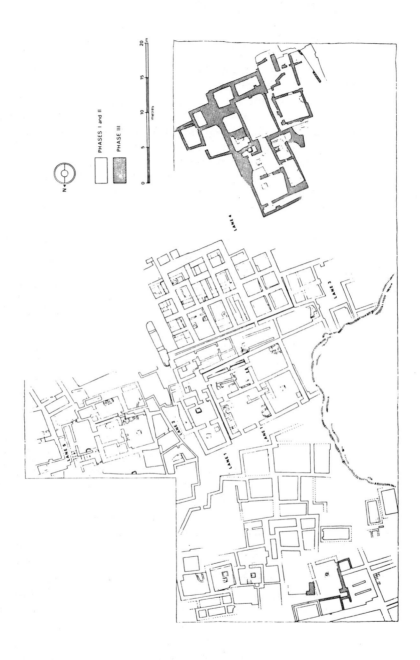

The residential quarter of Shahr-i-Sokhta with large multiroom dwellings. Mauricio Tosi, Early urban evolution and settlement patterns in the Indo-Iranian borderland, in **The explanation of culture change,** ed. Colin Renfrew (London: Gerald Duckworth, 1973), fig. 8.

and that the occupants of the large houses had greater access to wealth than the others. It may well be that they gained their wealth by controlling the production and exchange of lapis lazuli, the region's most valuable commodity.

ANCIENT TURKMENIA

People have lived in central Asia for more than 40,000 years. Temporary camps found in caves around the Caspian Sea and Lake Baikal have produced Mousterian stone tools that are not very different from those found in western Europe or the Levant. The tradition of living in caves for at least part of the year—probably during the winter months—persisted in central Asia well into the tenth millenium BC. After that time open sites appear in the archaeological record with increasing frequency.

The Kelteminar Peoples

By the sixth millenium BC the so-called Kelteminar peoples—hunting and fishing groups—were living in open settlements along the Amu Darya River, which flows out of the Hindu Kush Mountains east of Tashkent and empties into the Aral Sea. Their settlements usually consisted of a single large house built on a framework of wooden posts covered with wood, reeds, and earth. A fire burned in a large, permanent hearth in the center of the house; temporary fireplaces, perhaps for domestic use, were built around the edges of the building, which covered more than 2,400 square feet. It appears that the whole community—perhaps 25 to 30 individuals—lived together in a single house.

Early Farming Communities

The earliest farming communities of Turkmenia date from the sixth millenium BC. Their inhabitants built villages on small alluvial fans along the hills on the northern rim of the Iranian Plateau. They grew cereal grains in fields around their villages. Since the rivers on which they depended for water often changed their courses, the villagers had to move frequently in order to be close to the new river channels.

Dzejtun is one of the earliest of these settlements. It was occupied between 5800 and 5300 BC. During this time it probably had a population of 150 to 180. They lived in thirty small houses ranging in size from about 170 to 325 square feet. This suggests that each household had five or six members. Sometimes two or three houses shared a communal courtyard where various domestic activities were carried out. After the settlement had been occupied for several hundred years, the residents built a shrine, or meeting house, near the center of the village. This building was twice as large as the houses and had colorful geometric and zoomorphic designs painted on its walls.

The residents of Dzejtun probably used domesticated dogs in pasturing their sheep and goats. Throughout the occupation of the village, sheep and

The early settlement of Dzejtun in southern Turkmenia. V. M. Masson, Prehistoric settlement patterns in Soviet central Asia, in **Man, settlement and urbanism,** ed. Peter J. Ucko et al. (London: Gerald Duckworth, 1972), fig. 1, p. 266.

goats provided the bulk of the meat consumed. However, the villagers also hunted for meat. They liked gazelles but also killed onagers, wild pigs, and wild sheep for food. Fox, cat, and wolf were probably hunted for fur.

Chakmakli Tepe, located southeast of Dzejtun, was occupied between 5200 and 4900 BC. It, too, was a small village. Its inhabitants grew wheat and barley; domesticated sheep, goats, and cattle provided more than 60 percent of the meat they consumed. The presence of large numbers of spindle whorls indicates that they were already weaving textiles. In addition, they were using pottery that resembled the vessels being made by contemporary potters in northeastern Iran. They also used copper tools—awls, piercers, and knives. Since copper deposits are unknown in Turkmenia, the inhabitants must have gotten the tools or the ore itself from peoples living on the Iranian Plateau beyond the Kopet Dagh Mountains.

The village layout at Chakmakli Tepe was different from the layouts of earlier settlements. There were two blocks of buildings that were separated from each other by a street that ran down the middle of the village. Each block consisted of several household complexes, or apartments, with their own kitchens, living areas, and workrooms. In each building complex there was also a large room with red-painted walls and floors that was probably a shrine or a common room. The layout of the village suggests that the community was probably divided into two distinct groups, each composed of several households.

There were about twenty settlements along the foothills of the Iranian Plateau during the early part of the fifth millenium BC. Most of them were small, consisting of about twenty houses with their own courtyards randomly placed around a larger building that was probably a gathering place for the community. The population of these villages was probably about 100. However, two of the settlements were large. The earlier of the two was Kara Depe, which covered more than 35 acres and may have had a population of 2,500. The second large settlement developed in the Geoksyur Oasis, north of the foothills. This settlement was also surrounded by a number of small villages, several of which had fortification walls. The reason some of the villages in the oasis were fortified may well have been that they were a frontier region, which bordered on the area of central Asia occupied by nomadic hunters and gatherers.

These communities were still acquiring copper tools or ore from the peoples across the mountains in northern Iran. In addition, they were also getting semiprecious minerals like turquoise and carnelian from the same region. They made these stones into the jewelry that was worn by the living and buried with the dead. The presence of small quantities of these stones and the two-level settlement hierarchy suggest that there was an unequal distribution of wealth among the peoples of Turkmenia. It is probable that the wealthy individuals lived in the larger centers.

By 3000 BC settlements like Kara Depe and Geoksyur had similar plans. They consisted of a number of blocks separated from each other by narrow streets. Each block had a number of apartments with both living and domestic rooms. There were four to eight apartments in each of the blocks. In addition to the living quarters, there were communal yards and storerooms in each block. It appears that 20 to 50 people may have lived in a block. There were twenty-five blocks in Kara Depe, which suggests that it may have had a population of about 1,000 at the time. Two other features of these settlements are important. One is that there may have been technical divisions of labor among the townspeople, judging from the fact that a pottery kiln was found in one of the houses. The other is that there were communal burials; up to 28 individuals were buried in the same tomb. These graves may well have contained individuals who had lived in the same block.

During the last half of the third millenium BC, Namazga Depe and Altin Depe became the largest settlements in southern Turkmenia. They covered 175 and 125 acres, respectively, and may have had populations of 8,000 to 10,000. Altin Depe consisted of a number of multiroomed blocks separated by narrow streets. Each block had a series of apartments with their own courtyards. Again, it appears that the residents of a block formed the basic social unit of the community.

It is also clear that there was craft specialization at Altin Depe. The whole northern end of the site, some five acres in extent, was covered with broken and discarded pottery. Nearby were two-tiered pottery kilns located next to houses and workshops. The graves underneath these houses lacked grave goods, which suggests that the potters living in this part of Altin Depe were not wealthy.

In the eastern part of the settlement were large public buildings and the houses of wealthy individuals. Two caches were found bricked up in the walls of an apartment in this part of the city. One contained a seal, some pottery vessels, and some ivory objects; the other contained pottery vessels, a bronze vessel and mirror, a faience vessel and beads, and a pin. The inhabitants of this part of the city were buried on a hill to the north, close to the edge of town. Fourteen individuals were placed in one tomb along with a number of grave goods. A female figurine had a special place in this tomb. There were also single graves in the same area. One individual wore gold rings and beads made of agate, carnelian, and lazurite with a gold binding; in addition, a seal and two female figurines were found in the tomb. It is clear that the individuals in these tombs had access to much more wealth than the craftsmen who were buried under their houses.

There was a complex of public buildings located near the wealthy residential district. At the center of this complex was a 180-foot-long platform with a fifty-foot-high tower on it. The outer walls of the tower were decorated with projecting pilasters resembling those on a multi-roomed building immediately west of this complex. It also appears that there were earlier struc-

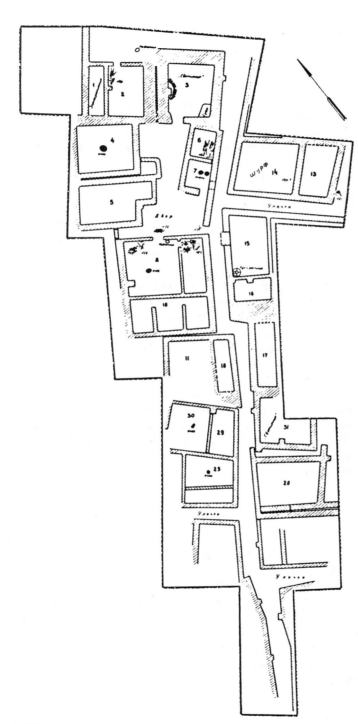

Plan of the settlement at Geoksyur, southern Turkmenia. V. M. Masson, Prehistoric settlement patterns in Soviet central Asia, in **Man, settlement and urbanism,** ed. Peter J. Ucko et al. (London: Gerald Duckworth, 1972), fig. 6, p. 272.

tures inside the platform–tower complex. This structure is reminiscent of those found in Mesopotamia. It was obviously a prestigious building whose construction required a great deal of labor.

Trade and
Social
Classes

The settlements of southern Turkmenia maintained close contact with other regions during the third millenium BC. In one hoard found at Altin Depe, there was a gray-ware jug that had been imported from northern Iran. In the same hoard were ivory rods with circles carved on their sides; similar objects were excavated at Mohenjo-daro in the Indus Valley.

It is clear that there were social classes in the large settlements at Altin Depe and Nemazga and that the elite had much greater access to wealth than the craftsmen did. They may well have controlled craft production and exchange through a temple complex patterned after those in Mesopotamia. Two of the major exports from southern Turkmenia may have been jade and tin ore from the area between the Amu Darya River and Lake Balkhash. In return, the elite middlemen of these cities received objects manufactured elsewhere: bronze implements, perhaps made from tin ores that they had exported; jewelry; and possibly even agricultural produce to feed those individuals who were not involved in food production.

During the second millenium BC the large settlements declined. People moved out of them into small villages that covered between three and five acres along the banks of streams and rivers. The inhabitants of these settlements lived in large semisubterranean houses with fifty or sixty residents. Why were the urban centers abandoned? One answer to this important question is that foreign markets for the commodities produced by these peoples disappeared. The focus of the communities in the Mesopotamian lowlands shifted northward to Anatolia and westward toward the Mediterranean world. The large cities of the Indus Valley were also abandoned, and it seems that the inhabitants of that region no longer demanded the commodities of Turkmenia.

THE INDUS VALLEY

People have lived on the Indian subcontinent for more than 300,000 years. Archaeologists have found the stone tools they made at various places along the Narboda River and in the foothills of northwest India and Pakistan. These early peoples left two different kinds of tool kits. One contains hand axes and cleavers; it resembles tool kits found in the Levant, Africa, and Europe. The other contains crudely shaped choppers and chopping tools; similar kits were found to the east, in Burma, China, Malaysia, and Indonesia.

Remains of the earliest domesticated animals come from the Adamgarh rock shelter in central India, 400 miles northeast of Bombay. The inhabitants of the shelter kept dogs, pigs, sheep, goats, and humped cattle. They also hunted deer and other animals, whose remains were as abundant in their refuse as those of domesticated animals. The residents of the shelter apparently lived there for short periods; it appears that they moved with their animals from one place to another during the year.

Farming Communities

The first farming communities appeared in the mountain valleys along the eastern edge of the Iranian Plateau. The earliest of these is Kile Gul Muhammad, located in the Quetta Valley near a pass leading from the Iranian Plateau to the Indus Valley. The settlement was first occupied around 4000 BC. Its residents kept domesticated goats, sheep, and cattle and grew cereal grains —presumably barley and wheat—judging from the sickle blades and grinding tools that were found at the site.

The earliest farming communities in the Indus Valley were somewhat later than those in the mountains overlooking the plain. They appeared about 3200 BC and have been found throughout the valley. These early villages

Early settlements in the Indus Valley.

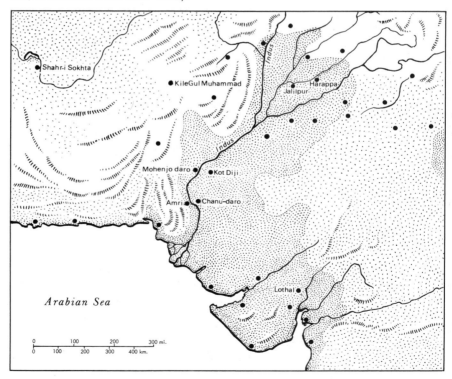

were remarkably similar, regardless of where they were located. Their architecture was similar; the residents of each village kept herds of sheep, goats, and humped cattle; and they all used two-wheeled carts. Even the pottery they used was similar from one end of the valley to another—a distance of nearly 900 miles. This pottery, which is called *Early Harappan,* also resembled the pottery used in the mountain valleys along the rim of the Iranian Plateau in northern and central Baluchistan. There were even similarities between it and the pottery made at Shahr-i Sokhta, more than 400 miles to the west. These similarities indicate that there were close ties between the peoples of the Indus Valley and those of the eastern part of the Iranian Plateau at the end of the fourth and the beginning of the third millenium BC.

Amri was one of the largest of the Early Harappan settlements. At its peak it covered about 20 acres and may have had several thousand residents between 3200 and 2500 BC. Like many other Early Harappan settlements, Amri was located on the edge of potentially arable land; it overlooked the flood plain of the Indus River. Its residents lived in rectangular houses about 20 feet long by 10 feet wide, with flat roofs and mud floors. After the settlement had been occupied for a while, the inhabitants built a large mud brick platform toward the edge of town; post holes on the top of the platform indicate that a wooden building stood on top of it. It is not clear how this platform was used. Farming was the community's economic base; the people grew wheat and barley and kept herds of domesticated sheep, goats, and donkeys. They hunted a wide range of animals, including gazelles, deer, rhinoceros, wild pigs, and turtles.

Other Early Harappan settlements such as Kot Diji or Jalilpur were smaller. They covered between 3 and 5 acres and probably had populations of a few hundred individuals. The size difference between settlements like Amri and the small villages indicates that there was a settlement hierarchy in the Indus Valley during the first half of the third millenium BC that had at least two distinct levels. This implies that a small elite class residing in the large towns dominated production in the villages around them. Furthermore, the members of these groups controlled exchange with other peoples. It is not yet clear what they exchanged, but it may have been perishable commodities like textiles or agricultural produce.

Mohenjo-daro   Mohenjo-daro emerged as the largest settlement on the Indus Plain during the last half of the third millenium BC. It is located near the river, 100 miles upstream from Amri, and covers more than 240 acres. At its height around 2200 BC it probably had a population of 30,000. Mohenjo-daro was a planned settlement. Its streets were wide and intersected at right angles. High walls made of fired bricks rose on both sides of the streets; they lacked doors and had only a few windows. To enter a building one turned off the main streets into alleys into which the doors opened.

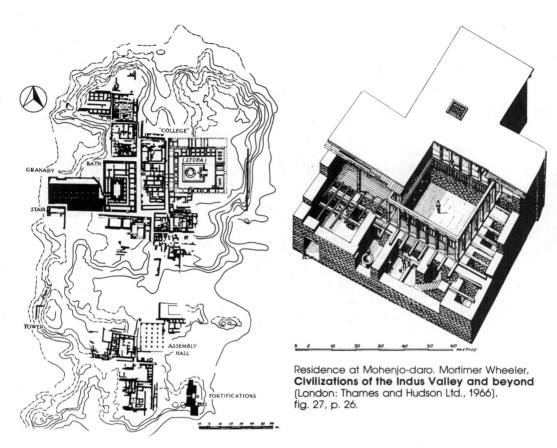

The citadel — the large, manmade rectangular platform — at Mohenjo-daro. Mortimer Wheeler, **Civilizations of the Indus Valley and beyond** (London: Thames and Hudson Ltd., 1966), fig. 4, p. 14.

Residence at Mohenjo-daro. Mortimer Wheeler, **Civilizations of the Indus Valley and beyond** (London: Thames and Hudson Ltd., 1966), fig. 27, p. 26.

There was a large rectangular platform—a manmade hill—west of the settlement that dominated the landscape. Thirty-foot-high towers with thick walls, pillars, and hallways stand on the platform even today. One of the buildings seems to have been a bath. Nearby is a large structure composed of brick blocks with passageways between them; it probably had a wooden superstructure and may have been used for storing grain.

East of the citadel, as this platform is called, lies the main residential district of Mohenjo-daro. It was separated from the citadel by a wide, open space, possibly a canal or a dried up branch of the river. In the residential quarters doorways opened off the narrow alleys. In one house a porter's room stood near the entry. Down a corridor was a bathroom with a large

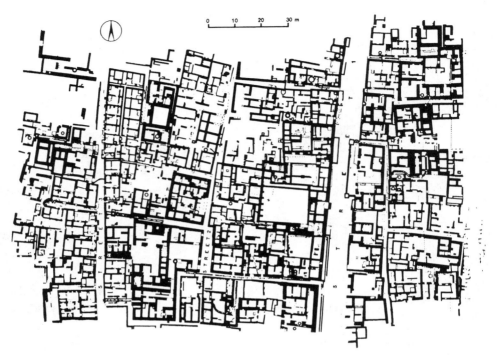

The residential quarter of Mohenjo-daro. Mortimer Wheeler, **Civilizations of the Indus Valley and beyond** (London: Thames and Hudson Ltd., 1966), figs. 14, 15, p. 22.

pottery pipe leading from a Western-style latrine to an open drain in the street outside. Other rooms opened off a square courtyard 30 feet on a side. A stairway led to an upper floor with more rooms. It seems that the domestic activities of a household were centered on the interior courtyard. Later the courtyards became crowded as the household members built flimsy mat- and cloth-covered structures to protect themselves from the weather as they carried out their domestic work.

Harappa

Harappa, another major center in the Indus Valley, was located 350 miles upriver from Mohenjo-daro. It had more than 20,000 inhabitants and shared many features with Mohenjo-daro. West of the residential area stood the citadel, a manmade platform 50 feet high that covered an area about 1,400 by 650 feet. High walls, 45 feet thick at the base, surrounded the platform. Outside these walls to the north stood a dozen warehouses with a total storage capacity about the same as that of the granary at Mohenjo-daro. The construction of these buildings at Harappa—the platform, the walls, and the warehouses—clearly involved the labor of a substantial work force and a great deal of planning.

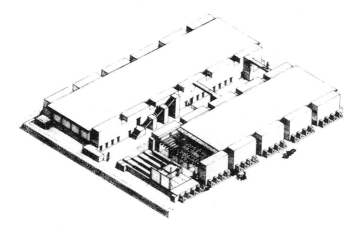

Reconstruction of the Granary at Harappa. Mortimer Wheeler, **Civiliations of the Indus Valley and Beyond** (London: Thames and Hudson Ltd., McGraw-Hill, 1966), fig. 32, p. 30.

Archaeologists used to believe that Harappa and Mohenjo-daro were the twin capitals of an ancient state in the Indus Valley that covered more than 400,000 square miles and had a population of at least a quarter of a million people. Recent studies suggest that the situation was much more complicated. Centers at least as large as Mohenjo-daro and Harappa have been found in the foothills of Baluchistan, southwest of Harappa, and in the desert to the south. These recent discoveries suggest that there were at least four, and perhaps as many as six, major centers in the Indus Valley. Each of these was significantly larger than the next-largest settlements and the 250 or more villages, large and small, that dotted the area. This four-level settlement hierarchy resembles that of Mesopotamia during the third and fourth millenia BC, suggesting that the patterns of political and economic domination in Indus Valley society were more complicated than the dual-capital model implies.

Indus Valley Society

Indus Valley society had an agricultural base. Its members grew wheat, barley, melons, and field peas for food, and cotton for clothing and twine, during the last half of the third millenium BC. In addition, the remains of rice embedded in clay have been found at Lothal, a trading settlement located on a bay of the Arabian Sea. The Indus peoples also had domesticated animals: dogs, sheep, goats, humped cattle, and donkeys. There were also cats in at least some of the Indus settlements. At Chanu-daro a dog chased a cat across a yard covered with undried bricks, and they left their footprints in a number of the bricks. The inhabitants also hunted a wide variety of animals that lived in the jungles along the rivers or in the tall grass beyond them; these included deer, gazelles, bison, tigers, rhinoceroses, and elephants as well as a number of smaller mammals and birds.

The Indus Valley peoples produced a variety of commodities: agricultural produce, textiles, beads, and metal objects, to name only a few. There were bronze foundries in Harappa and bead workshops in Lothal. It is clear that the Indus peoples engaged in foreign trade. They exported finished objects such as ivory tablets, which they obtained locally or from India, to areas like Altin Tepe, some 700 miles away. They imported minerals and other goods—turquoise, agate, carnelian, ivory, and perhaps rice. Some of these were transformed into finished commodities that were either consumed locally or exported. They imported finished goods—lapis lazuli from Shahr-i Sokhta and steatite bowls from Tepe Yahya on the Iranian Plateau. They also shipped goods—perhaps perishable ones—since chunks of clay stamped with Indus-style seals have been found at a settlement in southern Mesopotamia about 30 miles from the city of Uruk.

What was happening among the peoples of the Indus Valley during the later part of the third millenium BC? There may have been a number of quasi-independent city states centered on large settlements like Mohenjo-daro and Harappa. If so, these political entities maintained close ties with each other, for they had in common an elaborate system of weights and measures. Such systems are crucial for the maintenance of any economic system, in which equivalencies and exchange play prominent roles. Frontier settlements like Lothal may have served as ports of trade. Their residents shipped finished commodities—bronze tools or agricultural produce—into areas inhabited by peoples who did not produce them. In return they received minerals and other raw materials that were not available in the Indus Valley.

Many of the large settlements in the Indus Valley were abandoned during the first half of the second millenium BC. What caused the decline of urbanism in this area? As in Turkmenia, it may have been the breakdown of the export economy that provided jobs and direction for the rest of the population. Once the export economy became strained, the need for the specialized workers involved in the export sector of the economy diminished; these workers returned to their villages and became involved in the production of foods that were consumed locally by their own households and those of their neighbors. As foreign markets gradually disappeared, so did the specialists involved in the export economy. As the demand for raw materials from distant lands diminished, the amount of finished commodities exported probably declined. In the foreign areas, the goods exported by the Indus peoples were no longer considered necessary or were replaced by goods that were manufactured locally or in other places outside the Indus Valley.

EXTERNAL EXCHANGE AND SOCIAL DEVELOPMENT

Archaeologists have long recognized that there was an underlying unity or at least a close connection between what happened on the Mesopotamian plain and in the areas around it—the Nile River Valley, southeastern Europe, and the Indo-Iranian frontier. They use terms such as ancient East or oriental societies to express the underlying relationships between the ancient societies that developed in different parts of this vast area. One of the ties that bound people together in this area was the development of long-distance trade. After recognizing the importance of such trade, particularly the overland transport of goods, archaeologists were initially interested in where goods came from and where they ended up. More recently, however, they have begun to attack the problems of how external exchange integrates peoples with significantly different social and economic systems into larger social entities and the effects this has on social development in different parts of the larger area.

In the preceding chapters we noticed that communities developed along different pathways in various parts of the Near East because of the social and economic realities their members had to deal with. As a result, there were always significant differences in the ways of life of peoples living in different areas. For example, the inhabitants of one area lived in large, permanent settlements and sustained themselves on wild food resources, while their contemporaries in another area lived in transient settlements and relied to a greater or lesser degree on domesticated foodstuffs; later they lived in small city—states in southern Mesopotamia and dispersed farming communities in the north. As we saw in this chapter, uneven social development was also characteristic of the peoples of the Indo-Iranian frontier and those living elsewhere in the ancient East.

The continued existence of social and economic differences—reflections of uneven development—seems almost paradoxical in a social setting where the volume and variety of goods exchanged through the mechanism of long-distance trade were increasing, and we would logically expect the ways of life of the people involved to become more alike. In other words, how does a mechanism that brings people into closer contact with each other also function to maintain the differences between them? The solution to this paradox lies in the nature of the goods that were traded and in the exchange value they acquired.

Long-distance trade brings together societies that are ignorant of each other; that is, the members of one society are not familiar with the production costs of goods produced in the other society. Trade allows the members of a society to acquire scarce goods that cannot be produced locally or for which there are no substitutes available locally. This involves the transfer of part of the surplus production of one society to the members of another social unit. The particular good exchanged may have relatively low production costs and, therefore, low value in the society producing it. However, the same good—be it lapis lazuli, dried fish, or a spice—may have considerable value to the people who want to trade something for it, especially when they cannot produce it themselves or have no substitutes for it.

The social groups in each society that engage in and control long-distance trade hold monopoly positions. They can profit from these positions, particularly when the amount of the surplus product they can extract from other members of their society for the purposes of trade is small. For the society that acquires the small amount of this surplus good, its possession usually has little or nothing to do with the material well-being of its members; however, its possession is often absolutely indispensable for maintaining power relationships between different groups within the society. As a result, the transfer of prestige articles—goods that acquire high exchange values— form the basis for the wealth and power of those groups which control long-distance trade.

Such a situation can solidify the social relations that are developing in each society and lead to increased concentrations of labor in the export sectors of their economies. Hence, the social and economic differences that already exist between the two societies are maintained or even enhanced as each social unit structures itself around the transfer and acquisition of goods and the conversion of low-value, locally produced items into high-value foreign ones. It also leads to increased dependence of one society on the other, for a shift in the activities of one—a desire for items produced elsewhere or the discovery of a viable substitute that can be made locally— can have dramatic effects on those of the other. A shift in the patterns of long-distance trade can cause whole regions to decline or flourish. For example, there is some evidence to support the idea that the shift from overland to maritime trade around the Persian Gulf toward the middle of the third millenium BC was accompanied by a gradual decline in the settlements in Turkmenia and the Seistan area around Shahr-i Sokhta and by the development of new social forms in the Indus Valley.

FURTHER READINGS

Amin, Samir
1976 *Unequal development; an essay on the social formations of peripheral capitalism.* Monthly Review Press, New York and London.

Ekholm, Kajsa
1977 External exchange and the transformation of Central African social systems. *The evolution of social systems,* ed. J. Friedman and M. J. Rowlands, pp. 115–136. Gerald Duckworth, London.

Fairservis, Walter A., Jr.
1971 *The roots of ancient India; the archaeology of early Indian civilization.* Macmillan, New York.

Kohl, Philip L.
1975 The archaeology of trade. *Dialectical Anthropology,* 1, no. 1, November, pp.43–50.
1978 The balance of trade in southwestern Asia in the mid-third millenium BC. *Current Anthropology,* 19, no. 3, September, pp. 463–492.

Lamberg-Karlovsky, Carl and Martha
1971 An early city in Iran. *Scientific American,* 224, no. 6, June, pp. 102–110.

Masson, V. M.
1969 The urban revolution in southern Turkmenia. *Antiquity,* 42, no. 167, September, pp. 178–187.
1972 Prehistoric settlement patterns in Soviet central Asia. In *Man, settlement and urbanism,* ed. Peter J. Ucko, Ruth Tringham, and G. W. Dimbleby, pp. 263–278. Gerald Duckworth, London.

Mellaart, James
1975 *The Neolithic of the Near East.* Scribner's, New York.

Mughal, Mohammad Rafique
1974 New evidence of the Early Harappan culture from Jalilpur, Pakistan. *Archaeology,* 27, no. 2, April 106–113.

Pfeiffer, John E.
1977 *The emergence of society; a prehistory of the establishment.* McGraw-Hill, New York.

Tosi, Maurizio
1973 Early urban evolution and settlement patterns in the Indo-Iranian borderlands. In *The explanation of cultural change; models in prehistory,* ed. Colin Renfrew, pp. 429–446. Gerald Duckworth, London.

Wheeler, Mortimer
1968 *The Indus civilization,* 3rd ed. Cambridge University Press, Cambridge, England.

Wright, Henry T., and Gregory A. Johnson
1975 Population, exchange, and early state formation in southwestern Iran. *American Anthropologist,* 77, no 2, June, pp. 267–289.

Ancient Peoples of the Far East

The Far East is an immense area. It stretches from the Gobi Desert of Inner Mongolia southward through China, Indochina, and Malaysia into Indonesia and eastward from the Himalayas and the Tibetan Plateau to Japan, Taiwan, and the Philippines. It covers more than 10 million square miles and includes virtually every kind of ecological habitat found in the world today. There are tropical jungles in the south, arid deserts and steppes reaching from Chinese Turkistan to Mongolia, subarctic tundras in Manchuria and Tibet, and large temperate valleys carved by the rivers that flow out of the mountains to the west and empty into the China Sea.

People first lived in parts of the Far East more than a million years ago. Archaeologists have found human remains dating that far back in Java and more recent remains at various localities in China, including Choukoutien Cave outside Peking. In those days the people of the inhabited areas of the Far East hunted game and used some of the plant resources that were available. Their descendants have lived there ever since. By 10,000 years ago the inhabitants of the dunes and oases in the Gobi Desert hunted ostrich and other animals of the steppe and desert. Their neighbors in the forests around Peking hunted deer, bears, and other animals in the wooded areas and gazelles in the nearby grasslands; one group had marine shells, which suggests that they either traded for them or moved seasonally between the foothills of the Mongolian Plateau and the shores of the Yellow Sea. Below the Tsinling Mountains—that is, in the tropical forests of South China, Indochina, and the Philippines—the people used simple chopping tools that resembled those of their million-year-old ancestors; they hunted forest animals, harvested shellfish, and gathered a wide variety of plants.

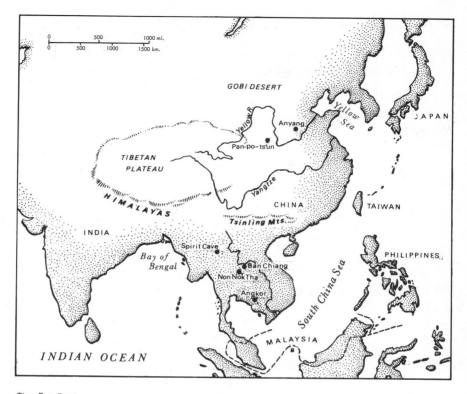

The Far East.

By the fifth millenium BC, peoples living on both sides of the Tsinling Mountains were farming, although they grew different crops. In the north, various kinds of millet were their staple food crops, and hemp and silkworms were raised for thread and fabrics. In the south, rice became the most important staple, though the inhabitants of the area supplemented it with a variety of roots, tubers, fruits, and seeds, which were used as food, spices, and even containers.

During the first half of the second millenium BC, the first of the Chinese political kingdoms emerged north of the Tsinling Mountains. This was the Shang state. Shang society was divided into three classes. At the top of the social hierarchy were the king and the royal family. Below them were court officials. At the bottom of the hierarchy were the craftsmen and farmers who provided the commodities and much of the labor that supported the king and his court. Outside the social system altogether were a few individuals without rights who worked on the farms, helped build large structures, and served as sacrificial victims for royal burials and the dedication of temples. Other states with different socioeconomic orientations appeared later both north and south of the Tsinling Mountains and on the islands offshore.

How did agricultural societies develop in different parts of the Far East? How did stratified societies like the Shang state develop in North China and elsewhere? What were they like? How did they change through time?

NORTH CHINA

The Yellow River and its tributaries rise in the highlands north of the Tsinling Mountains and flow eastward across the vast Hopei Plain before emptying into the sea. This plain and the low valleys leading into it make up North China. The summers are hot and the winters cold. What rain there is falls mainly during the summer months. The deciduous forests and grasslands that cover North China turn brown during the winter, and dust blows across the land.

Pan-p'o-ts'un   Lands like this supported the people of Pan-p'o-ts'un during the fifth millenium BC. The earliest known farmers of North China, they built their village on a hill overlooking the Wei River near the modern city of Sian. The village was oval in shape, with the long axis oriented north–south. It covered more than 12 acres and had a population of 500 or 600. A ditch 20 feet deep and 20 feet wide surrounded a residential area with more than 200 rectangular or circular houses built of logs covered with mud plaster. There was a cemetery north of the settlement beyond the ditch. To the east, also beyond the ditch, was a pottery-making district with a half-dozen kilns.

The villagers grew several species of millet and Chinese cabbage on the plains below the settlement. Judging from the decrease in tree pollen in the area, they burned the trees covering these lands. They then broke up the soil with stone celts (hoes) and planted their crops. After a few years the soil became progressively less fertile and the people had to clear new fields. This is called *slash-and-burn agriculture*. It took a great deal of land to support the villagers because they used fields in rotation. While one field was being used, other plots were lying fallow or had not been cleared. This pattern of shifting cultivation showed up in the debris around the village. The farmers lived in the village for a while, abandoned it when the fields became too unproductive, and returned to live there once again after the fertility of the soil had returned. Besides farming, the villagers kept domesticated dogs, pigs, and silkworms. They also hunted a variety of wild animals, fished in the river, and gathered nuts in the wooded areas around their homes.

The layout of Pan-p'o-ts'un, with its residential area, pottery-making center, and cemetery, resembled that of a number of other North Chinese settlements during the fourth and fifth millenia BC. In some of the later

The early farming village of Pan-p'o-ts'un in Sian, North China. A model at the Pan-p'o Museum. K. C. Chang, The continuing quest for China's origins, **Archaeology,** 30, no. 2 (1977), 119. Copyright 1977 Archaeological Institute of America.

Yangshao settlements, as the villages of this period are called, there was often a large communal structure in the central plaza. This was surrounded by smaller houses that opened onto the plaza. The later Yangshao cemeteries were different from the earlier ones. No longer were they located next to a village. Frequently several villages used the same cemetery, and their residents often carried the dead five or six miles up steep mountain paths to lay them to rest in hilltop graves, occasionally with a number of offerings. These graveyards were probably the burial places for groups of kinsmen from the same village or from a cluster of settlements.

The
Lungshan
Settlements

By 2500 BC the inhabitants of North China lived in permanent villages. This suggests that their agricultural economy had changed from one based on shifting slash-and-burn cultivation to a more permanent system of cultivation involving crop rotation or the rotation of fields. The principal crops were still millets, though wheat was grown in the Huai Valley and rice on the eastern plains. Cattle and sheep were economically the most important animals; however, the people continued to keep both dogs and pigs. They may also have kept poultry. The presence of hunting and fishing gear and of wild animal bones in the refuse around the villages indicates that wild game and fish provided significant amounts of animal protein.

The settlements that were occupied between 2500 and 1850 BC are known collectively as *Lungshan.* More than 100 of them have been discovered in North China and along the coast as far south as Taiwan. Large houses stood near the center of many Lungshan settlements. Individuals with wealth and power may have resided in them. Beyond these buildings were smaller houses where the rest of the villagers lived. High defensive earthworks surrounded a number of the villages. These walls—together with the development of offensive weapons and skeletons that show signs of violent death—suggest that organized warfare was taking place between different villages or groups of settlements. This implies that they had some way of distinguishing political groupings—of recognizing friend and foe.

Lungshan society was stratified. At the top of the social hierarchy was a small elite group whose members were buried with exquisite jade objects and large quantities of other objects, including specific kinds of tripod and ring-based pottery vessels that were used ritually in later times. These individuals were probably closely related to the powerful founders of the community, and they performed ceremonies honoring their dead relatives. By virtue of their close kinship with the founders, they had greater access to the community's wealth; they could call on others for labor or goods. There was some occupational specialization among the commoners. Besides farmers, there were potters, weavers, and perhaps even bronze workers. Many of the goods they produced were luxury items used exclusively by the aristocracy.

The Shang Dynasty

Chinese society changed dramatically by 1750 BC. Social relationships that had been hinted at earlier became fact. The descendant of a Lungshan chief named T'ang elevated himself above other chieftains to become the founder and first king of the *Shang dynasty,* which lasted from 1766 to 1122 BC. The Shang leader was no longer the chief of a tribe but an almost sacred king who ruled a domain by virtue of his genealogical proximity to important deified ancestors. The king and the royal lineage were at the top of the social pyramid. Below them was a corps of royal officials—scribes and officials who took care of the matters of state. A vast gulf separated these classes from the peasants and artisans who were the economic base of Shang society. At the bottom were slaves captured in warfare; they provided labor for the construction of monumental buildings and served as sacrificial victims.

The Shang kings resided in large, dispersed settlements, such as Anyang, that covered 11 to 15 square miles. The center of a settlement was the ceremonial and administrative precinct for a number of surrounding villages. In these precincts were large buildings, one of which was the king's palace. In one capital a large earthwork surrounded the ceremonial buildings. It was 4 1/2 miles long, 70 feet thick, and 40 feet high; its construction required a labor force of 10,000, working 330 days a year for 18 years. Other settlements were located at distances up to four or five miles from the royal compound These include dwellings and workshops where various commodities—carved bone, bronze, pottery, and fabrics—were produced. Some of the craftsmen—potters, for example—were highly specialized; one pottery workshop at Erh-li Kang produced only fine-textured vessels, while others must have produced domestic ware and glazed vessels. The artisans apparently lived in the precincts where they worked. Drainage channels ran between the settlements forming the capital; these probably drained off water and sewage. Agricultural fields and gardens were scattered through the capital and dominated the landscape outside. The farmers probably grew one crop each year. Millet was the staple, but wheat, barley, and rice were also grown, using the same short-term fallowing system that had been used in Lungshan times.

The Shang class structure was also apparent in the ways in which the dead were buried. More than 1,200 tombs were found at Anyang. All but eleven were the graves of commoners; they contained a single skeleton with a few pottery vessels as offerings. The other eleven were royal tombs. They were housed in structures that took more than 7,000 man-days of work to complete. One tomb contained a central coffin surrounded by many sacrifices, some of which had their own coffins, while others were only heads or human trunks. The tomb also contained objects made of stone, jade, bone, bronze, and pottery. Other royal tombs had chariots, the skeletons of horses, and the bodies of both adult and child sacrifices.

Farming was one of the main concerns of the Shang king, since the state's economy was based to a large extent on agriculture. However, agricultural technology had not changed significantly since Lungshan times. The farmers seem to have used the same tools, and there is no indication that they had devised new techniques to improve production. The fact that the Shang could support an aristocracy, a bureaucracy, and craftsmen implies that something had changed since earlier times, namely, the relations of production. No hamlet or village produced solely for its own consumption; instead, some of the commodities produced in each were exchanged for items from other settlements. There were thousands of storage pits located throughout the Shang capitals; nearly 4,000 stone sickles were found in storage pits in one village located near the ceremonial and political center of a capital. The fact that there were other storage pits containing different commodities near the central precinct suggests that there was some kind of central management or administration of commodity production, distribution, and exchange.

Many technological advances occurred in bronze metallurgy, which was almost unknown in earlier times. These innovations involved firing and casting techniques that increased not only the quality of the products but also the rate at which they could be produced. It is important that virtually all of the technological innovations in Shang society were oriented toward conspicuous consumption. This kind of production was stimulated by the requirements of

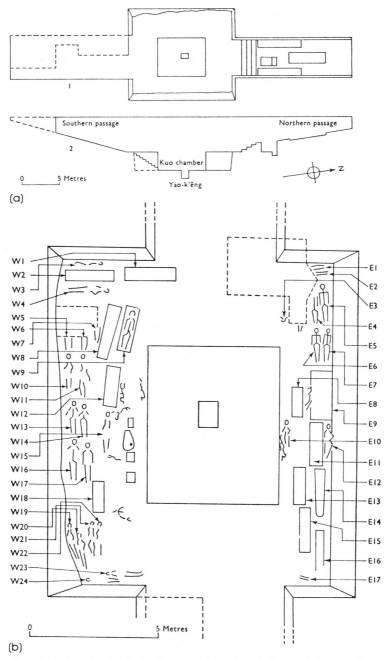

(a)

Southern passage   Northern passage

Kuo chamber

Yao-k'êng

0   5 Metres

(b)

W1
W2
W3
W4
W5
W6
W7
W8
W9
W10
W11
W12
W13
W14
W15
W16
W17
W18
W19
W20
W21
W22
W23
W24

E1
E2
E3
E4
E5
E6
E7
E8
E9
E10
E11
E12
E13
E14
E15
E16
E17

0   5 Metres

One of the Shang royal tombs found at Anyang. (a) Plan and cross-section of the tomb. (b) The arrangement of human victims on the raised platform of the royal tomb. One hundred and thirty-one victims, including eighty-nine human beings, were placed in the tomb of a member of the Shang royal family when he was buried. Chen Te-K'un, **Shang China** (Cambridge: W. Heffer, 1960), figs. 17, 18.

the ceremonial centers, by the royal lineages and aristocracies that needed luxury goods, and by the military retainers, who needed weapons and fittings for their chariots.

The Shang king sent out military expeditions to conquer other territories and to bring their peoples under his rule. By 1400 BC the Shang state had already reached its greatest extent. As the state grew larger, the king became progressively less able to run his domain as an extension of the royal household. A class of administrators gradually developed to govern the new territories. Some of the administrators were Shang aristocrats who were distant relatives of the king. Others apparently belonged to different ethnic groups that were at war with the Shang on some occasions and under their rule at other times. Some of these nobles lived near the Shang capitals; others lived in the territories they governed.

The Chou Dynasty

The Shang king actually had political control over only a small area of the Yellow River plain. Shang society may have influenced peoples living as far away as Chinese Turkestan or the South China coast, but the king did not have political control over them. Toward the end of the dynasty the Shang armies fought long, exhausting wars with neighboring political powers. During these wars, according to traditional sources, the Shang king was attacked by one of his vassals, a petty lord whose territory had been a gift of the Shang ruler himself. Ultimately this vassal overthrew the king and founded the *Chou dynasty,* which lasted from 1122 to 221 BC. After that date China was unified under a single monarch.

In many ways Chou society was similar to Shang society and is best viewed as its lineal descendant. In fact, there is no archaeological evidence that early Chou society, or Western Chou as it is called, was significantly different from its predecessor. After the conquest the Chou king established his vassals on lands strategically located throughout the old Shang state and on lands farther east that had never been part of the Shang domain. Many of the king's lords settled in old Shang cities; others built their own capitals in places where there had never been cities before. The most important of the Western Chou settlements was the imperial capital, where the king, his family, and their retinue resided. This was the administrative and ceremonial center of the state. The royal capital moved frequently during this period. At each location there was a central compound where the king lived and performed ceremonies honoring his ancestors; at one capital the central compound covered an area of nearly 19,500 square feet. There were also workshops in the compound where prestige items like bronze, jade, lacquer, and pottery objects were manufactured for the nobility. The cities of the provincial lords resembled the royal city; they also had central compounds with administrative and residential buildings as well as workshops.

The Western Chou cities were virtually self-sufficient. The lord, his family, and their retainers got their food from the surrounding countryside, and the workshops produced the luxury goods they demanded. As a result, markets were unimportant and money played an insignificant role in exchange. What merchants there were in the Western Chou cities were retainers of the noble households; they dealt in only a few commodities, perhaps salt and luxury goods, which moved from one noble household to another.

Western Chou society and Shang society were structured along similar lines. At the top of the social pyramid was the royal family, the king and his closest relatives. Immediately below the royal family were the king's ministers, who ran the state and were close relatives. They received both lands and titles from the king and ruled in his name. At the fringes of this powerful group was a class of men who were descended from rulers and ministers. This group did not own land; its members were minor nobles skilled in music, writing, and the martial arts. Far below the nobility were the commoners, who lacked surnames and did not worship the ancestors. They were landless farmers who worked the lands of their lord, or artisans attached to noble households.

At first the Chou king may have been as powerful as traditional sources claim he was; however, by the end of the eighth century BC he had lost almost all political power outside his own territory; several of his lords were as powerful as he was. The king was killed in 771 BC, and the royal capital was moved east to the city of Loyang.

The Eastern Chou period began at this time and ended with the political unification of China under a single ruler in 221 BC. There was an endless series of wars during this period. As the king's power waned, the lords became increasingly independent of royal authority. Because of the close kin ties between the king and the sacred ancestors, the royal throne was avidly contested by lords who wanted the prestige it offered in order to advance their causes.

A series of technological changes occurred during the Eastern Chou period. Agricultural production increased significantly after the eighth century BC. The farmers began to use heavy ox-drawn ploughs to break up the soil more quickly, and they used animal manure as fertilizer. They also built extensive canals to water their fields and transport goods to the cities. Some of the canals built during this period are still in use today. Traditional sources indicate that these innovations increased agricultural yields fivefold. Metalsmiths developed iron casting during the fifth century BC, and iron hoe blades and sickles gradually came into common use. The greatest effect of this advance was on weapons; long iron swords with single-edge blades came into use about this time and helped ensure the military superiority of the armies using them.

Land tenure patterns also changed during this period. It appears that farmers were beginning to pay taxes levied in the form of produce instead of labor service. In effect, they were paying rent to the lord for the fields they used. Some farmers brought new lands or abandoned fields under cultivation during this period; they owned those lands. What is important is that private ownership of land appeared during this period. Land thus became a commodity that could be bought and sold. During the later part of the period, merchants who had profited from the trade of luxury goods began to buy land from the peasants. The powerful lords also concentrated land ownership through heavy taxes that the peasants could not afford to pay. As a result, land ownership was increasingly concentrated in the hands of the wealthy, and a class of landless workers developed.

The Rise of Feudalism

An important series of transformations occurred in North Chinese society between the fifth millenium and the end of the first millenium BC. Very early, the North Chinese linked the ideas of surplus production and close kin ties to the gods. Groups that produced surpluses were viewed as more closely related to the gods than those that did not fare as well. As time passed, these groups became an aristocracy that could exploit the labor of the community in return for the performance of ceremonies to intercede with the gods. By the time of the Shang dynasty, one of the aristocratic lineages had become sacred. The king headed a conical clan and was entitled to a portion of the community's surplus production by virtue of his close relationship with his sacred ancestors. The ceremonies honoring their spirits were performed by him in the royal compound.

With the expansion of the Chou into lands beyond those controlled by the old Shang state, new kinds of social relationships developed between the king and his lords, on the one hand, and between the peasants and their overlords, on the other. The king granted lands and titles to the lords in exchange for their services. The lords used these apportioned lands to support warriors who would serve them in time of war. To provide the remuneration for these men, the lords received labor and tribute from their serfs in return for protection and other considerations. These new relationships were not based exclusively on kinship, though kin ties continued to play an important role. Because of this, they coincided with a significant weakening of the state in North China, which up to that time had been based on kin ties between the king and his nobles. These new relationships marked the beginning of a different kind of society, one that we call *feudal*.

As the lords became more independent of the king, they became more dependent on the production of their own lands. As a result, land itself became a more valuable commodity, one that ultimately could be held as private property and bought and sold. With the development of private property, the economically powerful lords and merchants began to accumulate it at the expense of minor lords and the peasantry, and the central state was weakened even further. Only when the social relationships that had appeared during the early part of the Chou dynasty began to change did feudalism begin to wane in China.

SOUTH CHINA AND SOUTHEAST ASIA

A slightly different story took place in the hill country below the Tsinling Mountains and on the plains of South China and southeast Asia, where tropical forests cover much of the land. One of the characteristics of tropical forests is that they contain an enormous variety of plants and animals; however, none of them is particularly abundant, nor are members of the same species often found in close proximity to each other. The plants are scattered, and the animals rarely congregate or live in groups.

<table>
<tr><td>

The Early
Hoabinhian
Peoples

</td><td>

To survive in this environment the people who were living there about 14,000 years ago belonged to small, highly mobile groups that exploited the plant and animal resources of a large area. These *Early Hoabinhian* peoples, as they are called, had to use a wide range of very specialized tools to exploit particular resources. They made these from locally available raw materials such as bamboo, many of which are perishable. They fashioned these tools with relatively simple stone implements—flakes with certain kinds of sharp edges and points. When they no longer needed the specialized tools, they discarded them.

</td></tr>
</table>

One of their settlements was at Spirit Cave in the extreme northern part of Thailand. People first lived there more than 11,000 years ago. They used simple Hoabinhian stone tools to make more specialized tools from the raw materials available along the stream in front of it or in the forest beyond. They hunted a variety of animals in the forests and along the stream: deer, pigs, antelope, monkeys, porcupines, and dugongs. They fished and collected molluscs and crustaceans from the stream, and they gathered cucumbers, betel nuts, almonds, peas, broad beans, water chestnuts, pepper, and gourds in the forest or grew them in gardens near the cave; all of these plants were later domesticated in the area. A typical meal at Spirit Cave was a stew made from small pieces of meat mixed with vegetables and spices and cooked in a bamboo container over an open fire.

A pollen core from central Taiwan shows the beginning of a significant trend around 12,000 years ago: Secondary forests began to grow near Sun-Moon Lake and fragments of charred trees began to accumulate in the sediments on the lake bottom. This suggests that the inhabitants of central Taiwan were disturbing the primary forests of the area by burning them to clear land for slash-and-burn gardens. Once they abandoned the gardens, plants characteristic of secondary forests gradually replaced the cultigens (cultivated plants). Cereal pollens appeared in the pollen profile a few thousand years later, and their prevalence increased progressively through time. This is a clear indication that the peoples of central Taiwan were engaged in agriculture by 4000 BC at the latest.

By 8000 BC peoples living in South China and Vietnam were using stone tools with polished edges and cord-marked pottery. Similar pottery has been found in sites dating from this period in central Taiwan, and from Japan through southern China into Indochina. It may well be that the inhabitants of these settlements used polished-stone tools to break up the soil after they had burned off the primary vegetation. A number of archaeologists believe that one of the crops they planted was rice, which is indigenous to the area. The settlements in South China and Vietnam have also yielded significant quantities of remains from pigs, chickens, dogs, sheep, and even water buffalo, some of which were probably domesticated. Settlements with polished-stone tools and cord-marked pottery continued to be occupied intermittently well into the sixth century BC.

Non Nok Tha lies on the flood plain of the Mekong River in northern Thailand, some 300 miles southeast of Spirit Cave. People first lived there during the fourth millenium BC. They raised cattle and grew rice on the flood plains. Their crop yields were probably much larger than those produced in highland garden plots around places like Spirit Cave. Non Nok Tha was a small settlement that covered about an acre and probably never had a population of more than 100. Some of the inhabitants of the village were skilled bronze workers; sandstone molds used for casting bronze ax heads were found there. This suggests that bronze metallurgy was developed in Indochina during the fourth millenium BC, more than 1,000 years before it appeared in North China.

Even earlier bronze work has been found at Ban Chaing, a village located about 100 miles northeast of Non Nok Tha. It was a mile square, with houses built on stilts over a cemetery. The tombs yielded red- and white-painted pottery associated with bronze tools and jewelry; some of these graves date as far back as 3600 BC. The ores from which the bronze objects were made probably came from the hill country of Indochina or South China. This implies the existence of an exchange network that linked the metalworkers of northern Thailand, Cambodia, and Vietnam as early as the fourth millenium BC.

The grave goods from more than 100 tombs at Non Nok Tha indicate that status differences already existed during the third millenium BC. Almost all of the bronze objects—beads, bracelets, and ax heads—were found in wealthy tombs that also contained a number of other items. It appears that a very small segment of the population at Non Nok Tha accumulated virtually all of the bronze objects in the community; these individuals may well have controlled the aquisition of copper and tin ores as well as the distribution and exchange of finished objects.

What happened south of the Tsinling Mountains during the first two millenia BC is still obscure, but one fact is very clear. The course of events in South China and southeast Asia was largely independent of what was happening on the Yellow River plain in North China. For example, in the first millenium BC there were more than 100 farming settlements in the hill country of Szechwan along the Yangtze River and its tributaries. Their inhabitants grew rice, raised a variety of domesticated birds and animals, and fished. Some individuals were buried with luxury goods—bronze, lacquer, and jade objects—that were manufactured in local styles that had little if anything to do with those of the Chou state. Farther south, on the shores of Lake Tien in Yunnan, a tomb bore a golden seal with a Chinese inscription, "Seal of the King of Tien." It dated to the second half of the first millenium BC and contained a number of bronze objects that were manufactured in the same style as contemporary items from Vietnam, Laos, and Cambodia. Tombs from other localities around Lake Tien that were contemporary with the royal tomb contained fewer objects; some contained none at all. This suggests that there was social stratification in the area and that the small elite group was wealthy enough to employ skilled bronzesmiths, perhaps from areas farther south, to produce luxury goods, including bronze coffins, for the royal court. Historical sources suggest that the King of Tien was powerful enough to slow down the unification of China for a few years toward the end of the third century BC.

The Development of Trade

During the early years of the first millenium AD, mainland Southeast Asia and the islands of Indonesia were gradually incorporated into a vast trade network that extended from the Red Sea and the coast of East Africa to China. The western half of this network was dominated by Arab sailors, the eastern half by Indian merchants who sailed along the coast carrying cloth and beads to exchange for gold and spices. With them they brought the ideas of divine kingship, priests, and temples. Small states focused on these temples emerged first in Burma, along the lower and middle parts of the Mekong River, and on the coastal plains of Vietnam. Later they appeared in Java.

One of the earliest of these trading kingdoms centered on the planned city of Oc-èo in the lower Mekong Delta of Vietnam. Canals connected the city with the sea and with villages located more than 40 miles inland. Oc-èo itself may have covered more than 1,100 acres; wooden palisades and a wide moat apparently surrounded the ancient city. Its residents built raised houses of bamboo that were set on stilts or pilings. At the center of the city was the king's two-story wooden house and the shrine. The towers of this temple were high enough to be seen from great distances in the surrounding countryside. Unfortunately, Oc-èo has not survived, except in Chinese historical accounts. What is clear from these accounts is the amount of centralized planning that was involved in constructing the city itself as well as the elaborate system of canals around it. The construction of these public works required massive amounts of labor.

Some of the temple capitals of these Southeast Asian trading kingdoms have survived. The most famous is probably Angkor, near the head of the

Mekong River in Cambodia. Angkor was the capital of Khmer, a kingdom that thrived from the ninth to the fifteenth centuries AD. In about 800 AD the Khmer king built his temple at Angkor Wat, an artificial island two-thirds of a mile on a side surrounded by a 600-foot-wide moat. The towers of this ornate shrine rise more than 200 feet above the surrounding countryside. It overlooks the king's palace, a mile to the north, and two enormous reservoirs. Angkor Thom, the king's compound, is also an artificial island; it is nearly two miles on a side and is surrounded by a 300-foot-wide moat. The palace, terraces with elaborately carved walls, and several reflecting pools are arranged around a shrine that stands at the middle of Angkor Thom. The reservoirs to the east are more than four miles long and a mile in width. Canals lead from them to Tonle Sap, the great lake in central Cambodia, and from there along the Mekong River to the South China Sea.

An inscription at Angkor Wat says that the temple had 18 high priests, 2,740 ordinary priests, and 2,232 assistants, 615 of whom were female dancers; they officiated at ceremonies held within the walls. Another 12,000 people resided at the shrine, and more than 66,000 men and women supplied food and performed other services for the temple. Its treasury contained more than 11,000 pounds of gold vessels and nearly as much silver, as well as 35 diamonds, 40,000 pearls, and more than 4,500 other precious stones. Khmer was a small state that was ultimately defeated by the Thai during the fifteenth century, when Angkor was finally abandoned. Imagine the labor power and resources of the larger trading kingdoms in Southeast Asia and Indonesia!

Small states developed south of the Tsinling Mountains more than 2,000 years ago. As time passed, the notion of divine kingship was either developed or adopted by a number of aristocractic groups, particularly those in the coastal and insular areas of Southeast Asia that were in contact with India and lands farther west. In these societies chiefs became kings who claimed to have descended from the heavens to rule on earth. They received massive amounts of tribute and labor from their subjects in return for their divine guidance and protection. The royal family and its retainers absorbed a large part of this surplus production; the rest was returned to their subjects in ways that reinforced the power of the state.

FURTHER READINGS

Chang, Kwang-chih
1976 *Early Chinese civilization: anthropological perspectives.* Harvard University Press, Cambridge, Mass., and London.
1977 *The archaeology of ancient China,* 3rd ed. Yale University Press, New Haven, Conn., and London.
1977 The continuing quest for China's origins. I. Early farmers in China. *Archaeology,* 30, no. 2, March, pp. 116–123.

Friedman, Jonathan
1975 Tribes, states, and transformations. In *Marxist analyses and social anthropology,* ed. Maurice Bloch, pp. 161–202. Malaby Press, London.

Gorman, Chester
1971 The Hoabinhian and after; subsistence patterns in Southeast Asia during the late Pleistocene and after. *World Archaeology,* 2, no. 3, February, pp. 300–320.

Hutterer, Karl L.
1976 An evolutionary approach to the Southeast Asian cultural sequence. *Current Anthropology,* 17, no. 2, June, pp. 221–242.

Levenson, Joseph R., and Franz Schurmann
1969 *China; an interpretative history from the beginnings to the fall of Han.* University of California Press, Berkeley and Los Angeles.

Meacham, William
1977 Continuity and local evolution in the neolithic of South China; a non-nuclear approach. *Current Anthropology,* 18, no. 3, September, pp. 419–440.

Moore, W. Robert, and Maurice Fievet
1960 Angkor, jewel of the jungle. *National Geographic,* 117, no. 4, April, pp. 517–570.

Pfeiffer, John
1977 *The emergence of society; a prehistory of the establishment.* McGraw-Hill, New York.

Treistman, Judith M.
1968 China at 1000 BC; a cultural mosaic. *Science,* 160, no. 3830, May 24, pp. 853–856.

von Dewall, Magdalene
1967 The Tien culture of South-west China. *Antiquity,* 41, no. 161, March, pp. 8–21.

Wheatley, Paul
1971 *The pivot of the four quarters; a preliminary enquiry into the origins and character of the ancient Chinese city.* Adline-Atherton, Chicago.
1975 Satyarta in Suvarnadvīpa; from reciprocity to redistribution in ancient Southeast Asia. In *Ancient civilizations and trade,* ed. C. C. Lamberg-Karlovsky and Jeremy A. Sabloff, pp. 227–284. University of New Mexico Press, Albuquerque.

Ancient Peoples of Egypt and Africa

11

Africa is an old continent. Two-billion-year-old sediments make up its southern part. The continent itself is a gigantic plateau whose highest part is its eastern edge; it dips gradually toward the north and west. Large rivers—the Niger, Congo, and Nile—drain much of the plateau before emptying into the Atlantic Ocean or the Mediterranean Sea. The Sahara Desert, an expanse of sand and rock more than 3,000 miles wide, stretches across all of North Africa. Tropical forests appear beyond the grasslands that fringe the southern margins of the desert in the west; they rim the coastline of West Africa from Nigeria to Zaire before they reach inland to the Ruwenzori Mountains. Below the forests lie the grasslands and deserts of Southwest Africa; they stretch from Angola and Rhodesia southward to the Cape of Good Hope, the southernmost tip of the continent. East Africa is covered with scrub forests and grasslands that reach northward into the Sudan, where they gradually merge with the Sahara.

More than 15 million years ago a massive rift developed in East Africa. Active volcanoes appeared along this fault and spewed lava over the countryside. Lakes formed and became progressively more saline as seasonal streams dumped their waters onto the rift floor. Several million years later water from Lake Victoria began to flow northward; ultimately it merged with tributaries of the old Nile River that rose in the Ethiopian highlands. The waters of these combined rivers flowed northward, plunging through narrow gorges and flowing slowly across the Sahara as they dropped from an elevation of more then 3,700 feet to sea level during the course of their 4,000-mile journey.

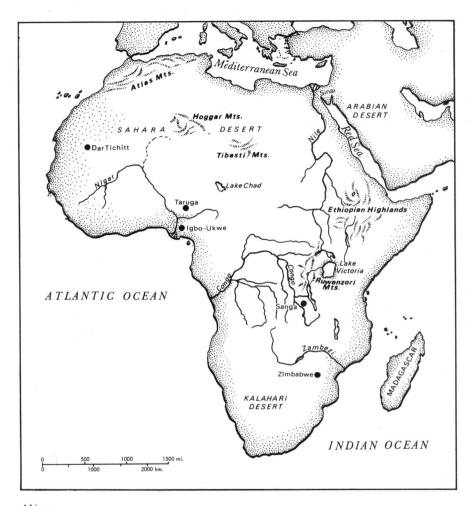

Africa.

The human species originated in the tropical grasslands of Africa. People have lived there for more than 2 million years, leaving their tools and remains at various localities in East and South Africa. These early inhabitants lived in small groups and used the plant and animal resources available to them. Their descendants have lived on the continent ever since, and they have developed a wide variety of economic orientations. Fifteen thousand years ago a group living at Nelson Bay on the Indian Ocean were harvesting the marine resources of the littoral. Their contemporaries on the Kom Ombo Plain, 300 miles south of Cairo, hunted cattle, gazelles, and hartebeest, ate hippopotamus, caught turtles and fish in the rivers, killed migratory birds between September and April, and processed wild grass seeds with stone grinding implements. At the same time, groups living along the Mediterranean coast of Algeria herded Barbary sheep, following these wild animals from one place to another as seasonal pastures appeared; they practiced herd management by consuming juvenile animals.

The earliest food-producing communities in Africa appeared during the seventh millenium BC. These peoples lived at scattered localities in the Sahara highlands of southern Algeria and Libya, along the Mediterranean coast, and in oases and high areas west of the Nile River. They kept a wide range of domesticated animals—cattle, sheep, goats, and pigs—and cultivated barley, emmer wheat, flax, and, in the Egyptian Sahara, dom and date palm. Their contemporaries along the Nile relied on local grasses, fish, and animals for food; it is doubtful that they domesticated any of these species. However, by 5000 BC there were farming communities along the Nile. Their residents were raising the same animals and growing many of the same crops that had already been brought under domestication in the Sahara highlands, the Near East, and southeastern Europe.

Peoples living elsewhere in Africa were also developing new ways of obtaining food. The inhabitants along the edges of the Sahara in Mauritania began to herd goats and cattle as wild game became scarce in the area; later they began to harvest wild millet, and ultimately they brought it under domestication. The peoples of the tropical forest from the Ivory Coast to Cameroon may well have cultivated yams—a staple food crop of the area even today—by the third millenium BC.

By 3000 BC Egypt was unified into a kingdom that stretched from the Nile River Delta on the Mediterranean to the First Cataract in Nubia—a distance of more than 800 miles. Hieroglyphic writing had been developed, and scribes were recording the deeds of Narmer, the king who unified Egypt, and his successors. These kings were divine rulers who were aided by skilled bureaucracies. They appropriated enormous amounts of surplus production to build water management systems and elaborate palaces and tombs for themselves and their families.

It is clear that a lot was happening in the Nile Valley and beyond. Let us consider a few questions. How did a primitive state based on an agrarian economy develop and evolve in the Nile Valley? What was it like? And what happened outside the Nile Valley in areas of the Sahara and to the south, where archaeological studies are still in their infancy?

ANCIENT EGYPT

The Nile River overflows its banks each year. The floods begin by mid-August in Upper Egypt and reach the northernmost areas of the valley four to six weeks later as the floodwaters surge toward the Mediterranean Sea. At the height of the floods four to five feet of water cover the areas next to the river, and fertile sediments are deposited in these flood basins. After a month or so the floodwaters begin to recede, and the alluvial flats gradually appear. They are muddy at first but dry out by early October in Upper Egypt. By late November they are dry all along the river, except for the backswamps, the oxbow lakes, and the delta next to the sea.

In ancient times, before farmers lived along the edges of the river, forests composed of figs, acacias, and evergreens fringed the channels of the Nile. Scrub–savanna and grasslands covered the seasonally flooded areas of the plain. Papyrus, sedges, and reeds covered the waterlogged soils of the backwater swamps and the delta. Fish abounded in the river, as they do today. Birds thrived in the wetland areas—the lagoons of the delta and the swamps along the river. A variety of game animals lived in the thickets beyond the river, and gazelles grazed in the desert grasslands that stretched out and merged with the sand and rock formations of the desert itself.

Ancient Egypt.

This environment was a rich one that, judging from the food remains found at Kom Ombo, provided the early inhabitants of the Nile Valley with a variety of food resources. It was a much richer environment than those found in the Sahara highlands or along the Mediterranean coast, where agricultural and pastoral economies first appeared on the African continent. When the inhabitants of the Nile Valley and the oases to the west first adopted agriculture and herding, these activities played only minor roles in their subsistence activities, which still had strong hunting, fishing, and gathering components. This emphasis on wild plant and animal foods continued well into the third millenium BC, long after the first water management systems had been built.

The Fayum A Settlements

The earliest farming communities in Egypt were the *Fayum A* settlements on the shore of an ancient lake. They were occupied about 4500 BC. Their inhabitants lived in temporary huts made of thatch or reeds. They planted emmer wheat and barley on the mud flats that appeared around the edge of the lake as the water receded during the dry season; they harvested these grains with small stone sickles set in wooden handles and stored them in basket-lined underground silos built on high ground next to the villages. They herded goats, sheep, and perhaps cattle in the savanna that stretched into the desert before disappearing. They hunted elephants in this savanna and hippopotamuses in the marshes around the lake; they harpooned fish and gathered freshwater mussels from the lake bottom. Some of the residents of these villages wore ornaments made of shells from the Mediterranean and the Red Sea; other ornaments were made of amazonite, a mineral that came from the Tibesti Mountains in the Sahara Desert to the west.

Farming Villages

The first farming villages along the Nile were settled around the beginning of the fourth millenium BC. They were not very different from the Fayum A settlements to the west. Merimde was built on high ground in the delta country. Its residents lived in semisubterranean huts and spread their debris over 44 acres during the 600 years they lived there. They broke up the soil with polished-stone hoes and planted wheat, barley, and flax on the flood plain. Their cattle, sheep, and goats grazed in the thickets around the village. The people hunted in the marshes and thickets and fished along the river. Their contemporaries in the Badarian villages, several hundred miles upstream, lived in much the same way.

The Gerzean Towns

Ways of life began to change after 3500 BC in Upper Egypt. Agriculture and herding had become more important, though wild plants and animals were still consumed by the villagers of these *Gerzean Phase* settlements. They had already built irrigation systems. These water control systems allowed them to plant in marginal lands along the edge of the desert and conserve water in the flood basins; this, in turn, permitted them to grow crops on good lands in drought years or to produce several crops in the same fields when the rains were abundant.

The Gerzean towns were built on the ruins of earlier villages. Hierakonpolis was one of the largest, with refuse covering an area more than three-quarters of a mile long. Toward the center the townspeople built a small temple on an elliptical mound. They lived in mud brick houses with wood-framed doorways and windows. A number of the townspeople may have been craft specialists. It appears that a lot of the pottery used by the Gerzean people was mass produced in a few workshops; this contrasts with the earlier pattern of small-scale production in each village.

The Gerzean craftsmen made use of a wide variety of raw materials imported from distant localities: copper and malachite from the Sinai; ivory from the south; basalt for stone vases from the Fayum; flint for stone knives and ornaments from the eastern desert; and lead, silver, and lapis lazuli from

Mesopotamia and beyond. The lapis lazuli probably came from northern Afghanistan and must have passed through Mesopotamia on its way to the peoples of Upper Egypt. For the Egyptians, this was clearly a time of increased commerce and contact with other peoples. Mesopotamian motifs appear with some regularity in their art, and Mesopotamian cylinder seals were placed in a Gerzean tomb at Naqada.

The wealth that came with this increased production and commerce was not evenly distributed among the members of Gerzean society. There seems to have been a small wealthy class and a larger group of not-so-wealthy individuals, judging from the continually increasing diversity of the tombs. Many of the tombs were small and poorly furnished. Others were large, elaborate structures with plank-lined walls and several chambers. At Hierakonpolis an exceptionally elaborate tomb had plastered walls covered with paintings. It may well have been the final resting place of a powerful man who led the peoples of this town and its environs. This tomb and the small temple found nearby probably foreshadow what was to happen later along the Nile.

<table>
<tr><td>

The
Unification
of Egypt

</td><td>

Traditional sources plus a lot of indirect evidence suggest that Egypt was divided into two independent kingdoms, or confederations, around 3200 BC. One was centered in the delta area of Lower Egypt; the other had its capital at Hierakonpolis in Upper Egypt. These sources also indicate that Narmer, a king or powerful leader of Upper Egypt, attacked the delta country and subdued its inhabitants. His predecessor, Scorpion, had already taken the first steps to unify the country; however, it was Narmer who actually carried out the unification and was the first ruler to wear the crowns of both kingdoms.

</td></tr>
</table>

Egyptian society was based on the idea that its rulers were divine. Throughout the early dynastic period every king bore the title of Horus, the falcon god, the patron deity of rulers. Annals describe coronations as the "Rising of the King of Lower Egypt, Rising of the King of Upper Egypt, Union of the Two Lands." This statement commemorates the division of Egypt into two lands with different insignias and customs and their ultimate unification under a single crown.

Because of their divine nature, the early dynastic kings were absolute monarchs who, in theory, had total control over everything that happened in Egypt. In practice, however, they relinquished some of their authority, for they were aided by a literate bureaucracy recruited on the basis of ability. The king's household was at the center of the administration, and the ruler himself dealt with matters that were his exclusive prerogative. Immediately below him were two chancellors, each of whom administered a treasury—one in Lower Egypt and the other in Upper Egypt. Their staffs included a number of important assistants, one of whom organized the census of fields and directed the collection and distribution of oil and other commodities that were levied as taxes. Each of the two kingdoms was divided into provinces, or *nomes,* that probably reflected the predynastic political organization of the land. The chief administrators of these districts may well have been the traditional leaders of the ethnic groups that occupied them.

Judging from the burials, there were three distinct classes in early dynastic society: the peasantry, a small group of officials and artisans, and an even smaller elite group composed of the royal family and the highest government officials. The tombs of the peasantry vastly outnumbered those of the upper classes and were the same as they had been earlier: an oval pit, a body covered with a reed mat, and perhaps a pot or two and some tools. The royalty, on the other hand, were buried in enormous tombs at Saqqara, a cemetery near the capital of Memphis, or Abydos, another cemetery nearby. For example, the tomb of an early queen was enclosed in a 185-by-83-foot structure consisting of five rooms, each with storage magazines containing gold, pottery, and other objects that the queen had used or accumulated during her lifetime. Outside the structure were 62 graves, each containing the remains of a slave. This particular tomb was somewhat large but in other ways not exceptional. The royal tombs contained goods that would satisfy every need of their occupants in the afterlife—servants, gardens, and even lavatories. The tombs of minor officials were located across the river from Saqqara and Memphis; they were small-scale versions of the royal tombs. Artisans were buried next to their masters; their tombs contained a few pots and the tools they had used during their lifetimes.

The royal families and their retinues were supported by the peasantry. The farmers grew the food and provided the tribute and labor that supported the king, his family, and the administrators and built water control systems and elaborate tombs for the nobility. They also provided food for the artisans—the potters, weavers, sailors, stoneworkers, metalsmiths, and merchants—who produced finished goods for the royal family. Both the size and the number of the tombs in the royal cemeteries at Saqqara and Abydos suggest that heavy demands for labor were placed on the workers.

It is difficult to determine exactly how great these demands were; however, we can make some rough calculations about what they were like during the fourth dynasty of the *Old Kingdom,* which lasted from about 2600 to 2500 BC. During this period the population of the Nile Valley was about 1 million or a little more; this was also the time when the three great pyramids of Giza were built. The largest of these, the Great Pyramid of Cheops, is more than 755 feet on a side at the base and covers an area of more than 13 acres. It rises 481 feet above the desert today and was even taller in ancient times, since some of the fine-grained limestone blocks that covered it have been stripped away. There are more than 2 million blocks in the pyramid weighing up to 15 tons each; the nine slabs that form the roof of the king's burial chamber each weigh about 50 tons. Many of these blocks came from nearby quarries; however, the fine-grained ones were brought by barge from quarries across the river.

Workmen's barracks were located next to the construction site; they housed between 2,500 and 4,000 men who were engaged full time in the construction work at the building site. This is 0.25 to 0.40 percent of the *total* population of Egypt at the time. In other words, 1 to 2 percent of the adult male working population was involved in full-time work at the building site. This does not include the gangs of men who worked in the quarries, those who transported the heavy blocks to the sorting area at the foot of the pyramid, or the people who supplied the workmen with food, or the people who were engaged in other projects. Herodotus tells us that it took 100,000 men working 20 years to complete the pyramid of a rather unimportant king. Many of these individuals probably did not work at the pyramid itself. What this implies, however, is that a much larger percentage of the total work force was directly involved in this project. (In terms of the capital investment required to build the Great Pyramid, it probably cost the ancient Egyptians an amount roughly equivalent to the defense spending of the United States in the 1970s—about 50 percent of the annual expenditures of the federal government.)

The kings who built the three pyramids at Giza placed an incredibly heavy burden on the human and material resources of Egyptian society for nearly a century. They used enormous amounts of surplus production to build and furnish their tombs and palaces. The tombs of their successors in the fifth and sixth dynasties were conceived in a much less grand style; they were smaller and often associated with royal palaces. This was a much more rational use of the country's economic resources; however, the decision to use them in this fashion may have been forced upon the kings by their provincial governors, whose offices had gradually become hereditary since the later years of the fourth dynasty.

Documentary sources indicate that the provincial governors became more important toward the end of the fourth dynasty and later. Prior to this time they were usually buried near the royal capital at Memphis; their tombs were near those of the king and the royal family. By the fifth dynasty, however, provincial cemeteries were becoming more important. The governors were having tombs built for themselves in the provinces they controlled, where they had growing economic and political interests and loyalties. The cemeteries where the provincial governors were buried were located in close proximity to their capitals. Apparently the governors of the richest provinces were the ones who initiated the trend of having their tombs built at home rather than near the royal capital. This suggests that the centralized political control of the king may have begun to erode.

Model in the Museum of Science, Boston, showing the construction of the third pyramid at Giza. To the right of the pyramid is an assembly and staging area where building materials arrived and were sorted before workmen hauled them up the long ramp that had been built against the face of the pyramid. The men used sledges and levers to move the heavy undressed blocks to their final resting places. Dows Dunham, Building an Egyptian pyramid, **Archaeology,** 9, no. 3 (1956), fig. 1, p. 159. Courtesy of the Museum of Science, Boston.

The First Intermediate Period

By the beginning of the *First Intermediate Period* (2181 to 2040 BC), there was no centralized political and economic authority in Egypt. The country was composed of a number of small, independent political units centered on the old provincial capitals. Goods like copper, lapis lazuli, and turquoise that formerly were acquired by agents of the state were no longer as common as they had been earlier. Pottery vessels that used to be standardized in size and shape throughout the country were highly varied; almost every province seemed to be producing its own particular kind of pottery. Some of the old provincial capitals were now fortified, and weapons appear in the tombs with increasing frequency. In fact, one ruler was buried with a large number of model warriors who would come to his aid during his afterlife.

A papyrus, *The Admonition of the Prophet Ipuwer,* written at the end of the sixth dynasty describes the conditions that prevailed when the Old Kingdom collapsed. The author wrote that the poor were jubilant while the wealthy lamented what was happening. Public offices had been sacked. Many fields were not planted, and others were not harvested as their crops ripened. There were shortages of everything from cloth, perfume, and oil to Lebanonese resin for embalming the dead.

The author of this papyrus was a literate man; his views, therefore, were those of the rulers and not those of the poor. The picture he painted was probably exaggerated; however, the specific conditions he described undoubtedly occurred, particularly around Memphis, where he lived. The poor were, in fact, better off in some ways during the First Intermediate Period than they had been earlier, judging from the fact that their tombs contain a wider range of objects than those of their ancestors; this suggests that they had access to more of the goods that were available in the country at the time. It is clear that governor fought governor in order to gain control over neighboring provinces. As the civil strife intensified, it is not difficult to imagine that fields were not planted or crops harvested. Shortages developed, famines occurred, and foreign goods became scarce as the daily lives of the Egyptians were disrupted.

The Middle Kingdom

By 2100 BC the rulers of two provinces that had been minor political centers in the Old Kingdom became dominant political figures. The rulers of Thebes in the south and Heracleopolis in the north had gradually subdued the lords of neighboring provinces and put together uneasy coalitions. The two rulers fought sporadically with one another as each tried to assert his rule over the entire country. This finally happened in 2040 BC, when a Theban king broke the power of the Heracleopolitans, unified Egypt, and founded the eleventh dynasty. This marked the beginning of the Middle Kingdom, a period that lasted from 2040 to 1640 BC.

The new king wore his crown uneasily, for he was still little more than first among a number of equals. His first act was to establish effective control over national affairs. He abolished the hereditary governorships, removed dissidents from office, and appointed a Theban to every key position in his new government. Even with these measures, it took the rulers of the Middle Kingdom more than 150 years to suppress the feudal lords. After suppressing the nobility the king turned his attention and armies toward Nubia to the south, where he established a series of fortified outposts between the First and Second Cataracts to safeguard the frontier and provide trading centers. His successor undertook projects that expanded the country's economy. The mines and quarries were worked as never before to provide building materials and valuable minerals, and an extensive water control system was completed in the Fayum, making it one of the most productive agricultural areas in the entire country.

The Hyksos Invasion

By 1785 BC the power of the monarchs had waned once again. They had become puppet rulers dominated by powerful court counselors. Their reigns were brief, for there were at least 60 kings during the next 153 years. In spite of these frequent changes, the central government continued to build palaces and tombs for the royal families throughout the country, and Egypt's prestige remained unblemished in Nubia and the Levant. It appears that a number of these kings were not descended from each other. At least one of them was of humble origin, according to the inscriptions on his tomb.

There had been Asiatic people in Egypt for more than five centuries. Many were attached to royal or noble households throughout the Middle Kingdom; for example, a minor official in Upper Egypt had 45 outlanders in his household. This situation probably describes the *Hyksos* "invasion" of Lower Egypt. Groups of nomadic peoples from the Sinai and beyond gradually moved into the delta country and established a kingdom there. Their influence and power slowly spread upriver toward Thebes, whose rulers maintained an uneasy independence by paying tribute to Hyksos overlords during the Second Intermediate Period (1640–1570 BC).

The New Kingdom

The Hyksos interregnum lasted seventy years. By 1570 BC Egypt was again unified under an Egyptian monarch who founded the *New Kingdom,* which was to last nearly 500 years. This time the king and his court dominated the political system. The power of the nobility was dramatically reduced; there were fewer subordinate members of the bureaucracy, and those who remained had very limited powers and owed their positions to the patronage of the king. The bulk of the country's 2 million or so people were farmers and herdsmen and were the ultimate source of its wealth. Since the existence of the country depended on managing the waters of the Nile, a considerable amount of labor was expended on maintaining the water control systems along the river. However, a great deal of labor was also involved in the construction and maintenance of temples and palaces. Some of these palaces were extensive; for example, Amenhotep III's palace at Thebes covered more than 80 acres, and his son, Akhenaten, had five palaces and villas at Amarna. These structures consisted of a series of buildings enclosed by massive walls built and maintained by slaves and peasants. Artisans provided the furnishings for these compounds and formed a respected class that produced primarily, if not exclusively, for their well-to-do patrons. Some of the most elaborate and extensive building sites in ancient Egypt were raised by the construction workers of this period.

The Egyptians had already adopted the idea of divine kingship by the beginning of the Old Kingdom. Because of his divine status, the king was able to appropriate enormous amounts of surplus production by claiming labor to build tombs and palaces for the royal family and court. Production declined during the waning years of the Old Kingdom because the amount of surplus available had not kept up with the demands of the royal family. The political hierarchy, with the divine king at its top, gradually withered away. The king was replaced by a series of less prestigious governors, each of whom controlled a province. They competed with each other for land and access to labor. As a governor emerged victorious from these conflicts, he soon adopted the symbols of divine kingship. Prestige goods were again imported from distant lands, and the new royal family began to appropriate continually increasing amounts of labor to build elaborate palaces and tombs. When the demands became too great and production declined, the system collapsed again.

AFRICA SOUTH OF THE SAHARA

The Sahara was different 15,000 years ago. There were still large expanses of land that were almost devoid of vegetation; however, they were located in different places than they are today due to the effect of glacial ice in the upper middle latitudes of Eurasia and North America. The trade wind belt was narrower then and located closer to the thermal equator than now. The southern margin of the desert had been pushed northward because of this intensified zonal nature of the weather. As a result, the mountains of the central Sahara—the Hoggar and the Tibesti—received more water than they do now. Forests grew in the highlands, and streams watered grasslands in the foothills. There were large permanent lakes—such as Lake Chad, which once covered more than 120,000 square miles—scattered through the grasslands along the southern edge of the Sahara. The weather patterns began to change about 10,000 years ago, around the end of the Pleistocene Epoch. The margins of the desert gradually shifted southward, and areas that had once been well watered became progressively drier. Lake Chad shrank to less than one-tenth of its former size, and smaller bodies of water disappeared altogether.

Early
Communities

During the fifth millenium BC and earlier, hunting and gathering communities lived along the southern margins of the Sahara. Groups of about 90 people or so lived in seasonal camps along the lake shores of the Adrar Bous area in northern Niger. They hunted the wild game that grazed in the desert savanna after the rains, and they fished in the lake as the game moved southward into areas where pasture was more plentiful. Their contemporaries, located 400 miles to the north and 2,000 miles to the east, along the edge of the Dar Tichitt escarpment in Mauretania, resided along the edges of the seasonal or semipermanent lakes that formed at the foot of the hills; they hunted giraffes, antelope, and wild cattle in the desert savanna, ground wild grasses with stone grinding tools, and fished in the lakes as the game animals became scarce. Like their contemporaries to the southeast, they moved out of the area during the summer as the grasslands dried up.

By 3800 BC the inhabitants of the seasonal camps around the lakes and swamps of Adrar Bous were no longer hunters and gatherers. They were pastoral nomads with herds of domesticated cattle and goats. Year after year they returned to the areas of restricted pasture that developed around the wetlands after the rains, for grass for their animals was plentiful and water was available. Perhaps as many as 500 or 600 people congregated in these temporary encampments. As their animals gradually reduced the pasture around the area to stubble, the nomads broke up into smaller groups and spread out in different directions in search of new grazing lands.

The inhabitants of the Dar Tichitt escarpment abandoned the area around the beginning of the second millenium BC because it had become too dry and the game that once thrived there had long since moved permanently into grasslands to the south, where better pasture was available. The human inhabitants of the area followed them. They returned to the escarpment around 1500 BC, but as pastoralists, not hunters; they had acquired herds of cattle and goats. They congregated in two large encampments, each with a population of 500 to 1,000, and herded their animals and harvested the wild millet that ripened in the savanna around their villages.

The desert began to expand again around 1100 BC, perhaps because of natural forces, perhaps because overgrazing had reduced the ground cover to such an extent that there was less rainfall in the region. Within a few centuries the environment had become harsher: The rainfall had decreased to half its earlier level. The lakes swelled during the rainy season and gradually evaporated under the hot summer sun. The people planted millet and other grass along the mud flats that appeared as the lakes vanished. Their settlements were dispersed. They lived in about twenty fortified villages on top of the escarpment that overlooked their fields. These fortified, easily defended settlements suggest that raiding may well have played an important role in the annual activities of the Dar Tichitt peoples. By 700 BC the villages in the area were no longer surrounded by defensive walls. This indicates that raiding was no longer as much of a problem as it had been earlier; it may also mean that some kind of centralized political control had emerged in the Dar Tichitt area.

At about the same time, the inhabitants of these villages imported materials from distant lands: shells from the Atlantic coast and amazonite from the mountains in the central Sahara 700 miles to the east. They had become part of a vast caravan network that stretched across the Sahara. This network brought Mauretanian copper, gold from the Sahara, and ivory and skins from further south to the Roman and Greek settlements beyond the Atlas Mountains on the shores of the Mediterranean. In return they received finished goods such as copper objects from the Moroccan coast. It is doubtful that these commodities were widely distributed in the community; in fact, they may well have been used to propitiate the dead.

About 500 BC or a little later, the inhabitants of the Jos Plateau of northern Nigeria began to smelt iron. Nine smelters, extensive slag deposits, and hundreds of pottery figurines have been found at Taruga, which lies in the forested hill country overlooking the Benue Valley. Fragments of wrought-iron figurines, some nearly 30 inches tall, have also been found in the area. Judging from what happened in historic times, these figurines were undoubtedly placed in family shrines to honor the deceased ancestors of large, extended kin groups. Perhaps the pottery figurines were used by the less affluent families while the wrought-iron ones were placed in the shrines of wealthy, powerful groups.

By the ninth century AD there were marked differences in wealth among the members of West African societies along the southern edge of the Sahara. An Islamic observer reported the existence of powerful kingdoms in the savanna country. A royal tomb was found at Igbo-Ukwe in southeastern Nigeria. The king was buried in a grave lined with wooden planks. He sat regally on a copper-studded wooden stool, clutching a copper fanholder next to his body while grasping a copper staff in his hand. An ivory tusk was placed at his feet, along with a number of copper and bronze vessels. Altogether, nearly 700 copper and bronze vessels and more than 160,000 glass beads have been found at three sites near the royal tomb. These commodities were imported. The fact that glass beads were exceptionally rare in West African sites that date to the first millenium AD suggests that foreign goods were concentrated at certain settlements and that some segments of the society had greater access to them than others.

Judging from historical accounts and evidence from North Africa, the rulers of these kingdoms sent gold from Niger, Senegal, and Mali, plus slaves, ivory, and skins from farther south, northward and eastward along the caravan routes that crossed the Sahara Desert. The prosperity of the West African kingdoms depended on the constant demand for gold and ivory to the north. It appears that this trade was controlled by the royal family and its retainers.

| Social Developments in Sub-Saharan Africa | The patterns of social development were somewhat different south of the equatorial rain forests that stretch from the mouth of the Niger River southward to the mouth of the Congo and inland almost to the lake country of the East African Rift. The reason for this is that sub-Saharan Africa had relatively few food plants that were particularly well suited to humid tropics. The plants that were present were oil palm, kaffir potatoes, and a few species of yams. It was not until Southeast Asian Food crops—bananas, Asian yams, and taro—arrived that agriculture began to become economically important in tropical Africa. These plants did not arrive in Africa until the Indian Ocean trade began, that is, during the early part of the first millenium AD. As a result, there is a substantial time lag between the development of agricultural |

economies in the savannas south of the Sahara and the development of such economies in the tropical areas of the continent.

Some of the earliest farmers south of the equatorial rain forest lived in the light woodlands and grasslands that stretch from the mouth of the Congo River through northern Angola and Katanga to the lakes of the East African Rift and northward to Lake Victoria. This country resembles the lightly wooded grasslands of northern Nigeria and the Cameroons, both in the kind of vegetation that covers it and in the rich deposits of copper and iron found there. Plant pollen from the bottom sediments of Lake Victoria indicates that there was a substantial reduction in the quality of tree pollen in the region during the early half of the first millenium BC. This probably indicates that the inhabitants of the western and southern shores of Lake Victoria were clearing the forests, presumably to plant millet and sorghum—grasses that had been introduced from the savanna areas north of the equatorial rain forest. By 500 BC or shortly afterwards, these groups were undoubtedly using iron axes to cut trees and iron hoes to break up the soil. Iron smelters dating from the second half of the first millenium BC have been found on the western and southwestern shores of Lake Victoria in Rwanda and Zaire.

These early Iron Age villages around Lake Victoria were probably seasonal. The residents planted their crops, grazed their animals, and made iron axes, hoes, spearheads, and arrow points during the summer months, when most of the rain fell. As the food from their harvests grew scarce, the villagers broke up into smaller groups and spread out over the countryside with their herds in search of game, fish, and wild plant foods. Some of them camped in rock shelters around the Kavirondo Gulf of Lake Victoria during the fourth century BC. Groups of five to ten individuals lived in these shelters. They ate fish and shellfish almost daily; occasionally, however, they had meals of goat, beef, or domesticated cat, judging from the animal bones in the refuse deposits. It is clear that hunting, fishing, and foraging for wild plants still played an important role in the subsistence economy of these early cultivators. As time passed, however, plant cultivation became increasingly important.

Ironworking spread rapidly. By the first century AD, there were ironworking communities north of the upper Zambezi River; a few hundred years later, there were ironworking settlements throughout Rhodesia. By the eighth century, ironworking had spread into Zambia and the northern Transvaal. The ironworking villages were composed of people who sowed some millet, had a few cattle, and hunted to supplement their diets. Their villages were small, containing perhaps 100 to 200 individuals. The people mined iron ore to make tools, and gold and copper for jewelry and trade with the east coast, for glass beads. The coastal peoples were, of course, already involved in the Indian Ocean trade network. The spread of the ironworking communities may reflect the spread of the Bantu languages throughout eastern and southern Africa.

Two sites dating from the eighth and ninth centuries suggest that wealth was not uniformly distributed among the peoples south of the equatorial rain forests. One is Ingombe Ilebe, located on the north bank of the Zambezi River in Zambia. Large amounts of copper and gold jewelry, welded-iron gongs, cloth, beads, and copper crosses have been found there. The settlement was probably a trading post with connections northward into the copper belt, southward into Rhodesia, and eastward to the coast. The other site is the Sanga cemetery in northern Katanga. It stretches for more than 10 miles along the shore of a lake and contains hundreds, if not thousands, of burials. The ones that have been excavated yielded elaborately decorated pottery, ivory bracelets, copper and iron knives, and copper crosses not unlike those found at Ingombe Ilebe. These were valuable commodities, and their presence in the tombs suggests that an elite segment of the society accumulated them and could afford to take them out of circulation by placing them in the tombs of the dead.

The copper crosses come in three different lengths: 1/2 inch, 1 inch, and 2 inches. Similar objects were used in northern Zambia less than a century ago as currency. The copper crosses at Sanga and Ingombe Ilebe may also have been a form of currency used to purchase commodities in marketplaces.

By the time the Portuguese arrived along the East African coast in the early years of the sixteenth century, there were well-established kingdoms centered at Zimbabwe, at Mapungubwe in the Limpopo Valley, and on the Rhodesian plateau near Salisbury. The king of the state on the plateau ruled his own kingdom and collected tribute from less powerful states in the highlands of eastern Rhodesia, along the southern bank of the Zambezi all the way to the coast, and in the lowlands of southern Mozambique. Judging from early descriptions, these kings had vast religious powers and centralized political organizations, which they used in the acquisition of raw materials to be used for foreign exchange.

FURTHER READINGS

Aldred, Cyril
1961 *The Egyptians.* Praeger, New York.

Butzer, Karl W.
1976 *Early hydraulic civilization in Egypt; a study in cultural ecology.* University of Chicago Press, Chicago and London.

Clark, J. Desmond
1970 *The prehistory of Africa.* Praeger, New York and Washington.
1971 A re-examination of the evidence for agricultural origins in the Nile Valley. *Proceedings of the Prehistoric Society,* 37, pt. II, December, pp. 34–79.

1972 Mobility and settlement patterns in sub-Saharan Africa; a comparison of late prehistoric hunter–gatherers and early agricultural occupational units. In *Man, settlement and urbanism,* ed. Peter J. Ucko, Ruth Tringham, and G. W. Dimbleby, pp. 127–148. Gerald Duckworth, London.

Dunhan, Dows
1956 Building an Egyptian pyramid. *Archaeology,* 9, no. 3, September, pp. 159–165.

Edwards, I. E. S.
1961 *The pyramids of Egypt,* rev. ed. Penguin Books, Baltimore.
1964 The early dynastic period in Egypt. *The Cambridge Ancient History,* vol 1, chap. 11. Cambridge University Press, Cambridge.

Emery, Walter B.
1961 *Archaic Egypt.* Penguin Books, Baltimore.

Fage, J. D., and R. A. Oliver
1970 *Papers in African prehistory.* Cambridge University Press, Cambridge.

Fagg, Bernard
1969 Recent work in West Africa; new light on the Nok culture. *World Archaeology,* 1, no. 1, June, pp. 41–50.

Hayes, William C.
1961 The Middle Kingdom of Egypt. *The Cambridge Ancient History,* vol. 1, chap. 20. Cambridge University Press, Cambridge.
1962a Egypt; internal affairs from Tuthmosis I to the death of Amenophis III. *The Cambridge Ancient History,* vol. 2, chap. 9. Cambridge University Press, Cambridge.
1962b Egypt; from the death of Ammenemes III to Seqenenre II. *The Cambridge Ancient History,* vol. 2, chap. 2. Cambridge University Press, Cambridge.

Kemp, B. J.
1972 Temple and town in ancient Egypt. In *Man, settlement and urbanism,* ed. Peter J. Ucko, Ruth Tringham, and G. W. Dimbleby, pp. 657–680. Gerald Duckworth, London.

Munson, Patrick J.
1976 Archaeological data on the origins of cultivation in the southwest Sahara and its implications for West Africa. In *Origins of African plant domestication,* ed. J. R. Harlan et al. Aldine-Atherton, Chicago.

O'Connor, David
1974 Political systems and archaeological data in Egypt; 2600–1780 B.C. *World Archaeology,* 6, no. 1, June, pp. 15–38.

Oliver, Roland, and Brian M. Fagan
1975 *Africa in the Iron Age, c. 500 B.C. to A.D. 1400.* Cambridge University Press, Cambridge.

Pfeiffer, John E.
1977 *The emergence of society; a prehistory of the establishment.* McGraw-Hill, New York.

Phillipson, D. W.
1977 The spread of the Bantu language. *Scientific American,* 236, no. 4, April, pp. 106–114.

Shinnie, Margaret
1970 *Ancient African kingdoms.* Mentor Books, New York.

Smith, Philip E. L.
1976 Stone-age man on the Nile. *Scientific American,* 234, no. 2, August, pp. 30–38.

Smith, W. Stevenson
1962 The Old Kingdom in Egypt. *The Cambridge Ancient History,* vol. 1, chap. 14. Cambridge University Press, Cambridge.

Trigger, Bruce G.
1968 *Beyond history; the methods of prehistory.* Holt, Rinehart and Winston, New York.

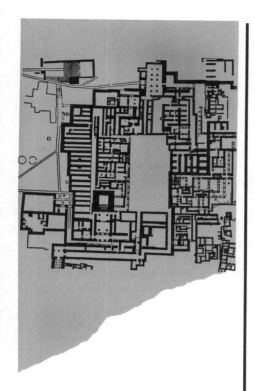

Ancient Peoples of Europe

Europe is a peninsula that juts into the sea. The landmass narrows as it stretches westward from the vast plains of Russia. The Mediterranean Sea borders Europe on the south, and the northern seas—the North Atlantic, the North Sea, the Baltic, and the Arctic—enclose it on the north. Like Caesar's Gaul, Europe is divided into three parts: the Mediterranean world, green Europe north of the Alpine barrier, and the rugged Scandinavian peninsula.

Mountains dominate the Mediterranean world. They stretch almost uninterrupted along the coast from Greece to Spain and northward to the Alps and the Carpathians, which seal off the Mediterranean lands from those lying to the north. Some of the mountains are high; others are parts of old ranges with deep, almost inaccessible valleys. Winters are long and severe in the mountains. Ten feet or more of snow can fall in a single night, while 100 miles away flowers bloom in the villages and towns that fringe the Mediterranean coast. Summers are hot and dry along the coast. Shrubs and underbrush, occasionally interspersed with trees, cover large areas of the coastal plain and piedmont country.

North of the Alps and Carpathians lies a great plain that reaches from France to the Ural Mountains in eastern Russia. A vast forest covers this plain. The climate is milder in the coastal regions and the lower latitudes, where mixed evergreen—deciduous forests predominate. The winters become more severe in the interior and the upland areas, where coniferous trees provide the dominant ground cover. Wide rivers, rising along the northern slopes of the Alps and Carpathians, cross the plain and empty into the North Sea or the Baltic. The Rhine, Elbe, Oder, and Vistula are only a few of the

12

waterways that provide communication and transportation links between the peoples of the plain and those living farther south.

The Scandinavian peninsula projects into the North Sea. Mixed oak and pine forests cover the lowland areas at its southern end. Farther north these give way to evergreen forests in the low-lying areas around the Baltic, and to fir trees and tundra in the mountains that form the backbone of Scandinavia. Arctic grasslands with occasional stands of fir trees in protected areas cover virtually all of the northern half of the peninsula and line the edges of the deep fiords that open into the Arctic Ocean and the North Sea. The winters are long and very cold; the summers are mild, with only a few months having average temperatures above 50°F.

Human beings moved into the land along the Mediterranean coast of Europe nearly a million years ago. Their numbers grew slowly. Half a million years later a few small groups had strayed north of the mountains into Germany and even England; however, as the climate cooled in the northern latitudes, with the onset of continental glaciation, they seem to have retreated

The European Peninsula.

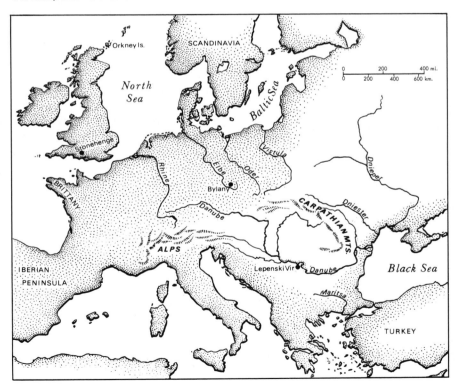

southward to the more pleasant environments of the Mediterranean coast. Only during the last 100,000 years have people lived north of the mountains on a more or less regular basis. Even so, their numbers were small at first, and it was not until much more recently that substantial numbers of people began to occupy the lowland country. The initial occupation of the Scandinavian peninsula on a regular basis may not have happened until sometime during the last 10,000 years.

While the peoples of Northern Europe were hunting game in the wooded areas that developed on the plain after the retreat of the glaciers, some inhabitants of the Greek mainland already had herds of domesticated cattle by 6000 BC. Shortly thereafter these herdsmen began to cultivate oats, millet, wheat, barley, and other crops. Unlike their contemporaries to the north or in the farming communities of the Near East, the early European farmers relied very little on wild game for food; domesticated animals provided most of the meat they consumed. In fact, they avoided living in the pine forests that were favored by the contemporary hunting and gathering groups of Europe. Instead, the early farmers built their villages, grew their crops, and raised their livestock on the rich alluvial soils deposited by the Danube and other rivers that flow into the Aegean Sea. North of the mountains the early farmers located in lightly wooded areas of the Danube Basin and along the upper reaches of rivers that empty into the Baltic and North Seas.

By 1500 BC city–states had emerged on Crete and the Greek mainland. Each of the Mycenaean states was dominated by a palace that organized virtually every detail of the local economy, from the production of food and manufactured items to their consumption by the local populace or their exchange for foreign goods. All of this was done without the benefit of money or markets. Scribes recorded many of the activities of these palaces on Linear B tablets, which have survived to the present and provide us with a picture of how these ancient states operated. The Mycenaean city–states were relatively short-lived; their power had declined by 1000 BC.

A new kind of social formation developed in the Mediterranean world during the first millenium BC. It was characterized by private ownership. Individuals not only owned land but also controlled manufacture and trade. This is a very different economic base from the one that prevailed earlier in the Mediterranean world or elsewhere in the ancient East. Palace or temple centers dominated the production, distribution, exchange, and consumption of goods in these primitive states, and individual ownership played only a minor role at best.

How did agriculture develop and spread in Europe? What were these early agrarian and pastoral societies like? How did primitive states develop in the Mediterranean world? What was happening elsewhere in Europe during the second and third millenia BC? And how did the development of a new economic orientation based on private ownership affect European society during the first millenium BC and afterward?

EARLY FARMING COMMUNITIES

Farming
Communities
in Greece

The earliest farming communities of Europe appeared in the low-lying areas of Greece. These areas have semiarid environments that resemble those of regions like Anatolia or the Zagros, where food production developed in the Near East. There is no evidence that agriculture developed independently in southeastern Europe; instead, the area seems to have been an extension of the early food-producing areas of the Near East. Many of the species grown by the early European farmers—wheat, sheep, goats, and barley—were probably first domesticated in the Near East. Other species, notably cattle, may well have been tamed in southeastern Europe during the seventh millenium BC while wild forms of the species were still being hunted in Anatolia and northwestern Europe.

The early farmers at Argissa in Thessaly had small herds of domesticated sheep and cattle by the middle of the seventh millenium BC. The sheep almost certainly came from the east, while the cattle were probably tamed in southeastern Europe. By 6000 BC the inhabitants of Argissa were also growing wheat, barley, peas, vetch, and lentils and harvesting pistachios, acorns, and wild olives. Their contemporaries at Franchthi Cave, which overlooks the Gulf of Argolis, a few hundred miles to the south, still hunted wild cattle, deer, and pigs and collected almonds and pistachios. They also built boats and caught deep-sea fish like tuna, and brought obsidian from the island of Melos, which was more than 100 miles away. By 5900 BC the inhabitants of Franchthi Cave were no longer consuming venison and wild pig; sheep and goats provided the bulk of the protein they consumed.

Farther south another group had crossed the Aegean Sea with sheep, goats, cattle, and pigs and established a settlement at Knossos on the island of Crete. The first village was small; it covered half an acre and had a population

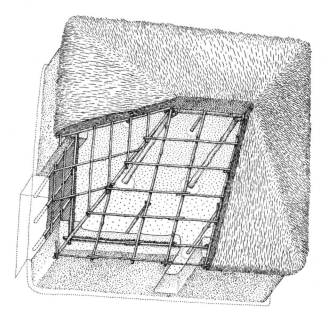

Reconstruction of a house at Nea Nikomedeia, Greece.
Robert J. Rodden, An Early Neolithic village in Greece.
Scientific American, 212, no. 4 (1965), 87.

of about 50. It grew during the next few centuries and eventually covered more than five acres and had a population of 200 to 300. Besides herding the animals, the inhabitants grew wheat, barley, and lentils.

Nea Nikomedeia, which lies on a knoll overlooking a lake in Macedonia, is the best known of these early farming communities. People lived there between about 5800 and 5400 BC in rectangular houses about 25 feet on a side. The residents put oak posts into the ground, wove reeds and rushes between them, and covered both the inside and outside walls with mud. The floors consisted of a layer of reeds plastered over with mud. The roofs were also made of reeds; they were probably pitched and had wide eaves. The villagers grew wheat, barley, and lentils; they supplemented these primary crops with cultivated einkorn, peas, and vetch, and harvested wild fruits and nuts. Sheep and goats predominated in their herds, although there were also a few cows and pigs around the settlement. These animals provided the bulk of the meat the people consumed, although they also fished and hunted a variety of large and small animals—notably red deer and hares. The villagers buried their dead in shallow graves outside the houses. The burials often consisted of an adult and a child placed in the same grave; occasionally groups of children were buried together. Judging from the skeletal remains, malaria was one of the diseases that caused deaths among the people of Nea Nikomedeia.

| Farming Communities in the Balkans | Farming communities began to appear in the Balkan countries—Yugoslavia, Hungary, Rumania, and Bulgaria—during the second half of the fifth millenium BC. The villages were located in lightly wooded areas along the Danube and a series of smaller rivers that empty into the Aegean Sea. These areas did not have abundant plant and animal resources; consequently, the hunting and gathering populations of the Balkans rarely visited them. They apparently were colonized by farming populations from the south, since food-producing villages are the earliest known settlements in the region. It is unlikely that the early farmers viewed themselves as colonists of a new land; instead, they probably moved gradually into new areas as their old fields became less productive and pastures were overgrazed. |

These early farming communities were known by a variety of names—Körös, Karanovo, Cris, Starčevo, and Kremikovci—that reflect regional differences in house construction, preferences in the location and arrangement of settlements, pottery styles, and the relative importance of various animals in the subsistence economy. For example, the Karanovo settlements in southern Bulgaria were frequently located in the middle of fertile plains; their inhabitants kept sheep and goats, grew wheat, and hunted red deer in the surrounding countryside. The Kremikovci settlements of southern Yugoslavia and western Bulgaria and the Cris villages of Rumania were river bank villages; their residents grew wheat, and the Rumanian groups raised domesticated cattle and hunted wild oxen at lower elevations and kept sheep and goats at higher ones. The Körös villages of the Danube basin in Hungary and northeastern Yugoslavia were located on river banks or on sandy hills in marshy areas; the residents of the settlements in the marshy areas had sheep and goats but relied to a considerable extent on the local wildlife. In other words, the Balkan farmers of the fifth and sixth millenia BC grew what crops they could, raised animals that survived well in the areas in which they lived, and utilized whatever fish, game, and (presumably) wild plants were available in the areas around their settlements.

Various kinds of economic orientations developed outside the lightly forested regions in which the early agricultural groups settled. In the area around the Bug and Dneister rivers in northeastern Rumania, the inhabitants relied heavily on hunting, fishing, and wild-plant collecting for food, and lived in year-round settlements, if only for a few years before abandoning them. However, they also adopted a few ideas from the farmers to the west. They kept a few cattle and grew some emmer wheat, which they processed the same way they processed other vegetable foods. Smilčić, another settlement from this period, was located near a spring about four miles from the Adriatic coast of Yugoslavia. The people of Smilčić collected marine shellfish, which they used for food as well as tools for decorating pottery vessels. They also ate sheep or goats, cattle, and red deer; it is not clear whether the sheep, goats, and cattle were domesticated animals, strays from neighboring farming communities, or wild species that lived in the area.

Not all of the Balkan peoples who were involved with the early farming communities lived on the periphery of the area in which agriculture and herding were economically important. Some of them actually lived in the middle of the farming areas and found argiculture and herding less productive than hunting and gathering. Usually they lived in environments that were exceptionally rich in natural resources like fish or game. Lepenski Vir, located on the banks of the Danube River at the bottom of the Iron Gates gorges, was one of these settlements. It was occupied nearly 7,000 years ago. The villagers built their houses on the river bank above a whirlpool where wels and barbels (large, voracious members of the carp family) were abundant. The villagers presumably used weirs or nets to catch them. They also hunted red deer, aurochs, bears, and lynxes in the pine and birch forests above the gorges; the large proportion of remains of domesticated dogs in their refuse deposits suggests that they may have used dogs to track, corner, and perhaps kill game. Eventually, as agriculture became more productive, the inhabitants of Lepenski Vir and settlements like it became farmers, although fishing and hunting remained important sources of meat in their subsistence economies.

The Western Mediterranean The rest of the Mediterranean world, from the Adriatic coast of Italy to France and Spain, was a peripheral area whose inhabitants adopted domesticated species from the east during the second half of the fifth millenium BC and integrated them into existing life styles and economic patterns. During the early part of the fifth millenium BC, for example, the inhabitants of Italy depended on wild pigs, red deer, and cattle. Pigs accounted for about half of the animals they consumed. The people may occasionally have herded them. However, it is more likely that they drove the animals into the forests and let them fend for themselves. When they wanted pigs they went into the forests and rounded them up. One of their major activities was following herds of red deer into mountain pastures during the summer months and returning with them to the coastal plain during the rest of the year. Small numbers of sheep and goats were easily accommodated into this economic pattern. The people merely took the animals to the mountains with them during the summer months. As the population grew larger, sheep and goats became economically more important and the value of red deer diminished. There were two reasons for this: (1) Sheep and goats reproduce faster than red deer, and (2) they need far less pasture to produce the same amount of meat. This kind of mobile economy was predominant in Italy during the first millenium BC, and it remained important well into the nineteenth century. It is still important in some areas of Spain.

Plant cultivation played a different role in the subsistence economy of the western part of the Mediterranean world. Initially the Italian pastoralists may have sown wheat around their lake shore settlements before they went into the mountains. They harvested what was left of the crop when they returned from the highlands in the fall. However, cereal grains played a minor role in their diet, judging from the plant remains that have been found in their garbage pits. Water chestnuts and other aquatic and woodland plants were many times more important. As time passed, however, cereal agriculture slowly became more important. Forests were cleared so that fields could be planted, and pigs and deer found their natural habitats becoming smaller and smaller. At the same time, sheep and goats were finding more and more open land as the people cleared away the forests.

The Linear Pottery Cultures Farming communities appeared north of the mountains during the early part of the fifth millenium BC. Agricultural and stockbreeding were well established in southern Holland by 4800 BC. Most of these early settlements were located in central Europe between the Rhine River on the west and the Vistula and Dneister Rivers on the east. These communities were remarkably similar; they shared a number of features, including the kind of pottery they used. As a result, they are known as the *Linear Pottery cultures.*

Linear pottery settlements were located in areas with windblown soils. Light oak forests covered these easily worked soils. The farmers cleared the trees with polished-stone axes and planted emmer and einkorn wheat. The rich foliage and undergrowth of the nearby forests provided excellent fodder for their cattle and pigs. They occasionally ventured into the forests, probably after their crops had been harvested, to hunt red deer, roe deer, wild pigs, and wild oxen; however, their herds provided most of the meat they consumed.

The settlements were located in the middle of areas covered with windblown soils rather than on their margins. This suggests that the farmers were interested in the soils themselves rather than in the plant and animal resources found on them.

Bylany, in western Czechoslovakia, was a typical Linear Pottery settlement. It had five to ten houses, some of which were more than 100 feet long and 20 feet wide. These buildings housed a number of people—possibly the members of an extended family—as well as granaries and possibly even livestock during the winter months. Altogether, about 200 people may have lived at Bylany at any given time. Bylany was a medium-sized Linear Pottery settlement; some of the larger ones had 20 or more houses and perhaps as many as 400 residents.

Judging from the size of the cattle corrals, it appears that the villagers kept about 100 to 125 animals. The kind of slash-and-burn agriculture they used can produce fairly high yields if the fields are rotated every three or four years. There were areas in Russia during the nineteenth century where slash-and-burn agriculture was practiced and plows were not used. The productivity of the poorest of these areas suggests that the Bylany farmers cropped 70 to 100 acres of land each year to produce the grain they needed for food and sowing. However, the windblown soils around Bylany and other Linear Pottery settlements erode quickly once they are stripped of natural ground cover. This means that the villages were probably occupied for relatively short periods.

Each year the inhabitants of Bylany burned the chaff and other residues remaining in their storage pits before relining them with new layers of clay. These underground silos were cleaned and relined an average of fourteen times before being abandoned. This suggests that the villagers lived at Bylany for about fifteen years before they moved away. During that time, they worked between 210 and 300 acres, assuming that they rotated their fields every four years. The soils regained their fertility and the forests regenerated after the settlement had been abandoned. The villagers apparently moved sequentially to at least two and probably three other settlements, living in each one for ten to fifteen years before moving on to the next. They returned to Bylany after about fifty years.

Agriculture and herding reached Britain and the Baltic shores of southern Scandinavia by the end of the fourth millenium BC. Beyond these areas

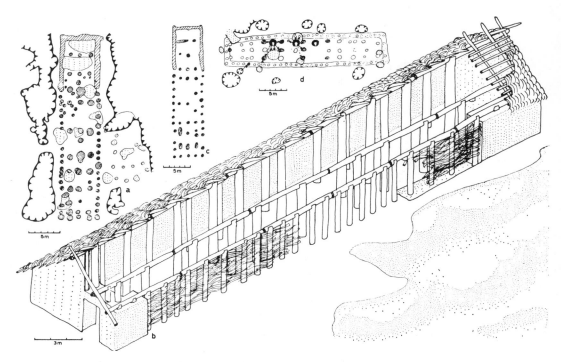

Early Neolithic house construction at Bylany, Czechoslovakia. Ruth Tringham, **Hunters, fishers and farmers of Eastern Europe, 6000–3000 BC** (London: Hutchinson University Library, 1971), fig. 20, p. 120.

stretch the Arctic and near-Arctic lands where economies based on mobile pastoralism or intensive hunting and fishing have persisted to the present day.

EUROPEAN SOCIETY FROM 4000 TO 2000 BC

The European peoples of the third and fourth millenia BC were farmers and herdsmen. They lived in small households of four to six individuals and villages with 50 to 400 residents. Many of their villages were surrounded by earth, stone, or wooden fortification works; this, along with the increasing frequency of weapons, suggests that intervillage raiding was more common than it had been earlier. Some of the farmers and herders took time off from their chores to become part-time craft specialists who produced metal tools and ornaments, shell jewelry, graphite-decorated pottery, bone figurines, and perhaps even flint tools used for harvesting and hunting. They also exchanged both raw materials and finished goods over considerable distances. By 4500 BC they had already organized themselves in ways that allowed them to undertake and complete construction projects that required 5,000 to 10,000 manhours of labor. By 1700 BC the peoples of southern England were able to muster more than 30 million manhours of labor to build Stonehenge. Some of the construction projects dating from this period were temples or public gathering places; others were tombs for what seem to be elite burials, which implies that some individuals had greater access to the resources of the society than others.

Agriculture

Slash-and-burn agriculture and herding used a lot of land. The productivity of this kind of agriculture as practiced in early Europe varied considerably from one area to another. In an area like the one around Bylany, it was fairly productive; the 200 or so inhabitants of the village needed 70 to 100 acres each year and 840 to 1,200 acres over a fifty-year period. In an area like the wetlands of southern England, a group of 100 people would have needed 100 to 200 acres for crops each year; this is roughly three to four times the amount of land required by the inhabitants of Bylany. Herds with 100 to 125 cattle, like the one kept at Bylany, may well have needed 1,500 acres or more of stubble, fallow fields, or marshlands each year to sustain themselves; the amount of grazing land required would have varied enormously, depending on the quality of the pasture available and the size and composition of the herd.

Villages appear to have been more numerous in Europe after 4000 BC than they had been earlier. Since these settlements were neither larger nor smaller than the earlier ones, this suggests that the population of Europe was increasing. In the Maritsa Valley of Bulgaria the people lived in settlements with about thirty houses and populations of 150 to 200. These villages were located about three miles from each other, which means that the inhabitants of each settlement had access to about 3,800 acres of land. If all of the settlements were occupied simultaneously, disputes over access to land might develop very quickly, given the land use patterns that prevailed at Bylany or in southern England. This demographic expansion may well have led to increased raiding and may have been one of the reasons for the fortifications that appeared around many of the settlements.

Metalworking and Other Crafts

During the sixth millenium BC the peoples of the northern Balkans began to use copper ores from the numerous deposits in the Carpathian Mountains to make cold-hammered tools and ornaments. This process required relatively little skill, and presumably anyone in a community could do it with sufficient practice. However, by the end of the fifth millenium BC the inhabitants of the Balkans and northern Greece were smelting ores, judging from the slag heaps that have been found at various sites in this area. Smelting and casting tools in open and two-piece molds requires considerable skill, which suggests that there were part-time metalworkers in the farming communities the area. Some of these farmer—craftsmen were also part-time miners; shafts dug to depths of more than 80 feet existed in Yugoslavia during the closing years of the fifth millenium BC. After extracting the ores from the earth, the craftsmen smelted them and cast them into axes, awls, daggers, fishhooks, and small ornaments. Copper was not the only metal they worked, for jewelry made of silver, gold, lead, and antimony has been found throughout the area. Other metalworking centers, possibly independent from the Balkan one, appeared elsewhere in Europe during the fourth millenium BC in Italy, the Aegean, and the southern portion of the Iberian peninsula. The inhabitants of these areas used ores that were available locally.

Many of the copper ores used by the early metalsmiths of Europe had impurities like arsenic that made objects manufactured from them harder or more durable than those made from purer ores. By 2500 BC the European metalsmiths were deliberately adding elements such as tin to copper ores in order to produce bronze, an alloy with many economically desirable qualities. Some of the tin used by the early bronzesmiths of the Balkans and the Aegean may have come from as far away as the upper Rhine, central Italy, Brittany, or Cornwall in the British Isles.

The metalworkers were not the only part-time craft specialists. Someone made small bone figurines in a workshop at Chotnitsa in northern Bulgaria; archaeologists have recovered a series of figurines in various stages of manufacture as well as the stone axe, flint blades, and bone and stone polishing tools the artisan used to make them. Another workshop was found in a settlement near the Black Sea; the craftsmen who used this shop made shell bracelets. There were other kinds of part-time workers as well—miners, flint workers, potters, and weavers.

Trade

At the same time that metal objects were becoming more important in Europe, there was a marked increase in the amount of exchange that occurred and in the variety of the goods that were moved. These included raw materials like obsidian and tin, copper, and bronze ingots that were manufactured by metalsmiths before being exchanged with peoples living in areas where these metals were scarce; ultimately, metalsmiths in these areas fashioned them into objects that met the needs, both technical and aesthetic, of the local inhabitants. Shell jewelry made in workshops along the Aegean was also exchanged. Bracelets, rings, and beads made from the brightly colored Aegean spondylus have been found as far north as Hungary and Germany. A cache of copper and spondylus objects was uncovered in the Soviet Union, more than 150 miles from the nearest copper deposits, located in the Carpathians, and over 500 miles from the Aegean Sea.

Tombs and Monuments

More than 6,000 years ago the farmers of Brittany began to build megalithic tombs, burial chambers made from large rocks with heavy stone roofs completely covered with earth. By 3000 BC many of the farming peoples from

Denmark to Spain—the lands bordering the Atlantic and the North Sea—
were also erecting megalithic tombs. Some of these tombs were very large;
one of them, for example, was entered through a passage more than 100 feet
long. The capstone of another tomb weighed more than 50 tons and required
200 individuals working together to raise it into place. The farmers of western
and northern Europe were the first people to develop a technology for moving and raising large stones.

These megalithic monuments seem to have been family crypts, judging
from the fact that they contain the remains of a number of individuals buried
at different times. The grave goods were not elaborate—a few pots, a stone
axe or two, and later perhaps a copper dagger. In most areas they were built
by farmers who lived in one place for ten to fifteen years. When their fields
became unproductive they moved to a nearby locality where fertile soil was
available. The megalithic tombs built by these farmers may well have been
the only permanent structures in the area. As such, they were focal points for
the activities of a family over a span of several generations.

Megalithic tombs are quite numerous in some areas, which suggests that
not many have been destroyed in those localities. Eighteen were built on the
island of Arran off the west coast of Scotland. They are all located near arable
land and are regularly spaced, with the exception of two that are located next
to each other. The regular spacing suggests that they were all in use at about
the same time and that there were seventeen "territories" on the island, assuming that the inhabitant of each territory built a crypt. When the tombs
were built the total population of the island was probably between 600 and
1,200, which means that each territory was occupied by groups with 35 to a
maximum of 70 members. Independent estimates from Rousay in the Orkney
Islands suggest that these "territorial" groups around megalithic tombs had
25 to 50 members. Building a tomb that required 5,000 to 10,000 manhours
of labor was clearly feasible for groups of this size. It meant that twenty individuals worked ten-hour days for one or two months. It is clear that this work
was not done all at once, for many of the tombs were built in a series of stages
over a number of years.

There is no evidence from Arran or Rousay to indicate that the residents
of one territory were more important than those of any other territory. This
egalitarian kind of social organization may well have been predominant in
northern and western Europe during the fourth millenium BC. However, it
may not have been characteristic in other parts of Europe, for example, Malta.
By 3000 BC the people of Malta had already built a series of underground
burial chambers carved out of rock in which 6,000 to 7,000 people were
entombed. They had also built six clusters of temples on different parts of the
island. Each temple cluster contained two to four structures built out of stone.
The largest temple had several courtyards and terraces with a 50-foot-high
retaining wall; its construction required more than a million manhours. Con-

struction projects of this scale were clearly beyond the manpower capabilities, though not the technical skills, of small groups like those on Arran or Rousay. They required centralized planning and the ability to mobilize significant numbers of people. The regular spatial arrangement of the temple clusters suggests that they served as the centers of territories, each with an area of about 125,000 acres and a population of 1,000 to 2,000—farming and herding peoples who built and maintained the temples and assembled there at regular intervals.

Evidence dating from the end of the third millenium BC offers clearer indications of what this new kind of social organization was like and how it developed in southern England. By 2500 BC the peoples of Wiltshire and Dorset were burying some individuals in wooden or stone mortuary houses known as long barrows. However, not all the members in the society seem to have been buried in a long barrow. Some members of the group were disposed of in a different way—perhaps by exposure—that left no evidence. The building of a long barrow required 5,000 to 10,000 manhours of labor and could have been accomplished by a small group. However, this does not seem to have been the case.

Other monuments were also being built in southern England. These included artificial mounds, causeways, and Stonehenge and other structures like it. These projects required many millions of hours of labor and were far beyond the manpower capacities of small groups. It appears that the peoples of southern England were divided into a series of regional groups during the third millenium BC, with each group centered on a henge monument. Judging from the size of the territories, each group may have had about 2,000 members. If one-fifth of the population could be mobilized for three months each year, then the group had 400,000 manhours of labor available for public works, and a henge monument like the one at Avebury could have been built in four or five years. A major henge monument like Stonehenge took much more labor—30 million manhours or more. It is conceivable that the various regional groups in southern England pooled their labor resources to build Stonehenge.

The existence of Stonehenge and similar monuments implies a degree of specialization and differential access to power and wealth. Someone had enough power to organize a vast labor force for a number of years. The tombs of southern England, as well as those of Denmark, show marked differences in wealth. Some individuals had lots of gold, silver, and other metal objects placed in their tombs, while others had only a few pieces of metal or none at all. It appears that many of the late neolithic societies in northern and western Europe were structured along the same lines as those found elsewhere in the Old World, namely, conical clans. Individuals who could claim closer genealogical ties with the founding ancestors had greater access to the wealth and productivity of the society than did other people. They used their kin ties to consolidate their positions; they directed the activities of their less fortunate relatives and repaid them for their services with feasts in which the surplus production of the society was redistributed.

THE MEDITERRANEAN WORLD

Like many other settlements in Europe, the towns of mainland Greece were often fortified during the third millenium BC. The inhabitants of these towns, with their well-defended citadels, were prosperous. They grew cereal grains, grapes, olives, figs, and spices in nearby fields, while large flocks of sheep grazed in the countryside beyond. They also kept smaller numbers of goats, cattle, and pigs. The townspeople engaged in commerce with the peoples of Anatolia, Europe, and the islands of the Aegean. As time passed, their trading ties with the peoples of Asia Minor declined in importance and their relationships with the Europeans and the Aegean peoples became more significant.

A number of the fortified towns on the Greek mainland were destroyed

The Aegean world during the second millenium BC.

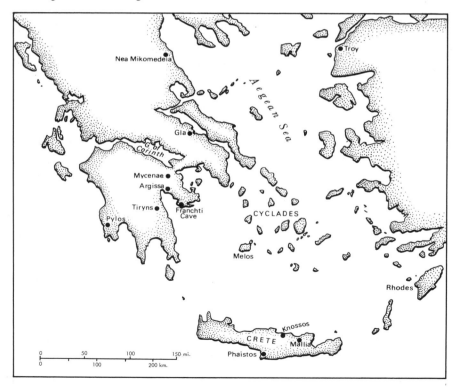

around 2000 BC. Their destruction was probably due to local convulsions rather than invasions by Greek-speaking foreigners, as some scholars have suggested. The ruler of one province may well have led his armies against the townspeople of another district in order to acquire booty, land, labor, or perhaps even tribute. The defeated peoples rebuilt their towns, though often on a smaller and more impoverished scale than had been the case earlier. Foreign commerce seems to have played a less important role in the economy of these new settlements than it had before.

Minoan
Culture

In some areas the fortified towns and country hamlets were not destroyed around the beginning of the second millenium BC. Crete and the Cyclades Islands of the Aegean were two such areas. There were a number of villages and hamlets on Crete during this period. The daily lives of their inhabitants

Plan of the Palace of Knossus, Crete. Moses I. Finley, **Early Greece; the Bronze and Archaic Ages,** (1970), fig. 1, p. 33. By permission of Williams & James, London, England.

50 M.

150 FT.

were probably organized by the residents and administrators of three palace centers located at Knossos, Mallia, and Phaistos. These palace centers shared a number of Minoan culture patterns; however, each had its own distinctive characteristics, such as pottery workshops that did not always develop in the same direction or at the same rate as those of the other palaces. Scribes at all three centers kept track of their accounts using Linear A tablets. The Minoan peoples of Crete established settlements in the Cyclades and maintained close trade relations with them as well as with the Egyptians and the coastal populations of the Levant. They do not seem to have maintained close relationships with settlements on the Greek mainland during the first few centuries of the second millenium BC, though sporadic contacts did take place. The Minoans expanded their overseas influence even further during the seventeenth century BC by establishing settlements in new areas—such as Rhodes and the coast of Asia Minor—and resuming trade with the Greek mainland.

Mycenaean
Culture

At the same time that Minoan influence reappeared on the mainland, Mycenae emerged as the most important town in the Argolid. Its importance was due to its position overlooking the major trade route between the Aegean and the Gulf of Corinth, rather than to its renewed contacts with Crete. The powerful leaders of Mycenae were buried in shaft graves that were grouped in two large circles. Both grave circles were part of a large cemetery located outside the settlement. The grave circles were used over successive generations; they were deliberately marked out and their boundaries were respected even 300 years later. The tombs in them frequently contained the remains of more than one individual and a number of grave goods, including swords and objects made from precious metals. One tomb alone contained 183 items; however, this figure is an understatement of what was actually there, since one of the "items" included 64 small gold discs engraved with butterflies.

Three cemeteries from Messenia, southwest of Mycenae, add to our understanding of the social milieu of the region. The one at Peristeria had three monumental beehive-shaped tombs, or *tholoi,* one of which contained a vast array of precious objects that resembled those from the later grave circle at Mycenae in both variety and style. A contemporary cemetery at Kleidi had tombs that contained only pottery vessels; however, the same kind of vessels were found at Mycenae and Peristeria. The third cemetery, not far from Pylos, yielded some pottery, a few gold ornaments, and bronze cauldrons—all of which resembled objects from the grave circle at Mycenae. The grave goods from these cemeteries indicate that there were marked differences in wealth and show clearly that there were highly stratified societies in several parts of mainland Greece as well as on Crete during the sixteenth and seventeenth centuries BC. The wealth of these principalities was undoubtedly based on their ability to produce significant surpluses. Some of the surplus was exchanged with peoples in distant lands, like Sicily, or other parts of Greece; ultimately it was converted into luxury goods that were used by the royal families and their close relatives.

The Structure of Mycenaean Society

In comparison to the buildings of the ancient East and even those erected later in the Mediterranean world, the palaces, tombs, and walls built by the Mycenaeans were of modest size. For example, the palace at Pylos covered less than two acres, while the entire citadel at Tiryns, including the palace, encompassed only about five acres. This does not mean that the Mycenaeans lacked the ability to undertake massive construction or move heavy objects. The lintel over the doorway of a beehive tomb at Mycenae weighs more than 100 tons and probably required the labor of 400 men to set it in place. The walls of the citadel at Mycenae have a perimeter of about 3,500 feet, while those around the palace at Gla in Boeotia have a circuit of more than a mile and a half. These walls are massive; they are over 50 feet thick in places and rise to heights of more than 20 feet today.

More than 400 Mycenaean settlements have been found in mainland Greece. Some of these were farming hamlets; others were palace towns that served as the administrative centers of small, independent states. A typical palace town had a palace enclosed by a walled citadel to which the townspeople retreated in times of danger. At Mycenae the royal tombs were located inside the citadel along with other buildings. Houses and other buildings covered the slopes outside the citadel walls.

Trade in the Aegean

Knossos had established some sort of hegemony over the island of Crete by 1500 BC. The residents of that district enlarged the palace on several occasions, while the palaces in the other provinces and many of the settlements had fallen into disuse or been destroyed by 1450 BC. The peoples at Knossos maintained extensive overseas contacts throughout the Aegean, Cyprus, the Levant, and even eighteenth-dynasty Egypt. However, during the fifteenth century BC, Mycenae and other mainland principalities began to rival Knossos for control of overseas trade in the eastern Mediterranean. The fact that both Minoan and Mycenaean pottery have been found at Ialysos on Rhodes indicates that the two areas maintained simultaneous trade relationships with the same overseas community.

The Mycenaeans initially traded with the peoples of Sicily and the western Mediterranean, presumably because the Minoans had fairly tight control over trade in the Aegean and eastern Mediterranean. However, as the Mycenaean states grew more wealthy as a result of their trade with the west and north, they gradually began to challenge the peoples of Crete for control of sea trade in the Aegean and the eastern Mediterranean. When peoples who speak different languages are in contact with each other for extended periods, they often develop some sort of common trading language or commercial jargon so that they can communicate. Apparently this is what happened when the Greek-speaking Mycenaeans came into contact with the Minoans, who spoke a different language. Scribes on both Crete and the mainland recorded pieces of this language on Linear B tablets, labels, and seals.

The palace of Knossos was destroyed about 1400 BC. After its fall Minoan influence in the Aegean and eastern Mediterranean was severely curtailed. The chief beneficiaries of its decline were the Mycenaean states on the Greek mainland, which expanded rapidly during the next two centuries. They built elaborate palaces by Mycenae, Tiryns, Pylos, and probably other localities, such as Thebes, as well. The offerings they placed in the royal tombs increased in number and variety. They erected an extensive water control system around Lake Kopais in Boeotia. And they established extensive trading contacts with peoples in northern Europe, the Mediterranean, and the Near East.

The Linear B tablets found at a number of the Mycenaean palaces provide information about the structure of these states. There seem to have been no clear-cut distinctions between what we call economic and political institutions, on the one hand, and religious and secular institutions, on the other. At Pylos, for example, the ruler received offerings from the community and made offerings along with the community to Poseidon the earthshaker, the most important of the four deities recognized by that community. His seconds-in-command were frequently mentioned in the context of cult activities, and some of them, like the ruler himself, held "lands leased from the community."

There was a great deal of occupational specialization in a Mycenaean state like Pylos; in each occupation there was a well-defined group of people, at least some of whom were probably slaves. Their work was directed and controlled by palace officials. A large staff of palace clerks recorded what the various occupational groups were doing, how many people were involved in a particular project, what the palace contributed in terms of raw materials and food, and what it expected to receive each year from these craftsmen or from the inhabitants of a particular place.

The tablets record a great deal about bronzesmiths. There were more than 400 of them in the domain controlled by Pylos, though there were none in the vicinity of Pylos itself, presumably because of the fumes they produced and their constant need for fuel. They worked in groups of up to 26 and were supervised by an overseer. Each smith received an amount of bronze from the state and directions about the specific objects he should make from this metal. Though each smith received a relatively small amount of metal, the total amount involved was quite large—perhaps two tons a year in Pylos alone. The state obtained copper and tin from distant lands. A shipwreck off the coast of Turkey had a cargo of more than a ton of copper ingots from Syria destined for the Greek mainland. This suggests that metal ingots were

A reconstruction of the archive room at Pylos showing a scribe recording information. John Chadwick, **The Mycenaean world** (Cambridge: Cambridge University Press, 1976), fig. 9, p. 19.

shipped to the mainland and manufactured into bronze ingots, and that pieces of these ingots were distributed to local smiths, who then produced specific items for the state.

Besides recording the state's assessments and the contributions made to it, the personnel of the various work units, and the details of land tenure, the palace scribes kept close track of the whereabouts of units of the Pylian army. The army had been mobilized to meet some imminent danger. Pylos ultimately succumbed to this danger, for it was destroyed around the end of the thirteenth century BC. This was an unstable time on mainland Greece. There was open warfare between states over control of land, labor, and resources; palaces were destroyed and townspeople dispersed. Local uprisings may well have followed on the heels of these battles, adding to the chaos, as farmers and slaves took advantage of the weakened powers of local rulers.

A new kind of social formation gradually developed in the Mediterranean world after the collapse of the Mycenaean states. No longer were the economies of the Mediterranean peoples dominated by palaces that administered and controlled the daily lives of their subjects. By the middle of the first millenium BC—after the appearance of Villanovan and Etruscan culture in northern Italy and the advent of ironworking among the Urnfield peoples of northern Europe—the prevailing economic pattern in the Mediterranean countries was one of private ownership. Individuals owned land as personal property that could be sold or willed to their descendants; individuals, rather than the palace or the state, controlled manufacture and commerce. Currency, and with it wage labor, appeared for the first time in this part of the world. Status and social position became major concerns of the Mediterranean peoples as they had not been earlier. People were no longer grouped in ways that depended on their genealogical ties to the ruler or the divine ancestor. Instead, these groupings were based on membership, freedom, degree of servitude, land ownership, and place of residence. In classical antiquity men struggled to gain imperial favor so that they could enhance their own status and that of their families. This kind of struggle could not have been comprehended earlier. This social milieu marked the end of kin-based societies as they had existed earlier.

FURTHER READINGS

Atkinson, Richard J. C.
1961 Neolithic engineering. *Antiquity,* 35, no. 140, December, pp. 292–299.

Barker, Graeme
1973 Cultural and economic change in the prehistory of central Italy. *The explanation of culture change; models in prehistory,* ed. Colin Renfrew, pp. 359–370. Gerald Duckworth, London.

Bloch, Raymond
1960 *The origins of Rome.* Praeger, New York.

Branigan, Keith
1975 *The foundations of palatial Crete; a survey of Crete in the Early Bronze Age.* Routledge and Kegan Paul, London and Boston.

Chadwick, John
1976 *The Mycenaean world.* Cambridge University Press, Cambridge.

Childe, V. Gordon
1951 *The dawn of European civilization,* 5th ed. Knopf, New York.
1958 *The prehistory of European society.* Penguin Books, Baltimore.

Clark, J. C. D.
1952 *Prehistoric Europe; the economic basis.* Methuen, London.

Daniel, Glyn, and J. D. Evans.
1967 The western Mediterranean. *The Cambridge Ancient History,* vol. 2, chap. 37. Cambridge University Press, Cambridge.

Finley, Moses I.
1970 *Early Greece; the Bronze and Archaic ages.* W. W. Norton, New York.
1973 *The ancient economy.* University of California Press, Berkeley and Los Angeles.

Hooker, J. T.
1976 *Mycenaean Greece.* Routledge and Kegan Paul, London.

Jarman, Michael
1971 Culture and economy in the north Italian neolithic. *World Archaeology,* 2, no. 3, February, pp. 255–265.

Muhly, J. D.
1973 Tin trade routes of the Bronze Age. *American Scientist,* 61, no. 4, July-August, pp. 404–413.

Pallotino, Massimo
1975 *The Etruscans.* Indiana University Press, Bloomington and London.

Pfeiffer, John E.
1977 *The emergence of society; a prehistory of the establishment.* McGraw-Hill, New York.

Phillips, Patricia
1972 Population, economy and society in the Chassey–Cortaillod–Lagozza cultures. *World Archaeology,* 4, no. 1, June, pp. 41–56.

Piggott, Stuart
1965 *Ancient Europe from the beginnings of agriculture to classical antiquity.* Aldine-Atherton, Chicago.

Renfrew, Colin
1973 *Before civilization.* Knopf, New York.
1973 Monuments, mobilization and social organization in neolithic Wessex. In *The explanation of culture change; models in prehistory,* ed. Colin Renfrew, pp. 539–558. Gerald Duckworth, London.

Rodden, Robert J.
1965 An early neolithic village in Greece. *Scientific American,* 212, no. 4, April, pp. 83–91.

Soudský, Bohumil, and Ivar Pavlu
1972 The Linear Pottery culture settlement pattern of central Europe. In *Man, settlement and urbanism,* ed. Peter J. Ucko, Ruth Tringham, and G. W. Dimbelby, pp. 317–328. Gerald Duckworth, London.

Tringham, Ruth
1971 *Hunters, fishers and farmers in Eastern Europe 6000–3000 B.C.* Hutchinson University Library, London.

PEOPLES OF OCEANIA AND THE AMERICAS

In the previous section we saw how stratified societies developed out of kin-based ones in various parts of the Old World, and the effects of this development. The social relationships that emerged in these societies were no longer relations between equals. Instead, there were classes of people, some of whom had greater access to the wealth and power of the society by virtue of inherited rather than achieved status.

In this section we will examine what happened in the Pacific Islands and the Americas during the same period. These areas are important because they provide us with an independent laboratory in which to study the development of ancient society. The processes of social development that occurred in the Americas and Oceania were largely, if not exclusively, independent of what happened in the Old World. As a result, they offer a way of testing theories of social change and development.

PART
FOUR

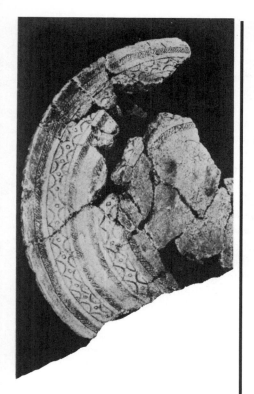

Peoples Out of Asia

For most of the last 5 million years, people lived exclusively in Africa, Europe, and Asia. No early forms of human life have been found in either Australia or the Americas. Sometime after people reached their modern form, about 50,000 years ago, they moved into previously uninhabited lands. Between thirty and forty thousand years ago, they crossed the Bering Strait and settled in the Western Hemisphere for the first time. About 30,000 years ago, they crossed the open water that separates Australia and New Guinea from the Indonesian Archipelago and the mainland of Asia. During the second millenium BC they moved into the large islands that stretch eastward from New Guinea. A thousand years later they began to cross vast expanses of open sea and settle in the islands of the Pacific.

EARLY PEOPLES OF AUSTRALIA AND THE PACIFIC

Australia, New Guinea, and the rest of the islands in the western Pacific are large; many have central mountain ranges, and some have active volcanoes. The islands of the central Pacific are smaller and more dispersed. For example, New Guinea covers more than 300,000 square miles; the fifteen islands of the Cook group have a combined area of less than 100 square miles and are spread over nearly 1 million square miles of ocean. Less than 100 miles of water separates New Guinea from Australia across the Torres Strait, while to the east Hawaii is nearly 2,300 miles from the Marquesas Islands, the nearest group that was inhabited in prehistoric times.

Lake Mungo and Kosipe

The oldest known habitation site was a seasonal camp on the shores of Lake Mungo in the interior of southeastern Australia. About a dozen people lived there between 25,000 and 30,000 years ago. They caught small burrowing animals in the bush and occasionally captured larger species like wallabys or kangaroos. They collected shellfish along the shores of the lake during the summer and fished for perch in the deeper waters. During the winters they ate emu eggs. The patterns of availability of the different kinds of foods they consumed suggest that they lived at the lake during the winter and again in the late spring and early summer.

Two of the people who camped at Lake Mungo died, at different times. One was a young adult woman. The rest of the group tried to cremate her; however, they did not use enough fuel, so her back and neck were singed rather than burned. The group smashed the burned skeleton, especially the head and face. They then gathered the broken bones and placed them in a shallow pit. Even in historic times some of the aboriginal peoples of southeastern Australia and Tasmania disposed of the dead in this fashion.

The Pacific.

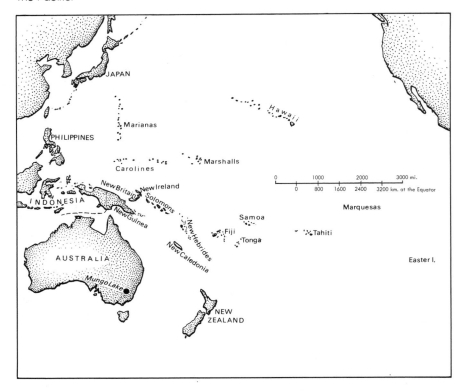

The people at Lake Mungo made their stone tools—heavy "horsehoof" cores used for pounding and scraping, and various kinds of scrapers used for scraping and cutting—from rocks that outcropped about ten miles north of the lake. The high proportion of finished tools suggests that they were made elsewhere and received final trimming or were resharpened at the campsite. The tools themselves resemble other early tool assemblages on the continent. They are different, however, from roughly contemporary stone implements found at Kosipe in the mountains of southeastern New Guinea. Waisted blades and ax-adzes with ground edges are the two main kinds of stone tools found at Kosipe.

Because of lower sea levels, New Guinea and Australia formed a single, continuous landmass at the time that Kosipe and Lake Mongo were occupied. Open water separated it from Indonesia, which was part of the Asian main-

Stone tools from Mungo Lake and Kosipe. (a) Lake Mungo: 1–2, core tools; 3–6, steep-edge scrapers; 7, flat scraper; 8, notched tool. J. M. Bowler et al., Pleistocene human remains from Australia; a living site and human cremation from Lake Mungo, western New South Wales, **World Archaeology,** 2, no. 1 (1970), fig. 13, p. 50. (b) Kosipe: a–c, e, waisted blades; d, flaked ax–adze; f, partly ground ax–adze. Drawings by Rhys Jones. J. Peter White et al., Kosipe; a late Pleistocene site in the Papuan highlands, **Proceedings of the Prehistoric Society,** 36 (1970), fig. 3, p. 162. Courtesy of the Prehistoric Society.

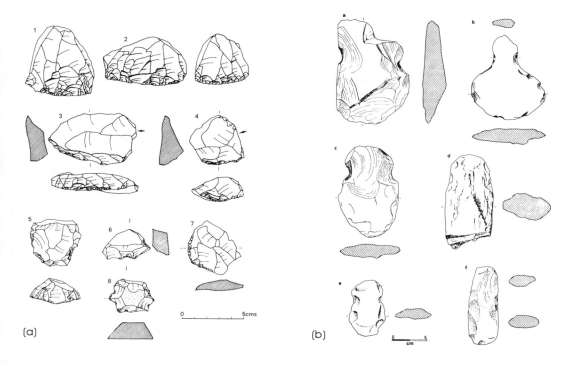

(a) (b)

land at that time. Why were the tool assemblages from the two localities so different from each other? The answer to that question reflects the kinds of resources that were available to the two groups. The people at Lake Mungo lived on a lake in a scrub desert; they needed digging implements and cutting tools. Those at Kosipe lived on a forested mountain more than 6,000 feet above sea level; they used ax-adzes to clear vegetation and waisted-blade hoes to dig up wild tubers. The Kosipe population may well have been low-land people who visited the ridge each year to cut the pandanus that grew in a nearby swamp. Like some of their contemporaries in the Australian grass-lands to the south, they may also have hunted giant marsupials.

Other Early
Settlements

The inhabitants of the Oenpilli region of Arnhem Land in northern Australia used edge-ground axes like those of New Guinea between 22,000 and 15,000 years ago. Their contemporaries at Koonalda Cave on the south coast of Australia mined flint from veins more than 200 feet deep in the ground; they also engraved drawings on the cave walls. The tools used in Australia until about 10,000 years ago resembled those found at Lake Mungo—horsehoof cores and large scrapers. These were replaced by a variety of small chipped-stone tools after that time. These small tools, which vary from one region to another, were being used when the Europeans arrived on the coast of the continent in the seventeenth century. At that time the peoples on the Australian side of the Torres Strait relied on the rich marine resources of the coast and gathered wild taro, yams, and arrowroot. Their neighbors across the strait in New Guinea cultivated these plants along with sugar cane and tree crops like bananas, breadfruit, and coconuts.

By 4500 BC the inhabitants of the Kiowa rock shelter in the south-central highlands of New Guinea were eating pigs. These were domesticated animals, since pigs were not native to the island and must have been imported from the Asian mainland. By 3000 BC they were using ground-stone ax-adzes to clear forested areas in the Mt. Hagen area of central New Guinea, judging from a reduction in the amount of arboreal pollen found in a pollen core. This suggests that they were already practicing slash-and-burn agricul-ture. By 300 BC (and perhaps 2,300 years earlier), the inhabitants of the Mt. Hagen area had built elaborate systems of ditches to drain swampy areas. These drainage systems were probably used for cultivating taro. Post holes and wooden farming implements have been found with the ditches, as have fragments of pandanus and gourds.

Perhaps as early as 6000 BC people moved into the large islands of the Bismarck Archipelago, which lie about 50 miles off the northeast coast of New Guinea. On one of these islands, New Britain, they used waisted-blade hoes similar to those found in the New Guinea highlands. This movement continued during the late second millenium and early first millenium BC as people moved eastward through the Solomon Islands to the New Hebrides, New Caledonia, Fiji, Tonga, and Samoa.

The Lapita Pottery Cultures

The people who moved from the Bismarck Archipelago and the Solomon Islands into the eastern archipelagoes used *Lapita pottery*. Most of this pottery consists of undecorated round-bottomed bowls and pots; however, a small portion of the pottery found at any settlement consists of flat-bottomed bowls with incised, appliqué, or "combed" decoration on their upper surfaces. The decorated Lapita bowls are very similar from one island group to another, not only in their appearance but also in the kinds of tempering materials that were added to the clay to prevent the vessels from breaking during firing. This suggests that tempering materials or even whole vessels were traded over considerable distances, along with other items like obsidian. The Lapita peoples of the eastern Solomons made tools out of obsidian that they acquired from a volcanic island off the coast of New Britain, more than 1,250 miles to the west.

The peoples who made Lapita pottery were fishermen and shellfish collectors at first. Later they raised pigs and grew taro, yams, and bananas. First

Lapita pottery dish from Reef Islands. Courtesy of Roger Green and the Department of Anthropology, University of Auckland, New Zealand.

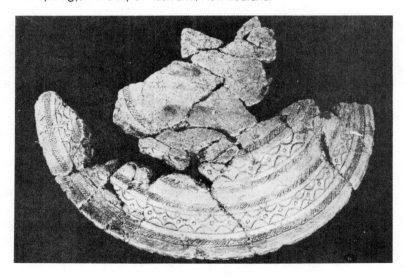

and foremost, however, they were skilled sailors who were able to cross hundreds of miles of open sea. These voyages were impressive accomplishments, given the fact that they had neither compasses nor charts. These ancient sailors used their powers of observation to guide them. They knew about the gentle swells produced by ocean currents and could distinguish them from storm waves, which move from different directions with a different rhythm. They knew about the small, fast waves produced when ocean currents are reflected from islands. During the day they used seamarks—such as coral reefs lying below the surface of the water—together with cloud formations, cloud color, and the presence of shore birds or pieces of land plants floating in the water to determine the presence and direction of land. By night, they used the stars or the phosphorescent flashes that appear in the water and streak toward land before disappearing. These signs increase the effective range of an island and allow the skilled sailor to detect its presence long before it appears on the horizon.

The Settlement of Polynesia

By AD 300 these ancient seafarers had already carried immigrants into the islands of eastern Polynesia. The first settlers in the Marquesas arrived at that time; shortly after their arrival they made a few pots like those that were being used in Samoa, which suggests that the immigrants may have come from there. Immigrants also settled in Hawaii and the Society Islands at about the same time. Within a few hundred years they crossed more than 1,000 miles of open sea to settle Easter Island. By the end of the first millenium AD, voyagers from eastern Polynesia established the first settlements in New Zealand.

It is not clear why people from Samoa, Tonga, and other islands of western Polynesia emigrated. There is some evidence that they moved because of conflicts over scarce resources. Shortly before eastern Polynesia was settled, the inhabitants of Samoa and Tonga began to raise pigs and grow plant foods. This increased the amount of food available to the islanders and probably led to an increase in the population of the two island groups. By the fifth century AD the Samoans were building forts. What was happening in Samoa at that time may well have been similar to what took place in New Zealand 1,000 years later. The Maoris of New Zealand, and presumably the ancient Samoans at an earlier date, were divided into a number of large, kin-based groups, each of which controlled the resources of a particular area. As the population increased, these groups began to compete with each other for arable land. As tension grew, they began to build hilltop fortresses. When conflict erupted, the groups retreated to their palisaded fortresses. Ultimately, some of them lost the fight for access to arable land, and the remaining members of these groups set sail to the east in search of uninhabited lands where they could settle and begin life anew.

The early settlers of eastern Polynesia brought the idea of social inequality with them. The highest-ranking group was composed of direct descendants of the founder. The next-highest group was composed of descendants of his younger sons. These noble lines kept close track of their genealogies; for example, the noble clans of the Cook Islands trace their ancestors back more than ninety generations. At the bottom of the social hierarchy were the commoners, who fished, farmed, and provided labor to build sacred plazas, stone-faced platforms, and even stone statues like the ones on Easter Island. By and large, the commoners did not keep elaborate genealogies. In return for their gifts of tribute and labor to the chiefs, they received commodities that they did not produce for themselves.

As time passed, social inequality increased in eastern Polynesia—particularly in Hawaii and Tahiti. The early settlements in Hawaii were located in coastal areas or in the well-watered valleys below the mountains. The inhabitants of these early villages farmed, raised pigs, and fished. As the population of the island grew, people had to move into marginal lands where farming could be practiced only with the aid of stone terraces and extensive irrigation systems. During the time that these terraces were built, sacred plazas with stone-faced pyramids and storage areas enclosed by stone walls were erected in various parts of the island. These were the centers of domains that were administered by minor chiefs. By AD 1500 the amount of labor expended in building tombs near these plazas suggests that there were no more than four distinct social ranks, the highest-ranking individuals were buried with stone walls demarcating their place of interment, while those of intermediate rank were buried with canoes or canoe parts, and commoners were buried without any grave goods. By the same criterion, there were six or seven distinct social status levels on the island 200 years later.

When Captain James Cook arrived in Hawaii in 1778, the eight islands were ruled by four paramount chiefs, each of whom had 200 to 300 attendants. Immediately below them in the social hierarchy were 33 chiefs, each of whom administered a district for one of the paramount leaders. At that time the paramount chiefs were replacing the district chiefs, who had ties to the local populations, with their own kin. This had the effect of centralizing political authority in the hands of the paramount rulers; it also had the effect of centralizing conflict at the top of the social hierarchy as the close kin of the paramount chief began to compete with each other, and with the ruler for social position. During the 1780s the paramount chiefs of Hawaii fought with one another and with their noble relatives as each sought to gain a competitive advantage over his kin that could be translated into an advance in social position and an increase in political power. At about the same time, the Pomares, a royal lineage of Tahiti, succeeded in consolidating their social and political position by defeating the other paramount chiefs of the island group and establishing themselves as the supreme rulers of the islands.

New Zealand The social situation had not progressed as far in New Zealand by the end of the eighteenth century as it had in Hawaii and Tahiti. New Zealand not only was settled 700 to 800 years later than the island groups to the east, but it also was many times larger than they were. However, the process of social development was following the same trajectory. Socially, the people of New Zealand were organized in the same way as their relatives in the islands to the east. There were conical clans, and the high-ranking groups were the direct descendants of the founder, while less prestigious groups were more distant kin of the founder or his immediate descendants.

The earliest settlements in New Zealand were located in the coastal areas of North Island and the northern part of South Island, where the people could farm and exploit marine and forest resources. As the population density in these areas increased, the Maori peoples began to build hilltop fortresses surrounded by up to seven wooden palisades, some of which had raised wooden platforms for fighting. They stored surplus food in these fortresses and used them as social centers. Most of the Maori lived in seasonal camps around the forts; however, some members of any given group may have lived in or near the fort, although their numbers fluctuated from one season to the next. In times of conflict all of the peoples of the district presumably sought shelter and protection in a fort. It appears that the leaders of neighboring districts even formed temporary alliances to fend off common enemies. These alliances were probably short-lived, and no paramount chiefs had emerged by the time the Europeans arrived in the closing years of the eighteenth century.

THE FIRST AMERICANS

The first immigrants to the Americas arrived 30,000 to 40,000 years ago, shortly before the Bering land bridge began to form between North America and Siberia. This suggests that these early immigrants crossed the 40 mile stretch of water called the Bering Strait that separates Alaska from Siberia. On clear days Alaska can be seen from Siberia, and both continents are visible from the Diomedes Islands, which are located in the middle of the strait. As a result, land would never be out of sight for anyone who wanted to cross the strait, even if sea level were as high as it is now. The strait was probably not as important a barrier to human traffic as we often think. Even today the ice is firm enough about once every decade for people to cross between Alaska and Siberia with dog sleds. And the cultural similarities between the American Arctic and Siberia during the past 10,000 years indicate that the peoples of these two areas continued to exchange ideas and techniques long after the Bering land bridge had ceased to exist.

When people moved into the perennially unglaciated area of central Alaska and the Yukon, they found it dotted with small lakes and streams and

The Americas.

covered with a variety of forest, tundra, and Alpine environments that stretched eastward across northern Canada and southward through the valleys and basins of the Rockies. The animals that thrived in this country—caribou, forest bison, steppe antelopes, and musk oxen, to name only a few—were the same ones, by and large that the immigrants had known in Siberia. These early peoples of the American Arctic often camped in the foothill country, where the forest, Alpine, and tundra environments converged and the plant and animal resources were not only more diverse but perhaps also more abundant at certain times of the year. The hills also provided them with vantage points from which they could watch animals moving along game trails or congregating at watering places.

The Old Crow Basin

People were living in the American Arctic more than 30,000 years ago. One of the areas they inhabited was the Old Crow Basin of the northern Yukon. Radiocarbon dates on a series of bone tools indicate that they were made between 26,000 and 29,000 years ago. The climate of the American Arctic was cooling slowly during that period, and glaciers were beginning to form in the mountains. Horses, bison, and woolly mammoths grazed in the grasslands of the basin. The presence of caribou indicates that at least some of these grasslands were steppes. Beavers lived in the streams and lakes of the basin, and moose browsed in nearby spruce woodlands. The human residents of the basin hunted these and other animals for food and materials like skins, sinew, and bone with which to make clothing and tools.

Other tool assemblages that may be as old as, if not older than, the one from Old Crow Basin are the British Mountain complex from Engigstciak on the Arctic shores of the Yukon and the Hughes and McLeod complexes from Fisherman Lake in the southwest corner of the Northwest Territories. Pollen and fossil animals from Engigstciak indicate that the climate there was at least as warm as it is today, if not warmer, when its human inhabitants left British Mountain tools there. This suggests that the site may be somewhat earlier than Old Crow Basin, where climatic conditions were deteriorating because of the onset of the last glacial cycle. All of these assemblages are very similar to the Mal'ta, Buret', and Irkutsk Military Hospital complexes of cenetral Siberia, which were incorporated into soil horizons that formed 30,000 years ago.

Migration to the South and East

The early immigrants probably moved rapidly throughout the unglaciated portions of the American Arctic and then into the foothill country of the Rockies. There they gathered wild plants and hunted the caribou and other animals that thrived in the area. In any given year they probably moved from one place to another as they followed the herds and waited for wild plants to ripen. However, as the climate cooled and glaciers began to spread over the mountaintops and through the intermontane valleys of Alaska and Canada, the plant formations changed, and animals that had once been plentiful became scarcer along the northern edges of their old hunting territories. Many of the animals were moving southward into areas where food was more plentiful. The early Americans followed them down the eastern slopes of the Rockies through the Mackenzie River basin and across the Pelly and Liard Rivers of the southern Yukon and the northeastern corner of British Columbia.

Human populations must have begun moving out of the American Arctic almost as soon as they arrived there. Stone tools found in one of the lower levels of the Meadowcroft rock shelter in western Pennsylvania were associated with organic materials whose radiocarbon date shows that they are more than 15,000 years old. The tools from the lowest level of Wilson Butte Cave in southern Idaho were used about 14,500 years ago. Some obsidian blades found at Tlapacoya, near Mexico City, were associated with hearths that were 23,000 to 24,000 years old. The earliest cultural remains at Pikimachay Cave in the south–central highlands of Peru are 19,000 to 20,000 years old. Burned bones, some of them cut and scored, from Muaco

The entrance of Pikimachay, a cave in the Peruvian highlands that contains some of the oldest cultural remains in South America. Richard S. MacNeish, Early man in the Andes, **Scientific American,** 224, no. 4 (1971), 102. Copyright © 1971 by Scientific American, Inc. All rights reserved.

and Taima-Taima in north–central Venezuela are from 13,000 to more than 16,000 years old. An early tool assemblage from the Alice Boer site in south-eastern Brazil is more than 14,000 years old. And people had reached Fell's Cave, near the southern end of South America, more than 11,000 years ago.

The locations of these early assemblages and others, as well as their antiquity, indicate that human populations were already living well south of the Canadian ice sheets before the time of the last glacial maximum, about 18,000 years ago. Furthermore, they had spread throughout many of the unglaciated portions of the New World by the time of the last glacial maximum or shortly thereafter.

The way people moved into the Americas probably resembled a wave that began in Alaska and northern Canada and spread southward. Secondary centers were established south of the ice sheets, and people began to spread from these centers as well. The availability and abundance of food resources changed in the New World because the size, shape, and location of major natural regions were modified by the advance and retreat of the glaciers. When human groups first moved into previously uninhabited areas, their numbers may have increased relatively rapidly because food was relatively abundant. Some of these food resources probably replenished themselves each year; others were not replenished because people overexploited them. When the population of an area became too large for its members to feed themselves adequately, the group divided. Some of its members remained in the area, for food was relatively more plentiful than it had been earlier since there were fewer people to feed. The other part of the population moved out and colonized a nearby area where the food resources had not yet been disturbed by people.

Cultural
Diversity

As people moved from one natural region to another—from forest to grass-land or from tropical grassland to jungle—they had to deal with environmental diversity. While they continued to use whatever familiar resources occurred in their new homelands, they had to learn which other elements of the new environments could also be used profitably. They had to recognize which of the natural products of the new area were potential resources; they had to decide to exploit them; and they had to develop tools and techniques to utilize them efficiently. When adjacent regions shared a large number of resources, the shift from one to the other may have been rapid. But when there were significant differences in the resource composition of adjacent regions, movement into the new area may have occurred more slowly because the group needed time to learn about the new land and devise ways to exploit its wealth. The resource differences between one natural region and the next was expressed not only in terms of the availability of certain resources at different times of the year, but also in terms of how people organized themselves to obtain food, when they worked, how long and hard they worked, and the tools and techniques they used to carry out certain tasks.

The cultural diversity produced by this process increased over time. Many of the earliest known tool assemblages are fairly similar to each other both in appearance and technology, regardless of whether they occur in North or South America. They contain cobble hammers and a wide range of crude, unifacially chipped stone tools made on flakes or blades, some of which have prepared striking platforms and were removed from discoidal cores. This kind of stoneworking technology occurs from the American Arctic to the deserts and mountains of western South America. The later tool assemblages in both North and South America are much more varied both in appearance and technology. It is possible to distinguish at least half a dozen toolmaking traditions that date from between 14,000 and 9,000 years ago. These include the Alaskan microcore tradition, the conical core tradition of the Yukon, the fluted-point tradition of North America south of the ice sheets, the stemmed-point and leaf-shaped point traditions of North America, and the Andean biface tradition of western South America. In general, all of the later assemblages belonging to one or another of these traditions include bifacially chipped projectile points, well-made scrapers, and various kinds of more specialized tools.

The cultural differences that developed are most apparent in the stone tools used by peoples living in different areas. This variation reflects differences in the kinds of foods they ate and how they acquired those foods. For example, the earliest occupants of Pikimachay Cave in the mountains of Peru, who lived there sporadically between 19,000 and 16,000 years ago, left Pacaicasa tools in the cave. They apparently chased giant ground sloths out of their den in the cave and killed these 10- to 15-foot-tall animals outside the cave. They butchered these animals along with horses and camelids outside and brought selected cuts of meat back to the shelter of the cave; judging from the high proportion of jaws and femurs among the remains, the human inhabitants were especially fond of tongue and round steak, both of which are relatively lean cuts of meat.

Subsistence Activities

By 7000 BC the inhabitants of the Ayacucho area, where Pikimachay Cave is located, moved from one place to another during the year as seasonal food resources became available. During the dry season, they hunted deer in low-lying wooded areas and camelids on the *puna,* or high alpine grasslands. After the rains came, they moved into the thorn forest, where they did a little hunting; however, small mammals—particularly guinea pigs—provided most of the meat they consumed. This indicates that for these people trapping was a much more important wet-season activity than hunting. In other words, both their patterns of work and their diet changed from one season to the next.

Their contemporaries on the Great Plains of southeastern Colorado near the Arkansas River were buffalo hunters who stampeded a herd into an arroyo and then butchered the animals. It is clear that the hunters had a lot of information about the animals. They knew that this buffalo, now extinct, lived in herds of 50 to 300 individuals and had a keen sense of smell but very poor vision. The animal bones and their associations tell us a great deal about what happened more than 8,500 years ago at the Olsen-Chubbuck site. Since some of the calves were only a few days old, the hunters must have stampeded the herd toward the end of May or the beginning of June.

A group of hunters approached the herd of 200 or so from downwind so that the animals could not smell them. They startled the herd, and the animals began to run away from the noise. As the animals approached the arroyo, they became aware of it; however, by then it was too late, for more

Bison kill at the Olsen-Chubbuck site in Colorado. Ancient hunters drove a bison herd into an arroyo. Joe Ben Wheat, The Olsen-Chubbuck site; a Paleo-Indian bison kill, **Memoirs of the Society for American Archaeology,** no. 26 (1972), fig. 1. Reproduced by permission of the Society for American Archaeology.

hunters had already moved in on both flanks of the herd to prevent the animals from veering away from the gulch. The lead animals plunged into the arroyo as they were pushed by those behind them. The dead or disabled animals were quickly covered by other animals, who also died in contorted positions. After the stampede was over, more than 200 buffalo lay in the arroyo. A few had projectile points in them, but virtually all had died as a result of the stampede.

The hunters moved in quickly and began to butcher the animals on top. They removed the forelegs and turned the animals onto their stomachs to skin them. The meat from the hump was removed, then the rib meat and the internal organs. As each cut was removed, it was placed in a pile with similar pieces from other animals. The hunters then removed the top round steak and the hind legs; finally, they took the neck meat and the tongue, and cracked open the skull to get brains. It took an hour or so to butcher a single animal, so a group of 75 to 100 individuals could carry out the work in a single morning.

By noon they had completely butchered about 150 animals; they left another 50 to 60 animals virtually untouched, presumably because they were either inaccessible because of the animals on top of them or too crushed to be butchered easily. The stampede produced more than 56,500 pounds of meat, 4,000 pounds of edible organs, and 5,400 pounds of fat. This was far too much for the hunters to carry, so they camped near the arroyo until the fresh meat became too gamy to be eaten. Depending on weather conditions, buffalo meat will last about a month before this happens.

There was enough fresh meat and fat to feed a group of 150 individuals for seven weeks, assuming that each of them ate 10 pounds of meat per day. It is likely, however, that some of the meat was dried before it spoiled. It takes 100 pounds of fresh meat to make 20 pounds of dried meat. If the group ate two-thirds of the kill fresh and preserved the rest, it could remain near the arroyo for four weeks and break camp with more than two tons of dried meat.

Hunting, trapping, and wild plant collecting were not the only subsistence activities of the early Americans, though they were important ones. The inhabitants of coastal areas like southern Brazil or central Peru began to gather marine molluscs more than 10,000 years ago. Groups in the Great Basin began to rely on the food resources of rivers and old glacial lakes for increasingly long periods each year. Peoples living along the rivers of Kentucky, Tennessee, and Alabama began to exploit freshwater mussels about 7,000 years ago; they supplemented them with the wild plants and small game that abounded in the forests that stretched away from the rivers.

The Extinction of Large Herbivores

One of the questions raised by the study of the early Americans is, what role did they play in the extinction of a number of species of large land mammals toward the end of the Pleistocene: mammoth, mastodon, horse, giant bison, ground sloth, saber tooth tiger? All of these species have been found associated with cultural remains; therefore, it is clear that people were exploiting them. It is also clear that these species became extinct, for the most part, after the last glacial maximum, which occurred some 18,000 years ago; people had already been preying on them for more than 10,000 years. This had led some scholars to believe that the earliest Americans were not particularly efficient hunters and that they had relatively little effect on the fauna they exploited. These scientists also believe that the descendants of the first Americans—those who lived 12,000 to 13,000 years ago, during the period when the extinctions began to take place—were efficient hunters and that they played a role in the extinction process, along with the environmental changes that were also occurring at this time.

What is not clear from this perspective is the precise role that people played in the extermination of the species in question. In other words, how did they upset the balance of nature? In answering this question it is useful to think about the relationship between a predator and its prey. When a predator specializes in hunting a single species as its sole source of food, then its numbers depend on the population size of the prey. When the prey are abundant, the number of predators increases. If the prey decline in number, so do the predators. Some predators are less particular about their food sources and hunt a number of species during the year. In this situation, if a given prey species is hunted to a point at which its numbers are significantly reduced, then individual members will be encountered less often, the hunters will turn to other quarry more often, and the prey will be saved from extinction because of reduced contact and lower rates of predation. This suggests that predation is not a major cause of extinction.

If predation is not the primary cause of extinction, what is? The answer to this question lies in direct competition for food resources or in the removal of something essential from an environment. Toward the end of the Pleistocene, as human predators became more efficient hunters of large herbivores like mammoths or bison, they increasingly entered into direct competition with carnivores for food resources. They began to deprive the carnivores of their normal food supplies, and this ultimately led to the disappearance of the carnivores in those areas where human hunters were operating. This process was probably most effective during those times of the year when the prey were most scarce and the competition for them was greatest.

The late-Pleistocene hunters of the Great Plains do not seem to have preyed on particular sex or age classes of mammoths and bison, the two herbivores they stalked. This behavior differs dramatically from that of the natural carnivores that preyed on the same species; they killed immature individuals, disabled adults, or the old, and avoided encounters with healthy adults. As a result, the survivorship curves of the herbivores preyed on by human hunters and those preyed on by natural predators were different. More young individuals survived under the kind of human predation that occurred on the Great Plains than under the kind practiced by carnivores. Since more of the young reached maturity under human predation, the population size of the prey species may actually have increased and their territory may have expanded. When this happened, the favored prey species—mammoths and then buffalo—were able to compete favorably with other herbivores for scarce food supplies. As these species declined in numbers, so did the natural predators that preyed exclusively on them. Ultimately, these herbivores and the carnivores that preyed on them became extinct.

Food production is the third way in which the early Americans eliminated elements of the native fauna in some areas of the New World. Both stock management and agriculture can affect local faunas; however, they do it in different ways. More than 8,000 years ago the inhabitants of the central Peruvian highlands were culling immature males from the camelid herds that grazed in the *puna* grasslands. Presumably, these animals were used for meat and were not wanted or needed for breeding purposes. The practice of culling permitted the number of females to increase; this ultimately led to significant increases both in herd size and in the total camelid population of the area. As a result, the stock-managing inhabitants of the area could consume much more of the herd each year than did their ancestors, who relied exclusively on hunting. It also meant that as the camelid herds grew in both size and number, they expanded into new lands along the edges of the *puna*, where they competed quite successfully with other herbivores.

Farming affected local faunas in various ways. It removed vegetation that may have been the major food supply for some animals; the clearing of farm land removed habitats as well as food resources; and the presence of people may have interfered with the normal activities of various species.

This does not mean that the environmental changes occurring at the end of the Pleistocene were inconsequential in bringing about the extinction of certain large mammals. The direct and indirect effects of human activity and environmental change worked in conjunction with one another. In some places, human activity was more important; in other places or at other times, environmental change predominated.

The early Americans grew slowly in number. The population probably multiplied rapidly immediately after people moved into a previously uninhabited area. A group may have doubled in size each generation over a short period; however, this would have been a short-term phenomenon, since demographic crises appear with repeated regularity among small populations because of famine or disease. Nonetheless, the long-term demographic process that occurred in the New World was growth. Population size increased slowly—at a rate of 0.1 or 0.2 percent a year or less—after people first entered the New World. There were two obvious factors in this long-term trend: one was movement into previously unoccupied lands, and the other was technological or organizational innovations that allowed people to exploit the food resources of their homelands more efficiently.

FURTHER READINGS

Bellwood, Peter
1971 Fortifications and economy in prehistoric New Zealand, *Proceedings of the Prehistoric Society,* 37, pt. I, July, pp. 56–95.
1975 The prehistory of Oceania. *Current Anthropology,* 16, no, 1, March, pp. 9–28.

Bowler, J. M., Rhys Jones, Harry Allen, and A. G. Thorne
1970 Pleistocene human remains from Australia; a living site and human cremation from Lake Mungo, western New South Wales. *World Archaeology,* 2, no. 1, June, pp. 39–60.

Davidson, Janet
1977 Western Polynesia and Fiji; prehistoric contact, diffusion and differentiation in adjacent archipelagos. *World Archaeology,* 9, no. 1, June, pp. 82–94.

Gould, Richard A.
1973 *Australian archaeology in ecological and ethnographic perspective,* a Warner module publication, module 7. Andover, Mass.: Addison-Wesley.

Irving, William N., and C. R. Harrington
1973 Upper Pleistocene radiocarbon-dated artefacts from the northern Yukon. *Science,* 179, no. 4071, January 26, pp. 335–340.

Krantz, Grover
1970 Human activities and megafaunal extinctions. *American Scientist,* 58, no. 2, January, pp. 44–52.

MacNeish, Richard S.
1976 Early man in the New World. *American Scientist,* 64, no. 3, May–June, pp. 316–327.

MacNeish, Richard S., Thomas C. Patterson, and David L. Browman
1975 The central Peruvian prehistoric interaction sphere. *Papers of the Robert S. Peabody Foundation for Archaeology,* 7.

Martin, Paul S.
1973 The discovery of America. *Science,* 179, no. 4077, March 9, pp. 969–974.

Patterson, Thomas C.
1973 *America's past; a New World archaeology.* Scott, Foresman, Glenview Ill., and London.

Pfeiffer, John E.
1977 *The emergence of society; a prehistory of the establishment.* McGraw-Hill, New York.

Shutler, Richard, Jr., and Mary Elizabeth Shutler
1975 *Oceanic prehistory.* Cummins, Menlo Park, Calif.

Tainter, Joseph A., and Ross H. Cordy
1977 An archaeological analysis of social ranking and residence groups in prehistoric Hawaii. *World Archaeology,* 9, no. 1, June, pp. 95–112.

Wheat, Joe Ben
1967 A Paleo-Indian bison kill. *Scientific American,* 216, no. 1, January, pp. 44–52.

White, Peter, K. A. W. Crook, and B. P. Buxton
1970 Kosipe; a late Pleistocene site in the Papuan highlands. *Proceedings of the Prehistoric Society,* 36, December, pp. 152–170.

Ancient Peoples of North America

North America is a wedge-shaped continent. It is widest in the north and tapers toward the south. Most of it lies north of the 30th parallel in temperate and subpolar latitudes. North of the Rio Grande there are mountain ranges along both edges of the continent. The Appalachian chain in the east consists of worn-down mountains that were formed more than 400 million years ago. The Rockies and the coast ranges of the west are composed of high, young mountains that were formed during the last 10 to 15 million years. The lowlands separating the two mountain chains include the ancient Canadian Shield, which is composed of rocks that are more than 2 billion years old, the Great Plains of the western United States, and the Mississippi Basin. Rivers rise in the mountains or along the edges of the Canadian Shield; most of them flow either north or south before emptying into the oceans that surround the continent.

The northern part of the continent, from Alaska to the coast of Greenland, is covered with polar tundra. South of this treeless, frozen area lies the taiga, with evergreen forests that stretch southward into New England. This gives way to deciduous forests with oak, maple, and beech, which cover much of the eastern United States. These forests thin out toward the west, where they gradually merge with the grasslands of the Great Plains. West of the grassland lie the steppe, desert, and alpine environments of the Rockies, the Great Basin, and the American Southwest. Evergreen rain forests line the Pacific coast of the continent from the middle of California northward to Alaska.

Various kinds of societies developed north of the Rio Grande. Here we will see how society developed in three very different areas—the Arctic, the eastern woodlands, and the American Southwest—and how people lived in these regions.

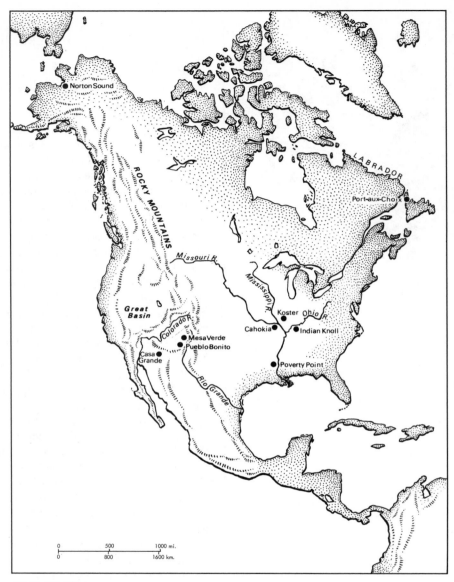

North America.

THE AMERICAN ARCTIC

Alaska and northern Canada were not abandoned when people moved southward into more temperate areas before the last glacial maximum. There is ample evidence that the unglaciated portions of the American Arctic, which were an extension of Eurasia, were inhabited more or less continuously during the waning years of the Pleistocene and afterward. The ancient peoples of the Alaskan interior made tools on small blades that they struck from microcores. The earliest of these toolmakers lived 12,000 to 14,000 years ago at Onion Portage in northern Alaska. Their successors, who lived in northern and central Alaska between 10,000 and 12,000 years ago, also made small tools on blades struck from microcores. These peoples and their contemporaries in the Yukon, who made their tools on blades and flakes struck from conical cores, hunted caribou, bison, and musk ox in the treeless tundra.

Toolmaking in the Arctic

Two other stone toolmaking traditions appeared in the Arctic about 8,500 years ago. These are the *Northwest Microblade Tradition* and the *Aleutian Blade and Core Tradition*. The former developed in the interior and is a continuation of the microcore technology that had existed several thousand years earlier in Alaska. The people who made tools in this fashion lived in evergreen forests where they hunted elk, caribou, buffalo, and smaller mammals, and fished. The geographic distribution of these tool assemblages increased significantly as evergreen forests spread into those parts of Canada which had been glaciated during the Pleistocene and became ice-free in postglacial time.

Tools of the Aleutian Blade and Core Tradition are known from sites on Anangula and Umnak Islands, off the coast of Alaska. The inhabitants of the older of the two settlements (Anangula) lived there 8,500 years ago and made a variety of stone tools on large flakes. Five thousand years later their descendants at Chaluka on Umnak Island were still making similar tools. These early peoples were hunters of sea mammals and collectors of marine foods from the intertidal zones along the shores. At first they hunted seals, sea lions, and walrus while the animals were on land; a few walrus bones have been found with projectile points still embedded in them. By 1000 BC, however, they ventured out to sea in tiny skin-covered boats. They fished and harpooned whales. In all likelihood the inhabitants of these settlements were the ancestors of the Aleuts who live in the islands today.

The *Arctic Small-tool Tradition* developed on the Bering coast of Alaska about 6,000 years ago. During the next three millenia people using these kinds of tools spread across the Arctic coast from Alaska to Greenland and southward to Labrador and Newfoundland. These peoples were the ancestors of the modern-day Eskimos, who still inhabit the same coastal areas. These ancient peoples were sea mammal hunters par excellence. They used thrusting harpoons tipped with slate blades to kill whales, seals, and walrus; they fished with bone and shell fishhooks; and they hunted caribou with bow and arrow. Like the Eskimos of today, they burned whale oil lamps to light their houses and made a variety of tools and decorative objects from carved walrus ivory and antler.

As time passed, the early Eskimos became increasingly adept at exploiting the resources of the cold north seas and at living in areas where snow, ice, and subzero temperatures are common for much of the year. Whale hunting is perhaps the most characteristic feature of Eskimo culture. The earliest whale hunters in the Arctic lived at Cape Krusenstern in northern Alaska nearly 4,000 years ago.

By 500 BC whaling peoples lived at a number of places along the Bering Sea and the Arctic Ocean. One settlement was on the shore overlooking Norton Sound in northwest Alaska. During the long winter months the inhabitants of this settlement lived in sturdy rectangular houses made of driftwood logs covered with earth; they entered through long passageways that helped keep out the wind and cold. The men hunted seals and walrus from kayaks, fished through holes in the ice, and tracked small land mammals. At night or when the weather was too severe for them to leave their homes, they repaired old tools and made new ones in preparation for the whale hunt that would begin in April. When the ice opened, the men set out in open umiaks (large kayaks) in search of the bow whale. If they harpooned one, the sixty tons of meat that they got ensured that everyone would eat during the winter. If they were fortunate enough to take three or four whales, the winter would be a very good one indeed.

In June the villagers dispersed. The households moved inland along the rivers. The women and children set up fishing stations, while the men moved into the wilderness in search of caribou. After a month or so they returned to the coast to hunt walrus with the other men of the community. By September the walrus hunt was over, and the people went inland once again to pick up the other members of their households and the fish that they had caught. As the first snows began to fall, the households began to move back to their winter quarters overlooking the ocean.

A different life style, known as the *Maritime Archaic Tradition,* developed in Labrador, Newfoundland, and the coastal areas of eastern Canada during the second millenium BC. The groups belonging to this tradition were originally inland hunters who began to exploit seals, walrus, and other marine resources with increasing efficiency during the summer months. They congregated at settlements like Port aux Choix on the west coast of Newfoundland in late spring in order to hunt seals that were drifting south with the pack ice. After the seal hunt the men returned inland for a short time to hunt the caribou that were migrating to their summer pasture in the north. Some of the meat was undoubtedly consumed on the spot, while the rest was probably dried and brought back to the coastal settlement, where it was eaten later. Back on the coast, they fished for salmon and cod, which abound in these waters, and preyed on geese and ducks, which nest in the area from late spring through the end of summer. They harvested wild plant foods such as gooseberries and blueberries. When the first snows came, the coastal community broke up into smaller social units that moved inland once more to follow the caribou and hunt elk, moose, and other animals in the boreal forest.

A burial mound built more than 7,000 years ago by a band of hunters and gatherers at l'Anse Amour in southern Labrador. The excavators estimate that it would have taken fifteen to twenty families more than a week to dig and refill the pit. James A. Tuck and Robert J. McGhee, An Archaic Indian burial mound in Labrador, **Scientific American,** 235, no. 5 (1976), 123. Copyright © 1976 by Scientific American, Inc. All rights reserved.

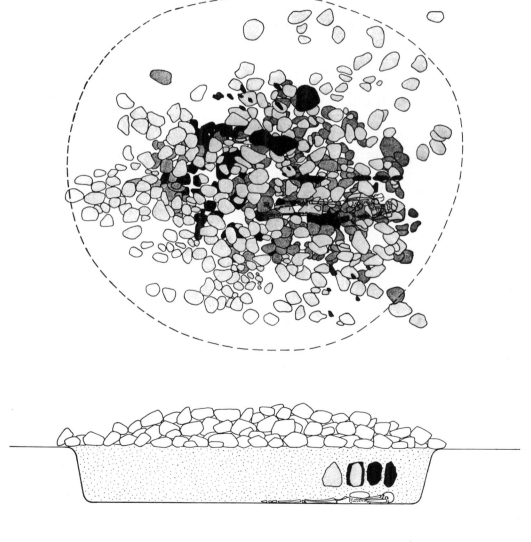

Though both the Eskimos of the north and the peoples of the Maritime Archaic Tradition exploited marine resources, there were striking differences between them. The Eskimos made extensive use of whales, while their contemporaries on the east coast of Canada largely ignored them, in spite of the fact that they occur with some frequency in the waters off Labrador and Newfoundland. The Eskimos moved inland to fish along rivers and to hunt caribou during the summer months. This was exactly the time that the maritime peoples congregated on the coast to hunt seals, walrus, and migratory birds, and to fish. The maritime orientation permitted both the Eskimos and the peoples of the east coast of Canada to congregate in significant numbers at certain seasons of the year. The reason for this lies both in the abundance of the marine resources and in the fact that these items are less subject to dramatic fluctuations in abundance than interior resources like caribou. As a result, the maritime settlements of the American Arctic were often much larger and more stable than those of the interior.

THE EASTERN WOODLANDS

People have lived in the eastern woodlands of North America for at least 15,000 years. They left tools in one of the lower levels of the Meadowcroft rock shelter in western Pennsylvania at that time; 4,000 years later people were presumably hunting caribou and mastodon in the forests around the Debert site in Nova Scotia. Between 9,000 and 11,000 years ago, the inhabitants of this area made a variety of fluted and basal-thinned spear points. These have been found throughout the area; they are particularly abundant in the region drained by the Ohio River.

The Koster
Site

As early as 6500 BC, the inhabitants of the Koster site in the lower Illinois River Valley north of St. Louis were already supplementing their late summer diet of hickory nuts and game with freshwater mussels that they collected from the river. Fifteen hundred years later, the practice of using this permanently available food resource was widespread among the peoples living along the rivers of Illinois, Kentucky, Tennessee, and Alabama.

Toward the end of the fourth millenium BC, the people at Koster resided there throughout the year, with the possible exception of a brief period each summer. Their homes resembled overturned wicker baskets covered with clay plaster. They used the riverine resources available to them more thoroughly and efficiently than their ancestors had. They continued to collect shellfish, and by 3500 BC they were harvesting millions of fish each year, some no more than an inch long, from the backwater lakes that form every spring as the flood waters recede. They also collected marsh elder from the flood plain and nuts from the forests and brought them back to the village for food. They butchered large animals like deer and dried some of the meat on wooden racks. They roasted the fresh meat in open pits, baked it in ovens covered with limestone slabs, or boiled it in clay-lined pits.

Poverty Point By the middle of the second millenium BC, peoples in the lower Mississippi River Valley could muster enough labor to build monumental earthworks in a number of localities. The largest of these was at Poverty Point on a bluff in northeastern Louisiana overlooking the Mississippi flood plain. It consisted of six concentric semicircular embankments, the largest of which has a diameter of 4,000 feet. A large earthen mound was attached to the outer ring. Its base measures 634 by 706 feet, and it rises nearly 70 feet above the bluff. A slightly smaller version of this mound lies a mile and a half to the north. There were also two smaller mounds at Poverty Point and its environs: one a few hundred yards north of the major mound and the other a mile and three-quarters to the south. Archaeologists estimate that it took a labor force of 1,350 able-bodied adults working 210 days to build just the embankments at Poverty Point. This was nearly 3 million manhours of labor solely for construction; it does not include the labor of those who provided food and other necessities for the construction workers.

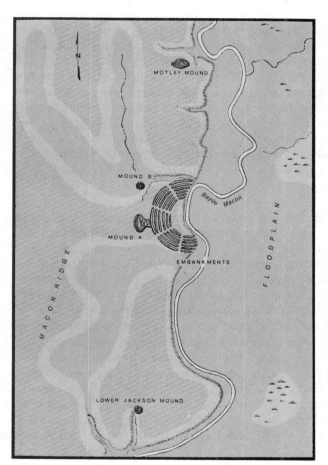

Earthworks at Poverty Point, Louisiana. Jon L. Gibson, Poverty Point, **Archaeology,** 27, no. 2 (1974), 98. Copyright 1974 by Archaeological Institute of America.

It is likely that between 4,000 and 5,000 people lived at Poverty Point; another 5,000 or so lived nearby in two parallel chains of small settlements. One chain was located along a stream that flows next to the ridge where Poverty Point was built; the other was located a few miles away along a bayou on the Mississippi flood plain. Most of these settlements were small hamlets with less than 100 residents each. Poverty Point and the hamlets nearby were located in an ecologically diverse area along the boundary between markedly different ecosystems. As a result, the residents of these settlements could exploit a wide range of food resources. Furthermore, human activity in the area undoubtedly produced a number of "disturbed" habitats that were invaded by economically valuable wild plants like wild millet amaranth, sunflowers, and chenopodia.

What is most striking about the cluster of settlements at Poverty Point and contemporary clusters in three other areas of the lower Mississippi Valley is that all of the food remains found so far are wild endemic forms. In other words, there is no direct evidence that the inhabitants of these settlements farmed to produce food surpluses. It is possible that they tended small patches of chenopodia and other economically important wild plants, as their contemporaries in southern Illinois did. What is important, however, is that they were able to use the rich natural food resources efficiently enough to support a large unskilled labor force for short periods each year so as to build monumental earthworks, as well as part-time stoneworkers who used rocks and minerals from areas as far away as 700 miles to make arrowheads, plummets, bird effigies, and beads, some of which may have been used exclusively by individuals with high social status.

Trade in the Eastern Woodlands

A widespread exchange network emerged in the eastern woodlands during the third millenium BC. By 2000 BC three of the more prized items among those being exchanged were copper from the Great Lakes area, chert from various places in the Midwest, and marine shells from Florida and other Gulf states. Chert was a valued material for making tools in areas like northeastern Louisiana, where it does not occur naturally. However, it was also exchanged in areas where it does occur naturally; as much as 30 percent of the stone tools in some of the Late Archaic settlements of southern Illinois were made from imported cherts, even though chert occurs locally and the imported material is not superior in quality. The most prized commodities, however, were Great Lakes copper and Gulf Coast shells. Copper objects are relatively more common the the North than in the South. Utilitarian objects outnumber ornaments in the North. In the South, at places like the Indian Knoll settlements in northern Alabama, only four of the thirteen copper objects found were tools; the rest were various kinds of ornaments. Objects made from marine shells were more common in the South, where both tools and ornaments were placed in burials.

Not everyone in these Late Archaic societies had equal access to objects made from marine shells and copper, judging from the burial offerings found in the cemeteries at the Indian Knoll settlements. At Indian Knoll itself, 503 of the 879 individuals buried in the cemetery could be identified by sex. Of these, only 14 of the 283 men and 5 of the 220 women had shell objects in their graves. In other words, less than 5 percent of the men and about 2 percent of the women had grave goods made from marine shells. Ten copper objects were found in the cemetery; half of them were placed in the tombs of infants or very young children. It is unlikely that these individuals accumulated the copper objects during their brief lifetimes. What the grave associations probably reflect is the social status accorded the individual by other members of the community.

<table>
<tr><td>

Burial
Practices

</td><td>

From 1000 BC on, the peoples of the eastern woodlands—particularly those living in southern Illinois, Indiana, and Ohio—built thousands of earth mounds. The largest of these were several hundred feet long and 40 to 50 feet high. The dead were buried in these mounds. More than 400 burials from two mound groups in the lower Illinois River Valley provide information about the social organization that prevailed in the area from 150 BC to about AD 400.

</td></tr>
</table>

There were six different kinds of tombs in the two mound groups; the differences reflect the varying amounts of energy expended on their construction. This suggests that there may have been six recognizable levels or ranks in woodlands society during this period. The mounds were built to house one or more centrally located tombs; these often had log sides and log or limestone slab roofs. The individuals buried in them, regardless of whether they were infants or adults, were accompanied by a wide array of grave goods, many of which were made from materials that came from distances as great as 1,300 miles. Some of these central tombs had been reopened, their contents removed, and new individuals placed in them. The former occupants were placed in pits dug adjacent to their former resting places. The fact that the highest-ranking individuals included both adults and infants suggests that this status was hereditary.

While the few individuals at the top of the social hierarchy were placed in specially constructed tombs, more than half of the 439 individuals were buried in rectangular graves dug into the surface of the mound and covered with dirt. These individuals came from the next-to-lowest social rank and rarely had grave offerings in their tombs. Individuals at the bottom of the social hierarchy were not even buried on the mounds; they were placed in pits dug along the edges of the mounds.

As mentioned earlier, the peoples of the eastern woodlands participated in a vast exchange network 2,000 years ago. They acquired grizzly bear teeth from the Rockies, obsidian from Yellowstone, steatite from the Carolina piedmont, copper from the Great Lakes, and marine shells from the Gulf Coast. Many of these items arrived in the southern Illinois and Ohio area as raw materials or partially worked goods. Craftsmen at various centers in the eastern United States finished them. For example, Hopewell in Ohio was apparently a place where Yellowstone obsidian was worked into finished commodities; more than 300 pounds of obsidian chipping debris has been found in one of the two dozen or more mounds at this site, even though the raw material was transported more than 1,300 miles. The other kinds of objects found in tombs in the eastern woodlands that date to this period were manufactured at other centers.

Because of the amount of exchange taking place, there was a great deal of similarity in the grave offerings placed in elite burials, regardless of their location. As a result of the similarities in these high-value commodities, archaeogists speak of the *Hopewellian interaction sphere,* in which peoples living in different parts of the eastern United States participated in this traffic of luxury goods, and of a *Hopewell burial cult,* in which high-status individuals were buried with these goods. There were marked differences in the kinds of utilitarian objects that were used or buried with the dead in different regions at this time. This reinforces the notion that exchange was limited primarily to

The Hopewell earthworks and mounds of the Edwin Harness group in Ohio. Gordon R. Willey, **An introduction to American archaeology** (Englewood Cliffs, N.J.: Prentice-Hall, 1966), fig. 5-23, p. 274.

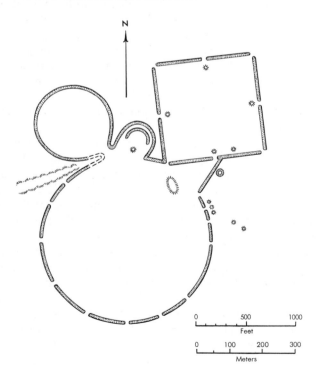

high-value items that were used mainly by the upper echelons of eastern woodlands society.

The
Hopewellian
Settlements

Many of the Hopewellian settlements were located in rich bottom lands along rivers. The people who lived at Scovill in the lower Illinois River Valley about AD 450 made selective use of a number of the food resources that occur in river bottom environments. Deer provided more than 90 percent of the meat they consumed, turkey about 4 percent, and fish and mussels from the river the remainder. Migratory birds like mallard ducks were particularly important in the late fall and spring, when the sky is often filled with flocks of mallards as far as the eye can see. The residents of Scovill also planted squash and gourds in the late spring before they split up into smaller units to hunt deer and other animals in the upland areas outside the river valley. They returned to Scovill in late summer to harvest the squash and gourds and other economically important plants such as nuts, chenopodia, knotweed, wild rice, marsh elder, grape, and plum that occur in the area.

The peoples of the eastern woodlands were already cultivating a number of plants, including sunflower, chenopodia, amaranth, and sumpweed, by the beginning of the first millenium AD. The seeds of these plants found in archaeological sites are larger than those of their wild relatives today. This indicates that they were harvested, stored for use during the winter, and the larger ones planted during the spring. These plants are also different from the ones that were brought under cultivation in the American Southwest or Mesoamerica; this shows that there were separate centers of plant domestication. Two thousand years earlier, around 2000 BC, the peoples of western Kentucky were already growing a thick-shelled squash—a species originally domesticated well to the south in Mesoamerica—not for food but to make containers. They ate chenopodia and other food plants that were indigenous to the eastern woodlands.

Cahokia

One of the most productive agricultural regions in the eastern woodlands was the American Bottoms, a large, fertile valley just below the place where the Mississippi, Missouri, and Illinois Rivers come together. The valley and the areas around it form one of the most environmentally diverse regions in North America. As a result, a wide variety of natural resources were available to the people who lived there. By virtue of their proximity to the confluence of three major river systems, the inhabitants of the American Bottoms had ready access to the transportation and communication network provided by these waterways; this network encompassed all of the Midwest. Given these assets, it is not surprising that the largest aboriginal settlement in North America developed in the central part of the American Bottoms. Archaeologists call it Cahokia.

People first lived at Cahokia about AD 600; however, there were also other settlements in the American Bottoms at that time. By the beginning of the tenth century Cahokia was clearly the social and political center of the area. The inhabitants were building large mounds and had erected a wooden "stonehenge" that indicates their knowledge of and concern with astronomical phenomena. Monks Mound, the largest of these public buildings, covered nearly 14 acres; it was more than 1,000 feet long, 700 feet wide, and 100 feet high. It took more than 200,000 man-days of labor just to bring the earth fill to the building site for this mound, and there were more than 100 other mounds in this 3,300-acre settlement. The central portion of the settlement was surrounded by a wooden palisade; this central precinct included a number of mounds and encompassed about 250 acres.

During the tenth and eleventh centuries, a small mound was aligned with Monks Mound on the north–south axis of the settlement. Two important individuals were buried in this mound within 100 years of each other. Little is known about the first burial. The second individual, however, was accompanied by a number of other people. He was buried on a platform made of more than 20,000 shell beads. Near him were bundles of bones from earlier burials. A little farther away six men were buried in separate tombs with lavish grave goods that included rolls of sheet copper, stacks of mica sheets, semiprecious stones, and caches of finely chipped arrowheads—masterpieces of stoneworking that apparently were never used. More than fifty young women of roughly the same age and size were buried at the same time in a nearby pit. Four men, lacking their heads and hands, were buried in a platform between the central figure and the young women. Other individuals, who had been placed on litters or stretchers, were entombed in long pits dug into the southwestern edge of the mound. As one archaeologist put it, "The central figure was clearly a guy with class," meaning that a large number of people were sacrificed when the central figure was entombed, and that the materials used to make the goods placed in the tomb came from as far away as the Gulf Coast, Yellowstone, the Great Lakes, and the Carolina piedmont.

At its height, 30,000 to 40,000 people lived in Cahokia. Four major settlements—each with several platform mounds, plazas, and large residential areas—surrounded Cahokia. They were located close to major watercourses, and their inhabitants probably controlled the collection and redistribution of resources from different parts of the Midwest. Farther away there were two other settlements with mounds, one located on the plains east of Cahokia and the other in southern Wisconsin. The residents of these settlements, which apparently had close ties with Cahokia, presumably controlled the accumulation and redistribution of resources from the prairie uplands, and perhaps copper from the north country. There were also smaller settlements in the American Bottoms, some with mounds and some without them. They were usually located near specific resource areas, and their inhabitants probably exploited these local resources, which were ultimately channeled to the people at Cahokia.

By 1400, the population of Cahokia had dwindled to 4,000 or 5,000. Three hundred years later, the first French explorers in the American Bottoms found only mounds overgrown with vegetation. The decline of Cahokia was the outcome of a process of social reorganization in which the residents of outlying settlements in the hinterlands of the Mississippi and its tributaries acquired more importance in the accumulation and redistribution of resources. At the same time, power gradually slipped away from the ruling elite at Cahokia as they lost access to local resources and to goods from other regions.

THE AMERICAN SOUTHWEST

The American Southwest is a small area. Most of it lies in Arizona and New Mexico; its outer edges lie in southern Colorado and Utah and in northwestern Mexico. In spite of its small size, the American Southwest had many different kinds of environments. Low-lying desert lands begin around Tucson and Phoenix and stretch westward to the Colorado River and southward into Mexico; in these arid lands there is little temperature variation from one season to the next. North of the desert lie the mountains of the Mogollon Rim, which stretch in a broad band from central Arizona to central New Mexico. Deep, narrow valleys separate steep mountains covered with pine forests and woodlands composed mainly of juniper and piñon. Average temperatures differ by as much as 40° F from summer to winter. The Mogollon Rim is rich in natural resources, and the inhabitants of this area always made more extensive use of wild species than did their contemporaries living elsewhere in the Southwest. North of the mountains lie the high mesas and deep canyons of the Four Corners area—the region where the boundaries of Colorado, Utah, Arizona, and New Mexico converge. Unlike the area to the south, much of the land in the Four Corners is flat or gently sloping; about half of it lies on wooded mesa tops, while the rest forms grass-covered bottom lands. As in the mountains, there are extreme variations in temperature from one season to the next.

Early Inhabitants

The first inhabitants of the American Southwest were hunters and gatherers. More than 11,000 years ago these early peoples hunted mammoths and other animals around springs. The group that camped at Blackwater Draw in eastern New Mexico killed a variety of animals and made more than one-third of their tools from stone that came from a quarry located more than 100 miles away. Their descendants living in the area 5,000 years later were also hunters and gatherers; however, these later peoples relied more intensively on plant foods and on fish and birds from lakes and rivers. They dug up tubers, roots, and whole plants with wooden digging sticks. They carried these plants, along with seeds and nuts, in baskets. They ground seeds, nuts, and other plant foods on flat milling stones, and boiled these vegetable foods, as well as meat, by dropping hot stones into baskets that had been waterproofed by a lining of pitch. They probably wore little clothing besides robes made of small animal skins that had been sewn together and sandals made of woven plant fibers. Some of them wore necklaces made of seashells from the Pacific Ocean that had been perforated and strung together.

By 2000 BC the inhabitants of the Mogollon Rim were growing a kind of corn that was first domesticated in the highlands of Mexico several thousand years earlier. Later they added other Mexican cultigens—beans, squash, and cotton—to their repertory of economically important plants. In some areas of the Southwest the ancient peoples probably planted crops in the spring and wandered away, returning in the fall to harvest them. They spent no time or effort caring for their crops. In other areas the ancient inhabitants devoted a great deal of time and energy to farming, even though wild plant foods always formed an important element of their diet. In the desert region of southwest Arizona they built an elaborate irrigation system. One of the ditches near Phoenix was more than 10 miles long; another was 18 feet across and 12 feet deep. Toward the end of the first millenium AD, the inhabitants of the 27 villages around Phoenix were irrigating more than 140,000 acres of land and were planting two crops a year—one in February and the other in July. In the mountainous country of the Mogollon Rim they built terraces and check dams in the natural drainage channels to impede the flow of water. This prevented erosion and allowed the water to soak into the ground. Crops were then planted on the terraces.

The Hohokam and the Hakataya

By 300 BC many of the inhabitants of the desert of southwest Arizona were sedentary farmers who lived in villages all year round. Their contemporaries on the Mogollon Rim and the plateau country beyond were nomads. Archaeologists call these desert farmers the *Hohokam* and the *Hakataya;* the Hohokam lived along the Gila, Salt, and Verde Rivers in southern Arizona, and the Hakataya occupied the desert area of western Arizona. At first the inhabitants of both areas lived in rectangular houses grouped in irregular clusters of two dozen or so huts. The earlier villages were generally smaller than the later ones, and the largest of them probably had fewer than 400 residents. By AD 1300, towns had emerged along the rivers of the Hohokam area. Many of the towns had one or more "great houses"—four-story adobe buildings measuring 40 feet by 60 feet or more at the base with four-foot-thick walls. At Casa Grande there were two great houses, one of which is still standing today in a 65-acre compound enclosed by a seven-foot high wall. The town at Los

Muertos outside of Phoenix and Tempe is said to have been more than five miles long and up to a mile wide; one estimate places its population at more than 13,000. It was probably the largest town in the American Southwest.

Large settlements were not characteristic of the mountain country north of the Hohokam desert; however, they did occur in the plateau country north of the Mogollon Rim. By 100 BC the inhabitants of the mountainous Mogollon area lived in small hamlets or villages with up to twenty circular pit houses. For nearly 1,000 years these settlements were systematically built on the edges of mesa tops located several hundred feet above the valley floors. After AD 900 the inhabitants of the area began to live in apartment houses with contiguous rooms formed by masonry walls. These later villages were usually located along or near streams and arable land.

Before AD 500 the average pit house had a floor area of about 330 square feet, which suggests that it was occupied by about ten people. In other words, the villages had about 200 residents. As time passed, however, the pit houses became progressively smaller. By AD 1000 the average dwelling room had a floor area of about 130 square feet. At the same time that the rooms were getting smaller, the number of rooms found in a village was increasing progressively. By AD 1000 there were almost three times as many rooms per village as there had been 500 years earlier. However, the population of the villages was about the same. What may have happened was that the organization of residential groups, or households, changed. In the earlier villages, extended families lived together in a few large houses; in the later villages, household units were composed of two to four individuals—a nuclear family. This shift was accompanied by a change in the size of cooking vessels, which indicates that patterns of food consumption also changed as the composition of the household units was modified.

The Anasazi

Archaeologists call the ancient inhabitants of the plateau country centered on the Four Corners area the *Anasazi*. Before AD 900, the Anasazi usually built their villages on low mesas or ridges that overlooked permanent streams. After that time, about half of their settlements were located on the tops and sides of mesas and the other half on valley floors near expanses of arable land. By 1150, some regions of the Anasazi area—such as the Grand Canyon—were abandoned, and the villages in the inhabited areas were on mesas or ridges rather than near arable land in the bottom lands.

The early Anasazi villages were small, with between ten and twenty houses. By AD 500 some of the villages had more than fifty houses; these pit houses were arranged in clusters of three to six arranged around communal storage pits. The later Anasazi villages—those occupied after AD 900—were generally larger than the earlier settlements. They were built above ground, and the pueblo apartment houses had several stories; some of them had more than 200 rooms.

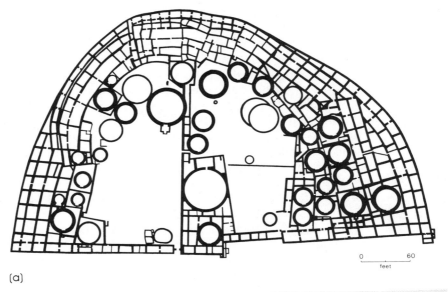

(a)

(b)

Pueblo Bonito. (a) Plan of the site. (b) Reconstruction of its appearance about AD 1050. Jesse D. Jennings, **Prehistory of North America**, 2nd ed. (New York: McGraw-Hill, 1974), figs. 7-16, 7-17, pp. 306, 307. Copyright © 1974 McGraw-Hill Book Company. Used by permission.

270

The largest of the late Anasazi settlements was probably Pueblo Bonito in the Chaco area of northwestern New Mexico. It was one of 12 towns and more than 100 villages in the 20-mile-long Chaco Canyon that were occupied after about AD 850. Initially Pueblo Bonito consisted of a crescent-shaped block of rooms. Later the open edge of the crescent was enclosed by another block of rooms. By the time it was completed there were more than 800 rooms in the four-story building that sprawled over three acres and enclosed more than 30 *kivas,* or ceremonial buildings. At its height, more than 1,200 people lived in Pueblo Bonito. The other eleven villages that were contemporary with Pueblo Bonito were built on the same plan—a crescent-shaped block of rooms rising up to four stories above the ground and enclosing a plaza where kivas were located. The largest kivas, several of which are more than 60 feet in diameter, were probably used by the community as a whole. The smaller ones, some of which were built within blocks of apartments, may have served only the residents of those units.

There were originally doors and windows in the buildings at Pueblo Bonito and the other towns of the Chaco Canyon. As time passed, however, the residents of these settlements filled in the windows and even the main entrances. The towns were entered by ladders placed against the outer walls of the pueblos. These were obviously defense measures. Perhaps the relatively large size of Pueblo Bonito and the other Chaco Canyon towns was also a product of the need for protection against raiders. These were troubled times; villages were burned, people mutilated, and the dead left unburied. It was also a period of drought, when crops often failed and food was scarcer than it had been earlier.

North of the Chaco Canyon in the Mesa Verde region of southwestern Colorado, the people lived on mesa tops or, more commonly, in caves on cliff faces. There were nearly 1,000 cliff houses at Mesa Verde alone. The most famous of these is the Cliff Palace. Nearly all of the mesa-top villages and cliff dwellings at Mesa Verde were inhabited between AD 950 and 1300. The preferred habitation sites during this period were caves and cliffs, which could be easily defended against troublemakers. The villages on the mesa tops frequently had towers several stories high that afforded excellent views of what was happening in the surrounding countryside.

Before AD 500, the Anasazi grew some corn and harvested about half a dozen species of wild plants. After AD 1000, they grew corn, beans, and squash and harvested the fruits, nuts, and seeds of nearly a dozen wild species. During the period when agriculture provided the bulk of the plant food consumed—about AD 500 to 1000—the Anasazi villagers were relatively independent and did not rely extensively on the inhabitants of neighboring settlements. However, with the onset of drought conditions the social distance between adajacent villages diminished and cooperation seems to have increased.

FURTHER READINGS

Bohrer, Vorsila R.
1970 Ethnobotanical aspects of Snaketown, a Hohokam village in southern Arizona. *American Antiquity,* 35, no. 4, October, pp. 413–430.

Fitzhugh, William W.
1972 Environmental archaeology and cultural systems in Hamilton Inlet, Labrador; a survey of the central Labrador coast from 3000 B.C. to the present. *Smithsonian Contributions to Anthropology,* no. 16.

Fowler, Melvin L.
1974 Cahokia; ancient capital of the Midwest. *An Addison-Wesley Module in Anthropology,* no. 48.

Gibson, Jon L.
1974 Poverty Point; the first American chiefdom. *Archaeology,* 27, no. 2, April, pp. 97–105.

Jennings, Jesse D.
1974 *Prehistory of North America,* 2nd ed. McGraw-Hill, New York.

Laughlin, Willian
1967 Human migration and permanent occupation in the Bering Sea area. In *The Bering land bridge,* ed. David M. Hopkins, pp. 409–450. Stanford University Press, Stanford, Calif.

Longacre, William A., ed.
1970 *Reconstructing prehistoric Pueblo societies.* University of New Mexico Press, Albuquerque.

Martin, Paul S., and Fred Plog
1973 *The archaeology of Arizona; a study of the Southwest region.* Doubleday/Natural History Press, Garden City, N.Y.

Munson, Patrick J., Paul W. Parmalee, and Richard A. Yarnell
1971 Subsistence ecology of Scovill, a Terminal Woodland village. *American Antiquity,* 36, no. 4, October, pp. 410–431.

O'Brien, Patricia J.
1972 Urbanism, Cahokia, and Middle Mississippian. *Archaeology,* 25, no. 3, June, pp. 189–197.

Pfeiffer, John E.
1974 Indian city on the Mississippi. *Time–Life Nature/Science Annual,* pp. 125–139. Time–Life Books, New York.
1977 *The emergence of society; a prehistory of the establishment.* McGraw-Hill, New York.

Schroeder, Alfred H.
1960 The Hohokam, Sinagua, and Hakataya. *Archives of Archaeology,* no. 5.

Struever, Stuart, and John Carlson
1977 Koster Site; the new archaeology in action. *Archaeology,* 30, no. 2, March, pp. 93–101.

Struever, Stuart, and Kent D. Vickery
1973 The beginnings of cultivation in the Midwest-riverine area of the United States. *American Anthropologiest,* 75, no. 5, October, pp. 1197–1220.

Tainter, Joseph A.

1975 Social inference and mortuary practices; an experiment in numerical classification. *World Archaeology,* 7, no. 1, July, pp. 1–15.

Tuck, James

1970 An Archaic Indian cemetery in Newfoundland. *Scientific American,* 222, no. 6, June, pp. 112–121.

Willey, Gordon R.

1966 *An introduction to American archaeology,* vol. 1, *North and Middle America.* Prentice-Hall, Englewood Cliffs, N.J.

Winters, Howard D.

1968 Value systems and trade cycles of the Late Archaic in the Midwest. In *New perspectives in archaeology,* ed. Sally R. Binford and Lewis R. Binford, pp. 175–227. Aldine-Atherton, Chicago.

Ancient Peoples of Mesoamerica

Mesoamerica stretches southward from the Tropic of Cancer in northern Mexico to a line that runs from central Honduras through western Nicaragua and Costa Rica to the Nicoya Peninsula. Northern Mexico is a high plateau that lies between mountain ranges that parallel the coasts. Farther south lies the volcanic country of central and southern Mexico; this area of mountains, basins, and river valleys stretches southward from the Valley of Mexico through Oaxaca to the lowlying Isthmus of Tehuantepec, which separates the Yucatan Peninsula and the mountains of southern Mexico from those in the north. Mountainous country with numerous intermontane basins and valleys continues southward through western Guatemala to the Nicoya Peninsula of Costa Rica. The Pacific coastal plain of Mesoamerica is narrow, while the eastern one, bordering on the Gulf of Mexico and the Caribbean, is composed of a broad belt of low-lying areas.

Mesoamerica is a tropical area; however, its rainfall and temperature are moderated by elevation. As a result, it is an environmentally diverse area where hot, humid lowlands lie in close proximity to cool mountain country. In general, northern and western Mesoamerica are dry, while the eastern and southern portions of the area are more humid. Tropical forests and grasslands cover much of the low-lying area of the east coast. East of these lie montane forests and grasslands that merge into scrub steppe and desert in the north and the scrub and deciduous forests and grasslands of the west. In other words, Mesoamerica is a vast ecological mosaic where peoples living in neighboring areas might produce entirely different goods because of the environmental differences between their homelands.

15

These differences had important effects on where people went to acquire what they needed and how they got those items. Since many of the goods that the ancient peoples of Mesoamerica viewed as desirable or essential could not be produced locally or even in nearby areas with different environmental conditions, they had to rely on peoples in distant lands to produce and provide these items. These conditions seem to have favored the development of markets and far-flung commercial networks. When the Spaniards arrived in central Mexico in the early years of the sixteenth century, they found enormous markets where thousands of people came together to barter for goods produced in distant lands. They found towns with 20,000 or more houses, irrigated agricultural fields that covered thousands of square miles, sumptuous temples, and powerful political entities in which one ethnic group dominated and controlled the activities of a number of other groups.

Let us consider three questions: How did ancient societies develop in Mesoamerica? Were the processes of social development the same for peo-

Mesoamerica.

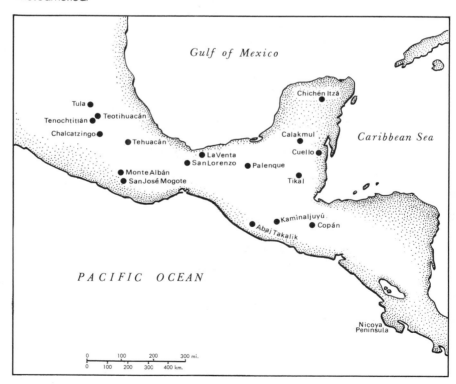

ples living in areas with markedly different environmental settings? What kinds of relationships existed between societies that evolved in different parts of Mesoamerica?

THE EARLY PEOPLES OF MESOAMERICA

People have lived in Mesoamerica for more than 20,000 years. Archaeologists have found their tools and traces of their activities at a number of localities in highland Mexico. Toward the end of the Pleistocene Epoch, when the vast continental ice sheets covering Canada began to recede, the inhabitants of the Mexican highlands had to deal with environments that were changing in response to the climatic changes. In regions like the Valsequillo Reservoir or the Tehuacán Valley of Puebla, their old food resources were gradually being replaced by new ones. As horses, mammoths, and other Pleistocene animals became less plentiful, the peoples of these regions gradually turned their attention to pronghorn antelope and jack rabbits. When these animals began to move northward into more favorable habitats around the end of the Pleistocene, they again turned to new animal resources—white-tailed deer and cottontail rabbits. Since each of these species had different behavior patterns, their human predators had to devise new ways of hunting and trapping them.

By 7000 BC the ancient peoples of Mesoamerica were exploiting literally hundreds of wild plant and animal species. Some of their food resources, such as white-tailed deer, maguey, and wild corn, were found in a number of different environmental settings, while others, such as acorns and piñon nuts, occurred in only a few habitats. People used widespread resources continually and those with more limited ranges whenever they were available. As a result, what distinguishes the economic orientation of one group from that of another is the way each group used the resources available in its homeland. For example, groups living in Oaxaca at this time relied extensively on acorns and piñon nuts during the winter months, while their contemporaries in the Tehuacán Valley ate ceiba roots, maguey, and prickly pear leaves.

The Tehuacán Valley
Archaeologists estimate that about a dozen people lived in the Tehuacán Valley around 7000 BC. During the winter months these people hunted deer, peccaries, and other large animals that congregated around permanent springs. They also collected maguey, ceiba roots, and leaves, though meat constituted nearly three-fourths of their winter diet. Toward the end of March, the first of a series of wild plants ripened, and the people of Tehuacán harvested prickly pears and amaranth. Later in the year, they gathered a variety of wild fruits and grasses. As fall approached, they collected mesquite beans and other fruits. From early spring through fall the people of the valley de-

voted most of their energy to plant collecting. Most of the food they consumed, perhaps 65 percent, was plant food; what meat they ate came from
small animals—rabbits, gophers, and lizards—that they trapped near their
seasonal campsites. Hunting became important once again in late fall as the
large animals returned from the hills and began to congregate in increasing
numbers around the permanent water holes in the valley, and as the stores of
fall fruits, seeds, and pods dwindled.

By 5000 BC about 100 people lived in the Tehuacán Valley. They still
hunted, trapped, and collected wild plants; however, they had increased
the size of their harvests by planting wild fruits like avocados and zapotes
around springs and along the banks of streams and rivers, and by sowing wild
seed plants like amaranth and corn in the barrancas and canyons that line the
edges of the valley. They recognized that these plants had requirements that
could be satisfied with a little care in places where they did not occur naturally or were not very abundant. The first fruits and annuals that they planted
undoubtedly were native to the valley. Within a short time, however, they
began to plant species—gourds, common beans, and chili peppers, to name
only a few—that had been imported from elsewhere. By introducing these
plants to new habitats—regardless of whether they were native to the valley
or not—the people of Tehuacán and those living in other parts of highland
Mesoamerica were subjecting them to new selective pressures that led to
changes in the plants' genetic composition and ultimately enhanced their
economic importance. As time passed, the peoples of highland Mesoamerica
brought an ever-increasing number of these economically important plants
under domestication.

By 3000 BC the inhabitants of the Tehuacán Valley and other parts of
highland Mesoamerica were able to live for longer periods each year in a
series of small villages with populations of 100 or so. They were producing
enough surplus from their crops and from their summer and fall harvests of
wild plants to live in sedentary settlements. During the fall and winter small
parties made brief forays into the countryside to hunt, trap, and collect the
wild-plant produce that was available during the dry season. These supplemented the foods that they produced and collected during the summer and
fall.

During the next two millenia the inhabitants of the Tehuacán Valley,
and other areas as well, gradually expanded their agricultural production by
increasing the amount of land under cultivation and the intensity with which
the fields were used. By 800 BC irrigation canals carried water from permanent springs, the river, and manmade reservoirs to fields located in parts of
the valley where crops had not been grown earlier. As a result, virtually all of
the Tehuacán Valley became potential farmland; the inhabitants were no
longer limited to the areas around permanent water sources or those in which
the water table was close to the surface. Agricultural surpluses increased as

the valley peoples began to cultivate more of these newly opened farmlands. At the same time, food production was intensified even further when they began to harvest more than one crop each year from the same plot of land. At this point in the developmental process, agricultural production was relatively elastic, given occasional droughts and famines, and could meet the needs of a steadily increasing population. Processes similar to those that occurred in the Tehuacán Valley undoubtedly happened elsewhere in Mesoamerica during this period.

Permanent Villages and Social Stratification

By 1000 BC substantial numbers of people throughout Mesoamerica were living in permanent villages. In some areas—such as the Pacific coast of Guatemala or the Tehuacán Valley—all of the early villages were small, with a dozen households or less and populations of 50 to 60. In other regions—the Valley of Mexico, Oaxaca, and the Gulf Coast of Mexico—a single large settlement with a population of 500 to 1,000 was surrounded by a number of small hamlets with populations of less than 100. Socioeconomic factors, rather than environmental ones, led to the formation of these large settlements toward the end of the second millenium BC.

With agricultural production more secure than it had been earlier, part-time craft specialization developed. One hamlet in the Oaxaca region specialized in quarrying obsidian. At first the residents of other hamlets and villages in the valley dealt individually with the inhabitants of this settlement. Later the obsidian from this and other sources in Mesoamerica was pooled by a central agency—perhaps an elite household—before being redistributed to the various communities in the valley. Other part-time craft specialists emerged at about this time as well. They included shell workers, people who made magnetite mirrors, stoneworkers, and perhaps even potters. In some of the smaller communities, the range of craft specialization was limited; in the larger ones, there were many different craft specialists.

Shortly after permanent villages appeared in Oaxaca and elsewhere, there was a substantial increase in the amount of social stratification, judging from marked differences in the quantity and quality of the goods buried with different individuals. At about the same time, public buildings became more common and elaborate. Platforms, some of them faced with stone, supported massive temples. On the Gulf Coast the inhabitants of San Lorenzo and La Venta erected enormous earthen mounds whose construction required millions of manhours of labor. The labor forces for these public works were drawn from beyond the communities in which they were built. This suggests that there were administrative authorities with sufficient power and prestige to organize construction on a massive scale. Ritual, controlled by a chief who had special access to a powerful household or community diety, was undoubtedly one form of social and ideological control that existed in these early Mesoamerican communities.

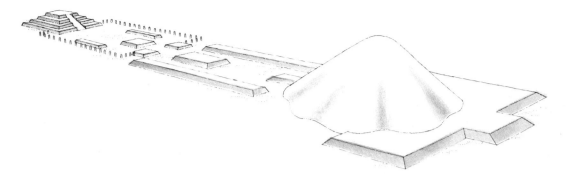

Perspective reconstruction of the fluted pyramid at La Venta and its accompanying structures. They were erected during the first part of the first millenium BC. Michael D. Coe, **America's first civilization; discovering the Olmec** (New York: American Heritage, 1968), pp. 64–65. © 1968 American Heritage Publishing Company.

The distribution of certain free-standing design motifs on pottery in the early villages and hamlets of Oaxaca suggests that there were at least two major descent groups in the valley. The "fire serpent" and the "were-jaguar" were the mythical ancestors of these groups. The households in two residential districts of San José Mogote were associated primarily with fire serpent motifs, while those in another residential district of the same settlement were associated primarily with were-jaguar motifs. Both groups of motifs depict themes identical to those found on Olmec stone sculpture and pottery at San Lorenzo, La Venta, and other settlements on the Gulf Coast and elsewhere in Mesoamerica during this period. Other design motifs found at San José Mogote were not part of the Olmec repertory and probably depict the mythical ancestors of descent groups that had local or regional importance rather than international significance.

The San José Mogote households associated with the were-jaguar motifs also contained most of the exotic materials found in the village. This suggests that their residents controlled the accumulation of these goods and had extensive commercial ties with other settlements in the Mesoamerican area. The fact that some of these commodities were used in outlying hamlets implies that the same individuals controlled the redistribution of these goods. And the fact that some of the exotic materials found in these households were used for ritual purposes suggests that this group used its descent from important ancestors to control ritual and the means for acquiring and redistributing exotic materials.

THE OLMEC

The first burst of extensive long-distance exchange in Mesoamerica occurred about 1100 BC and was associated with the spread of *Olmec* influence from the Gulf Coast lowlands of Vera Cruz and Tabasco to other parts of

279

Mesoamerica. The people of San Lorenzo—a settlement that was to become a major Olmec center—were already importing obsidian from a number of different sources in highland Mexico and Guatemala by 1400 BC. Some of these quarries were more than 300 miles from San Lorenzo. By 1100 BC the Gulf Coast peoples were importing a wide range of materials—such as jade, magnetite, hematite, and basalt—that do not occur in the tropical lowlands where they lived. The Olmec communities on the Gulf Coast imported impressive quantities of these exotic materials; for example, more than 5,000

A colossal Olmec head from Tres Zapotes that weighs approximately 18 tons. Each head is believed to be the portrait of a ruler. Michael D. Coe, **America's first civilization; discovering the Olmec** (New York: American Heritage, 1968), p. 46. © National Geographic Society.

tons of imported serpentine have been found at La Venta. The volume of this commerce is even more impressive given the fact that these commodities—including a number of 25- to 30-ton basalt blocks—were carried by human porters.

By 1000 BC the Olmec rulers were exchanging prestige goods with the lineage leaders of highland groups like those centered at San José Mogote. The highland leaders redistributed these items in such a way as to maintain their position in the social hierarchy. In less than two centuries these interregional trade networks had become so complex that important pooling and redistributive centers began to develop in those places where regional trade could be easily controlled. One of these was San José Mogote in Oaxaca; another was Chalcatzingo in Morelos, whose residents controlled trade and commerce throughout much of the central highlands of Mexico. These communities, with their relatively large populations, dominated the commercial exchange networks of central Mexico during the early part of the first millenium BC.

The acquisition of exotic materials from distant localities allowed the elite groups of both the coastal lowlands and the highland valleys to enhance their prestige within their own communities. The rulers of La Venta even buried a serpentine pavement in order to take this commodity out of circulation and make it more valuable. By doing so, they maintained the value of this good, and by continuing to maintain trade relations with its suppliers, they ensured that a steady supply would arrive at La Venta. By controlling its availability within their own community, they were able to maintain the status differential that existed within it.

The exotic materials that flowed along these comercial networks changed over time. Magnetite, hematite, and ilmenite were important at first. After 900 BC jade seems to have become increasingly important while the value of some of the other commodities diminished. There were undoubtedly a number of reasons for these changes. Whatever the reasons, their effect was that the various elite groups participating in these commercial networks were entering into social and economic relationships with a continually changing series of groups that had access to different economically important materials. As a result, exchange relationships that were important in 1000 BC may have been unimportant or even nonexistent 500 years later.

By the middle of the first millenium BC, the commercial networks dominated by the elite groups of the Olmec heartland in the tropical lowlands gradually dwindled. They were replaced by a series of regional networks in the highland areas that were dominated by different regional elite groups such as those in the Oaxaca Valley or the Valley of Mexico to the north. These highland elite groups established new ties with other peoples that would allow them to maintain the status differentials that existed in their own communities.

These post-Olmec commercial networks appeared at different times; for example, the one centered in the Oaxaca Valley appeared about 500 BC, while the one that included Tlatilco in the Valley of Mexico and other localities in the central Mexican highlands may have emerged as early as 800 BC.

THE DEVELOPMENT OF CITIES

Toward the middle of the first millenium BC, peoples of the central highlands of Mexico began to plan, build, and live in cities that ultimately covered several square miles and contained tens of thousands of residents. One of the earliest of these was Monte Alban in the Oaxaca Valley. The construction of Monte Alban began about 500 BC and continued intermittently for nearly 1,000 years. Workers were drawn from San José Mogote and other settlements in the three arms of the Oaxaca Valley. The first settlement at Monte Alban consisted of three separate areas that may have been residential areas for leaders from the three arms of the valley. As time passed, the distinction between the three areas vanished as more and more buildings were built in the areas between them. By 100 BC, the 55-acre main plaza had already been built, as had many of the 2,300 house terraces, some of which had dozens of residences. By this time, 5,000 to 10,000 people lived in Monte Alban and were ruled, along with the other inhabitants of the Oaxaca Valley, by a single ruler who resided in this hilltop city. As time passed, the population of Monte Alban swelled to more than 30,000, and by AD 400 the city covered more than three square miles.

Teotihuacán

During the first millenium BC the inhabitants of the Valley of Mexico exported obsidian and other commodities to groups living elsewhere in Mesoamerica. Cuicuilco was the largest town in the valley and probably the most important one, judging from the large public buildings found there. It may have had a population of more than 10,000. There were other towns in the valley as well; these were located around the edge of the ancient lake that filled most of the central part of the valley. By the end of the first century BC, two towns located side by side at Teotihuacán, in a small valley northeast of the lake, had become the largest settlements in the valley. They covered about one and one-half square miles and had about 7,500 residents. The two settlements eventually merged as houses, workshops, and other buildings gradually filled up the space between them. By AD 150 Teotihuacán was the largest and most imposing settlement in the valley. Massive public construction had occurred—the major north—south and east—west avenues had been laid out and two enormous pyramids built. More than 45,000 people resided in Teotihuacán at this time.

The 55-acre central plaza at Monte Alban. John E. Pfeiffer, **The emergence of society,** (New York: McGraw-Hill, 1977), p. 355. Courtesy of Richard E. Blanton, Purdue University.

By AD 250 the city was spread over nine square miles and housed at least 65,000 people. The inhabitants had established close ties with the peoples of the Gulf Coast and were shipping obsidian to places as far away as British Honduras. During the next three centuries, the city's population swelled to more than 150,000 persons living in over 2,200 single-story apartment houses located throughout the urban area. Surface remains from these buildings indicate that some of their residents were craft specialists—potters, stoneworkers, weavers, and feather workers, to name only a few.

By AD 450 Teotihuacán was many times larger than any other city in Mesoamerica; in fact, it was probably the largest city in the world at that time. It was located at the crossroads of several major trade networks that let to other highland regions and to the Gulf Coast, and was the hub of the most extensive commercial network the peoples of Mesoamerica had ever seen. It was also the most important ritual and market center of the area, as well as the capital of an empire that influenced the course of events as far away as the jungles of eastern Guatemala. Pilgrims and traders from virtually every part of Mesoamerica visited Teotihuacán; sections of the ancient city were inhabited by foreigners from places like Oaxaca; and soldiers and officials from the city left buildings and traces of their activities in places like Kaminaljuyu and Tikal in Guatemala.

A number of factors contributed to the growth of Teotihuacán and to the spread of its influence through much of Mesoamerica. It was located in a

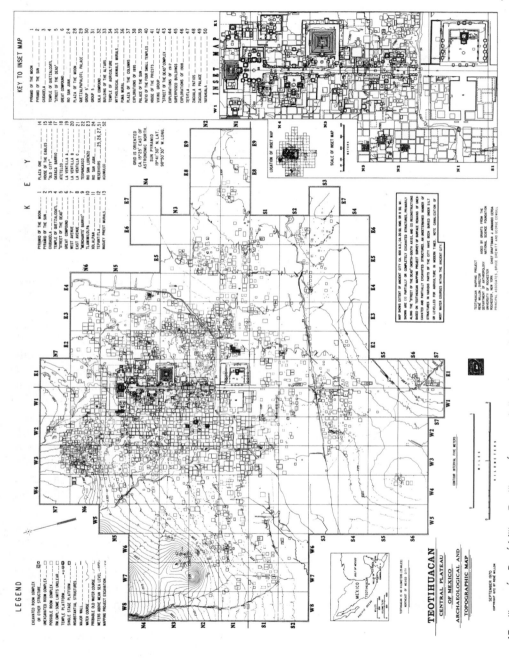

Plan of Teotihuacán. René Millon. Teotihuacán; completion of map of giant ancient city in the Valley of Mexico. *Science*, 170, no. 3962 (1970), 1078. Copyright 1970 by the American Association for the Advancement of Science. From **Urbanization at Teotihuacán, Mexico**, v 1, **The Teotihuacán Map.** Copyright © 1973 by René Millon.

rich agricultural area whose productive capacity was continually expanded to meet the growing needs of the city and its residents. Not only was production intensified in this rural sustaining area, but the size of the area itself was probably increased during the period of Teotihuacán's ascendency. Besides being a major seat of power—political, commercial, and religious—the city was also the most important manufacturing center in Mesoamerica. It is clear that the rapid growth of the city after AD 250 was at least partly a result of what was happening to its industries and its export economy. The obsidian industry apparently was one of the more important ones in the city and, from the perspective of the archaeologist, among the more informative.

As time passed, a number of things happened to the obsidian industry at Teotihuacán. It became more specialized; the early obsidian workers in the city produced a wide range of goods, while the later ones became much more specialized in their production. These craftsmen, particularly the ones who made prismatic blades and cores, began to use ever-increasing amounts of obsidian from quarries located outside the Teotihuacán Valley; in other

The Pyramid of the Moon and the Plaza of the Moon are in the foreground; the Palace of Quetzalpapalotl lies on the right side of the Plaza; the Street of the Dead extends from the plaza to the top of the picture; and the Pyramid of the Sun, the largest pre-Columbian structure in the Americas, lies on the left beyond the plaza. René Millon, **Urbanization at Teotihuacan, Mexico,** V. 1, **The Teotihuacan map.** Copyright © 1973 by René Millon.

words, they were importing unworked obsidian from distant localities to make objects, some of which were then shipped to other parts of Mesoamerica. As obsidian production became more specialized, the number of workshops increased; for example, the number of workshops tripled between AD 300 and 400.

The obsidian workers added new work to old work. At first, obsidian collecting was their most important activity. Later, they began to make cores and blades. Once this had become an established activity, they added the manufacture of arrowheads and ornaments to the obsidian work carried out in the city. This ever-increasing specialization produced a greater division of labor within the city's work force. As this happened, the older activities did not become obsolete. In fact, there was probably an even greater demand for unworked obsidian and for blades than there had been before the new craft specialities emerged. The effect of this process was that more and more people became involved in the obsidian industry of Teotihuacán.

At first, most of the obsidian quarried in the Teotihuacán Valley was probably used locally for the production of tools; a small portion of the un-worked stone apparently was exported to other areas, including Oaxaca and the Gulf Coast. After the beginning of the Christian Era, the peoples of Teotihuacán began exporting their obsidian to new areas, and some of the craftsmen who had formerly produced objects for local consumption began to export their finished products to these new markets. Eventually the export of these finished objects became more important to the city's economy than shipping unworked obsidian to distant lands.

As the volume of Teotihuacán's obsidian exports increased, the local economy grew. More and more people became involved in one aspect of the industry or another. Some were craftsmen; others worked in the quarries to meet the needs of the craftsmen for more obsidian and for different kinds of obsidian; and others were involved in exporting the finished commodities to distant markets. Each new job created by the increased demand for obsidian added still other jobs to the city's economy as more people had to be employed to meet the needs and demands of the ever-increasing number of people involved with obsidian production.

| The Effects of Import Replacement | As the city's export economy grew, the people of Teotihuacán were able to import a greater quantity and variety of goods produced in other areas. These imports also added to the local economy. Some of them—like obsidian from distant quarries—went directly into the export economy. Other imports apparently were used by the growing population. Teotihuacán grew steadily as its inhabitants generated new exports from the local economy. |

However, by AD 250 two new conditions had developed in the local economy. There was enough demand for certain imported goods so that it became feasible for the people of Teotihuacán to produce them locally. And the inhabitants of the city had the technical capacity to produce these goods by adding the new work to tasks that were already being carried out. This process is called *import replacement.* Its most important effect on the people of Teotihuacán was that they no longer had to pay for certain imported goods with the commodities they produced and exported. As a result, they were able to shift the composition of their imports to include new goods and services without increasing the size of their export economy. Some of the new imports—raw materials like jade—were probably incorporated immediately into locally produced items that had been imported in the past. The rest of the imported items had not been available earlier.

Import replacement created new jobs at Teotihuacán. Some of them consisted of producing goods and services that had been imported earlier; others were aimed toward satisfying the needs and demands of the new producers. Since the residents of Teotihuacán replaced a number of imports at about the same time, the number of jobs available increased very rapidly after AD 250. As a result, the population of the city grew, and demand for the items produced in the city also increased. This kind of growth took place without an increase in the volume of either imports or exports. Since a greater quantity and variety of goods and services were now available within the city, it was possible for the urban producers to generate new exports.

The influence of Teotihuacán diminished rapidly after AD 650. Within two centuries or less the city was in ruins; its only residents were a few hundred individuals who hid out or camped in some of the abandoned apartment complexes. There are a number of reasons why Teotihuacán declined so dramatically. For one, the rural area around the city could no longer produce enough food to meet the needs of the townspeople. As food and other goods produced in the countryside became scarce, people left the city. This reduced the size of the urban labor force and may have created manpower shortages in the export industries. As the volume of goods produced declined, so did the size of the city's export economy. The residents of Teotihuacán lost markets for their goods as other groups seized control of the old commercial networks and new networks emerged. These groups, including peoples from other towns in the Valley of Mexico that had once been subordinate to Teotihuacán, gradually began to challenge the people of Teotihuacán for political and economic supremacy in Mesoamerica.

The collapse of Teotihuacán reverberated throughout Mesoamerica. It created a power vacuum in central Mexico that lasted for nearly 350 years. Many of the large settlements in the Maya lowlands of eastern Guatemala and Belize were abandoned within a century of the time that Teotihuacán fell. It was a time of warfare; people lived in fortified settlements; and scenes of raiding and the taking of captives appeared with increasing frequency.

THE MAYA

The Maya lived in the southern part of Mesoamerica—in Chiapas, Guatemala, Belize, and western Honduras. They lived in both the highland areas of Chiapas and western Guatemala and the lowland jungles that lie to the east. The climate is hot in the lowlands. Trees tower more than 150 feet above the jungle floor, and animal life is varied; deer and peccary are plentiful in the drier areas of the northern lowlands, while monkeys abound in the wetter forests of the south.

Early
Settlements
in the
Lowlands

The first evidence of human occupation in the Maya lowlands comes from the site of Cuello in the northern part of Belize, or British Honduras. By 2500 BC the residents of Cuello were living in thatch-and-timber houses built on small circular platforms made of earth and covered with plaster. They hunted deer and agouti in the nearby forests and collected edible snails from the swamps around their settlement. When people died, they were buried in the house platforms. Five individuals were found in one platform—a child, an adult woman, and three adult men. Jade beads, seashells, and hematite had been placed in their graves. Some of these objects—notably the jade—had been transported up to 200 miles. This suggests that there were already extensive commercial networks operating in the Maya lowlands by the second millenium BC. All of the adults buried in the house platform at Cuello showed abnormally advanced tooth wear; this indicates that there was some abrasive substance in their diet such as lime or grit from grinding stones. Since suitable materials for grinding stones are not generally available in the Maya lowlands, the inhabitants of Cuello must have obtained them elsewhere. The evidence also suggests that they may have been growing maize—a crop grown by the modern Maya, who process it with lime to make maza (corn meal).

By 1250 BC or earlier the peoples of Belize were draining the swampy lowlands and burning the remaining ground cover to make the land more suitable for cultivation. Along the Río Hondo they dug ditches and piled up the soil to form long ridges where they planted crops. Extensive ridged field systems like the ones along the Río Hondo have been found elsewhere in the Maya lowlands. Their construction indicates that there were many people in the area and that they were able to plan and carry out large-scale communal work projects that increased agricultural production.

The early settlements in the lowlands of eastern Guatemala and the neighboring areas of Belize and southern Mexico—the core area of the lowland Maya—were probably smaller and more impoverished than those located in the highlands or areas adjacent to the mountains, where essential resources were available and access to the commercial networks of the first millenium BC was easier. The earliest stone monuments with Maya Long Count calendrical dates occur at Abaj Takalik on the Pacific slopes of the mountains in southwestern Guatemala. The earliest monument at this settlement was erected no later than the first century BC—300 to 400 years earlier than the first dated stone monument in the Maya lowlands.

Peoples living in the core area of the Maya lowlands during the first millenium BC devoted much of their labor to producing food and shelter; however, some of their efforts apparently went into building small temples and other public structures. The rest was used to produce decorated pottery, cotton textiles, and status items—ritual and ideology—that could be exchanged for essential items, such as salt and grinding stones made of igneous rock, that were not available in the lowlands. They acquired these items from peoples living in the highlands or in the buffer zone along the eastern slopes of the mountains and the coast. This commerce required some degree of organization. The goods had to be produced and collected before they could be carried by porters to the highland settlements to be exchanged. The goods for which they were traded were then transported back to the lowlands, where they were distributed to the local groups that had produced the commodities to be exported. Presumably, the distribution of the highland items took place at some central place, such as a settlement with a small temple.

At first, individuals representing a number of different social units may have directed this trade and accumulated status, wealth, and power as a result of their commercial activities. As time passed, progressively fewer groups or families were involved in the commerce. Those that were gained more wealth and authority within their communities; instead of living away from the temples, as some of their ancestors had, they began to live in elaborate residences or palaces located near the shrines. The earliest of these palaces was built about AD 100 at Holmul in the northern Peten; others appeared at all of the other important lowland Maya settlements within the next few centuries. No longer, it seems, were power and authority accorded to anyone who accumulated wealth. As time passed, wealth and, with it, power and status became concentrated in the hands of a few closely related individuals.

Individual households in the core area were not able to produce the artificially scarce products and services—ritual paraphernalia and esoteric knowledge—that were used for long-distance exchange. This reinforced the concentration of power and authority in the hands of those wealthy families who represented the wider community and organized and promoted the accumulation of these resources, their production, and their exchange with outsiders. These families resided in the ceremonial centers and provided the capital, organization, and integration for the scattered households that they represented. Their newly acquired wealth was used to build lavish temples and palaces, to erect stelae commemorating the deeds of particular rulers, to acquire exotic materials that reinforced status differences, and to furnish tombs that reflected the status hierarchies that existed in the Maya communities of the core area.

After AD 250, these activities took place at an ever-increasing pace in the major lowland Maya centers. Ultimately, four centers—Tikal, Copan, Palenque, and Calakmul—gained paramount importance in the core area. Each was surrounded by a hierarchy of settlements—a few minor or secondary ceremonial centers, more villages, and a larger number of hamlets and isolated households.

The Buffer Zone Settlements

The concentration of wealth and power did not occur as dramatically in the buffer zone settlements as it did in the core area of the Maya lowlands. As a result, the peoples of the buffer zone lacked the complex social hierarchies of their contemporaries in the core area, and there was a much greater degree of social mobility since social status was something a family could achieve through its own efforts. The peoples of the buffer zone exchanged a wide range of goods (either locally produced items or goods acquired through highland commercial networks) with the residents of the core area of the Peten. In return, they received the artificially scarce goods associated with ritual; however, these goods were made available to a wider number of people than they would have been in the core area, and families used them to enhance their prestige among the buffer zone communities.

Sometime during the fifth century AD Teotihuacán took over direct control of Kaminaljuyu in the Guatemala highlands and thereby acquired a virtual monopoly over the obsidian trade in Mesoamerica. At about the same time, it established a gateway community at Tikal that gave it direct access to the resources—both real and artificial—of the core area of the Maya lowlands. This probably had the effect of drawing people from the buffer zone to Tikal and other centers in the core area to procure and produce commodities desired by Teotihuacán. Many of the core area settlements grew significantly in both size and population during this period.

When Teotihuacán's influence collapsed during the sixth or seventh century AD, a power vacuum developed in the Maya lowlands. The leaders of the Sky dynasty—the ruling family of Tikal—continued to have enormous tombs built for themselves during the eighth century; however, their wealth and power was waning as the settlements of the buffer zone gradually took over control of the old exchange network and became larger and more socially diversified than they had been earlier. These buffer zone communities were beginning to compete directly with Tikal and the other major centers in the core area by the end of the seventh century. In order to reduce the effects of this competition, the rulers of the Sky dynasty, who still possessed considerable power, began to marry off their daughters to the rulers of Maya communities located in the buffer zone. By creating alliances through marriage they hoped to stave off the impending economic disaster.

By AD 800 or perhaps a little earlier, a new trading system centered in Tabasco in southern Mexico on the Gulf coast was producing and exporting a type of pottery called Fine Orange on a scale previously unknown in the Maya area. This pottery was mass produced. The buffer area settlements received Fine Orange pottery and other commodities decades before they reached the communities located in the core area. As the new trade networks developed and the economic power of the buffer zone communities increased, the wealth, prestige, and power of Tikal and other centers in the Peten core area diminished even further. They grew progressively smaller, and foreigners eventually gained political and ideological control over several of them. However, as the core area Maya communities no longer had anything to export, the peoples of the buffer zone settlements also felt the pinch in their dealings with the peoples of the highlands and Tabasco. These settlements on the periphery of the core area, which had once acted as middlemen, were no longer functional, and eventually they too ceased to exist, as new markets and sources of desirable goods emerged.

These new sources and markets were not located in the Maya lowlands. The area's population declined dramatically after AD 800. In fact, some regions seem to have been abandoned altogether, while others were inhabited by only a small fraction of the people who had lived there earlier. By 1950, the population of the Maya lowlands still had not reached the level it had attained 1,500 years earlier. The reason for this lack of recovery was economic. The inhabitants who remained there after 800 had few resources, if any, to contribute to what the rest of the people of Mesoamerica wanted.

THE TOLTECS AND THE AZTECS

Between AD 850 and 1200 the *Toltecs,* with their capital at Tula in northern Mexico, gained political and economic dominance over Mesoamerica. Their capital was located in the Teotlalpan region north of the Valley of Mexico on the edge of the old Teotihuacán Empire. Economically, the Teotlalpan was and is an unstable area. When the rains are good, the people farm; however, when they become irregular or insufficient, farming becomes difficult in this marginal farming area. Farming peoples lived in the Teotlalpan when Tula was founded, about AD 500. When the Spaniards arrived 1,000 years later, nomadic bands of hunters and gatherers had moved into the area from the north.

The Toltecs established frontier garrisons north of Tula to prevent the *chicimeca,* or wandering peoples, from overrunning their territory. They attempted to incorporate these groups into their own society, much as the Romans did with the Germanic tribes. The Toltecs looked to the south to acquire goods that they could not produce themselves. They seem to have established gateway communities in the rich lands to the south and east where cacao, jade, and feathers were found. In one residence at Tula there was a cache of pottery vessels that had come from distant lands. The Plumbate vessels in the cache were probably manufactured in Guatemala, while the Nicoya Polychrome pots were made on the Nicoya Peninsula of Costa Rica. Costa Rica lies more than 1,300 miles southeast of Tula. Like their predecessors, the Toltecs traded, conquered, and collected tribute to get what they needed.

The historical annals of the Toltecs indicate that power was divided between sacred and secular rulers. When one of the sacred rulers tried illegally to pass his office to a member of his own family, a civil war was fought and the victor drove the sacred ruler and his followers from the city. The internal strife accompanying this dispute seriously undermined the power of the state. Groups in different areas seized control of various parts of the old commercial network dominated by the Toltecs and gradually became economic and political forces in their homelands. There were several of these successor states in the Valley of Mexico alone, and others emerged elsewhere in Mesoamerica; examples, are Chichen Itza on the Yucatán Peninsula, Cholula, and others in the highlands of Guatemala. *Chicimeca* groups moved into the Toltec domain from the north and eventually carved out economic and political niches for themselves. One of these was the Mexica, or *Aztecs,* who settled in the Valley of Mexico about AD 1200.

When the *Chicimeca* groups arrived they were little more than clients to wealthier, more powerful groups that gave them agricultural land in exchange for military service. But toward the middle of the fifteenth century the Aztecs, who had served the most powerful group in the valley, rebelled against their lords and allied themselves with two other groups that lived on the island of Texcoco on the western side of the valley. The Aztecs and their allies conquered their enemies in 1430. The members of the "Triple Alliance" then divided the Valley of Mexico and much of Mesoamerica into separate spheres of influence.

During the next seventy years the Aztecs brought most of the peoples of central Mexico under the rule of the Triple Alliance and raided or conquered areas as far south as Guatemala. Like their predecessors, they conquered and occupied those areas where there were particularly prized resources. In other areas they established gateway communities or ports of trade. By 1515 the Aztecs were the dominant power in the alliance because they had put puppet rulers on the thrones of their erstwhile allies. As a result, they were able to keep much of the wealth that they received as tribute from conquered or subject peoples in their own treasury. Part of the tribute was redistributed among the warrior groups, but the bulk of it was used to purchase luxury goods for the nobility and the king.

Tenochtitlan, the Aztec capital that is now located beneath Mexico City, had a population of 200,000 or more on the eve of the Spanish conquest. Many of its residents were immigrants from other areas—craft specialists, refugees, foreigners with special privileges, and individuals who spent part of each year there. They resided in various parts of the city and intermingled freely with the native inhabitants. In addition, thousands came to the city on

Reconstruction of the great temple of Tenochtitlan. The temple is on the left, the northern canoe basin in the foreground; the palaces of Axayacatl and Motecuzoma flank the Great Temple. Courtesy of the American Museum of Natural History.

market days, and hundreds arrived each day with tribute from various parts of Mesoamerica. They often remained in the city for days and were accommodated in different ways; some had their own houses, while others stayed with Aztec families or lived in hotels.

The residents of Tenochtitlan worked at many different occupations. Some were administrators or warriors; others engaged in commerce or craft production. Still others grew some of the food consumed in the city on *chinampas,* raised fields surrounded by water from the lake. The city itself was divided into quarters, each with its own market, shrines, and facilities. Each quarter, in turn, was divided into districts that had local markets and shrines. As a result, there was a great deal of duplication and diversity in the city.

Commerce played a major role in creating wealth, status, and power in Mesoamerica. The ancient peoples of the area often preferred raids over permanent occupation, and tribute over some form of permanent political control. When permanent occupation did occur, it was frequently in the form of a gateway community that opened up whole areas for commerce with the invaders. Many of the items that were exchanged were clearly useful. Others were not so useful and were artificially scarce. These included ceremonies, ritual paraphernalia, esoteric knowledge, and the prestige, status, and power that went with possessing them.

FURTHER READINGS

Becker, Marshall Joseph
1973 Archaeological evidence for occupational specialization among the Classic Period Maya at Tikal, Guatemala. *American Antiquity,* 38, no. 4, October, pp. 396–406.

Calnek, Edward E.
1970 The internal structure of pre-Columbian cities; the case of Tenochtitlan. Paper presented at the 39th International Congress of Americanists, Lima, Peru.
1972 The organization of urban food supply systems; the case of Tenochtitlan. Paper presented at the 40th International Congress of Americanists, Sevilla, Spain.
1972 Settlement pattern and chinampa agriculture at Tenochtitlan. *American Antiquity,* 37, no. 1, January, pp. 104–115.

Coe, Michael D.
1968 *America's first civilization; discovering the Olmec.* American Heritage, New York.

Cowgill, George
1974 Quantitative studies of urbanization at Teotihuacán. In *Mesoamerican archaeology; new approaches,* ed. Norman Hammond, pp. 363–396. University of Texas Press, Austin.

Diehl, Richard A., Roger Lomas, and Jack T. Wynn
1974 Toltec trade with Central America; new light and evidence. *Archaeology,* 27, no. 3, July, pp. 182–187.

Flannery, Kent V.
1968 Archaeological systems theory and early Mesoamerica. In *Anthropological archaeology in the Americas,* ed. Betty Meggers, pp. 67–87. Anthropological Society of Washington, Washington, D.C.
1968 The Olmec and the Valley of Oaxaca; a model for inter-regional interaction in formative times. In *Dumbarton Oaks Conference on the Olmec,* ed. Elizabeth P. Benson, pp. 79–117. Dumbarton Oaks Research Library and Collection, Washington, D.C.
1976 *The early Mesoamerican village.* Academic Press, New York.

Graham, John A.
1977 Discoveries at Abaj Takalik, Guatemala. *Archaeology,* 30, no. 3, May, pp. 196–197.

Hammond, Norman
1977 The earliest Maya. *Scientific American,* 236, no. 4, April, pp. 116–133.

Haviland, William A.
1967 Stature at Tikal, Guatemala; implications for Classic Maya demography and social organization. *American Antiquity,* 32, no. 3, July, pp. 316–325.
1970 Tikal, Guatemala and Mesoamerican urbanism. *World Archaeology,* 2, no. 2, October, pp. 186–198.
1977 Dynastic genealogies from Tikal, Guatemala; implications for descent and political organization. *American Antiquity,* 42, no. 1, January, pp. 61–67.

Hirth, Kenneth G.
1978 Interregional trade and the formation of prehistoric gateway communities. *American Antiquity,* 43, no. 1, January, pp. 38–45.

MacNeish, Richard S.
1964 Ancient Mesoamerican civilization. *Science,* 143, no. 3606, February 7, pp. 531–537.

1967   Mesoamerican archaeology. In *Biennial review of anthropology,* ed. Bernard J. Siegel and Alan R. Beals, vol. 5, pp. 306–331. Stanford University Press, Stanford, Calif.

1968   Some implications of changes in population and settlement pattern of 12,000 years of prehistory in the Tehuacán Valley of Mexico. In *Population and economics,* ed. Paul Deprez, pp. 215–250. University of Manitoba Press, Winipeg.

1971   Speculation about how and why food production and village life developed in the Tehuacán Valley, Mexico. *Archaeology,* 24, no. 4, October, pp. 307–315.

Marcus, Joyce

1973   Territorial organization of the lowland Classic Maya. *Science,* 180, no. 4089, June 1, pp. 911–916.

Millon, René

1967   Teotihuacán. *Scientific American,* 216, no. 6, June, pp. 38–48.

1973   *Urbanization at Teotihuacán, Mexico,* vol. 1. University of Texas Press, Austin and London.

1974   The study of urbanism at Teotihuacán, Mexico. In *Mesoamerican archaeology; new approaches,* ed. Norman Hammond, pp. 335–363. University of Texas Press, Austin.

Molloy, John P., and William L. Rathje

1974   Sexploitation among the Late Classic Maya. In *Mesoamerican archaeology; new approaches,* ed. Norman Hammond, pp. 431–444. University of Texas Press, Austin.

Patterson, Thomas C.

1973   *America's past; a New World archaeology.* Scott, Foresman. Glenview, Ill., and London.

Pfeiffer, John E.

1977   *The emergence of society; a prehistory of the establishment.* McGraw-Hill, New York.

Rathje, William L.

1970   Socio-political implications of lowland Maya burials; methodology and tentative hypotheses. *World Archaeology,* 1, no. 3, February, pp. 359–374.

1971   The origin and development of lowland Classic Maya civilization. *American Antiquity,* 36, no. 3, July, pp. 275–285.

1973   Classic Maya development and denouement; a research design. In *The Classic Maya collapse,* edited by T. Patrick Culbert, pp. 405–454. University of New Mexico Press, Albuquerque.

Sanders, William T., and Barbara J. Price

1968   *Mesoamerica; the evolution of a civilization.* Random House, New York.

Willey, Gordon R.

1968   *An introduction to American archaeology,* vol. 1. Prentice-Hall, Englewood Cliffs, N.J.

Winter, Marcus C.

1974   Residential patterns at Monte Alban, Oaxaca, Mexico. *Science,* 186, no. 4168, December, 13, pp. 981–987.

Wolf, Eric R.

1959   *Sons of the shaking earth.* University of Chicago Press, Chicago.

1976   *The Valley of Mexico; studies in pre-Hispanic ecology and society.* University of New Mexico Press, Albuquerque.

Ancient Peoples of South America

South America is shaped like a gigantic triangle. The equator runs through the widest portion of this triangle; as a result, most of the landmass lies in the tropics. However, the narrow tip of the continent projects farther south into the subpolar latitudes than any other landmass in the Southern Hemisphere. The Andes Mountains extend along the entire western edge of the continent; these are young, active mountains that were formed during the last 10 to 15 million years as the South American Plate overrode the Pacific Plate. Earthquakes are frequent in the geologically active areas of coastal and mountainous western South America. East of the Andes lie the Brazilian and Guiana uplands—among the most ancient landmasses in the world. More than 100 million years ago this enormous shield was connected with the ancient landmasses of southern and western Africa. South of the Brazilian highlands and east of the Andes lies the Patagonian plateau.

Tropical rain forest covers much of the eastern lowlands north of the Tropic of Capricorn. Tree-studded savannas and grasslands replace these forests in Paraguay and northeastern Argentina. These eventually merge with the desert scrub vegetation that covers the parched plateau of Patagonia. To the west, rain forests cover the northern and southern coasts of the continent; one of the driest deserts in the world separates the tropical forests of coastal Colombia from the temperate rain forest of southern Chile. The Andes, with vast plateaus at 12,000 feet or more above sea level and mountain peaks more than 20,000 feet high, possess an incredible range and variety of alpine environments.

When the Europeans arrived in South America during the sixteenth century, the first explorers

1b

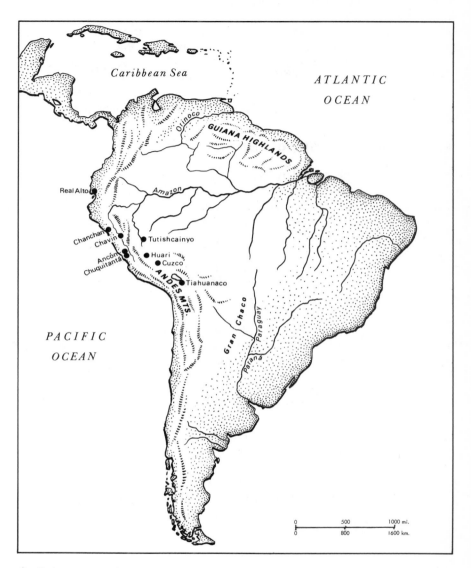

South America.

found highly stratified states in the Andes. The largest of these was the Inca Empire, with an elaborate bureaucracy that controlled the daily lives of millions of people who lived in the mountains and along the coast from what is now northern Ecuador through Peru and Bolivia into northern Chile and northwestern Argentina. At the same time that the Incas dominated the activities of numerous ethnic groups in the Andean area, hunting and gathering peoples roamed the Patagonian plateau much as their ancestors had 10,000 years earlier. Farming peoples lived in the forests east of the Andes. Some of these forest-dwelling groups displayed the same kind of social stratification that existed among the coastal and mountain peoples of the Inca Empire. Yet, the life style of the Andean peoples and those of the tropical forest were different. Let us consider how societies developed in these two areas and what kinds of mechanisms produced the differences between them.

ANCIENT PEOPLES OF THE ANDES

The central Andes—the coastal area and mountain ranges from northern Ecuador to northern Chile and northwestern Argentina—is one of the most environmentally diverse regions of the world. A journey of only a few hours can take one through three or four very different habitats, each of which is characterized by its own particular set of resources. Much of the environmental diversity is patterned. One pattern consists of a series of environmental zones that repeat themselves every 15 to 20 miles; this pattern is most apparent on the west side of the Andes, where fertile river valleys are separated from each other by desert and barren hills at low elevations and by *puna* grasslands at higher ones. The other important pattern is a linear one that consists of a series of environmental zones that do not repeat themselves; this again is most apparent on the western slopes because of the steep elevation gradients that occur there.

The distinction between these patterns had important implications for where the early inhabitants went to get food. The food resources immediately available to a group living near the mouth of a river were roughly the same as those available to groups residing in similar habitats in other coastal valleys; they were very different from the resources that were immediately available to groups residing in the middle or upper portions of the same river valley. As a result, if the coastal group sought new resources, its members would be more likely to find them in the higher parts of their own valley than in similar settings in other valleys. If the local supply of a particular resource was insufficient, then the group would most likely find additional supplies in similar environments in the valleys located to the north or south.

The Ideal of
Self-Sufficiency
The Andean peoples worked out a distinctive way of dealing with the environmental diversity of their homelands. This has been described as "the ideal of community self-sufficiency," "vertical control," and "the archipelago model." The first term—*community self-sufficiency*—indicates what the various Andean peoples were trying to do; they wanted to have access to all of the resources they needed to sustain themselves throughout the year so that they did not have to rely on outsiders for essential commodities. The other terms emphasize the spatial arrangement of resources in

the Andes. Most of these do not occur naturally or cannot be produced in a single environmental setting; consequently, the members of a group had to exploit a number of different environmental settings in order to produce what they needed. Since these settings usually were not contiguous, the group members were dispersed in clusters over a considerable area. As a result, their land use patterns, as well as their settlements, resembled chains of islands; each "island" was located in a different environmental zone where particular resources were available, and was separated from other "islands" by lands that were often controlled by other ethnic groups.

The members of these ethnic groups—scattered over the landscape and often separated from each other by several days' travel—were bound together by kin ties. The individuals in one locality shared the fruits of their labor with kin living in other places where those goods were absent or in short supply. In return they received goods that they could not produce for themselves. Judging from historical records, these transactions took place in various ways: traffic between kin living in different localities; redistribution centers where goods were accumulated, stored, and reapportioned among the various segments of the group; and regular ceremonies that brought different segments of the group together in the same place. The records also indicate that markets and market exchange were not important in the Andean area before the arrival of the Europeans in the sixteenth century.

The ideal of community self-sufficiency is apparently an ancient one in the central Andes. By 7000 BC groups living in the Ayacucho-Huanta region of the central highlands were moving from one habitat to another as the seasonal resources of those localities became available. They hunted deer and camelids during the dry season and consumed a variety of wild plants, including some that were not native to the area, judging from the contents of their feces. At least one group kept large numbers of guinea pigs, which they ate with a wide range of wild plants during the wet season. By 5000 BC one coastal group was able to live in the same place all year round because the seasonal resources its members needed were all found within three miles of each other. Their contemporaries 50 miles to the north had to move from one place to another during the year because in their territory the same seasonal resources were more than 15 miles away from each other. This was too far for them to travel in a single day; furthermore, when seasonal resources were plentiful in one area, supplies of other food resources in different settings were either inadequate or absent.

The pattern of moving from one place to another as seasonal food resources became available persisted for several thousand years in the Andes. It appears that members of highland groups occasionally ventured to the coast for shellfish or into the fringes of the tropical rain forests for jungle foods; however, during the fourth and fifth millenia BC these seem to have been sporadic forays rather than established patterns of movement. This seasonal pattern of movement occurred even after both plants and animals had been domesticated in the central Andes. For example, by 4000 BC the inhabitants of the Ayacucho-Huanta region were beginning to rely increasingly on domesticated guinea pigs and cultivated plants like chili peppers, squash, corn, and perhaps beans. As a result, they were able to reside in their wet-season camps for longer periods each year because of the agricultural surplus they could produce, store, and consume after the beginning of the dry season. Their contemporaries on the high plateaus of central Peru, who were in the process of domesticating camelids, still moved from place to place with their herds. By the end of the fourth millenium BC, coastal populations still relied almost exclusively on wild plant and animal foods; however, they were gradually beginning to adopt squash, chili peppers, corn, and other plants that were cultivated in the highlands.

The
Development
of Agriculture

The development of agriculture ultimately had an important impact on the ideal of community self-sufficiency and the way peoples spaced themselves over the landscape to produce the food they required. No longer were the resources of different localities exploited on a seasonal basis, with people moving from one environmental setting to the next as resources became available. Instead, groups began to establish villages and hamlets in localities where different resources were available or could be produced. They lived in these settlements all year round. Judging from the remains found in their garbage dumps, the residents of the various settlements exchanged food and other products with each other.

One of the earliest of the settlements is Real Alto in coastal Ecuador. A group of fisher—gatherers lived there toward the end of the fourth millenium BC and used molluscs from coastal mangroves as a major source of protein. They lived in small houses made of flexible poles bent inward and tied over the middle of the enclosed space. A few hundred years later the residents of Real Alto lived there year round and supported themselves by farming; corn was one of the crops they grew. By 2300 BC Real Alto covered more than 20 acres and probably had a population of about 1,500. Its residents lived in large elliptical houses with vertical log walls and gabled roofs; judging from their size, each household probably had about ten members. The houses were arranged around a series of rectangular courtyards on two parallel mounds, each of which was more than 1,200 feet long. The mounds were separated by a 300-foot plaza in which there were two public buildings. One of these buildings was a "fiesta house" surrounded by pits containing the remains of clams, lobsters, scallops, sea turtles, deer, and drinking bowls. Since nearly all of the pieces of each bowl were found in the same pit, it seems that each pit was dug after a particular feast. Across the plaza was a charnel house where individuals of high status and their retainers were interred. In

Reconstruction of the settlement at Real Alto, Ecuador, showing the two parallel ridges with houses (A, D), the fiesta or club houses (B), and the inner plaza (C). Donald W. Lathrap et al., Real Alto; an ancient ceremonial center, **Archaeology,** 30, no. 1 (1977), p. 6. Copyright 1977, Archaeological Institute of America.

one stone-lined tomb were the remains of a woman. Next to her was the body of a dismembered male; a few feet away the remains of seven men had been stacked in a pit.

After 2200 BC the population of Real Alto declined, but the amount of ceremonial activity taking place at the settlement seems to have increased. What happened was that the inhabitants of Real Alto created a number of satellite settlements in the surrounding countryside.

Agricultural production became increasingly important in the coastal valleys of central Peru after 2500 BC. However, none of the early settlements was anywhere near as large or impressive as Real Alto. At first only a small portion of the population of the central coast of Peru engaged in farming activities in the lower parts of the valleys near places where the rivers overflowed or the water table was high. Most of the population lived in villages with about 200 residents near rich fishing grounds and shellfish beds. The proportion of farmers to fishermen changed dramatically over the next 600 years as cultivated plant foods became more varied and important. By 1900 BC most of the population of the central Peruvian coast lived in farming settlements located in the lower and middle portions of the river valleys. The fishing villages were as numerous and as large as they had been earlier. What was different was that there were many more farming settlements, and some of them were many times larger than they had been before. For example, the largest farming commuinity on the central coast of Peru in 2300 BC covered less than an acre and probably had no more than 50 residents. Four hundred years later, Chuquitanta (El Paraiso), the largest settlement in the same area, covered more than 100 acres and probably had a population of over 1,000.

Construction and Water Management	All of the really large settlements located on the central Peruvian coast at the beginning of the second millenium BC covered more than 20 acres and contained a variety of stone structures, including houses, residential terraces, platform mounds, courts, and large complexes of rooms. Two of the room complexes at Chuquitanta are more than 1,000 feet long and 150 wide. It is estimated that more than 100,000 tons of stone were quarried for the construction of the buildings at Chuquitanta alone. Since they were remodeled frequently and were used for little more than a century, just the quarrying and transportation of the stone represents a massive investment of labor that was

Chuquitanta, an early collection and redistribution center on the central coast of Peru. The structure shown here is about 160 feet on a side and is one of nearly a dozen structures at the site. Gordon R. Willey, **An introduction to American archaeology** (Englewood Cliffs, N.J.: Prentice-Hall, 1971), vol. 2, figs. 3-16, 3-17.

undoubtedly well beyond the power of the approximately 1,000 people who lived there. Large-scale construction of the kind that took place at Chuquitanta, and at the other large settlements on the central Peruvian coast, strongly suggests that the labor force was drawn largely from the villages and hamlets in the surrounding countryside.

These peoples lived in fishing villages with marine-oriented economies or in small farming settlements located in the lower and middle parts of the river valleys. They were coping with the linear arrangement of resources on the west side of the Andes. The farmers in the lower valleys probably grew a wide range of crops. Their contemporaries in the upper valleys may well have specialized in one or two crops that were particularly well suited to these settings—for example, coca and avocados, which occur in the garbage dumps of coastal fishing villages. Given the fact the rivers are fast and have cut deep channels in the middle valleys, the residents of these areas probably used short ditches to bring water from the rivers to the lands above them where crops could be grown.

By the end of the second millenium BC, water management systems were in use in many of the agricultural areas of the Peruvian coast and highlands. These systems enormously increased the productive capacities of the peoples living in the regions where they were built. By this time virtually all of the economically important plants that were brought under cultivation in the Andes had already been domesticated, even though they were not grown or consumed everywhere. It is also probable that the inhabitants of some of these regions, particularly those along the coast, were growing two crops a year, instead of one, as their ancestors had 1,000 years earlier. Increased productivity—a result of the increase in the amount of land under cultivation as well as the introduction of multicropping—provided enough food to support a much larger population than before. The population growth that occurred during this time was undoubtedly a product of the expanded productive forces of these societies.

Communication Networks

There was uneven social and economic development in the central Andes by the second millenium BC. Some groups were already beginning to cope with the repetitive arrangement of resources and had access to lands in similar environmental settings in adjacent valleys. Many of these groups had large populations that were capable of producing enough food and other items to support craft specialists and some degree of social differentiation among the various segments of the society. Other groups, living in regions with less agricultural potential or fewer natural endowments, were smaller and less socially and economically differentiated than the larger ones.

The various social groups in Peru did not exist in isolation. Widespread similarities in architectural and pottery styles, in weaving technology, and in the organization of labor indicate that they were in close contact with each other. They were bound together by communication networks that crossed the coastal deserts and grasslands of the *puna* and even the mountain ranges of the western Andes. Sometimes, a single group participated in a number of these networks.

(a)

(b)

The two major deities found at
Chavin de Huantar. (a) The
smiling god, so named because
his lips turn upward. (b) The staff
god. Gordon R. Willey, **An
introduction to American
archaeology** (Englewood
Cliffs, N.J.: Prentice-Hall, 1971),
figs. 3-39, 3-40.

305

The groups that participated in these communication networks were dealing with the linear arrangement of resources mentioned earlier. They took part in these networks in order to obtain what they could not produce for themselves. One of the early networks was based on the movement of obsidian from the south–central highlands of Peru; it existed toward the beginning of the second millenium BC. One of the most interesting of the communication networks, the Chavin network, developed nearly 1,000 years later and was centered at Chavin de Huantar in the Mosna Valley of the north Peruvian highlands. It tied together groups living in the north highlands of Peru and along the north, central, and south coasts of the country. One of the items that moved from Chavin de Huantar to other centers in the area of the network was information.

The Chavin Influence

Chavin was a religious cult in which oracles probably played a prominent role, as they did in later cults in the Andean area. Chavin de Huantar was the center of this cult. The first stone statues carved in the Chavin style depict caymen (a crocodile-like animal), eagles, felines, tropical forest plants, and mythical beings; they were set in place about 1200 BC. At that time the most important deity was the "smiling god"—so called because his lips turn up at the corners, exposing his teeth. The earliest and most important representation of the smiling god was a large stone statue housed in a small, dark room near the center of the old temple.

There is relatively little evidence for Chavin influence outside the Mosna Valley before about 1050 BC. It occurred on the central coast of Peru, where there was already a tradition of large pyramids, but not on the north coast or in the Callejón de Huaylas, a large, fertile valley separated from the Mosna by a narrow range of mountains. This suggests that the peoples of Chavin were dealing with the linear arrangement of resources and were interested in areas where products that they could not produce themselves were available.

By 800 BC Chavin influence was much more apparent than it had been earlier. Temples with Chavin decorative themes were built in the Callejón de Huaylas and elsewhere in northern Peru, and cotton shirts with Chavin designs painted on them were made and apparently stored in quantity on the south coast. At Chavin de Huantar itself another deity, called the "staff god," had replaced the smiling god at the top of the religious pantheon. What probably happened at this time was that a number of semi-independent branch oracles were established at strategic places throughout Peru; these oracles gave advice to the residents of the areas in which they were located in return for textiles, the most prized commodity in the Andes, and other goods. The peoples of Chavin de Huantar were no longer dealing exclusively with the linear arrangement of resources, judging from the facts that the same crops are grown in the Callejón de Huaylas and the Mosna Valley and that cotton is produced in all of the coastal regions. It appears that the demand for particular commodities—such as cotton cloth—increased dramatically after the beginning of the first millenium BC. This necessitated the creation of new sources of supply, which took the form of tribute given to the branch oracles.

The influence of the oracles at Chavin had all but disappeared by 300 BC though representations of Chavin mythical beings reappeared in the Andean area for the next 2,000 years. However, the problem of scarce resources, first faced and dealt with by the peoples of the Mosna Valley and their associates elsewhere in the Peruvian Andes at the beginning of the first millenium BC, remained. After 300 BC ethnic groups in many areas were beginning to raid and conquer peoples in neighboring areas where similar resources were available. The residents of the conquered areas were incorporated into small states. A number of small independent states existed after this time. The boundaries between these political units, as well as their size and number, fluctuated continuously. At one moment, the inhabitants of four or five adjacent valleys may have belonged to the same political entity. A century or so later, there may have been two or three political units in the same area, or the same area may have been incorporated into an even larger political unit. The patterns of dominance and subordinance that existed among the various ethnic groups in these states also changed over time as first one group and then another gained control of the political apparatus.

The Huari Empire	Two large, multiethnic states emerged in the central Andes between AD 550 and 750. The smaller of the two apparently was centered at Tiahuanaco, near the southern end of Lake Titicaca; it included most of the Bolivian highlands, northern Chile, and the southernmost part of Peru. At its greatest extent it was several times larger than any of the earlier Andean states. The other state, *the Huari Empire,* had its capital near Ayacucho; by AD 750 it included most of the coast and highland areas of Peru. Since we know much more about the Huari Empire, let us consider it in more detail.

About AD 600 the inhabitants of the Ayacucho area were no longer able to support themselves with the goods they could produce locally. They gained access to needed items by acquiring lands elsewhere where those items could be produced. They acquired these lands by conquest, by subjugating foreign populations, and by exacting tribute from the peoples they incorporated into their state. They built large storage complexes at various places throughout the empire; there locally produced goods were collected and stored before being redistributed to supply armies engaged in conquest, feed and clothe state officials, or assist peoples in drought-stricken areas.

Large numbers of people were needed to govern the empire. The higher echelons of the state bureaucracy were undoubtedly drawn from the Huari ethnic group itself, while the lesser officials in the provinces probably

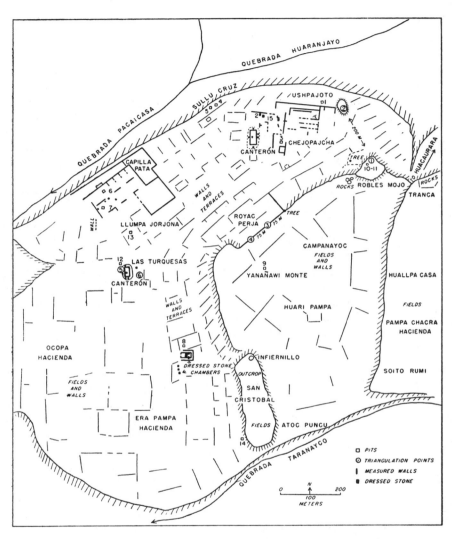

Plan of Huari, Peru. The plan shows the outlines of the unexcavated compounds at the settlement. Wendell Bennett, Excavations at Wari, Ayacucho, Peru, **Yale University Publications in Anthropology,** 49 (New Haven, Conn., 1953), fig. 2.

came from the traditional elite groups of the conquered peoples. Officials drawn from these groups must have had mixed loyalties. They served the state, yet they belonged to the groups that they governed and represented. In the long run their mixed loyalties probably undermined any attempt by the people of Huari to create a politically unified state in which all power and authority emanated from the small ruling class of the Ayacucho area.

It is almost impossible to separate religious spheres of influence from political or economic ones in ancient Andean society, since the three are so intertwined. It is clear that the people of Huari used religion, probably as the Incas did later, to justify their conquests. They imposed a religion, one that used new representations of the staff god, to justify their conquests. This state religion and others that were closely tied to it including Tiahuanaco, involved oracles. Like their predecessors, the peoples of Huari tried to maintain self-sufficiency by exporting a scarce commodity—predictions or statements about the appropriate courses of behavior to achieve desired goals—and receiving land and other resources in return. By doing so they were gaining access to the labor and wealth of other groups in the Andean area.

The Huari Empire collapsed rather suddenly during the first half of the ninth century. The capital city was virtually abandoned; some coastal areas apparently were depopulated and suffered severe economic depressions as a result; and small successor states appeared in the north, where the economic demands placed on the conquered peoples may have been smaller than those placed on the coastal peoples during the waning years of the empire. By AD 850 the pattern of small regional states with continually changing boundaries had reemerged in the central Andes.

The collapse of the Huari Empire probably occurred for a number of reasons. The demands of the state undoubtedly increased as its bureaucracy grew. These were met easily as long as the state was incorporating new ethnic groups from which it could exact tribute. Once the state had stopped expanding, any additional demands produced by the growing bureaucracy had to be made on peoples that had already been incorporated into the empire. As time passed, the burdens placed on them grew each year and must have become a source of dissatisfaction as they saw an ever-increasing portion of their productive capacity drawn off by the state. At the same time, there were no technological or organizational innovations during this period that might have increased the productive capacity of the subject group. As a result, total production in the empire remained constant or declined slightly during the ninth century. However, there is no evidence that the state reduced its demands on its subjects. When these demands became too great, the provinces rebelled. Provincial officials, often with dual loyalties, sided with their neighbors against the central government. The ethnic groups that fared best were those in the north, where the demands were smaller and labor shortages had less impact.

The Incas

During the early years of the fifteenth century, ethnic groups varying in size and degree of political complexity competed for access to resources. Ultimately, two of them emerged as supreme in the central Andes—the *Incas*

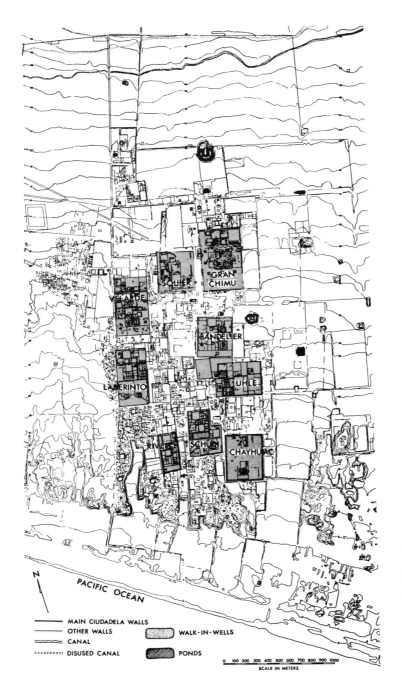

N

PACIFIC OCEAN

Map of the central area of Chanchan on the north coast of Peru. The central area is dominated by nine compounds, which served as residences, storage areas, and mortuaries for the hereditary leaders of the Kingdom of Chimor. Michael E. Moseley, Chan Chan; Andean alternative of the preindustrial city, **Science,** 187, no. 4173 (1975), fig. 1. Copyright 1975 by the American Association for the Advancement of Science.

from Cuzco in the south highlands and the Kingdom of Chimor, with its capital at Chanchan on the north Peruvian coast. By 1460 the two groups had entered into direct competition for political supremacy in the central Andes. The Incas won, and by 1525 *Tawantinsuyu,* the Inca Empire, stretched from

Map of Cuzco, the Inca capital, in the south highlands of Peru. The heavy dark lines show ancient Inca walls. E. G. Squier, **Peru; incidents of travel and exploration in the land of the Incas** (New York: Harper & Row, 1877), p. 428.

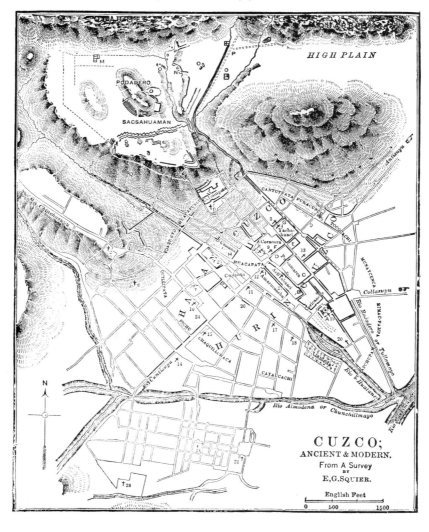

the northern border of Ecuador to northwestern Argentina and central Chile. The Incas conquered other ethnic groups in the name of religion: They imposed their ideology on other groups while allowing their subjects to keep their own religious beliefs as long as they served the state. They used ideology to justify their conquests so that the people of Cuzco could maintain their self-sufficiency by imposing labor taxes and tribute on subject peoples.

The Inca emperor rebuilt Cuzco, the capital city of the empire, after 1450. At the same time, he had the entire Cuzco basin rebuilt. Rivers were rechanneled, the valley floor leveled, and terraces built on the hills that enclosed the basin. This reclamation project increased the valley's agricultural productivity and made the capital, with its palaces, royal tombs, storehouses, and surrounding villages, one of the most impressive areas in the central Andes. Enormous amounts of labor were required to complete these public works, and entire ethnic groups were moved out of the Cuzco Basin while the project was carried out.

The Inca political system was a hierarchical one. The emperor ruled by divine right. Immediately below the emperor were his close relatives. Below them were the provincial leaders—the traditional leaders of subject ethnic groups. The Incas probably attempted to solve the problem of regional differences between political systems by making or creating hereditary leaders. To ensure loyalty, the Incas took the sons of traditional leaders to Cuzco, where they were indoctrinated into the ways of the Inca state. This guaranteed the loyalty of their fathers and provided leaders who were trained in the ways of the Inca state.

Such a political system was inherently unstable. No ruler could inherit anything from his predecessor. The property of the dead ruler passed to his other descendants, who formed a royal corporation; these individuals used his lands and the labor obligations that were owed to him to support themselves and their descendants. The new emperor had to establish his own corporation, which involved acquiring lands, labor, and tribute that were distinct from those of his father, the state, and the state religion. This process placed a continually increasing burden on the provincial communities as they were required to provide land and labor to four new rulers between 1438 and 1532. This must have been particularly burdensome after 1493, when the empire virtually stopped expanding and new sources of labor were no longer available. In addition, there was no recognized succession to the Inca throne. As a result, there was a great deal of tension as rival groups put forward their candidates. Each emperor dealt with this problem in a different way. One resigned; another married his sister and named his son as his heir; still another died without naming his successor, thereby plunging the Inca state into a civil war as rival groups fought over the throne. During the civil war the power of the Inca state declined considerably as groups broke away and joined various factions, which at times included the Spanish conquistadors.

The Spaniards arrived in 1532 in the midst of this civil war and ultimately played a role in bringing down the Inca state; one of the reasons for their success was that so many of the Andean peoples were dissatisfied with Inca rule. These peoples ultimately became close allies of the Spaniards.

THE TROPICAL FOREST AND BEYOND

Enormous river systems rising in the Andes and the Brazilian and Guiana highlands are the major feature of eastern South America. The largest of these is the Amazon, which drains most of tropical South America; it is the largest river system in the world. Only a narrow ridge separates the tropical forests of the Amazon Basin from the forests and savannas of the Orinoco to the north; in fact, the two drainage systems share a common water source in the Casiquiare swamp. A similar situation prevails in the south, where low hills separate the tributaries of the Amazon from the upper reaches of the Paraguay–Paraná drainage system. As a result of the proximity of their headwaters, the river systems of eastern South America provided an excellent communication and transportation network in ancient times. At various times this network connected the inhabitants of the Amazon Basin with peoples living in the Orinoco Basin, the deciduous forests and grasslands of the Guiana highlands, the savannas that cover the interior plateaus of the Brazilian Shield, and the seasonally flooded savannas of the Gran Chaco and the Paraná–Paraguay drainage system.

People have resided in eastern South America for more than 10,000 years. Nearly 15,000 years ago, the inhabitants of northern Venezuela were butchering and cooking extinct animals like mastodons, native American horses, and glyptodons. Peoples living on the Brazilian Shield were hunting horses and other mammals with spear points resembling those used in Patagonia more than 10,000 years ago. By 7000 BC, groups of fishermen and shellfish collectors lived along the south coast of Brazil. Two millenia later, peoples with a similar economic orientation left shell heaps along the Caribbean coast of Venezuela.

| The Amazon Basin | There is indirect evidence that widely dispersed groups inhabited the tropical forests of the Amazon Basin by the seventh millenium BC. These peoples were beginning to put new selective pressures on a wide variety of local plants that were ultimately brought under domestication. Judging from what happened elsewhere in the world, this process probably took between 3,000 and 4,000 years. Seeds from one of the economically important plants of the tropical forest—achiote, a condiment and dye—were brought to a 9,000-year-old archaeological site in the Ayacucho area of the central Andes. By 2700 BC the inhabitants of Rancho Peludo in Venezuela were processing |

bitter manioc flour on pottery griddles. Peanuts, manioc, sweet potatoes, chili peppers, and achira—all brought under domestication in the tropical forests and their environs—appeared in domesticated forms at archaeological sites in the desert coast of western South America by the end of the third millenium BC.

The earliest direct evidence for human occupation of the Amazon Basin comes from Tutishcainyo on an oxbow lake north of Pucallpa, Peru. People first lived there about 2000 BC. Although much of the site has been destroyed by the meandering Aguatía River, what remains stretches for several hundred yards along the edge of the old flood plain. The size of the site, as well as the depth and density of the deposit, suggests that the population of the settlement numbered in the hundreds. Modern settlements of the same size in the tropical forest have 1,000 or more residents.

The inhabitants of Tutishcainyo clearly used the resources offered by their riverine environment. More than 10 percent of their pottery was tempered with crushed shells from freshwater molluscs; presumably, the meat was consumed. A significant proportion of the pottery contained accidental inclusions of fish bones and scales, which suggests that fish were another important source of animal protein. The presence of large pottery vats, cups, and strainers—items that in later times were used to make manioc gruel and beer—suggests that the residents of Tutishcainyo were also doing so; it also implies that they were growing root crops and perhaps other cultigens along the edge of the alluvium and in small fields that they had cleared with stone axes on the high ground away from the river. Clay fragments with impressions of woven cane and poles indicate that they lived in wattle-and-daub houses; they also suggest that the people got rid of the swarms of mosquitoes that infest the area at night by building smoky fires in their tightly shut homes.

By the beginning of the second millenium BC, the inhabitants of Tutishcainyo and other settlements in the tropical lowlands of eastern Peru and Colombia, and undoubtedly those along the flood plains of the middle and lower Amazon, already possessed many of the characteristics of tropical forest culture as it was known when the first Europeans arrived more than 3,500 years later. They lived in large settlements along slow-moving rivers and oxbow lakes; they fished; and they grew a wide variety of cultivated and semicultivated plants, many of which were originally brought under domestication by peoples living elsewhere in the eastern lowlands of South America. They presumably acquired the cultigens and other commodities, such as stone axes, through extensive trade networks that followed the river systems.

We have a clearer picture of the nature of production and exchange in the Amazon Basin and its environs at the end of the second millenium BC. The village of Tutishcainyo, which had been abandoned for five centuries or more, was reoccupied about 1200 BC. Nearly 5 percent of the pottery used by the later inhabitants of the village was tempered with unrolled crystals of volcanic rock that could not have been acquired locally. In fact, the temper must have been imported from a considerable distance, as other commodities, such as stone axes, were. This suggests that the people of Tutishcainyo produced a surplus of some items, which they used for trade. It also suggests that various groups of villages specialized in the production of particular commodities and that they exchanged some of these products with other groups for goods that they could not produce for themselves. In other words, the extensive trade networks that linked economically specialized communities together also appeared early in the tropical forest.

Exchange Networks and Fiestas

Given the biological and geological diversity of the tropical forests, it is not surprising that complicated exchange networks developed; these often included groups that lived over 1,000 miles apart. Groups living at the ends of the trade networks oriented along the rivers undoubtedly were at a disadvantage in comparison to those living toward the middle of the network. They were less likely to acquire exotic goods produced at the other end of the network than groups living closer to those distant productive centers. One way of alleviating this situation was to incorporate communities producing exotic goods that lived beyond the limits of the old exchange network; as a result, marginal communities were gradually replaced by other groups that lived farther up or down the river.

Evidence dating from the middle of the first millenium BC gives us a clearer picture of some of the activities involved in these exchanges. In Nazaratequi settlements in the Alto Pachitea of eastern Peru, archaeologists have found urns in standard sizes, large beer-making vats, and cylinder roller stamps that in historical times were used to apply paint to the faces and bodies of the peoples using them. Judging from what happened in historical times and what takes place today, *fiestas,* or parties, brought together people from different communities or ethnic groups. Body painting, beer drinking, and the exchange of commodities are only a few of the activities that occur at such ceremonies today. The presence of artifacts that are typical of these activities in archaeological settlements more than 3,000 years old suggests that the fiesta pattern was an important element of the ancient trade networks as well.

Hostility, Raiding, and Migration

By 1500 BC many of the riverine peoples lived in large villages with populations of 1,000 or more. They had chiefs with political authority that extended beyond the limits of the community itself, and they usually maintained hostile relations or fought with their neighbors. These too may be ancient patterns in the Amazon Basin. One effect of hostility between neighboring groups was to confirm the prevailing trade patterns by keeping people inside their own territories and away from the resources controlled by other peoples. For exchange to take place between hostile neighbors, the hostility had to be suspended at regular intervals—probably when an intervillage fiesta was to take place.

When intergroup hostility failed to prevent one group from seizing the resources of another, the losing group often moved into a new territory that was sparsely inhabited or not occupied at all. This migration pattern seems to have been characteristic of the tropical forest area for more than three millenia. It produces major discontinuities in the archaeological record of particular areas. For example, one group with a particular repertory of tools and art styles inhabits an area for a while and leaves its remains. When its members are forced out of the area by another group with distinctive tools and styles, the remains left at archaeological sites are quite different and lack antecedents in that area. This has happened on numerous occasions in the tropical forest area of South America. It suggests that hostility, raiding, and migration are also old features of tropical forest culture.

It is clear that the societies that developed in the tropical forests of eastern South America were not watered-down versions of what happened in the Andes or even reflections of what was taking place in the mountains to the west. Instead, the tropical forest societies developed along somewhat different lines in which much greater emphasis was placed on the exchange of commodities between different ethnic groups and different groups specialized in the production of certain commodities. In other words, exchange was a much more developed idea among the lowland peoples of the Amazon Basin than it was among the peoples of the central Andes.

FURTHER READINGS

Browman, David L.
1974 Pastoral nomadism in the Andes. *Current Anthropology,* 15, no. 2, June, pp. 188–196.
1976 Demographic correlations of the Wari conquest of Junin. *American Antiquity,* 41, no. 4, October, pp. 465–477.

Cordy-Collins, Alana, and Jean Stern
1977 *Pre-Columbian art history; selected readings.* Peek, Palo Alto, Calif.

Harris, David R.
1972 The origins of agriculture in the tropics. *The American Scientist,* 60, no. 2, March–April, pp. 180–193.

Lathrap, Donald W.
1968 The "hunting" economies of the tropical forest zone of South America; an attempt at historical perspective. In *Man the hunter,* ed. Richard B. Lee and Irven Devore, pp. 23–29. Aldine-Atherton, Chicago.
1970 *The upper Amazon.* Prager, New York.
1973 The antiquity and importance of long distance trade relationships in the moist tropics of pre-Columbian South America. *World Archaeology,* 5, no. 2, October, pp. 170–186.

Lathrap, Donald W., Jorge G. Marcos, and James Zeidler
1977 Real Alto; an ancient ceremonial center. *Archaeology,* 30, no. 1, January, pp. 2–13.

Lumbreras, Luis G.
1974 *The peoples and cultures of ancient Peru.* Smithsonian Institution Press, Washington, D.C.

MacNeish, Richard S., Thomas C. Patterson, and David L. Browman
1975 The central Peruvian prehistoric interaction sphere. *Papers of the Robert S. Peabody Foundation for Archaeology,* 7.

Menzel, Dorothy
1964 Style and time in the Middle Horizon. *Ñawpa Pacha* 2, 1964, pp. 1–105.
1968 New data on the Huari empire in Middle Horizon Epoch 2A. *Ñawpa Pacha* 6, 1968, pp. 47–114.

Morris, Craig
1976 Master design of the Incas. *Natural History,* 85, no. 10, December, pp. 58–67.

Moseley, Michael Edward
1975 *The maritime foundations of Andean civilization.* Cummings, Menlo Park, Calif.
1975 Chan Chan; Andean alternative of the preindustrial city. *Science,* 187, no. 4173, January 24, pp. 219–225.

Murra, John V.
1962 Cloth and its functions in the Inca state. *American Anthropologist,* 64, no. 4, August, pp. 710–728.
1969 An Aymara kingdom in 1567. *Ethnohistory,* 15, no. 2, Spring, pp. 125–142.

Patterson, Thomas C.
1971 Central Peru; its economy and population. *Archaeology,* 24, no. 4, October, pp. 316–321.
1971 Chavin; an interpretation of its spread and influence. In *Dumbarton Oaks Conference on Chavin,* ed. Elizabeth K. Benson, pp. 29–48. Dumbarton Oaks Research Library and Collection, Washington, DC.
1973 *America's Past; a New World Archaeology.* Scott, Foresman, Glenview, Ill.
1974 Inca civilization. *Encyclopaedia Britannica,* 15th ed., vol. 1, pp. 847–854. Encyclopaedia Britannica, Chicago.

Rowe, John H.
1967 Form and meaning in Chavin art. In *Peruvian archaeology; selected readings,* ed. John H. Rowe and Dorothy Menzel, pp. 72–103. Peek, Palo Alto, Calif.
1967 What kind of settlement was Inca Cuzco? *Ñawpa Pacha* 5, 1967, pp. 59–76.

Willey, Gordon R.
1971 *An introduction to American archaeology,* vol. 2, *South America.* Prentice-Hall, Englewood Cliffs, N.J.

Epilog

Human history began when people began to make tools, share food with their peers, talk with each other, and leave traces of their activities on or in the ground. All of these distinctly human attributes seem to have developed at about the same time—roughly 2 million years ago—judging from the archaeological evidence left by our early ancestors and the anatomical evidence provided by their skeletons. In the preceding pages we have seen how peoples living at different times and places in the past worked out ways of meeting the necessities of life—ways of producing enough to satisfy the needs of their own generation plus enough to ensure the survival and well-being of future generations.

One of the first things we noticed was that there were vast differences in the ways in which various societies went about solving these problems. We might feel overwhelmed by the diversity of the archaeological record; at the same time, we cannot help admiring the creativity of ancient peoples as they continually devised new ways to solve the problems of daily life and existence. We can appreciate the fact that no two societies seem to have changed in exactly the same way or at the same rate. Each seems to have followed its own developmental trajectory.

Underlying this diversity, however, was a great deal of repetition. When we peel away the cultural peculiarities, or form, of each society and examine its underlying structures and the transformations that occurred in those structures, we begin to see similarities. It is precisely the *repetition* in the history of different human societies that allows us to get at the essence of how ancient societies evolved—to determine what their underlying structures were and work out the processes that governed their development.

By focusing on the relationships into which people entered as they were satisfying their needs, archaeologists are beginning to formulate questions about the development of human society in ways that make them comprehensible to other scholars concerned with human history and society. They are beginning to develop a common language and a theoretical framework that give meaning to the different kinds of evidence we use today to understand what happened yesterday and what is happening now. Like history and other fields concerned with the past, archaeology can begin to tell us something about the present, provided that we pose our questions in ways that make archaeological evidence meaningful, and provided that we take the time to ponder the significance of what we find.

Glossary

Absolute date—A date that is expressed in terms of calendar years or some other unit of calendar time, such as decades, centuries, or millenia.

Acheulian tradition—The earliest standardized stone toolmaking tradition in the Old World. It appeared about 1.5 million years ago, and its assemblages are characterized by a high proportion of bifacially flaked hand axes. Other toolmaking traditions, with less standardized tool assemblages, were contemporary with it in Asia and parts of southern Europe.

Adaptation—Any morphological, physiological, or behavioral characteristic of a group of organisms that allows them to survive and reproduce in the environment where the members of the group live.

Adaptive radiation—The process that occurs when an ancestral group adapts broadly to a new environmental situation and its descendants develop a wide variety of minor adaptations to specific parts of the environment.

Aleutian blade and love tradition—Stone tool assemblages in the American Arctic characterized by tools made on large numbers of blades. These assemblages date between about 7000 and 6000 BC.

Anasazi culture—An archaeological cultural area in the Four Corners area of Arizona, Colorado, Utah, and New Mexico—essentially the Colorado Plateau. After 100 BC, the Anasazi peoples became increasingly dependent on agricultural production by various methods of water management.

Archaeological site—A place where some form of human activity was performed in the past.

Archaic prosimian—The earliest primates, which lived from about 65 to 68 million years ago and still shared a number of anatomical features with insectivores.

Arctic small-tool tradition—Arctic tool assemblages that date from about 4000 to 1000 BC and contain large numbers of pressure-flaked artifacts of small size.

Artifact—Any object that has been manufactured by people.

Assemblage—The array of contemporary objects and associations found at an archaeological site.

Association—The spatial relationships of objects and artifacts with respect to each other and to features of the natural environment.

Aurignacian—Tools made largely on stone blades that were used in France between 30,000 and 24,000 years ago.

Aztec culture—An ethnic group that settled in the Valley of Mexico (Mexico City) about 1200 AD as clients of politically powerful groups. By the middle of the fifteenth century, the Aztecs established themselves as the most powerful political and economic force in Mesoamerica.

Bus Mordeh Phase—The cultural remains of the people who lived on the Deh Luran plain in southwestern Iran between 7500 and 6750 BC. They relied on a combination of wild and domesticated food resources for their subsistence.

Châtelperronian—Tool assemblages composed largely of stone implements that were used in France between 37,000 and 30,000 years ago.

Chavin influence—Toward the end of the second millenium BC, there were several ceremonial centers in north-central Peru. By about 750 BC, one of these, centered at Chavin de Huantar, established hegemony over the others and influenced political and economic developments for the next several centuries in the central Andes.

Chou dynasty—A political dynasty founded in north China that lasted from 1122 to 221 BC.

Chronometric dating method—Any method of absolute dating that measures the rates of natural phenomena, such as the disintegration of radioactive carbon, and translates them into absolute dates.

Comparative method—The eighteenth-century idea that non-European societies represented earlier stages in the development of civilization—particularly European civilization—than the peoples of classical antiquity. By studying various aspects of the behavior of these non-European peoples, scholars sought to reconstruct the early stages in the development of European society.

Conical clan—A group of individuals related by descent from a common ancestor. The relative rank of individuals in the group depends on how closely related each is to the founding ancestor.

Cultural ecology—The study of the relationship between specific features of a society's culture and the adaptation of the group to its environment.

Cultural evolutionism—The theory that the cultures of human societies become more complex as their members make increasingly efficient use of their natural environments.

Culture—The combination of materials, activities, and norms that are characteristic of a particular society; they are learned and transmitted from one generation to the next.

Dendrochronology—A system of dating that is based on the fact that trees add growth rings each year. The age of the tree can be determined by counting the number of concentric rings; it can be used as a calendar, if we know when the tree was cut down.

Diffusion—The spread of objects, ideas, or forms of organization from one society to another through historical contact.

Early Harappan—A widespread pottery style in the Indus Valley between 3200 and 2500 BC found in many of the earliest farming communities known in the area.

Early Hoabinhian—A stone tool assemblage composed of tools used to make other implements found in Thailand and other parts of southeast Asia between 14,000 and 11,000 years ago. At Spirit Cave in Thailand, people who used Early Hoabinhian tools also collected a wide range of plant foods or grew them in gardens near their homes.

Ecology—The study of the relationships between organisms and their environments.

Evolution—For biologists, it means change through time, or descent with modification; the plant and animal species of today are the modified descendants of ones that lived in the past.

Fayum A Settlements—A series of early farming settlements located along the shores of an ancient lake in the Fayum Depression west of the Nile River in Egypt. These settlements were occupied about 4500 BC and provide the earliest evidence of agriculture in Egypt.

Feudal society—A type of society based primarily on agrarian economies in which neither labor nor the products of labor were commodities for sale. The basic production unit of the rural economy was the large landed estate surrounded by peasant-owned plots. The peasants, whether they worked on the estate or the strips of land adjacent to it, submitted to the authority of the manorial lord and were obligated to provide him with various services and goods. The lord owned his land by virtue of his obligation of service to a superior lord; the hierarchy of dependency created by the political system of decentralized authority effectively precluded the formation of extensive bureaucracies.

First Intermediate Period—The period from 2181 to 2040 BC in Egypt, when there was no centralized political or economic authority.

Forces of production—The natural objects used by the members of a society, the tools they use to modify these objects, and the labor power they invest in these activities.

Gene—Hereditary factor found on chromosomes; genes exist in pairs in which one gene is contributed by each parent.

Gene pool—The total of the genetic make-up of a population; it involves counting and tabulating all of the different varieties of genes found in a population.

Gerzean Phase—A culture characteristic of early farming settlements along the Nile River that date from 3500 to 3200 BC, which was a period of increased contact between the peoples of Egypt and Mesopotamia.

Hakataya culture—An archaeological cultural area straddling the Colorado River, which separates Arizona and California. Between 100 BC and AD 1500, the inhabitants of the Colorado River valley practiced flood plain agriculture, made pottery that resembled wares found elsewhere in the American southwest; and traded with peoples on the Pacific coast for seashells to make jewelry.

Halaf Phase—A culture that is widespread in northern Mesopotamia and beyond that dates between 5300 and 4400 BC. The people who lived in Halafian settlements farmed, produced luxury goods, and may have controlled overland trade between the Mesopotamian plain and eastern Anatolia, where rich mineral deposits were found.

Hassuna Phase—A culture defined on the basis of more than forty settlements in northern Mesopotamia that date between 5500 and 5000 BC and contain Hassuna pottery and other tools.

Historical materialism—A social theory based on the ideas that the development of society is a product of human activity and that different forms of society—such as feudalism or capitalism—operate according to different sets of laws, which are independent of the consciousness and activity of people.

Hohokam culture—An archaeological culture centered in the deserts of southcentral Arizona that emerged about 100 BC. It was characterized by intensive irrigation farming in the desert and perishable wattle-and-daub houses or massive adobe structures.

Hominid—A biological family composed of fossil and modern human beings.

Hominoid—A biological superfamily consisting of fossil and modern great apes and human beings.

Hopewell burial cult—High-status individuals in different parts of the eastern woodlands were buried with similar luxury goods that circulated throughout the Hopewell interaction sphere.

Hopewell interaction sphere—A widespread exchange network centered in the eastern woodlands of the United States about 2,000 years ago that extended from Yellowstone and the Rockies in the west to the Carolina piedmont in the east and the Gulf Coast in the south. High-value goods moved over this exchange network.

Huari Empire—The first pan-Andean conquest state. It emerged about AD 600 and incorporated much of central and northern Peru into a short-lived polity.

Hyksos invasion—Groups of nomadic peoples from the Sinai and beyond who moved into the delta country of northern Egypt and established a kingdom that dominated the political affairs of the area from 1640 to 1570 BC.

Import replacement—A process in which goods that were originally imported eventually are manufactured in the local economy.

Inca culture—An ethnic group whose homeland was centered at Cuzco in the south highlands of Peru during the fourteenth century. Incas began to conquer their neighbors during the fifteenth century and quickly established a state that extended from the northern borders of Ecuador to central Chile and northwestern Argentina.

Kiva—Semisubterranean, circular structures found in the American southwest that were used for ritual purposes.

Lapita pottery—Pottery that was manufactured in the Bismarck Archipelago, the Solomon Islands, Fiji, Tonga, and Samoa during the first millenium BC.

Levallois technique—A method for making stone tools that involves removing flakes from a cobble in such a way that the shape of the final flake to be removed is predetermined.

Linear A script—Between the eighteenth and fifteenth centuries BC, the peoples of Crete used a handwritten language for keeping accounts and probably dedicatory inscriptions. It is not clear what language the script was written in. Similarities between it and the later Linear B script allow archaeologists and philologists to decipher some of the messages contained on tablets found at the Palace of Knossos.

Linear B script—During the fifteenth century, the Greek-speaking Mycenaean scribes borrowed or adapted the Linear A script to represent the Greek language. These scribes recorded economic transactions, which provide a great deal of information about the structure of Mycenaean society.

Linear pottery culture—Early farming settlements located on the wind-blown soils of northern Europe during the fifth millenium BC. They are named after the kinds of pottery found in these settlements.

Lungshan settlements—More than 100 early farming communities on the plains of north China that were occupied between 2500 and 1850 BC. There are indications of differences in social rank among the inhabitants of these settlements. High defense walls around many of the settlements indicate that organized raiding or warfare was taking place between different villages or groups of settlements.

Magdalenian—The technology of the Magdalenian peoples of western Europe included a wide variety of small tools made on stone blades removed from specially prepared cores, as well as a number of implements made from bone and antler. These assemblages date between 17,000 and 12,000 years ago.

Mammal—A large group of animals, including humans, that have body hair and constant body temperature, give birth to live infants, and suckle the young. Mammals have adapted to constant expenditures of energy over prolonged periods of time.

Maritime archaic tradition—A life style that developed in Labrador, Newfoundland, and the coastal areas of eastern Canada during the second millenium BC. The inland hunters who originated this tradition exploited seals, walrus, and other marine resources during the summer months.

Maya culture—An archaeological culture area located in the southern part of Mexico, Guatemala, Belize, and western Honduras. The ancient Maya lived in both the mountains and the lowlands to the east. Their remains have been found at a number of sites and indicate that their society was highly stratified by the middle of the first millenium AD.

Mesoamerica—An archaeological cultural area that extends from north-central Mexico to a line running from northwestern Costa Rica through central Honduras.

Mesopotamian civilization—The stratified, urban societies based on agricultural production that emerged in Mesopotamia during the fourth millenium BC.

Middle Kingdom—The period of political unification in Egypt from 2040 to 1640 BC.

Minoan culture—Assemblages found on the island of Crete that date from the later half of the second millenium BC. At that time the island was divided into three distinct polities, the most imposing and best-known of which was centered at Knossos, where scribes recorded what were presumably economic transactions in the still-undeciphered Linear A script.

Modes of production—The underlying structure abstracted from social reality that expresses the relationship between the forces of production and the relations of production. Each mode of production has its own laws that govern its functioning and development.

Mogollon culture—An archaeological cultural area centered in southern New Mexico and southeastern Arizona that emerged about 300 BC. The Mogollon peoples relied on agriculture to a lesser degree than did their neighbors to the north and west.

Mohammad Jaffar Phase—The cultural remains of the people who lived on the Deh Luran plain in southwestern Iran between 6000 and 5600 BC. These peoples farmed and raised herds of sheep and goats.

Mousterian—Stone tool kits used between about 120,000 and 40,000 years ago in western Europe and other parts of Eurasia and in Africa north of the Sahara. These kits are characterized by multipurpose tools made on flakes struck from carefully prepared stone cores.

Mycenaean culture—A group of politically independent city-states found on the Greek mainland that replaced Minoan culture on the island of Crete during the later part of the second millenium BC. The economic and political organization of these polities, judging from the transactions and information recorded on Linear B tablets found at their centers, resembled those of the temple and palace corporations of the ancient Mesopotamian city-states.

Natufian Phase—A series of assemblages found at various sites in the Levant from southern Turkey to southern Israel that date between 10,000 and 8000 BC. The peoples of the area hunted and fished at first; later they herded and farmed the territory around their permanently occupied settlements.

Natural selection—The evolutionary force that limits the range of genetic variation by permitting advantageous genes or gene combinations to accumulate in a population, at the expense of those that are less favorable. By doing so, natural selection modifies the gene pool of a population.

Neolithic revolution—A major shift in the development of human society that involved increased reliance on domesticated plant and animal resources and established new patterns of work to coordinate a series of tasks (such as plowing, planting, weeding, and harvesting) that had to be carried out sequentially over an extended period of time. It was a gradual process that occurred slowly and unevenly. The new social relations of production that arose out of the process permitted high population densities, the formation of permanent settlements, and the development of stratified societies with marked class distinctions.

New Kingdom—The third period of political unification in Egypt, which lasted from 1570 to 1180 BC. During this period the king and his court dominated the political system, and the power of the nobility was dramatically reduced.

Northwest microblade tradition—A series of closely related stone tool assemblages found in Alaska, the Yukon, and the Northwest Territories that date between about 6500 and 4000 BC. The peoples who used these tools lived in evergreen forests, where they fished and hunted elk, caribou, and other mammals.

Object—Any item in an archaeological site that has been moved, modified, or manufactured by people.

Oceania—A vast cultural area that includes Australia, New Guinea, and the islands of the Pacific Basin. Anthropologists divide the latter into three areas—Melanesia, Micronesia, and Polynesia—each of which has its own ecological and social characteristics.

Old Kingdom—The first period of political unification in Egypt, which lasted from about 3200 BC, when the country was unified politically for the first time, to about 2181 BC.

Olmec culture—An archaeological culture that emerged toward the end of the second millenium BC on the Gulf Coast of Mexico at San Lorenzo, Tres Zapotes, and La Venta. The Olmecs built large platform mounds and exported ritual knowledge to peoples living elsewhere in Mesoamerica.

Population—A number of individuals who live in the same place at the same time and who can mate successfully with each other.

Positivism—A philosophical position that assumes that social or historical facts are analogous to the facts studied by physical scientists and that these facts are linked to each other by sets of constant and unchanging relationships that reflect universal laws. In other words, what is true about the behavior of one person is also true about the behavior of all other people, regardless of when or where they lived.

Potassium-argon dating—A chronometric dating technique based on the disintegration of radioactive potassium into argon gas. It is used to date materials that range in age from about 500,000 to 4 billion years.

Primate—An order of mammals composed of fossil and modern prosimians, monkeys, apes, and human beings. The members of this order are distinguished from other mammals by having relatively large brains, small snouts, flattened faces, stereoscopic color vision, nails instead of claws, and paired nipples located high on the chest.

Punch-blade technique—A method for making stone tools that involves splitting a cobble in half and removing long, parallel-sided flakes, or blades, by placing a bone or antler punch on the edge of the exposed split surface of the cobble and then striking it with a hammer.

Radiocarbon dating—A chronometric dating technique based on the disintegration of a radioactive isotope of carbon. It is used to date organic remains associated with archaeological assemblages that have ages up to about 60,000 years.

Relations of production—The social relations that people enter into as they satisfy their basic needs through work. They include the patterns of specialization and cooperation involved in the process of production, the exchange of labor resulting from the division of labor, and the ways in which goods circulate through the society. The relations of production also express different forms of property relations, depending on whether the means of production (materials and the tools used to modify these natural materials) are owned by all the members of the society, by some group within the society, or by individuals.

Relative date—A date that is expressed in terms of whether something is older, younger, or the same age as something else. It does not specify how much older or younger two objects or assemblages are.

Samarra Phase—A series of settlements located upstream from Baghdad along the flood plain of the Tigris River near Mandali. They were inhabited between 5500 and 5000 BC by farmers who apparently utilized small-scale irrigation systems.

Second Intermediate Period—A period of political instability in Egypt that lasted from 1640 to 1570 BC. Local Egyptian rulers maintained some independence during this period by paying tribute to Hyksos overlords.

Seriation—A technique used by archaeologists to arrange objects or assemblages in a sequence. It is based on the assumption that objects or assemblages that are most similar to each other are closer together in time than those that are less similar. In other words, change is gradual.

Shang dynasty—The first dynasty in north China, which lasted from 1766 to 1122 BC, in which the leader was viewed as almost sacred. He and the other members of the royal family constituted the top of a social pyramid and were separated by a vast gulf from the peasants and artisans, who provided the economic base of Shang society.

Slash-and-burn agriculture—An agricultural system in which land is cultivated for a shorter period of time than it is fallowed.

Soil horizon—Soils are divided into three horizons, which reflect different kinds of chemical and physical processes that have resulted from changing climatic conditions. In the top, or *A horizon,* there is the gross breakdown of organic matter. Minerals and other chemical materials produced from such processes are washed into the *B horizon,* producing various chemical and morphological changes in the soils. The effects of weathering are not so advanced in the lowest, or *C horizon.* When two or more buried soil horizons, or palaeosols, are found intact, the exact climatic conditions of the period of time when they were formed or deposited can be reconstructed.

Solutrean—A number of stone tool assemblages in France that date between 20,000 and 17,000 years ago.

Species—A more inclusive biological unit than population. It consists of a number of similar but geographically isolated populations whose members are capable of mating and producing viable offspring. The populations of one species are reproductively isolated from those of another.

Stratigraphy—The study of relations between deposition units. The first principle of stratigraphy states that the assemblages found at the bottom of an undisturbed deposit are older than the ones on top of it (the law of superposition). The second principle states that different assemblages can be distinguished from one another by differences in the kinds of objects and associations they contain (the law of strata identified by their contents).

Temple corporation—A political, religious, and economic institution in the Mesopotamian city-states that controlled agricultural and commodity production, administered long-distance trade, rented agricultural fields, collected tribute in exchange for the performance of important rituals, provided rations to work forces composed of men, women, and children, and recorded the day-to-day economic transactions that occurred in the polity.

Three Ages—The idea of a succession of three technological stages: first an age in which stone tools were used, followed by ones in which bronze and then iron tools were used. This system was first used in 1816 to organize archaeological collections by the Danish antiquarian Christian Jurgensen Thomsen.

Toltec culture—A group of people who moved into central Mexico during the tenth century AD, established a capital at Tula, and achieved political dominance over the area until the twelfth century.

'Ubaid Phase—The earliest farming cultures of southern Mesopotamia, which date between 4800 and about 3500 BC.

Uniformitarianism—The principle that the geological processes operating today are identical to those which operated in the past and that they operate at the same rate.

Upper Perigordian—A series of stone tool assemblages from France that date between 24,000 and 20,000 years ago.

Yangshao settlements—The earliest farming settlements in northern China, which date from the fifth to the third millenium BC.

Index

Abaj Takalik (Guatemala), 288–89
Abbeville (France), 23, 27
Absolute dates, 11–15
Abydos (Egypt), 201
Acheulean assemblages, 72–73
Acheulean tradition, 72–73, 85
Adamgarh (India), 170–71
Adams, Robert, 34
Adaptation, 46
Adaptive radiation, 47
Adrar Bous area (Niger), 206–7
Adriatic Sea (Italy, Yugoslavia), 218–19
Aegean Sea (Greece, Turkey), 215–17, 223, 226–30
Afar Valley (Ethiopia), 81
Afghanistan, 126, 159, 200
Agriculture, 33, 112–13, 119–24, 128, 136–37,
    140–42, 151–52, 155, 161, 165, 167, 170–71,
    175, 176, 182–83, 185, 188, 190–91, 197–99,
    203–5, 207–9, 215–22, 240, 262, 268–69, 271,
    277–78, 288, 298–302, 314
Agrissa (Greece), 216
Ain Gev (Israel), 114
Ain Mallaha (Israel), 129–30
Akhenaten, 205
Akkad (Iraq), 153
Alabama (U.S.), 251, 260, 262
Alaska (U.S.), 244–48, 255–58
Aleutian Blade and Core Tradition, 257
Alice Boer site (Brazil), 247
Ali Kosh (Iran), 125–27, 138, 161
Alliances, 155–56, 244, 290, 292
Alps (France, Switzerland, Italy), 213
Altin Depe (USSR), 168, 170, 176
Amarna (Egypt), 205
Amazon River Basin (Brazil), 313–16
Amenhotep III, 205
American Bottoms region, 265–67
Amphipithecus, 48
Amri (Pakistan), 172
Amu Darya River Valley (USSR), 165, 170
Anangula Island (Alaska), 257
Anasazi culture, 269–71
Anatolian Plateau (Turkey), 132–37, 170, 216, 226
Ancestors, 137–38, 155–56, 184, 279
Ancón (Peru), 5
Andes Mountains, 296–313
Angkor Thom (Cambodia), 193
Angkor Wat (Cambodia), 192–93
Angola, 195, 209
Anthropology, 27, 35, 53, 67
Antiquarians, 21, 26–27
Anyang (China), 184–86
Apes, 42, 49–53, 68
Apidium, 49
Arabian Peninsula, 147
Arabian Sea, 175

Arabs, 192
Aral Sea (USSR), 165
Archaeology:
associations as evidence, 4, 9–10
and cultures, 10–11
and dating, 11–19
defined, 4, 6
objects as evidence, 4, 6, 8–9
research and theories, 21–36
Archaic prosimians, 47–49
Arctic Small-tool Tradition, 257
Arcy-sur-Cure (France), 104–5
Argentina, 296–98, 312
Arizona, 267–69, 271
Arkansas River Valley, 249
Arpachiyah (Iraq), 145–46
Arran Island (Scotland), 224–25
Art, 108 , 110, 115, 157, 163, 185, 199, 205, 223, 279
Artifacts, 6, 27
Asia Minor. See Turkey
Assemblages, 10–15, 68, 72, 90, 101, 104
Associations, as evidence, 4, 9–10, 27
Assyria, 21, 26
Astronomy, 22
Atlas Mountains (Morocco), 207
Aurgnacian assemblages, 101–2
Australia, 99, 237–40
Australopithecines, 53–60, 70
Australopithecus afarensis, 56–58, 70
Australopithecus africanus, 57–58
Australopithecus boisei, 58–59
Australopithecus robustus, 58–59
Avebury (England), 225
Axes, 72–74, 220, 223, 239–40, 315
Ayacucho-Huanta region (Peru), 299–300, 307, 309, 313
Aztec culture, 291–93

Babylonia, 22
Badari (Egypt), 199
Bahrein, 147
Baikal, Lake (USSR), 165
Balkans, 217–18, 222–23
Baluchistan region (Iran, Pakistan), 160, 172, 175
Ban Chaing (Thailand), 191
Bands, 34
Barrows, long, 225
Beehive-shaped tombs, 228
Behaviorism, 29, 35
Beidha (Jordan), 129, 131
Belize, 274, 283, 287–88
Bering Strait and Sea, 237, 244, 257–58
Bible, 22–23
Biology, 41–47
Bismarck Archipelago, 240–42
Blackwater Draw site, 267–68
Boaz, Franz, 35
Bolivia, 297, 307
Borneo, 64
Bows and arrows, 106–7

Brazil, 247, 251, 296, 313
British Honduras. *See* Belize
Britons, 26
Brittany (France), 223
Brixham Cave (England), 23, 27
Broca's area (of the brain), 82
Bronze Age, 27
Buffer zone settlements, 290–91
Bug River Valley (Poland), 218
Bulgaria, 217–18, 222–23
Bureaucracies, 142, 157, 185, 200–201, 205, 297, 307, 309
Burial rites and sites, 3, 6, 92–93, 105, 110, 116, 129–30, 137–38, 152, 168, 183–86, 200–202, 210, 217, 223–26, 228, 230, 238, 243, 259, 262–66, 300–301
Burma, 48, 192
Bus Mordeh Phase, 125
Bylany (Czechoslovakia), 220–22

Cahokia site (U.S.), 265–67
Calakmul (Mexico), 290
Calendrical systems, 13, 22, 288
Callejón de Huaylas (Peru), 306
Cambodia, 191–93
Cameroon, 197, 209
Canada, 244–53, 255–71
Cannibalism, 79, 81
Carpathian Mountains, 213, 222–23
Casa Grande site (U.S.), 268
Caspian Sea, 159, 161, 165
Catal Hüyük (Turkey), 132–36, 138, 155
Cave paintings and carvings, 108, 115, 240
Caves, 79–81, 86–93, 102–5, 108, 110, 159, 165, 249
Cayönü (Turkey), 131
Celts, 14
Cemeteries. *See* Burial rites and sites
Chaco Canyon (U.S.), 271
Chad, 206
Chakmakli Tepe (USSR), 167
Chalcatzingo (Mexico), 281
Chaluka (U.S.), 257
Chanchan (Peru), 310–11
Channel Islands, 90
Chanu-daro (Pakistan), 175
Châtelperronian assemblages, 101–2
Chavin de Huantar (Peru), 304–7
Cheops, Great Pyramid of, 201–2
Chert, 69–70, 262
Chiapas region (Mexico), 288
Chichén Itzá (Mexico), 292
Chicimeca, 291–92
Chiefdoms, 34, 193, 243–44
Childe, V. Gordon, 27, 33–35
Chile, 296–98, 307, 312
Chimor kingdom, 310–11
China, 13, 22, 60, 79–80, 119–20, 180–93
Chinampas, 293
Choga Mami (Iraq), 144–45

Cholula (Mexico), 292
Chotnitsa (Bulgaria), 223
Chou dynasty, 187–89, 192
Choukoutien cave (China), 79–81, 180
Christian calendar, 11, 13, 15
Christianity, 22–23, 26
Chronometric dating methods, 13
Chuquitanta (Peru), 302–3
Cobbles, 68, 72–74, 248
Colombia, 296, 314
Colorado, 249–51, 267, 271
Commerce. See Trade
Community self-sufficiency, 298–300
Comparative method, 24
Comte, Auguste, 24
Congo River, 195, 208–9
Conical clans, 156–57, 225
Copán (Honduras), 290
Copernicus, Nicolaus, 22
Costa Rica, 274, 292
Crete, 215–17, 227–30
Cris (Rumania), 217–18
Cuello (Belize), 288
Cultural ecology, 32–33
Cultural evolutionism, 33–35
Culture history, 35–36
Cultures, 10–11, 27–28
Cuzco (Peru), 311–12
Cyprus, 229
Czechoslovakia, 107–10, 115, 213, 220–22

Danube River, 215, 218
Dar Tichitt area (Mauretania), 206–9
Darwin, Charles, 44
Dating, 11–19, 22–23
Debert site (Canada), 260
Debt slaves, 156–57
Deh Luran Plain (Iran), 127–28
Demotic script, 9
Dendrochronology, 13–14
Denmark, 26–27, 106, 224–25
Differential survival, 45–46
Diomedes Islands, 244
Djetis Beds, 60
Dneister River Valley, 93–94, 218–19
Dolni Vestonice (Czechoslovakia), 108–10
Domestication of plants and animals, 119–24, 136–37,
    170–71, 191–92, 197, 209, 215, 300
Dordogne River Valley (France), 86, 104, 107
Dorset (England), 225
Dryopithecines, 50–51, 53
Dryopithecus africanus, 51
Dzejtun (USSR), 165–67

Early Harappan Phase, 172
Early Hoabinhian peoples, 190
East African rift, 208–10
Easter Island, 243
Ecology, 43, 261–62

Ecuador, 298, 300–301, 312
Egypt, 3, 9, 21–22, 28, 49, 195–206, 228–29
Egyptian hieroglyphics, 9, 197
Elam (Iran), 161–62
Elburz Mountains (Iran), 159
Engels, Friedrich, 24
Engigstciak (Canada), 246
England, 4, 21, 23–24, 26–27, 214, 220, 222–23, 225
Environmental conditions, 28, 45–47, 253
Environmental determinism, 33
Eocene epoch, 47–49
Erh-li Kang (China), 185
Eridu (Iraq), 146–47
Eskimos, 257–60
Ethiopia, 56, 58, 70, 81, 195
Etruscan culture, 231–32
Euphrates River Valley (Iraq, Syria), 130, 140, 142,
    145–47, 159
Evidence, archaeological, 4, 6, 8–10, 24, 26
Evolution, 43–65
Exchange. See Trade
Extinction, 251–53

Farming. See Agriculture
Fars region (Iran), 160
Faunal dissimilarity, law of, 12
Fayum A settlements (Egypt), 198–99
Feyum Depression (Egypt), 45, 198–99, 204
Feudalism, 189, 204
Fiestas, 315–16
Fiji, 241
Fine Orange pottery, 291
Fishing, 216, 218, 221, 257–58, 260, 300, 302, 313
Flannery, Kent, 34
Food supply and production. See Agriculture; Hunting
    and gathering
Fossil record, 23, 27, 47, 52–53, 85
Fox, Cyril, 28
France, 21, 23–24, 26–27, 60, 73–77, 86–93, 96–97,
    101–8, 114–15, 213, 219, 223
Franchthi Cave (Greece), 216
Franks, 26
French Guiana, 296, 313
Fuel, 90

Galilei, Galileo, 22
Gauls, 26
Genealogies, 243–44
Gene pools, 45–46
Genes, 44–46
Genetic variability, 46
Geoksyur (USSR), 167–69
Geology, 22–23, 26–27
Germany, 21, 24, 26, 88–89, 106, 214, 223, 291
Gerzean Phase, 199–200
Gigantopithecus, 50
Giza, pyramids at, 201–3
Gla (Greece), 229
Glaciers, 214–15, 246–47, 256

329

Gobi Desert, 180
Grand Canyon, 269
Great Basin (U.S.), 32, 251
Great Britain. *See* England; Scotland
Great Plains (U.S.), 249, 252
Greece, 9, 21, 23–24, 26, 207, 215–17, 222, 226–32
Greenland, 255, 257
Grids, use of, 7
Guatemala, 13, 274, 278, 280, 283, 287–92
Guilds, 150
Guyana, 296, 313

Hadar area (Ethiopia), 56, 70
Hagen, Mount (New Guinea), 240
Hakataya culture, 268–69
Halaf Phase, 145
Harappa (Pakistan), 174–76
Hassuna Phase, 143
Hawaiian Islands, 237, 242–44
Heracleopolis (Egypt), 204
Herculaneum, 10, 13
Herding, 112–13, 121–24, 128, 140, 151, 161, 165,
    167, 191, 197, 205, 207, 209, 215, 217–22
Herodotus, 202
Hierakonpolis (Egypt), 200
Hieroglyphics, Egyptian, 9, 197
Hindu Kush Mountains (Pakistan), 159–60, 163, 165
Historical materialism, 24, 28–32
History, 4, 27, 35
Hoabinhian peoples, 190
Hohokam culture, 268–69
Holmul (Guatemala), 289
Homeostatic mechanisms, 33
Hominids, 53–65, 68–69, 74, 82
Hominoids, 49–53
Homo erectus, 54–55, 60–63, 74
Homo habilis, 54–55, 59–61, 68–69, 82
Homo sapiens, 62–65, 67, 85
Hondo River Valley (Guatemala), 288
Honduras, 274, 288, 290
Hopei Plain (China), 182
Hopewell burial cult, 264
Hopewell sites (U.S.), 263–65
Hopewellian interaction sphere, 264
"Horsehoof" core technique, 239
Horus, 200
Huai River Valley (China), 183
Huari Empire, 307–9
Humanism, 21–23
Hungary, 73, 217–18, 223
Hunting and gathering, 33, 61, 68, 81, 89–90, 96,
    105–7, 114–15, 129–31, 167, 177, 190, 206,
    209, 215, 217–21, 245–46, 249–53, 257–60,
    265, 267, 276–77, 307, 313
Hutton, James, 23
Hyksos, 204–5
Hylobatids, 50

Ialysos (Rhodes), 229
Igbo-Ukwe (Nigeria), 208
Illinois, 260, 262–63
Illinois River Valley, 4, 260, 263, 265
Import replacement, 286–87
Inca culture, 297–98, 309–13
India, 160, 170–71, 192
Indian Knoll sites (U.S.), 262
Indians:
    Mesoamerican, 7–8, 13, 119, 274–93
    North American, 4, 14, 22, 25, 32, 244–53, 255–71
    South American, 5, 13, 22, 246–53, 296–316
Indochina, 180, 190–93
Indonesia, 60, 62, 64, 99, 180, 192–93
Indus River Valley (Pakistan), 120, 159–60, 163,
    170–76
Ingombe Ilebe (Zambia), 210
Iran, 21–22, 27, 120, 124–28, 136, 140, 147, 159,
    161–65, 167
Iranian Plateau, 124, 159, 161, 163, 165, 167, 171–72
Iraq, 92–93, 97, 140–57
Iron Age, 27, 209
Israel, 111–14, 129–31
Italy, 21, 92–93, 213, 219, 223
Ivory Coast, 197

Jalilpur (Pakistan), 172
Japan, 180, 191
Java, 60, 180, 192
Jericho, 130–31
Jewelry, 108, 116, 122, 130, 138, 145, 168, 170, 176,
    199, 210, 222–23, 262, 278, 288
Jordan, 112, 114, 129–31
Jordan River Valley, 112–14, 129
Jos Plateau (Nigeria), 208
Juvenile peer groups, 86, 88

Kaminaljuyu (Guatemala), 283, 290
Kara Depe (Soviet Union), 168
Karanovo (Bulgaria), 217
Kayaks, 257–58
Kelteminar peoples, 165
Kentucky, 251, 260, 265
Kenya, 53, 60, 68–69, 78–79, 82
Kermanshah region (Iran), 127
Khmer kingdom (Cambodia), 192–93
Khuzistan Plain (Iran), 125, 128, 147, 160
Khyber Pass (Afghanistan, Pakistan), 159
Kidder, Alfred, 35
Kile Gul Muhammad (Pakistan), 171
Kiowa Cave (New Guinea), 240
Kivas, 271
Kleidi (Greece), 228
Knives, 73–74, 90–91, 199, 210, 223
Knossos (Crete), 216–17, 227–30
Kom Ombo Plain (Egypt), 196, 198

Konya Plain (Turkey), 132
Koobi Fora (Kenya), 68–69
Koonalda Cave (Australia), 240
Körös (Hungary), 217–18
Kosipe (New Guinea), 238–40
Koster site (U.S.), 260–61
Kot Diji (Pakistan), 172
Kremikovci (Yugoslavia), 217–18
Krusenstern, Cape (Alaska), 258

Labor, division of, 96, 107–8, 115, 138, 155–56, 168, 243, 287, 303
Labrador, 257–60
La Chapelle-aux-Saints (France), 97
La Colombière (France), 107
Laetotil (Tanzania), 56
La Ferrassie (France), 93
Lagash (Iraq), 152–54
La Magdeleine (France), 102, 104
Land ownership, 152, 157, 188–89, 215, 230, 232, 299
Language, 54, 60, 68, 81–82
Laos, 192
Lapis lazuli, 163, 165, 176, 199–200
Lapita pottery, 241–42
Laugerie Haute (France), 102
La Venta (Mexico), 278–79, 281
Le Moustier (France), 93
Les Eyzies (France), 86
Levallois technique, 73, 86, 90–91
Levant, 111–14, 121, 128–32, 136–37, 205, 228–30
Libya, 197
Limpopo River Valley (South Africa), 210
Linear A and B tablets, 228, 230
Linear pottery cultures, 219–21
Long barrows, 225
Los Muertos site (U.S.), 268–69
Lothagam (Kenya), 53
Lothal (Pakistan), 175–76
Louisiana, 261–62
Loyang (China), 188
Lugal, 153–54
Lungshan settlements (China), 183–85
Luristan region (Iran), 127, 161

Magdalenian assemblages, 101–2, 104–5, 107
Mali, 208
Mallia (Crete), 228
Malta, 224
Mammals, 41
Mandali Plain (Iraq), 144, 147
Maori peoples, 242, 244
Mapungubwe (South Africa), 210
Maritime Archaic Tradition, 258–60
Maritsa River Valley (Bulgaria), 222
Marquesas Islands, 237, 242

Marx, Karl, 24
Materialism, historical, 24, 28–32
Mathematics, 22
Mauritania, 197, 206–7
Maya Long Count, 13, 288
Mayans, 13, 287–91
Meadowcroft Cave (U.S.), 246, 260
Megaliths, 223–24
Mekong River Delta (Vietnam), 191–93
Memphis (Egypt), 9, 201–2, 204
Mendel, Gregor, 44
Merimde (Egypt), 199
Mesa Verde sites (U.S.), 271
Meshed (Iran), 159
Mesoamerica, 274–93
Mesopotamia, 13, 21–22, 26, 28, 119–24, 130, 140–57, 159–63, 170, 175–77, 200
Messenia (Greece), 228
Metal working, 222–23, 230–32
Mexico, 6, 13, 246, 267–68, 274, 276–88, 290–93
Mexico, Valley of, 281–87, 291–93
Migrations, 67, 74, 99, 242, 291–92, 315–16
Mill, John Stuart, 24
Mining, 162–63, 170, 199, 222–23, 230
Minoan civilization, 227–30
Miocene epoch, 49–53
Mississippi River Valley, 255, 261–62, 265, 267
Modes of production, 31
Mogollon Rim site (U.S.), 268–69
Mohammad Jaffar Phase, 126
Mohenjo-daro (Pakistan), 170, 172–76
Molodova (Soviet Union), 93–94, 96
Mongolia, 180
Monkeys, 42, 48–53, 68
Monte Alban (Mexico), 282–83
Monte Circeo (Italy), 92–93
Morelos region (Mexico), 281
Morocco, 207
Mosna Valley (Peru), 306–7
Mounds, burial, 259, 263–64, 266
Mousterian assemblages, 90
Mousterian tools, 90–91, 165
Mozambique, 210
Muaco (Venezuela), 246
Mungo, Lake (Australia), 238–40
Mureybet (Syria), 130
Mutations, 45
Mycenea (Greece), 215, 228–31

Nahal Oren (Israel), 112–13
Namazga Depe (USSR), 168, 170
Naqada (Egypt), 200
Narmer, 197, 200
Natufian Phase, 130
Natural selection, 45–46
Navigation, 242
Nazaratequi settlements (Peru), 315

Neanderthals, 62–64, 85–97
Nea Nikomedeia (Greece), 216–57
Necrolemur antiqus, 49
Negative feedback mechanisms, 33
Nelson Bay Cave (South Africa), 110–11, 196
Neolithic (New Stone Age), 27
Neolithic revolution, 119
Newfoundland, 257–60
New Guinea, 99, 237, 239–41
New Mexico, 267–68, 270–71
New Stone Age (Neolithic), 27
Newton, Isaac, 22
New Zealand, 242, 244
Niah Cave (Borneo), 64
Nicaragua, 274
Nicoya Polychrome pottery, 292
Niger, 206–8
Nigeria, 195, 208–9
Niger River, 195, 208
Nile River Valley (Egypt, Sudan), 3, 120, 195, 197–201, 205
Nippur (Iraq), 147
Nobility, 142, 153–54, 157, 184–85, 188–89, 201, 210, 243–44, 292
Nomes, 201
Non Nok Tha (Thailand), 191
North America, 255–71
Northwest Microblade Tradition, 257
Northwest Territories (Canada), 246
Nubia (Sudan), 197, 204–5

Oaxaca region (Mexico), 276, 278–83, 286
Objects, as evidence, 4, 6, 8–9, 27
Obsidian, 263–64, 278, 280, 283, 285–86
Oc-eò (Vietnam), 192
Oenpilli region (Australia), 240
Old Crow Basin (Canada), 245–46
Oldowan assemblages, 69, 72–73
Old Stone Age (Paleolithic), 27
Olduvai, Gorge (Tanzania), 60, 69–72, 76, 79, 81
Oligocene epoch, 50–51
Olmec culture, 279–82
Olorgesailie (Kenya), 78–79
Olsen-Chubbuck site (U.S.), 249–51
Omo Basin (Ethiopia), 58
Onion Portage (Alaska), 257
Orinoco River Basin (Guianas), 313
Orkney Islands (Scotland), 224–25

Pacaicasa tools, 249
Pacific Ocean cultures, 237–44
Pakistan, 120, 159–60, 170–76
Palenque (Mexico), 290
Paleoanthropology, 53
Paleobiology, 41
Paleolithic (Old Stone Age), 27
Palestine, 111–14
Panama, 274

Pan-p'o-t'sun (China), 182–83
Papua New Guinea, 99, 237, 239–41
Papyrus, 203–4
Paraguay, 296, 313
Parapithecus, 49
Patagonia region (Argentina), 296–97, 313
Peasantry, 189, 201, 205
Pennsylvania, 246, 260
Perigord region (France), 86–93, 96–97, 101–8, 115
Peristeria (Greece), 228
Persia (ancient). *See* Iran
Persian Gulf, 146–47, 178
Peru, 5, 28, 246–47, 249, 251–52, 297, 300–315
Petén area (Guatemala), 289–91
Phaistos (Crete), 228
Phoenix (U.S.), 268–69
Physics, 22
Pikimachay Cave (Peru), 246–47, 249
Pincevent (France), 105
Pleistocene epoch, 64, 67–83, 85–97, 99–116, 122, 206, 251–53, 257, 276
Plesiadapidae, 48
Pliocene epoch, 53–56
Plumbate pottery, 291
Poland, 213, 218–19
Polynesia, 237, 242–44
Pomares, 243
Pompeii (Italy), 10, 13
Pondaung Hills (Burma), 48
Pondaungia, 48
Populations, 44–47, 122, 253
Port aux Choix (Canada), 258
Poseidon, 230
Positivism, 24, 28–32
Potassium-argon dating, 18
Pottery, 143–44, 146–48, 162–63, 172, 185, 191, 199, 203, 208, 210, 219–20, 228–29, 241–42, 279, 291–92, 303, 314
Poverty Point site (U.S.), 261–62
Pownall, Thomas, 26
Predator-prey relationship, 251–53
Predmost (Czechoslovakia), 107, 109
Prepared-core technique, 73
Primates, 41–43, 47–53, 67
Production, relations and modes of, 30–31
Production units, 128, 155–56
Progress, 100
Prosimians, 42, 47–50
Ptolemy Epiphanes, 9
Puebla region (Mexico), 276
Pueblo Bonito site (U.S.), 270–71
Punas, 249, 252–53, 298, 304
Punch blade technique, 101–2
Punjab region (India), 160
Pylos (Greece), 228–31
Pyramids, 147, 201–2, 243, 306

Quarries, 69–70, 202, 278, 280, 286, 302
Quetta (Pakistan), 171

Radiocarbon dating, 14–18
Ramapithecines, 50–53
Ramapithecus wickeri, 52
Rancho Peludo (Venezuela), 313–14
Ras al 'Amiya (Iraq), 147
Rationalism, 23–24, 26
Real Alto (Ecuador), 300–301
Recombination, 45
Reductionism, 29
Reformation, 22
Reisner, George, 35
Relations of production, 30
Relative time, 11–12
Religion, 142, 147, 150, 224–25, 278–79, 289,
     304–6, 309, 312
Renaissance, 21
Reproduction, 45–46
Rhine River Valley, 213, 219, 223
Rhodes, 228–29
Rhodesia. *See* Zimbabwe
Rocky Mountains, 245–46, 263
Rome (ancient), 4, 6, 10, 13–14, 21, 23–24, 26, 207,
     291
Rosetta Stone, 9
Rousay (Scotland), 224–25
Royalty, 142, 154, 157, 184–89, 193, 200–202, 205,
     208, 210, 229–30, 292, 312
Rumania, 217–18
Russia. *See* Soviet Union
Ruwenzori Mountains (Uganda, Zaire), 195
Rwanda, 209

Sacrifices, human, 181, 185, 203
Sahara Desert, 195, 197, 199, 206–7
Saltgitter-Lebenstadt (Germany), 88–89
Samarra Phase, 144
Samoa, 241–42
Sanga (Zaire), 210
San José Mogote (Mexico), 279, 281–82
San Juan de Pariache (Peru), 5
San Lorenzo (Mexico), 278–80
Saqqara (Egypt), 201
Saudi Arabia, 147
Scandinavia, 213–15, 220
Scotland, 26, 220, 223–25
Scovill site (U.S.), 265
Scrapers, 73, 90, 248–49
Seistan region (Iran), 162–64, 178
Senegal, 208
Serengeti Plains (Tanzania), 69
Seriation, 12
Sex roles, 82–83, 96–97, 116
Shaft graves, 228
Shahr-i Sokhta (Iran), 162–65, 172, 178
Shang dynasty, 181–82, 184–89
Shanidas Cave (Iraq), 92–93, 97
Sharing, 83, 97
Shoshones, 32
Siberia, 99, 244–46

Sicily, 228–29
Sinai Peninsula, 199, 205
Sind region (Pakistan), 160
Sinjar Hills (Iraq), 143–45
Sites, location and excavation, 3–6
Sivapithecus, 50
Sky dynasty, 290
Slash-and burn agriculture, 182–83, 220, 222, 240
Slavery, 153, 156–57, 184, 205, 208, 230–31
Smilčić (Yugloslavia), 218
Social change, 24, 26–32
Social organization, 33–35, 67, 82–83, 94–97,
     115–16, 136–37, 152–54, 157, 170, 175–76,
     178, 232, 243–244, 278–79, 303
Society Islands, 242–44
Solomon Islands, 241
Solutré (France), 105, 107
Solutrean assemblages, 101–2
Solvieux (France), 104
Somme River Valley (France), 23, 27
South Africa, 59–60, 110–11, 195–96, 209–10
South America, 296–316
Soviet Union (USSR), 93–94, 96, 99, 105, 116, 160,
     165–70, 176, 213, 220, 223, 244–46
Spain, 13, 77–78, 115, 219, 224, 275, 291–92,
     312–13
Spears, 90, 106, 248–49
Speciation, 57
Species, 44
Spencer, Herbert, 24
Spirit Cave (Thailand), 190–91
Starčevo, 217
States, 35, 157, 193
Steatite bowls, 162–63, 176, 263
Steppes, 93–94
Steward, Julian H., 32–35
Stone Age, 27
Stonehenge (England), 222, 225
Strata identified by their contents, law of, 12
Stratigraphy, 12
Sudan, 3, 195, 204–5
Sumer (Iraq), 153, 162
Sungir (USSR), 105, 116
Superposition, law of, 12
Survival, differential, 45–46
Susa (Iran), 149–50, 161–63
Susiana Plain (Iran), 128, 148, 161–62
Swartkrans (South Africa), 59
Switzerland, 213
Syria, 130, 140, 147, 230
Szechwan province (China), 192

Tabasco region (Mexico), 290–91
Tablets, clay, 141–42, 215, 228, 230
Tahiti, 242–44
Taima-Taima (Venezuela), 247
Taiwan, 180, 184, 190–91
T'ang, 184

Tanzania, 56, 60, 69–72, 81
Taruga (Nigeria), 208
Tasmania, 238
Taurus Mountains (Turkey), 131–32
Tawantinsuyu, 311
Taxes, 188–89, 312
Tehuacán Valley (Mexico), 276–78
Tell es-Sawwan (Iraq), 144–45
Tell es-Sotto (Iraq), 143
Tell 'Uqair (Iraq), 148
Temple and palace corporations, 142, 150–52, 157
Tennessee, 251, 260
Tenochtitlan (Mexico), 292–93
Teotihuacán (Mexico), 6, 282–87, 290–91
Teotlalpán region (Mexico), 291
Tepe Asiab (Iran), 161
Tepe Guran (Iran), 127, 161
Tepe Sialk (Iran), 162
Tepe Yahya (Iran), 162–63
Terra Amata (France), 74–77
Teshik-Tash (USSR), 93
Texcoco Island (Mexico), 292
Thailand, 190–91, 193
Thaya River Valley, 108
Thebes (Egypt), 204–5
Thebes (Greece), 231
Tholoi, 228
Thomsen, Christian Jurgensen, 26
Three Ages, 26–27
Tiahuanaco (Bolivia), 307, 309
Tiberias, Lake (Israel, Jordan), 114
Tien, Lake (China), 192
Tigris River Valley (Iraq), 140, 142, 144–45, 159
Tikal (Guatemala), 283, 290–91
Tiryns (Greece), 229–30
Titicaca, Lake (Bolivia), 307
Tlatilco (Mexico), 282
Tlapacoya (Mexico), 246
Toltec culture, 291–93
Tombs. See Burial rites
Tonga, 241–42
Tonle Sap Lake (Cambodia), 193
Tools, 6, 27, 60, 67–83, 85–86, 90–91, 101–3, 122–23, 141, 165, 176, 190–91, 221–23, 239–40, 245–46, 248–49, 257, 260
Torralba (Spain), 77–78
Tortoise core technique, 73, 90
Trade, 115–16, 122–23, 138, 150, 155–56, 165, 170, 176–78, 188, 192, 207–8, 210, 215, 221, 223, 229–30, 232, 262–65, 275, 279–82, 286–87, 289–91, 292, 314–15
Tree ring dating, 13–14
Tres zapotes (Mexico), 280
Tribes, 34
Tsinling Mountains (China), 181–82, 190–91, 193
Tula (Mexico), 291–92
Turkana, Lake (Kenya), 60, 68, 82
Turkey, 126, 131–36, 140, 170, 216, 226, 228, 230
Turkmenia (USSR), 160, 165–70, 176, 178
Tutishcainyo (Peru), 314–15

'Ubaid Phase, 146–48
Uganda, 195
Uhle, Max, 35
Ukraine, 93–94
Umm Dabaghiyah (Iraq), 142–44
Umma (Iraq), 154
Umnak Island (Alaska), 257
Uniformitarianism, 23
United States, 4, 32, 242–53, 255–71
Upper Perigordian assemblages, 101–2
Ur (Iraq), 147, 152
Urban society, development of, 146–54, 282–87
Urnfield peoples, 232
Uruguay, 296
Uruk (Iraq), 148–49, 151, 161, 176
Ussher, James, 22

Vallonet Cave (France), 60, 73
Valsequillo Reservoir (Mexico), 276
Van, Lake (Turkey), 126
Variability, genetic, 46
Venezuela, 246–47, 313–14
Vertesszöllös (Hungary), 73
Vesuvius, Mount (Italy), 10
Vézère River Valley (France), 86, 107
Victoria Lake, 195, 209
Vietnam, 191–92
Villanovan culture, 231–32
Vistula River Valley (Poland), 213, 219
Volcanic ash, 9–10, 13

Wadi Madamagh (Jordan), 112
Waisted blades, 239–40
Warka (Iraq), 146, 148–49
Water management systems, 302–3
Wealth, 116, 120, 124, 137–38, 145, 152, 155–57, 165, 191–93, 200, 205, 207–8, 210, 228–29, 248, 289, 291, 293
Whaling, 257–58, 260
White, Leslie, 33–35
Woolley, Leonard, 3
Writing, 141–42, 215, 228, 230–31

Yangshao settlements (China), 182–83
Yangtze River Valley (China), 192
Yarim Tepe I and II (Iraq), 143–45
Yellow River Valley (China), 182, 187, 191
Yucatán Peninsula (Mexico), 274, 292
Yugoslavia, 217–18, 223
Yukon (Canada), 244–46
Yunnan province (China), 192

Zagros Mountains (Iran), 124–28, 136, 161, 216
Zaire, 195, 209–10
Zambezi River, 209–10
Zambia, 209–10
Zawi Chemi (Iran), 125
Ziggurats, 147
Zimbabwe, 195, 209–10